T0164565

KILLING

THE

POORMASTER

A SAGA OF POVERTY, CORRUPTION,
AND MURDER IN THE GREAT DEPRESSION

HOLLY METZ

Lawrence Hill Books
Chicago

For more information, visit www.thepoormaster.com

Published by Lawrence Hill Books
An imprint of Chicago Review Press, Incorporated
814 North Franklin Street
Chicago, Illinois 60610
ISBN 978-1-61373-651-7

Library of Congress Cataloging-in-Publication Data
Metz, Holly.
  Killing the poormaster : a saga of poverty, corruption, and murder in
the Great Depression / Holly Metz.
    p. cm.
  Includes bibliographical references and index.

1. Murder—New Jersey—Hoboken—Case studies. 2. Poor—New Jersey—
Social conditions—20th century. 3. United States—Social conditions—
1933–1945. I. Title.
  HV6534.H63M48 2012
  364.152'3092—dc23
                                    2012021790

Interior design: PerfecType, Nashville, TN

Printed in the United States of America
5 4 3 2 1

For my parents,
who met these hard times
across the river.

CONTENTS

Hoboken, New Jersey, 1938

This map was produced by the Federal Writers' Project of the Works Progress Administration for the State of New Jersey.[1] It has been modified to include locations mentioned in *Killing the Poormaster* and to indicate the city's division between "uptown" (east of Willow Avenue) and "downtown" (west of Willow Avenue) prior to and during the Great Depression.

---

1. City hall, "the Hall"
94 Washington Street, headquarters of the poormaster, mayor, police, and the Recorder's Court (the municipal court.)

2. *Jersey Observer*
111 Newark Street, newspaper with a cozy connection to the Hall.

3. Home of Joseph Scutellaro
611 Monroe Street, home of the man accused of killing the poormaster.

4. Apartment of Herman Matson
812 Willow Avenue

5. Apartment of the Hastie family
1203 Willow Avenue

6. Volk Mortuary
631 Washington Street, where the poormaster's funeral was held.

7. Church Square Park
Where Herman Matson held his first public meeting.

8. Hudson Square Park
Where Herman Matson attempted to hold a second open-air meeting.

9. Pier at the east end of Fifth Street
From which longshoremen descended into Hudson Square Park during Matson's second meeting.

Map layout by Rose Daniels Design; original map © 1939 by New Jersey Guild Associates, Inc., reprinted 1986 by Rutgers University Press

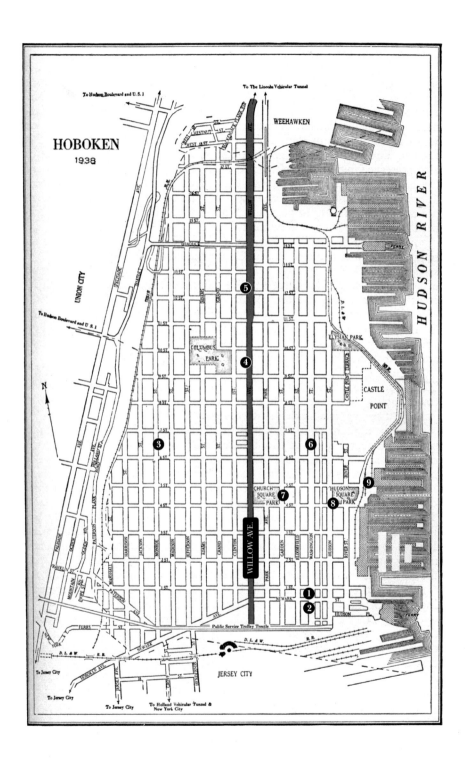

FEBRUARY 25, 1938
CITY HALL, HOBOKEN, NEW JERSEY
AROUND 10:15 AM

THE METAL SPIKE, PROPELLED with weight and force, punctured the poormaster's striped dress shirt at center chest, slicing through his undervest. It tore through downy chest hair and age-toughened skin, the accumulated fat of years, cut through membrane to pierce muscle. The skewer punctured bone; with great velocity it clipped through the cage meant to protect the heart and lungs. The spike tip continued, lancing the sac enclosing Harry Barck's heart, and then, with its sudden, sharp withdrawal, ripped a jagged hole in his aorta.

Now the swift gush of blood could not be routed but flooded into the gap between Barck's flailing heart and its fibrous sheath. Blood rushed and pooled inside the girdling case, pounding the contained muscle, desperate to work and failing.

This was the deadly sequence determined at autopsy, for the body's exterior had displayed little of the violence the medical examiners later found within. The puncture wound to Barck's chest, an eighth of an inch in diameter, had issued virtually no blood. But inside, the doctors discovered the cause of the poormaster's death: the massing force of his own blood had compressed his heart and choked it, until its beating ceased.[1]

1

1 | WAITING FOR NOTHING

THE MORNING THE POORMASTER was killed, twenty-three men and women were waiting for him outside his office. Just a few weeks earlier, a nationwide recession had returned them to the desperation of the Depression's early days, when millions had been forced to scavenge for scraps of food. Grim, already exhausted despite the hour, they lined the reception room and the walls of the narrow adjoining hallway. They waited to plead with Harry Barck for some bread tickets, or a check for a few dollars. Their spouses and children waited, too, on the other side of town from city hall, in tenement rooms gone cold and dark through unpaid bills.[1]

The poormaster made quick work of the line that morning. In fewer than fifteen minutes he had dismissed six aid-seekers, not even bothering to fill in the section on his printed Relief Client list that called for the number of relatives dependent on each interviewee. "Next case!" the waiting men and women heard him shout each time his door was opened by a rejected applicant. "Next!"[2]

Around 9:30, at the sound of the interior door suddenly yanked ajar, sixteen men and women turned their heads expectantly, listening for the seventy-four-year-old poormaster's customary dismissal of the last applicant and his summoning of the next. Instead, there was a woman's indistinguishable shouting and the huffing sound of someone moving quickly. Young, dark-haired Lena Fusco rushed from Barck's inner office

3

into the reception room penned in wood and pebbled glass. The towering, thickset poormaster followed immediately behind her, pausing to wipe the woman's spit from his face before summoning patrolman Thomas Carmody. The officer had been posted in the hallway ever since an altercation between Barck and a relief applicant two weeks before.[3]

"Lock her up!" Barck ordered Carmody, who grabbed Fusco's elbow as she swore in an Italian dialect he didn't understand. The elderly poormaster's face was colored with anger, and flecks of the woman's spit were splattered on his tweed suit. He had removed his round, wire-frame glasses. "Take her out!" he demanded. Then he added, starkly, "I won't give her any more [bread] tickets."[4]

View of the poormaster's private office from the waiting room, showing the secretary's desk. Forensic photograph taken by a police photographer on February 25, 1938, following the killing of Poormaster Barck.

From the case file *State v. Joseph F. Scutellaro*, 1939. Courtesy of the Hudson County Prosecutor's Office.

The clutch of aid-seekers outside Barck's door would have known what that meant: the only person who could approve aid to Lena Fusco had just cut her off.

Not that this power was new. Harry Barck had been Hoboken's gate-keeper of poor relief for forty-two years, and like local officials in municipalities, townships, and counties all across the country, he had been authorized to determine how much aid was to be granted the destitute of his region. And Barck and his colleagues were not inclined to be charitable. Harsh treatment of the jobless poor had been, from colonial times, a deterrent against claims on public funds, as well as an established expression of community disapproval. Local politicians had long extolled their poormasters' meanness, portraying it as both a benefit to taxpayers and a way for the poor man to regain self-worth. "Under the philosophy of this ancient practice, the applicant is in some way morally deficient," protested Harry L. Hopkins, who sought to eradicate that notion when he became federal emergency relief administrator during the Depression. Despite cycles of economic downturn and unemployment during the late nineteenth and early twentieth centuries, local overseers had maintained, as their predecessors had done, that work was always available for any able-bodied man who truly wanted it. If a man was poor, they insisted, he had only himself to blame: he drank too much or he was lazy.[5]

Even when the Depression struck and made millions of men and women jobless, traditional overseers like Harry Barck persisted with their entrenched beliefs and practices. During a cross-country tour of local relief offices commissioned by Hopkins, writer Lorena Hickok repeatedly encountered these hardliners and noted with disgust their habitual withholding. Aid-seekers in Calais, Maine, she reported, were subjected to treatment that was "almost medieval in its stinginess and stupidity." More than two thousand miles away, Hickok had found more of the same. "They think there is something wrong with a man who can-not make a living," she wrote of relief administrators in Bismarck, North Dakota. "They talk so much about 'the undeserving' . . ."[6]

But the knowledge of shared misery would not likely have com-forted the Hoboken relief applicants who waited for the poormaster that February morning. All who heard Harry Barck's sharp retort to Lena

Fusco would have been able to picture its consequences. Without Barck's authorized tickets for day-old bread or a grocery order from his office—a check, to be redeemed at a specific local store for explicitly prescribed portions of rice, meat, coffee, vegetables, or milk—Fusco's survival, and the survival of her children, would be left entirely to chance, and their odds were pitiful. Every day, for lack of supplies to meet the ever-increasing need, hungry men and women were turned away from Hoboken's few clergy-run soup kitchens. And Fusco's family was already near ruin. Her three children had rickets. Her husband spent his days lining up with thousands of other men to apply for jobs that didn't materialize. The family had no savings, no money even for necessities such as kerosene for the single stove they used for cooking and heat. When one of the Fuscos' children had outgrown her clothes, Lena had salvaged an empty flour sack and covered her. When she could find no substitute for stockings, her children had gone without.[7]

Just a few years earlier, it must have seemed to unemployed workers and their families that the "new deal" offered by their newly elected president, Franklin Delano Roosevelt, would dispel such misery. Certainly they had seen the failure of local relief efforts. When the Depression had taken hold, needy applicants had swiftly overwhelmed private and public aid offices nationwide, and most agencies were virtually bankrupt by the time of Roosevelt's inaugural. But under the new administration, the federal government had become—for the first time—directly involved in the distribution of poor relief. And aid, mercifully, had come quickly. Within one month of the passage of the Federal Emergency Relief Act in 1933, Hopkins, as the federal relief agency's new administrator, ushered through grants to forty-five states, keeping millions of people from destitution.[8]

And then, almost as suddenly as that intervention had been initiated, it was terminated. By 1935 the federal government had essentially withdrawn from what the president called "this business of [direct] relief." In its stead came "work relief" through the Works Progress Administration, a public works program. For as Roosevelt explained, jobs created by the government would "preserve not only the bodies of the unemployed, but also their self-respect, their self-reliance and courage and determination."[9]

But for most of the jobless, the promise of work relief went unfilled. There were simply not enough WPA jobs for all of the able-bodied and unemployed—not in Hoboken, not in cities and towns all across the United States. The vast majority of those eligible for work relief could not get it. And though the states were meant to pick up responsibility for "the dole" when the federal government withdrew, most could not do so adequately. California and Texas offered needy families less than "a subsistence budget." Some states offered nothing.[10]

In 1936 New Jersey abolished its direct relief program, shunting responsibility for the "employable unemployed" to hard-hit municipalities and to public agencies administered by local poormasters. For Harry Barck, it meant the restoration of his uncontestable power to grant or to refuse assistance. He returned to authority with vigor, cutting off aid. His New Jersey colleagues proved to be stingy when they, too, resumed control—the average relief family was made to live on about half the minimum amount required for mere survival—but Harry Barck denied more, with swifter actuation, than any of his fellows. Within a few weeks of his return to complete command, the Hoboken poormaster had slashed relief rolls from two thousand cases—representing more than seven thousand jobless men, women, and dependent children—to ninety, insisting to incredulous reporters that most applicants were "chiselers."[11]

Barck's cast-off relief clients could not expect much from state bureaucrats. Although New Jersey had been the second state, after New York, to set up an emergency relief administration in 1931, Trenton only allowed municipalities to apply for reimbursement of a percentage of their relief costs *if* they first met the state's standards for adequate relief. Hoboken would do neither. County officials, no longer involved in the distribution of aid, declared themselves powerless to intervene—though several, including the Hudson County supervisor, went on record to object to Barck's purging of clients and his drastic cuts in relief to those who remained on the rolls. "You cannot keep a family of nine alive with $1.90 worth of food orders a week," the supervisor complained. "The great majority of people on relief today are respectable working people who are unemployed through no fault of their own. They would rather have jobs than relief, but they must live."[12]

"I'm in favor of giving the old American pioneer spirit a chance to assert itself . . . ," Barck replied, adding that the lack of any rebellion in response to his actions was proof that he had been right to cut off aid to so many. There had been no food riots or public disturbances in Hoboken, he'd boasted to reporters—not like other places.[13]

For the unemployed had taken to the streets from the earliest days of the economic crisis. They had orchestrated "hunger marches" to state capitols and rallied for aid at relief centers and municipal buildings across the country. In Chicago, organized groups initiated "rent riots," countering evictions by reversing landlords' curbside dumping of delinquent renters' furniture. In New York City—just a brief ferry ride across the Hudson River from Hoboken—over a hundred thousand demonstrators crowded Union Square to call for relief.[14]

Though leftists often organized their public meetings, jobless protestors included in their ranks penniless Americans of every political stripe. They were mostly peaceful, but reaction to them, fueled by fear of their potential to upturn the established order, was not. On one march to Capitol Hill, three thousand marchers were detained on a highway, while jeering, armed policemen, empowered by their superiors to "open fire" on insubordinates, dared the marchers to leave their enforced encampment.[15]

Some relief officials and politicians responded to demonstrators as nineteenth-century industrialists had reacted to trade unionists: they called in squads of police to brutally subdue them. But such confrontations made reporters take notice of the protestors' demands. "Bleeding heads converted unemployment from a little-noticed to a page one problem in every city in the United States," one writer later noted. "No one could any longer afford to ignore it." Aid was then stepped up, to quell dissent. Later in the Depression, a survey of relief officers in New York City determined that when organized groups of jobless men and women shouted demands and picketed relief bureaus, administrators readily made concessions.[16]

But that was not about to happen in Hoboken—there would be no demonstrations to receive widespread attention, no ground to be gained by anyone who disagreed with the way things were done in the city. For what Harry Barck did not say to reporters when he'd noted the absence of street protests in Hoboken was that Mayor Bernard McFeely, known to all as "Boss," did not tolerate dissent in his city.

Though many in Hoboken whispered that the city's true boss was the chief of police—who also happened to be the mayor's brother Edward—Boss McFeely had earned his title. He had followed the direction of other urban bosses—cunning men who ruled cities and states after the Great War. And like them, he had outfoxed, bullied, enticed, or beaten all who stood in his path. Across the country, tin pot municipal dictators had seized control of local governments weakened by public apathy and postwar cynicism: Tom Pendergast in Kansas City, Ed Crump in Memphis, Jim Curley in Boston, and, in neighboring Jersey City, Frank Hague. Through his ability to deliver hundreds of thousands of votes, the blustery Jersey City mayor was the state's ultimate wirepuller. He

Rare photo of Bernard McFeely, taken in 1921
when he was Hoboken's commissioner of public
safety under Mayor Patrick Griffin.

Courtesy of the Hoboken Historical Museum.

commanded power over New Jersey legislators, judges, and governors; and Boss Hague's political sway and attention-grabbing suppression of free speech and assembly in his own city had kept reporters from troubling much with goings-on in Hoboken.[17]

"Barney" McFeely, like some of the other reigning urban bosses, had found opportunity in the widespread lawlessness of the Prohibition era. These men steered elections and often enriched themselves and their cronies as their political forefathers had done before them, but they were also frequently in cahoots with or influenced by gangster rumrunners, and they used force to gain their ascendancy. When they did not use baseball bats, they used police muscle to punish and dominate their cities' populations. They eagerly claimed or rewrote the law for their own purposes.[18]

McFeely cleaved to this newer model, and Hoboken's poor, weakened by hunger and worry, took note.

Few in the city would forget McFeely's punishment of a lone protestor, a downtown resident named Anthony Bezich who had been handing out leaflets on an uptown street not long after the Depression struck. His flyer had announced a march on Washington and had called upon his neighbors to "fight against starvation" and to reclaim their government.[19]

A report by a McFeely ally likely set Bezich's arrest in motion. He was tossed into the city jail before he could circulate all of his leaflets and was charged with violating an ordinance that made a permit mandatory for the distribution of handbills. Such a permit, all of Hoboken knew, was never going to be approved. No one was going to organize the poor in Boss McFeely's city.

And after a cursory visit before a Hoboken judge, Bezich was removed to the county penitentiary. He had appealed for leniency because of his wife's poor health, but the judge had imposed the maximum sentence— three months. That was meant to teach him a lesson. But Bezich was also physically frail, and while in prison he contracted pneumonia and died. Days later, his wife died of heart failure.

Outraged by the result of near-starvation combined with repression, a few neighbors appeared on Hoboken streets with leaflets protesting the "miserable conditions imposed upon [Bezich] by the bosses and their henchman in City Hall" that had made two children orphans.

McFeely again called out his police and had the new protestors hustled off the streets. They too were charged with violating the city ordinance. The First Amendment to the US Constitution and its promise of freedom of speech, as well as the rights to peaceably assemble and to petition the government for redress of grievances, were not extended to the dissenters. A Hoboken judge sentenced them to serve time in the penitentiary.

The streets were cleared for a while. Then, as the economic slump continued and deepened, a few protestors cried out, attempting to roust fellow sufferers. And then McFeely and *his* supporters rallied, too, sometimes subduing dissenters with fists and boots as well as jail time. No claims of democratic process were to be tolerated, no mercy shown.[20]

For many, the threat of beatings alone had not been sufficient to maintain their silence, for these longshoremen and masons and shipyard workers had seen their share of scrapes and battles. No, it was McFeely's thorough domination of virtually every vehicle of survival and redress that had each poor resident standing alone during the Depression years. What good would it do them to object? To speak up was to be publicly marked as an enemy. How would they ever get any work then? Even if someone *could* hire them, the neighborhood McFeely men would turn against the employer. No permits or permissions would ever be granted them to do business in the city. The police would hound them. They would go to jail and their kids would have nothing.[21]

Relief from the poormaster, already in short supply, would be even harder to come by for those who sided against Boss McFeely. The city's poorest residents had nothing to offer the mayor but their obedience. And so they narrowed their sights on the little bit of aid eked out by Poormaster Barck, on the bakery seconds granted through tickets from his office. Yes, the bread was so stale it had to be soaked in water to eat—but it *was* bread. They waited on line to beg for it. For what was the alternative? To die?

————— ◆ —————

Patrolman Carmody tightened his grip on Lena Fusco's elbow and quickly led her away from the other aid-seekers. He stopped in the corridor, just before stairs that led to a ground-floor exit. From there steps led to the dingy basement headquarters of the Hoboken police, and the chilly confines of the city jail.[22]

A few weeks prior to Carmody's posting outside the poormaster's office, Fusco had had another run-in with Barck and had knocked over an inkwell on his desk. Barck had later sworn she had threatened him— "I haven't got a crowbar on me," he'd claimed she'd shouted, adding, "but I'll use my fists on you"—but the poormaster had not called for the woman's arrest. Rather, she'd been taken down to police headquarters and detained until they'd quieted her. Then she had been released.[23]

On the morning Harry Barck was killed, Carmody had again tried to calm a raging Lena Fusco, as twelve applicants were speedily dispatched from the poormaster's inner office. Four men remained waiting, gazing fitfully at the secretaries who walked in and out of the nearly cleared room. The women would have been looking forward to the noon lunch hour when the office closed, and their rooms were cleared of the insistent, needy crowds.

Only one of the waiting men had some work lined up—John Galdi Jr., a factory hand. The others had described themselves on their applications by the work they could no longer find: Ralph Corrado, baker; Nicholas Russo, laborer; Joseph Scutellaro, mason and carpenter.[24]

To most observers, Joe Scutellaro would have seemed a beaten man. And indeed, the previous five years had been especially rough for him. There had been almost no work in construction in the state for quite some time—not even for skilled carpenters like his father, Frank, who had developed a reputation for fine craftsmanship before launching his own successful contracting business. During the construction boom that had flourished in New Jersey after the Great War, Frank had trained his son to do building estimates and masoning, and they had worked together. Many of their jobs had been for the city, back when Frank was still in McFeely's favor. But then, just before the nationwide financial collapse, Frank had taken a notion to support the mayoral aspirations of a *paesan*, a man named Bartletta, who had dared to challenge the political machine. After McFeely crushed his opponent, the Boss made sure the city assignments that had sustained the Scutellaros were withdrawn and handed over to loyalists. For a time, father and son had cobbled together their livelihoods with little carpentry jobs and cement work for neighbors, but now, with the Depression entering its eighth year, there was nothing for either of them, and builders and masons all over were on relief.[25]

Joe sat in the waiting room. At thirty-six, he had lost the sinewy strength of his youth, when he had been fit and purposeful. Always a small man, he had been rendered frail and hollow-eyed by joblessness, worry, and hunger.[26]

The poormaster's shout—"Next!"—issued from inside his office as another man left. Ralph Corrado now headed the line, but he turned to Scutellaro and said, "Joe, you go in first."[27]

Scutellaro nodded and ran his hands down his drab suit, shiny with wear. He crossed the dull linoleum floor and entered Barck's private office. It was just after 10:00 AM. Within a half hour, Harry Barck would be dead.[28]

2 | A CITY DIVIDED

BY 1938 CITY HALL had occupied a square block in Hoboken's business district for nearly six decades. Stodgy, with a monumental façade fronting a main street named after the first American president, the sallow brick and brownstone hall was fairly typical of civic architecture of the 1880s: designed to convey sureness of purpose and the constancy of the government that operated within. Here the city's political machine ran smoothly, without interruption. From the day it opened its doors, "the Hall" remained the source of all civic improvement or neglect, of comfort or its lack.

For many longtime residents, the Hall's thorough domination of everyday life was a given. "Hoboken was a tough place," recalled Charles DeFazio Jr., who was born in the city in 1905. "You couldn't be a Pollyanna and live here. You had to be able to hold your ground. And meet a challenge. You had to be up to it. But you could only get so far because they had the strength, they had the resources, they had the police, the fire department, the majority of favor. So you had to go carefully. . . . If you tried to fight them physically, it was unfair competition. You didn't stand a chance."[1]

The city's size and geographical constraints had surely made it easier to control. A little more than a mile square, Hoboken was contained by neighboring municipalities to the north and south and by natural boundaries to the east (the Hudson River) and west (the rocky face of the Palisades)—a layout that could be traced back to the land's late eighteenth- and early nineteenth-century ownership. Members of the wealthy Stevens family had divided their Hoboken holdings into two sections: an upland strip along the river, developed first with comfortable single-family brownstones and an extensive park that bordered the Stevens estate, and the far larger, marshy lowland to the west, where tenants lived in shacks and navigated the mosquito-hazed "Meadows" on a mud-lapped plank road.[2]

The landowners organized a street grid. After the city was incorporated in 1855, the Stevens family retained ownership of most of the vacant land and, through their development company, marketed upscale apartment buildings on the uplands and encouraged new industries—and, inevitably, their workers—to move to the lowlands. The upland parcel, where the well-to-do settled, became known as uptown; the lowlands became downtown, the section for the working poor.

By the time city hall was built in 1881, uptown was mostly settled with German immigrants, who represented more than half the city's population. Germans had arrived in the 1850s and '60s highly educated and skilled in their trades and had settled comfortably—unlike the Irish, who had also arrived during that period, though in lesser numbers. Over time, the Irish would make up about 20 percent of Hoboken's population.[3]

At first, poor Irish families had crowded into the hastily constructed wooden dwellings and brick tenements of downtown, laboring ten- to twelve-hour days and six-day weeks for near-subsistence wages in the noxious factories and iron works of the burgeoning industrial age. Later they would shift to the more lucrative but equally dangerous building trades, constructing many of uptown's regal stone and brick structures, as well as area roads, railroads, and tunnels, where on-the-job injuries and death were common.[4]

Uptown residents faced no such work hazards. German bankers conducted business on the eastern shores of the Hudson River, in Manhattan offices, and returned to Hoboken on ferries owned by the Stevens family. Joined by others from their native country—professionals, merchants, skilled tradesmen, and hotel and tavern owners—they made their imprint on the young city, transforming uptown with beer gardens, theaters, and societies devoted to marksmanship, equestrianism, and German arts and literature.[5]

The Stevens family, too, retained their presence uptown, in a walled-in estate on Castle Point; and, with their development company, they continued to hold economic sway in the city for many years. But in the mid-1880s, they sold their docks to two German shipping companies, a simple transfer of ownership that was to precipitate vast changes in Hoboken's population and to affect its residents' prosperity for generations.

North German Lloyd and Hamburg American ocean liners were already transporting European passengers to America on a regular basis when the companies bought the Hoboken piers; by the turn of the century, their trans-Atlantic liners (and those of their competitors) would convey thousands of poor immigrants per crossing. The new arrivals debarked at Castle Garden on the tip of Manhattan or at Ellis Island—often with stoppages for initial immigration processing en route, at the Hoboken pier. Over the next three decades, more than twenty-four million Europeans would make the crossing to America, lured by hard-selling shipping agents, American immigration myths, and the need for opportunity.

Well over four million Italians left the southern provinces and hard-scrabble villages of Sicily and settled in American cities—including Hoboken—where they joined transplanted Eastern European Jews. The new immigrants shared a suspicion of police and authority, mixed with a deep devotion to family. They established separate, close-knit communities meant to protect their own in a new and hostile world that also promised them prosperity.[6]

As the population of Hoboken doubled and grew still more, city hall was bulked up. A third story was added in 1911 to house additional municipal offices and an armory; a two-story jail was appended. By then the city had reached a population of just over seventy thousand.[7]

Nevertheless, uptown Hoboken, with its established German cultural organizations and civic institutions, maintained its identity as America's "Little Bremen" until the conflict began in Europe in 1914. Then the German-owned docks were immobilized; their owners had feared what might happen to their ships if they left the neutral harbor, but war came to the docks instead. In 1917, when President Woodrow Wilson called upon Congress to declare war against Germany, Hoboken's German ships were seized by federal agents and armed soldiers. River Street, which fronted the piers, was declared a military zone for the duration of the war. Government officials evicted hundreds of German families—many with children born in the United States—and closed their shops. Hundreds were arrested and deported, and many more left the city, if they could. Those who stayed often obscured their ancestry.[8]

With the decrease in its German population, Hoboken experienced a postwar shift in ethnic power from Germans to the Irish—or, more properly, to Irish Americans, who had already begun to fill the ranks of the police and fire departments and to establish themselves in trade unions when the Italians began arriving in Hoboken. Americans of Irish ancestry were rising as a new American-born power, joining with the remaining heelers and standard-bearers of German heritage—men like Poormaster Harry Barck—to shape the political organizations of the twentieth century. Some would move uptown, into the northeastern reaches of the city, or, like Mayor Bernard McFeely, into offices in city hall. The Italians—poor, politically unorganized, and disregarded—would inherit the downtown streets.[9]

All through the Great Depression, every workday, the narrow streets downtown filled and emptied in waves—first the men and women heading to their jobs, trailed by little gangs of street-tough kids, sparring on their way to public schools identified by the order of their construction: 3, 5, 8, and 9. Then quiet—only to be filled with the rumblings of job-seekers and street scavengers; then plaintive mothers looking to barter or borrow, calling out to neighbors, gathering on corners to briefly commiserate. And, at day's end, when the working men and women returned, the sidewalks were claimed again by wives and mothers doing double duty, shuttling needlework to distributors on Fifth and Adams Streets, seeking the next night's work ornamenting dress collars, or, for those with lesser skills, sewing buttons on cards to earn four cents a gross.[10]

And the next workday, it began again. By 6 AM the men and women who lived downtown and who had work had already left for the windowless garment shops, the hulking American Lead Pencil factory, the smaller brick buildings on the fringes that housed factories for the manufacture of sheet metal, furniture, varnish, and paint. Most of those workers were Italian American, first and second generation, though there were still some poor Irish downtown and a fair number of more recent arrivals from Eastern Europe. Along with a fraction of African Americans originally from the southern states, Russians, Poles, and Slavs had found jobs in the Ferry Street tannery, one of the city's harshest industries. Men spent their days there scraping the flesh off of hides and mixing vats of poisonous chemicals.[11]

Downtown men also worked at the uptown docks, if they were selected to do so, hauling off freight from liners owned by Holland-American, Gdynia-American, Scandinavian-American, Navigazione Libera Triestian Lines, Red Star, and Wilson. And for some, there was pick-and-shovel work or other day labor referred by their *paesani*—men from Genoa, Patti, Molfetta, or Monte San Giacomo who had settled in Hoboken in large numbers and who passed along job tips to those who came from their village, town, or city on "the Other Side."[12]

But the *paesani* could offer little assistance to their countrymen during the Depression. The vegetable and fruit vendors, the downtown owners of live poultry markets were barely getting by. Italian purveyors on the far west side had taken to putting out "contribution boxes," hoping that more fortunate patrons would help them take care of the desperate neighbors who were not receiving relief from Poormaster Barck. They could only extend so much credit without going under themselves.[13]

Some families tried to make do as they had in the Old World. Even though Hoboken was the nation's most densely populated city, and downtown's unremitting rows of four-story walkups were backed by little more than patches of dirt, many families kept chickens behind their tenements, and some owned goats. The skittish, bandy-legged animals were meant to supply milk to the youngest children, but they were often unreliable producers, as they had to forage in gutters for their sustenance.[14]

Here and there older boys, out of school and in between jobs, would search the streets for wooden crates they could break up for fuel or would build a fire in a vacant lot while they waited for the factories to signal lunchtime. One or two might then be hired to carry beer from a corner speakeasy to thirsty workmen, and their coins could be turned into bags of charcoal, to be carted home for heat and hot water. If you were enterprising, some said, you would find a way—and there was always a way in Hoboken.[15]

For anyone so inclined, there was a thriving criminal network in the city, nurtured during the Prohibition years and mostly focused on gambling and selling swag from the docks and railroads. But an even more prevalent way to get by, for those willing to trade in political capital, was to go through the Hall for favors.

It was the time-honored way of urban bosses—and not only in Hoboken. Most of the immigrants who'd arrived at the turn of the century had settled in cities, where, for political and sometimes financial reward, local bosses brokered the services and jobs the new arrivals needed. Political machines had long had a lock on millions of votes in Chicago, Philadelphia, and New York.[16]

In the Depression's early days, Democratic presidential candidate Franklin Roosevelt had speculated to an advisor that the federal administration of relief might finally destroy these political machines. As a state senator and, later, as governor of New York, Roosevelt had been bedeviled by New York City's notorious Tammany Hall, the nation's longest-lived urban political machine. "People on relief would have no use for Tammany's services," he proposed.[17]

But in the short term, the federal programs Roosevelt introduced as president did not loosen the hold most urban bosses had on their populations; rather, the new arrangement strengthened their grip, as federal aid moved through local channels. And Roosevelt was inclined to favor the local politicians who supported his programs and kept him in power. When work-relief money began to flow out of Washington, dependable urban Democrats—including Chicago boss Edward J. Kelly, Memphis autocrat Edward H. Crump, and New Jersey powerbroker Frank Hague—were rewarded with generous funding for WPA jobs, to be doled out as they wished.[18]

And if the ruling politicians might require get-out-the-vote efforts or a tithe from your WPA paycheck, what was that in exchange for gaining the necessities of life? In Hoboken, such exchanges had long been everyday occurrences. For if you were considered a friend of the McFeely administration, if you had proved your loyalty, you could be on the receiving end of small benefits: bags of coal from the city's stocks or a nod to receive relief, a permit to hold a public meeting or to engage in a religious celebration on Hoboken's streets, or, most precious of all, a secure job on the city payroll. It mattered little what your qualifications were for the work you were supposed to do. Everyone knew about nursing staff at the baby welfare station who were not nurses. There were whispers about men who had met the Hall's requirement for supplication and suddenly found work as city hall cleaners. Others had found work in the office of the overseer of the poor. These little jobs could be brokered directly or, more likely, by trusted ward representatives of most every heritage and from both sides of Willow Avenue's class dividing line—men and a few women who were ambitious and who valued their own security.[19]

That cold morning in February 1938, the day the poormaster was killed, more than a few downtown residents left for jobs gained through the Hall, and some came there with recommendations for special treatment. With the starved budget for poor relief, the Boss's nod could make all the difference. The last aid-seeker Harry Barck would see before Joseph Scutellaro entered his office had been recommended by Boss McFeely's brother Edward, chief of police. On the list of applicants the poormaster kept on his desk, he had placed a mark beside this man's name, indicating approval for assistance—the only applicant okayed that morning—along with a reminder as to its impetus: "E. McF."[20]

Joseph Scutellaro, born in Hoboken in 1902, couldn't help but know about the city's political machinery, the way favors were dispensed and withheld. There had been his father's political miscalculation and its consequences, but there was also the knowledge that this was the way it was in Hoboken—the way, his older neighbors on Monroe Street surely recalled, it had *always* been. The McFeely regime was only the most recent in Hoboken's long line of political dynasties. When Joe's father, Frank, arrived from Naples as a teenager in 1889, he found in Hoboken—despite what had been said about American democracy—a city where one-party rule was well entrenched. The man who controlled the local Democratic Party organization—the chairman in charge of its coffers—had undisputed control of Hoboken. He was the man to be reckoned with, no matter what titles were conferred upon others.[21]

Most of the work-hungry immigrants who'd swelled the city's population just before and after the turn of the century did not question the political structure they found, and many found its paternalism beneficial. They helped keep the bosses in power, trading votes for the assurance of work, and noted that work for the party could grant an otherwise disenfranchised immigrant and his striving sons opportunity for advancement. The immigrant who became a ward heeler would not only gain favors for his broadly extended family, but gain a certain personal status. He might even allow himself to hope that his position was a sign from the powers-that-be of a growing respect for his people. At the very least, he would be reminded day after day of his neighbors' need for his services.[22]

In February 1938, like so many before him, Joe Scutellaro turned to his contact in the Democratic Party, an Italian committeeman, to ask for help in getting work. State and federal work programs seemed to change every day, and it did not hurt to ask about jobs suited to laborers. McFeely stalwarts had secured most of the long-term, government-sponsored desk jobs. But that was not for Joe. The committeeman listened sympathetically to his account of his family's struggle and said he had heard there might be more jobs coming up through the WPA—though he added that willing workers were always plentiful and jobs scarce. There had never been enough funding to supply government pay to every eligible worker. He promised to get back to him. Maybe something would come up by March 1.[23]

Joe had not worked in six months, and his last job had been only temporary, at the General Electric plant on Grand Street, where they manufactured mercury-vapor lamps. A factory job was light work compared to cement and masonry projects, but he often felt unwell while there. And taking WPA work had begun to feel almost shameful to him. Popular opinion across the country had turned against WPA jobholders—despite a previously stated preference for work relief over the dole—and Joe would have known that taxpayers had taken to complaining about "pampered poverty rats." Still, the position had briefly allowed him to take care of his wife, Anna, and their two children: Marie, who was in grade school at No. 8, and little Joseph, then just over a year old.[24]

Now, without work, he would have to stave off despair while pursuing any opportunity, no matter how vague or unlikely. As it was, the meeting with the committeeman had been a welcome interruption from the miserable pursuit of aid from the poormaster. At least Joe and the committeeman had conversed like men. During his first visit to the poormaster's office, at the beginning of the year, Harry Barck had not even looked up when he had ordered Joe to "send in an application." The official had then thrust a stack of printed cards across his desk, as if to suggest that mailing in just one would not do.

Joe sent an application every other day for ten days. When he had heard nothing from the poormaster, and had no cards left to fill out, he returned to city hall and was told to come back with his wife.[25]

The following day, Joe and Anna made their way to the poormaster's office. Barck ignored Joe, fixing his gaze instead on Anna. She was a plump woman, thirty-two years old, with a sweet, oval face framed by dark curls. "What did you do, bring her in a baby carriage?" Barck asked, without taking his pale blue eyes off of Anna's face. She did not say anything but turned quickly toward Joe to plead silently that he not respond to the old man's insinuation that he was a cradle-robber. Joe kept silent.[26]

After smoothing his trim salt-and-pepper mustache with his forefinger, the poormaster had reached for a small envelope among the jumble of papers on his desk and handed it to Anna. It held a check for $5.70, made out to a local grocer. "Don't give this to this rummy," Barck said, tilting his head toward Joe. "He is liable to spend it." Joe had begun to protest that he was not a drinking man, but the poormaster had already dismissed them both with a wave of his hand. That was all.[27]

The grocery check, received after a month of pursuit, did not bring much relief to the Scutellaros, for the debt they had accumulated while waiting for it far exceeded its value. Anna had managed thus far to keep a separate line of credit going with another grocer, but Joe continued to worry that they would be cut off any day. Even the relative security of his housing did not ease his fear and guilt. Although Joe's parents owned the frame house they all shared—a rarity for Hoboken, where just 9 percent of housing was owner-occupied—Joe had been hard-pressed to pay them the thirty dollars in monthly rent they had agreed upon in better times.[28]

In the five weeks that followed his receipt of the poormaster's grocery check, Joe had returned often to Barck's office to ask for more help and had always left empty-handed. His children's shoes were worn through. Could the poormaster help them get something to cover their feet for the winter? He begged for bread tickets, but Barck would hear none of it. "I went regular, every week, twice a week," Scutellaro would recall later. "No matter what I'd ask him, he'd say 'Get out, nothing doing.' "[29]

———————————— ✵ ————————————

On February 25, 1938, after a fitful night's sleep, Joe Scutellaro woke determined to make something happen for his family. He left his sleeping wife and children in their beds and walked downstairs to the cellar of 611 Monroe Street to chop up a wooden basket for a fire. He did not want to wake them—Anna was not feeling well, and Marie and little Joe were recovering from measles—and besides, Anna would not want him to break up wood in rooms she worked so hard to keep clean.

There was no coal in the bin downstairs. A fire, even a small one, would at least *seem* to burn off some of the numbing cold, and Joe could use it to boil the coffee he'd borrowed from his mother.

After he built a fire in the kitchen stove and had a few sips of coffee, Joe walked to the bakery down the street, and with the change he had left over from the half-dollar he'd borrowed from his father the day before, he bought three rolls for six cents. He owed the grocer twenty-five dollars and could not go there for food.

Joe quickly ate one roll on the short walk home and left the other two on the table for his family. There was one bottle of milk Anna had miraculously been able to get from the milkman after eight weeks of credit. They could not borrow any more money from his parents; his father had twenty dollars left in the bank. Joe bent over his sleeping children and kissed each one. He went into the bedroom and kissed Anna. Then he left the house, with nine cents in his pocket.[30]

Joe walked one block east and one south to meet Ralph Corrado at his home, 520 Adams Street. The two knew each other casually, and when Corrado had seen Joe on the street and mentioned an idea he had about starting a luncheonette, Joe had readily agreed to meet him to talk about it. Joe knew Corrado was a bit of a tough guy. The forty-year-old former handler of prizefighters had done nine months in federal prison on a liquor charge. The vast majority of the city's poor had not turned to crime when the Depression cut off their legitimate livelihoods, but some were now more willing to look the other way when their neighbors did. When a person is down and out, Joe reasoned, he'll do anything to make a dollar. And besides, Corrado had skills. He knew the baker's trade. Maybe they could work something out and Joe could feed his family.[31]

Joe rang Corrado's buzzer around 8:30 that morning, and they walked north together while Corrado described his plan. They were going to meet the owner of a building on the corner of Ninth and Madison Streets. If the landlord would let Joe's father do the work to turn the storefront into a luncheonette—everyone knew Frank Scutellaro was an excellent contractor—maybe they could get a few months' free rent. Joe could work in the restaurant with Corrado, and the two would finally get ahead.

But when they got there, the landlord didn't buy the idea of free rent. He had bills to pay, too, he told them. He thought he could make the necessary alterations himself and have a renter move in right away.

Their meeting concluded, the two men walked down to Eighth Street in silence, then east, past Willow Avenue, to the city's main commercial street. They were both headed for the poormaster's office, to see about getting relief. They began walking south on Washington Street, toward city hall. Joe saw the trolley moving in the wide road, saw it stop now and then to let off women with shopping bags balanced on their arms. He watched with what must have been a mixture of amazement and shame. How did they have the money to take the trolley at five cents a ride, to fill their bags with food? Historians would later note that those who *had* jobs actually lived very well compared to those who did not, considering that prices for just about everything had fallen. But Joe would only know for sure that his Anna was rising to a fourth day of weak coffee and dry bread.[32]

Joe surveyed the uptown street, the three-, four-, and five-story painted brick and stucco buildings that formed unbroken lines along both sides of Washington, most with storefronts one step up from street level. Unlike the wooden buildings downtown, few of these old-style storefronts were shuttered. Where Joe and Corrado lived, it seemed every other building bore a notice: FOR SALE, FOR RENT, or FOR EXCHANGE. A few had been simply abandoned. Uptown was bearing the weight of the Depression with fewer signs of strain, they could not help but notice.[33]

The two men reached First and Washington Streets and turned west, preparing to enter city hall. When they arrived, they did not go through the main entrance, which was fronted by heavy doors embellished with ironwork and led to a spacious entrance hall with vaulted ceilings. Nor did they climb the marble stairs McFeely's friends and supporters ascended to reach his office. Instead, Scutellaro and Corrado used a side entrance, one of two installed on opposite sides of the building. These were entries for people in trouble. The Newark Street entrance led to the local court; the First Street door, which the two aid-seekers used, opened to a plain black iron staircase that brought them directly to the waiting room outside the office of Harry Barck.

The four women who worked for the Hoboken poormaster had settled into their adjoining office by 9:00 AM that February morning, preparing themselves for another workday—set between the hours of 9:00 and 2:00, with an hour break for lunch. Three of the four were employed as typists, and their work, though unhurried, was completely mechanical. They were there not to make independent decisions but to fulfill the orders given them. Long breaks stretched between tasks, one of which was to type the addresses of some of the approved applicants on to envelopes, for mailing relief checks. The two youngest employees—Adeline Cerutti, a slim blonde, and dark-haired Romayne Mullin, at the opposite desk—were both in their twenties, and they looked forward to interruptions, often orchestrated by garrulous policemen who came to visit from their station in city hall. It wasn't that the women weren't grateful for their jobs. Cerutti, Mullin, and another typist, thirty-four-year-old Josephine Shea, were WPA hires, and they knew they had been given positions in the poormaster's office during the very month Harry Barck had cut more than seven thousand people from Hoboken's relief rolls. But there was no established professional standard for them to follow, and their boss widely dismissed the need for trained social workers. He often commented that "anyone with a high school education can handle this kind of work."[34]

In their inexperience, and as beneficiaries of the patronage system, the women who worked for Harry Barck would have been familiar to relief-seekers in other cities. They could just as easily have been working in relief offices in Pennsylvania, where Lorena Hickok discovered "a majority of the poor directors had a grand chance to make use of patronage—and did." Or they could have been found behind desks at one of New York City's relief bureaus, where the average hire, Hickok observed, was unlikely to be "qualified by experience and temperament for the job," yet was also "just another victim of the Depression."[35]

The Hoboken employees would have been keenly aware of the small but official benefaction that separated them from the jobless poor; and yet, like so many employed in financially strapped local relief agencies, their workdays were also consumed with constructing barriers to the transmission of relief. Offices around the country would periodically close their doors to thwart aid-seekers, or broadly refuse assistance to new applicants, or deny aid to anyone who was designated "employable," regardless of the job market.[36] The Hoboken relief workers had been pushing around a lot of paper since Mr. Barck had mandated that every person who had previously received state aid re-petition his office.

In time, some of the needy simply stopped returning to inquire about the status of their petitions for aid, and Barck declared this proof of the effectiveness of his system, the application of principles he had followed for decades as overseer of the poor. He had always routed out the "real chiselers." Those who were not fundamentally dishonest, he said, ". . . were people who could get along all right if they had to." The trouble with the system run by the state, he announced, was that poor people ". . . didn't have any incentive to get out and scratch for a living. They got their rent, clothing, and enough food to eat, so why should they try to get a job?" He concluded that those he had cut off ". . . must have gone out and found enough work to keep themselves from starving or they'd be back here asking for relief."[37]

Eleonore Hartmann, the fourth employee in the poormaster's office pool that morning, had surely heard Mr. Barck make such pronouncements before, and not only during the two years she had worked for him. Now in her midforties, Miss Hartmann had known the poormaster for twenty-eight years, since 1910, when Mr. Barck and his wife, son, and two daughters had lived at 621 Bloomfield Street, a brick row house six doors south of the Hartmann home. Miss Hartmann and Mr. Barck's eldest daughter shared the same given name, and, just two years apart in age, they had shared a friendship, too—though that closeness had not continued after the Barcks moved to upper Washington Street.[38]

During the years the Barcks lived on Bloomfield Street, newspaper articles had regularly detailed Harry L. Barck's accomplishments: election to the presidency of the New Jersey State Association of Overseers of the Poor, extensive work shaping the state poor laws, and consideration for possible appointment as state commissioner of charities and corrections. Another man eventually received the governor's nod, but Harry Barck, "a staunch Democrat," continued to command respect. Repeatedly elected president of a local division of the Rumson Club, Mr. Barck hobnobbed with his country club fellows on their three-hundred-acre Rumson, New Jersey, estate, and society pages took note of his standing alongside prominent men from both sides of the Hudson. "A big man with a big voice," was how Miss Hartmann later described him, acknowledging both his imposing physical presence—nearly six feet tall and weighing well over 215 pounds—and his city- and statewide stature.[39]

And when she had needed a job, well . . . Mr. Barck had always been kind to her. Despite her own advance into middle age, signaled by the graying of her carefully bobbed hair and the tight, downward pull of her mouth, Miss Hartmann thought of Mr. Barck as a genial old man, a kind of paternal figure. Although she could not take shorthand dictation, was not a stenographer, and was a minimal typist at best, Miss Hartmann had, in 1936, been hired by her former neighbor as a clerk, under his direct supervision and care. Until recently, her lack of skills hadn't mattered much: she had worked out of the No. 7 school, three blocks west of city hall on Park Avenue, where she doled out clothing to approved clients. In January, when Mr. Barck had reassigned her to the Hall to fill in for his usual secretary, he had again carefully assigned her a task—interviewing applicants—that in his office only required the employee to fill out forms with an ink pen. The work was clear-cut and left her with plenty of time to observe her boss. Miss Hartmann soon noticed that she was not asked to interview every person who came to the poormaster's office for assistance. There were some applicants Mr. Barck chose to see himself.[40]

On the morning he was killed, Harry Barck had excused Eleonore Hartmann from conducting *any* of the day's interviews. He was going to do them all, he'd announced. He would have wanted to reassert himself with relief seekers who might consider challenging him and to show those professional social workers and state officials, who were still complaining to reporters about his cuts, that he was in charge. State law was behind him, Barck knew. He had helped to shape those very laws years before, and he was not about to coddle anybody on the say-so of the new "relief trust" in Trenton and Washington.[41]

Until the Depression, Barck and his fellow poormasters had kept the New Jersey legislature from interfering with their decision-making. They'd blocked so-called "attempts to modernize poor relief," including requirements that they follow "social case-work methods." Poormasters had been handling relief the same way for generations and they had done all right, Barck was certain. Hadn't they always done what the taxpayers demanded, and kept relief appropriations to a minimum?[42]

But the economic collapse had allowed first Trenton and then Washington to meddle in local relief. For a while, the professional social workers and indiscriminate bureaucrats had muscled in to tell Harry Barck how to do the job he'd been doing for years.[43]

He'd signed off on their decisions. While they were in power, *that* was his job. And he'd watched as they floundered around, making up programs as they went along, as Washington launched and discontinued one emergency or work-relief scheme after another. Now they'd rediscovered the old, tried-and-true way of handling poor relief.[44]

Once power was restored to him, Barck knew what to do. He immediately applied the principles he had followed for more than forty years in the office of overseer of the poor. Those social workers—and federal relief administrator Harry Hopkins had started out in that field, too—had pitied the client "who was forced to plead his destitution in an offensively dreary room" and had expressed their profound regret when relief investigators "pried into private matters." Hopkins had even written a book—its very title, *Spending to Save*, admitting his freehandedness—in which he described his attempts to replace poormasters with relief officials "who understand that the predicament of the worker without a job is an economic predicament not of his own making."[45]

Harry Barck knew better. There were fit men like Herman Matson, a former merchant marine who claimed he was struggling to feed his wife and six children but who spent precious time writing letters to mooted state agency higher-ups, protesting the local poormaster's aid practices. Or so it seemed to Harry Barck. Cunning applicants like Matson didn't want work, they wanted to use the economic downturn to advance a Red agenda, to stir rebellion. Or maybe the claimants were foreigners, Barck said, who ". . . look on the government as a paternal institution. They thought they didn't have to work for a living because the government would take care of them. . . ." Harry Barck was sure to send them away empty-handed. "Now they know differently," he announced.[46]

He had certainly made an example of that out-of-work presser, Joseph Zitani.

The Hoboken poormaster had a daily reminder of that shameful episode—his loose teeth, which his tongue could touch upon throughout the day. The blow to his face, which had left him bloodied, had actually been struck by Zitani's wife, Rose, an attractive brunette, who had been begging for aid for days before the physical attack.

Barck had studied her face as he'd informed her that the requisite fourteen days had not passed since he'd issued her family's last food order, an official check for groceries. "Too bad," he repeated, when she told him again about her two little girls, the food she'd had to deny them when she had to spend $1.80 of their last food order on kerosene, the unpaid electric bills, and the two months' rent her family owed on their four-room apartment downtown. Her pretty face was flushed when she finished telling her story. "Watch the mail," he said, for he thought he might mail the next check, when the proper time came.[47]

Barck was about to say it again on February 7, when he found Rose and Joseph Zitani standing outside his office. The poormaster was leaving to go to lunch. But that woman, half his size, leapt in front of him, a real spitfire, he later recalled. She raged that she had been waiting two hours and would not wait for him to eat lunch while her children starved. He had to push her aside.[48]

And then, before he could take another step, she turned, swinging her handbag in a half-arc, clocking him on the mouth with such force that the bag released from her grasp and skittered to the floor. His mouth stung. He lost his balance for a moment, and when his foot came down, it landed on her fallen bag, smashing the clasp and cracking something inside. When he kicked the bag away, she set upon him, a tiny fury, hitting him again, this time with her fist. As she swore, Barck grabbed her arms to hold her back until Joseph Zitani stepped in, wrestling his bitterly crying wife out of the poormaster's grasp.

Barck called the police and had *Joseph* Zitani arrested. It would not do to say that the poormaster had been beaten by a woman; his cut lip swelled immediately. And Zitani had seemed more than willing to do the manly thing, Barck noticed—to take his wife's punishment. Waiving his right to grand jury action, Zitani pleaded guilty in police court to an assault and battery charge, though he denied the added accusation that he was a "disorderly person," a charge often leveled against drunks and others accused of unseemly behavior. When he was found guilty on both charges, with a suspended sentence for the disorderly person charge and a ninety-day sentence in the county jail for the assault, Zitani had fainted to the floor.

The poormaster let him sit in the county penitentiary for a week before he offered him an out, the results of which were trumpeted in Hudson County's three daily newspapers. "Please accept my deepest apologies," the papers quoted Joseph Zitani's contrite letter to Harry Barck, "I must have been out of my head to do what I did." He was rearraigned and confirmed under oath that the poormaster had previously presented his family with several checks. The allowances had not been extraordinary, and none had ever been in question, but they were presented cumulatively in court as a generous sum, to damn the ungrateful recipient.

Zitani was placed on probation for one year. The police court recorder said he was suspending the guilty man's sentence because of

Barck's intervention but warned, "If any one else follows the course you did, he'll go away for ninety days and serve the full term." For his part, the Hoboken poormaster informed the *Hudson Observer:* "I regretted having to do what I did in Zitani's case, but it was necessary to discourage like antics by other people."[49]

By February 25, however, the poormaster's threats were beginning to lose their potency for aid applicants. Joe Scutellaro, sitting on a bench in Barck's outer office that morning, had seen Lena Fusco's rage against her children's unallayed suffering and her contempt for the poormaster overwhelm any fear. It was splattered all over his clothes. "She had spit on him something terrible," Joe would later recall. He had watched the final moments of Lena Fusco's argument with Barck and heard his vow to cut off her relief. Joe remembered his own dealings with the poormaster. Harry Barck had always been unpleasant, had always abused him. He had shouted at him to get out when he returned to ask for food for his family.[50]

Barck returned to his office after the scene with Fusco and continued to call and dismiss aid-seekers. As the line that morning was reduced to four applicants, Joe heard the poormaster shout "Next!" Corrado was seated in front of him, but he turned and told Joe to go in first.

Joe stood and pushed back his glasses against his face. His green suit hung off of his five-foot, five-inch frame. He had lost a lot of weight in the past few months and weighed less than 120 pounds. He walked across the worn linoleum toward Harry Barck's private office and likely noted, with his builder's eye, that the poormaster's inner office was not truly a separate room but, like the reception area and the enclosure for secretaries, a small space carved out of a larger one, created by the addition of false fronts built with milky glass and wood panels, interrupted by doors. He stepped inside the poormaster's office.[51]

And there, perpendicular to the door, sat Harry Barck, hulking behind a boxy wooden desk that listed a little from the uneven settling of the old Hall's floors. Except for a small framed photograph of Barck in his younger days, surrounded by his cronies, there was nothing on the dingy painted walls to suggest the personal life of a man who had worked in the same office for forty-two years. Even that one old photo had been mounted casually, at a slight angle, as if the room barely deserved that little adornment.

Joe could see the poormaster in profile. As he would later describe it, he had to come around to the front of Harry Barck's desk to greet him. "Mr. Barck, good morning," Joe said.

The official did not answer; his head was bent over his desk as he scribbled notes about the last applicant. His desk was completely covered with papers and cards—loosely spread beneath his heavy arms as he wrote, and in wire trays, stacked in piles, jutting from cardboard boxes.

"I want my relief check," Joe Scutellaro said.

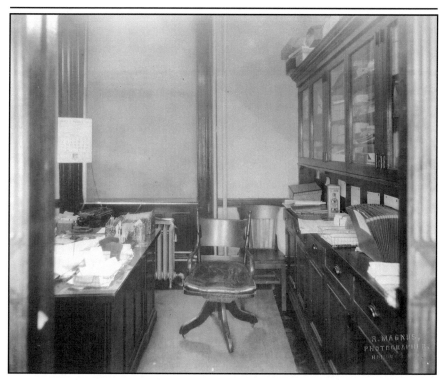

Harry L. Barck's desk in the poormaster's private office.
Forensic photo taken February 25, 1938.

From the case file *State v. Joseph F. Scutellaro*, 1939. Courtesy of the Hudson County Prosecutor's Office.

"Watch the mail, watch the mail," Barck replied without looking up. His response implied that he had ordered one of his typists to prepare an envelope to send Scutellaro's food order.

Joe had heard that before. And he remembered the last check, when Barck had instructed him to bring Anna to his office and had handed it to her after insulting them both. Maybe there was no check—in the mail or anywhere else. "It's been four weeks since you gave me the last food order, the one for $5.70," Joe said to the official. "When can I have another?" He swallowed deeply, thinking of Marie and little Joseph. "My children are home sick," he added, his throat tight with emotion. "They're starving. We have no food."

Barck raised his chin slightly, looking up from his paperwork. "What's the matter with your wife?" he asked, raising his eyebrows, still black despite his gray temples. "Can't she go down and swing her bag along Washington Street?"

Joe stared at the poormaster. "What do you mean by that?" he asked.

"Can't she make some money?" Barck proposed, a slight smile lifting the corners of his mustache. His ice-blue eyes were lit with amusement.

Joe suddenly understood what the poormaster was suggesting. "You can't talk about my wife that way!" he protested, his voice rising. He could feel the heat in his face and knew he was shouting.

"*You* get out of my office!" Barck yelled and abruptly rose to his feet, pushing back his chair, which slid along on metal casters and slapped into the porcelain corner sink that blocked the right corner of his desk. Barck's potbelly seemed to expand as he leaned in toward Joe. "You guinea," he boomed. "I'll break your goddamn neck!" He grabbed the lapels of the little man's coat, his face a dark red as he moved in closer. "Get out of this office!" he shouted into Joe's face.

Joe tried to pull back and felt the poormaster's thick fingers grip his coat still tighter. He was going to shake him until his neck cracked. Joe swung, hitting Barck in the face with his fist. The poormaster's head snapped back. Then the big man doubled over, falling face first, his barrel chest hitting the desk with a loud bang. He grunted and drew himself up slowly. And as Barck leaned back, Joe gasped; there was something sticking out of his chest. It looked like a metal desk spindle, one of the sharp files the poormaster kept on his desk to pierce rejected applications into a stack.

Joe reached across and yanked out the six-inch spike by its square base, throwing it to the floor. Barck gurgled and slumped forward, then began to drop. Joe began to feel dizzy. Everything whirled around him. He heard voices—people coming into the room, shouting, everyone running around—but he was in a fog, unable to think or move. He stood in front of the poormaster's desk, waxy pale and still, until Officer Thomas Carmody entered the office and grasped his arm to take him downstairs to police headquarters.

This was how Joe Scutellaro recalled what had happened in the poormaster's office. The only other person who could have described what had happened there, Harry Barck, was pronounced dead at 10:25 AM. Joseph Scutellaro, who had just been charged with "atrocious assault and battery," was about to be rebooked on a charge of murder.

3 | SUFFER THE LITTLE CHILDREN

JOE HAD NO WAY of knowing how long he'd been sitting in the Hoboken jail. He was numb. *What had happened?* He had tried to help his family. Now he was in this dingy basement cell, waiting . . . waiting for something worse to take place. He couldn't even turn around; the cell was as narrow as a coffin.[1]

He could barely focus. They had taken his glasses away. Was the old man going to die? That son of a bitch had insulted Anna, and now Joe had been charged with assault.[2]

He couldn't think of what the police might do to him. Would he ever be able to see his wife and his children again? He sat in his cell and covered his face with his rough hands. What would become of Marie and little Joe? When he imagined his children's upturned faces, he surely felt he'd be overcome by grief.[3]

But then he would have thought of Anna and grown calmer. Anna would do what she had to do to protect their children. Family was everything—a buffer against hardship, a leg up when needed. It could be a source of vindication, too, when that was called for. He'd known Anna ten years before they married, and this month they had celebrated their nine-year wedding anniversary. Anna would find a way.[4]

During the long Depression nightmare, he had seen how she could marshal her strength. She had certainly coped with their diminished income far better than Joe—probably because she had been poor before their marriage.[5]

Joseph Scutellaro in the Hoboken jail.

New York *Daily News* Archive/Getty Images.

One of eight children born to Italian immigrants, Anna Angelo had enjoyed the companionship of her many siblings and had also suffered with them when their longshoreman father, John, had fallen short on earnings.[6] The older men downtown still spoke wistfully of the once-thriving wharves and industries of prewar Hoboken, but dock work had long been subject to the schedules of shipping companies and the whims of hiring bosses.

And even after John Angelo had turned to running a corner grocery, the family had struggled financially. To help make ends meet, one of Anna's brothers, Christy, a chimney sweep during mild weather months, had worked for the Hoboken poormaster at Christmas. Christy Angelo knew Harry Barck as "a big politician" and the public face of city hall charity. Under Barck's direction, he had distributed Christmas baskets to McFeely supporters who may or may not have been in need. Some people downtown grumbled that the city's gifts of toys and candy were not really designed to help poor people anyway; the poor needed food or cash most of all.[7]

Anna remembered that Christy had asked Joe to join him in doling out Christmas baskets. This was before competition for city jobs—for any job—was so fierce. But Joe, she recalled, had vigorously declined to involve himself in "the vote-winning generosity of politicians."[8]

It had been easy for Joe to say that then, when the Scutellaro family was flush. Unlike the Angelos, who, like other laborers across the country, routinely lacked steady employment, Joe and his father had enjoyed a certain employment security—or so they had thought.[9]

The Scutellaros' financial descent—first with the loss of city jobs, then with the loss of *all* jobs—had been unexpected and, for the family patriarch, uncharacteristically humbling. Now in his sixty-fourth year, Frank Scutellaro had spent most of the preceding fifty vigorously establishing himself as an accomplished carpenter and contractor. He had been so driven, so intent upon advancement, that even on his wedding day in 1901, he had left for a job right after the celebration ended, peddling away on his bicycle. The twenty-seven-year-old groom's single-mindedness had likely bewildered his nineteen-year-old bride, Marie Thomas, but she had been smitten by the handsome, ambitious carpenter—as many women had been. Frank Scutellaro had been quite the ladies' man and an all-around charmer. And Marie, a Hobokenite by way of Alsace-Lorraine (she had left Europe at age four) must have sensed that his charisma and tenacity, combined with his carpentry skills, would help him succeed in a city with so many hungry workmen.[10]

In the years that followed, Frank Scutellaro could boast—and he did—that he'd made a good life for his family. But building it hadn't been *easy*. When he was a teenager arriving in the United States, Italian immigrants had faced vicious bigotry. For some their harassment had begun as soon as they'd debarked at the Hoboken pier. German dockmen had shouted ethnic slurs at the swarthy, dark-haired strangers and had set upon them with sticks.[11]

But the men who had left their native villages had been desperate for jobs. Unlike Frank, who arrived as a trained artisan, many had disembarked with only their strong backs to sell. They settled in Hoboken for the work the city offered. Though the labor they were hired to do was arduous and often dangerous, and Italian workers were subjected to abuse by Irish foremen, at least they *had* work.[12]

For every other necessity, the new arrivals had drawn upon the Old World. They had re-created societies and feasts to honor the saints that had so ably protected their towns on the other side. The faithful marched through the downtown streets carrying ornately ornamented banners and jewelry-clad statues; and behind them, clusters of children followed, eager to hear the sizzle and rapid-fire pops of fireworks that punctuated the marchers' path. When the weather was good, many gathered behind their tenements to celebrate. A backyard strip of dirt or poured cement—already narrowed by the installation of a henhouse or a grapevine—could be outfitted with a long communal table, around which family and friends would gather to eat a meal prepared in the tradition of the host's native province, and homemade wine was sure to inspire jubilant music.[13]

In those prewar years, the Scutellaro household had cause to celebrate. A year after they were married, Frank and Marie became parents. They would have been very unusual indeed, if they had doubted that their American-born son, whom they named Joseph, would inherit and build upon the success of his immigrant father—a prospect that became an imperative after Marie's later pregnancies failed.

Joe's position as an only child was sufficient to set him apart from his schoolmates, who mostly lived in homes crowded with siblings, but his increasingly prosperous parents had also spoiled him. After she knew she was going to marry him, Anna informed Joe that when she'd first seen him around town, she thought he was a show-off, with his new clothes and nice things. Not until they'd begun dating did she realize that Joe was unpretentious and even a little timid—nothing like his self-important father.[14]

Frank had become well known downtown, and he'd enjoyed his elevated stature. Never one to be shy, he'd been especially fond of grand public gestures. If something was going on in town, if the local Democrats were sponsoring an event, Frank Scutellaro wouldn't buy two or three tickets—he would buy a hundred. He was out to make an impression.

Over the next twenty-odd years, Frank bought and built properties, proudly showing off his series of brick apartment buildings and making neighbors aware of his string of west-side garages. The Scutellaros could now afford luxuries that many in the city could barely imagine. When Joe, just out of his teens, seemed tubercular and in need of a health retreat, Frank sent him to a resort in Pinehurst, North Carolina, where his recuperation included playing rounds of golf. And soon after, Joe became one of the first young men in town to have his own automobile— a gift from his father.

Joe's car might have added to Anna's perception that he was a show-off, but in the end, the car had helped him win her. The small parlor over the Angelos' corner store had been filled with suitors drawn to Anna's sunny nature and her splendid night-black hair. Joe gained a place in Anna's affections when he offered to take her infirm mother along with them on a drive—and then continued to ferry them to the countryside, after seeing how deeply the older woman enjoyed the views beyond her apartment window.

When they were alone, the smitten young man, who rarely spoke while in the Angelos' crowded apartment, would serenade Anna, singing in a clear and melodious voice Neapolitan love songs, tunes from popular American films, and German songs he'd picked up from his multilingual mother. And though a mutual friend had introduced Joe to Anna as "Harold Lloyd"—a reference to his striking resemblance to the handsome, dark-haired, bespectacled 1920s comedic film star—the man Anna fell in love with was not the go-getting character Lloyd most famously portrayed. No, Anna Angelo fell in love with a man who was mostly out of step with the noisy, frenetic, Jazz Age strivers; Joe Scutellaro was quiet and gentlemanly and—she would have had to admit—coddled. He had won her first with his slow, one-sided smile and then with his nearly desperate love. For Joe's proposal of marriage to Anna had had great force, coming from one so often silent. He had cried out to her that he could not live without her and could not bear the thought of her with another.[15]

As he sat in the cold Hoboken jail, Joe would have pictured Anna and their children. Every day, before he'd set out to search for work and the day's meager rations, he had drawn them close. He had noted his tiny son's pallor. When he bowed to kiss Marie, she would scan his face and offer a small, hopeful smile—a gesture both uplifting and heartbreaking. Each day he would leave the apartment with them in mind, as if they were accompanying him on his anxious rounds.[16]

Along with his son and daughter, perhaps, there had been the specters of other children. For following reports of children dying of starvation in faraway cities like Oakland, California, and even across the river in seemingly distant New York City, had come terrifying local news that would have haunted Joe Scutellaro: a little boy named Donald Hastie had starved to death in Hoboken after his parents had been denied more relief by Poormaster Harry Barck.[17]

———————— ⟨⟩ ————————

"Three-year-old Donald Hastie died of starvation at 9 o'clock yesterday morning at St. Mary's Hospital, Hoboken," the *Hudson Dispatch* declared on July 15, 1936, three months after the federal government, and then the state of New Jersey, had withdrawn from emergency poor relief and left Harry Barck in charge. By then the city's poor would have been unlikely to afford a daily newspaper, but with vendors hawking tabloids on the street, most would have seen the startling headline and the accompanying photograph of the boy's hollowed parents mourning beside a small white coffin.[18]

It would have been a difficult picture to forget.

The image would have instilled in Hoboken parents fear for the future of their children. For Joe and Anna Scutellaro, it surely stoked worries they already had. Their son, Joseph Jr.—born just a few months prior to Donald Hastie's wasting death—was terribly small and frail.[19]

Word of the local boy's starvation and his parents' protracted struggle to keep him alive had spread quickly in Hoboken. The poorest families would have heard about the state of Donald's body—"mere skin and bones," according to one observer—and eyed their sons and daughters with alarm. For the Hasties' story was all too familiar. Poormaster Barck had made the main breadwinner, thirty-five-year-old James, scurry for aid, and when it was finally granted, the unemployed father of three had received $5.40 in a biweekly check, or thirty-eight cents a day, to feed five people.[20]

The Hasties had left Scotland just before the onset of the Depression, hoping for a better future for their children in the United States. By 1936, faced with massive unemployment in their new location and lacking any relatives nearby, they sought simply to sustain themselves. James had begged the poormaster to approve more aid, so he could buy milk for his boys—eleven-year-old Jimmy, three-year-old Donald, and baby John, just over a year old. But Harry Barck had upbraided him for his audacity. "He told me I was no better than anyone else, that there was no money for 'extras,' and that I should be glad to get as much as I was getting," James would later recall, adding that Barck "told me there were plenty of jobs if I would look for them."[21]

After her son's death, thirty-two-year-old Margaret Hastie said she prayed her family's loss might bring about a change in the way relief was handled in Hoboken, "so that other babies of the unemployed will not go hungry or die like Donald." She did not want his passing to be put down to hard luck or neglectful parenting. Nor would she stand for later attempts by the city to obscure the cause of her child's death.[22]

Margaret told whoever would listen that two days before he died, Donald had been taken by ambulance from their first-floor Willow Avenue apartment to be treated for malnutrition in Hoboken's St. Mary Hospital. City funds supported the hospital's care for the destitute. Donald's undernourished state was recorded in the police blotter, and, after an examination, a hospital intern noted the same condition.[23]

But after Donald died and Margaret viewed his death certificate, she discovered that another doctor at the hospital had cited "lead poisoning" as the cause of death. And though the hospital was required to report the death and its cause to the county, the county physician did not learn of Donald's passing until contacted by a newspaper reporter.[24]

Margaret and James acknowledged that they had seen Donald eating chips of dried paint, peeled from the walls of their threadbare apartment, and they had tried repeatedly to stop him. But he had continued to do so, they asserted, to satisfy his unyielding hunger. "Donald often cried for milk and complained of being hungry," Margaret Hastie said. "I would explain to him that we had no money for milk." She protested that her son's death had been from starvation and requested an autopsy.

Her appeal went unfulfilled. The doctor who signed the death certificate professed to newsmen that the undertaker had somehow claimed Donald's body before a necropsy could be conducted. Nevertheless, he went on to assure them, the hospital had made X-rays and "other tests" to determine that the child's death was "definitely" the result of lead poisoning.[25]

The night the doctor issued Donald's death certificate, his parents held his wake in their front parlor. Neighbors helped with funeral expenses despite their own strained budgets. One contributed a suit for the boy's burial. Others paid for sprays of white flowers, the hearse rental, and the cost of two professional pallbearers to carry the coffin from the home to the funeral car. They even paid the Hasties' electric bill, so the tiny casket—donated by a local funeral director and opened to display Donald's body—would not sit in the dark, as the family had for so many weeks before.[26]

No city officials attended the wake. Mayor Bernard McFeely was not available for interview at his office, and when a *Dispatch* reporter reached him by telephone at his home and asked if he intended to investigate the death, the mayor replied, "I have no comment to make at this time."[27]

The reporter had pressed again. "Do you intend to check up on the relief situation to determine whether there are other cases like the Hastie case?" he asked.

"I have no comment to make at this time," responded the mayor.

The poormaster was, at first, said to be "bewildered by the developments," but his later published remarks were cool and unsentimental. Harry Barck informed a reporter that, regarding Donald Hastie, his conscience was clear. He had done all he could, he said, including making an offer to have his office pay for the child's burial in the potter's field, which the family had refused.[28]

On the morning of July 16, the Hasties, a few parishioners from the First Baptist Church, and its young minister, Reverend C. Robert Pedersen, assembled around Donald's coffin for a brief home service before making the journey to Hoboken Cemetery. Margaret Hastie wailed as she viewed her child for the last time. A friend held her tightly, gripping one of her spindly wrists to keep her from tearing at her hair.[29]

Hundreds of the Hasties' neighbors had gathered at the family's Willow Avenue tenement. They crowded the room adjoining the parlor, packed the hallway and stairs, and spilled over into the street. Four policemen were posted at the address to keep clear an aisle for the pallbearers and mourners to accompany the coffin out of the building.

Newspapermen arrived in force, too. Hoboken's more comfortable residents, the ones who could yet afford their daily newspapers and adequate food and who might have continued to believe that the poor were responsible for their own suffering, would now be faced with a damning account of the failure of the relief system.

The story would extend to readers well beyond Hoboken's borders, including state lawmakers. More than a dozen journalists covered the boy's funeral, and just as many photographers perched on fire escapes to best capture the developing scene. "Widespread publicity has been given the case," one reporter commented, "and from its repercussions and the welter of conflicting opinions attending it, there has been sounded a note of its possible use as a political issue, involving the question of whether relief administration may be best handled by the state or by municipalities."[30]

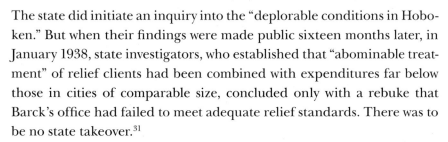

The state did initiate an inquiry into the "deplorable conditions in Hoboken." But when their findings were made public sixteen months later, in January 1938, state investigators, who established that "abominable treatment" of relief clients had been combined with expenditures far below those in cities of comparable size, concluded only with a rebuke that Barck's office had failed to meet adequate relief standards. There was to be no state takeover.[31]

"We did all we humanly could . . . ," a state official charged with overseeing relief standards later declared, "but we cannot go into a municipality and dictate. We have no police powers and can only tell them what we think they should do in maintaining relief standards." Under the law, he explained, ". . . administration is a local matter, with the state only an indirect supervisor. We make our investigations, and do what we can, but the matter of who gets relief and how much is up to the local overseers."[32]

Mayor McFeely, who could have removed Barck from his appointed post, made no changes and issued no statements reproaching his overseer. Harry Barck remained in power for a few weeks after the state shrugged off responsibility for Hoboken's poor. Then came the fatal altercation with Joe Scutellaro on February 25.

4 | IN THE DARK

AFTER JOE LEFT HER side that February morning, Anna Scutellaro had stayed in bed, trying to trap under the blankets the extra bit of warmth left by her husband's body. This is what poor people had learned in the Depression: to stay in bed as much as possible, to save fuel and to cut back the amount of food they needed to keep warm.[1]

At least Joe's parents owned their house, so they would not be forced on to the street in the bitter cold. Who hadn't seen the pathetic bundles of evicted tenants? Those people had been doubly shamed. The bedding and clothes they'd been unable to mend or even wash—the sign of utter destitution they had once been able to hide in their private rooms—had landed on the street, for all to see.[2]

The bedroom had been so cold; it would have been hard to get out of bed. But Anna could hear her son coughing. First she'd taken her daughter out of school when she came down with the measles, and just as Marie was getting better, little Joe had started to get symptoms.[3]

The coughing had continued, accompanied by the sounds of her daughter washing. Anna rose from her bed to see to the children, first pulling on a dark housedress. She'd noticed the previous day that Marie was well enough to be out of bed, though she was not yet ready to return to school.[4]

Anna saw that Marie had dressed herself in a cotton frock and a wool cardigan she had almost outgrown. As the stove fire died down, she would top the sweater with a heavy robe. Her daughter's dark eyes were sad, beseeching. She seemed older than her six years.

Though her understanding of her family's troubles was incomplete, Marie had learned things that had subdued some of her childishness. She knew she shouldn't complain about having to eat onion sandwiches or potatoes with chutney; she knew she should be good and not make demands. Most of all, she knew she was supposed to help care for her sickly younger brother.[5]

Marie watched her mother cut the rolls Joe had left for them, looking on with steadfast concentration, and ate the squares with equal purpose. Perhaps she also knew if she ate each small piece very slowly, she could trick her stomach into feeling full.

Anna had left Joseph in his pajamas, as he was still recuperating. She could put him back in bed after she had fed him some bread and a bit of the milk she had managed to get on credit. She covered him in a robe and carried him to the kitchen, along with a blanket, in case he grew chilly during the short meal. He coughed in short, staccato bursts, then stopped, exhausted.

Anna set out to wash windows in the railroad apartment's front room. A fine ash from the stove fires had settled on the panes, and it must have seemed to her that she was always cleaning them. Her mother-in-law remembered how she had labored in the days before electric home appliances and gas heat; and now Anna found herself cast back to the turn of the century, when housewives had battled the accumulation of soot every day, wiping down lamps, scrubbing everything by hand.[6]

Just after 10 AM, Anna heard her mother-in-law call to her from their vestibule. The mail had arrived, including a letter addressed to Joe that was marked PERSONAL. It had been mailed in Hoboken the day before, at 5 PM. The return address was a Hoboken post office box.[7]

When Anna opened the envelope, she saw that it had been sent by the poormaster's office. It contained a book of thirty salmon-colored coupons for bread (one loaf per ticket) to be picked up from the Continental Baking Company, Ninth and Clinton Streets, and a grocery check for eight dollars, made out to grocer William Schmidt at 941 Garden Street. That was where she would have to go to exchange the order for food.

A month had passed since the family had received their last food check, the one for $5.70, which the poormaster had handed over after summoning them to his office and insulting them. Then Joe had returned, again and again, and Barck had told him each time to make out a new application. But they didn't want applications, they wanted food. How could a family live on $5.70 for four weeks? After one visit to the poormaster's office Joe had returned to tell Anna that Barck had advised the family to save on electric bills by using candles. "Candles were good enough for us in the old days," the poormaster had told him.[8]

But at least the eight-dollar grocery check had arrived. Anna didn't know what they were going to do about their other bills; they had borrowed five dollars to pay what they owed for electricity, but the utility said it would cut off the gas in three days if that bill wasn't paid. They had been trying so hard to ration their use. She didn't know what was going to happen to them.[9]

PUBLIC RELIEF

OVERSEER OF POOR

HOBOKEN, N. J.

To

Continental Baking Company

9th and Clinton Streets

Hoboken, N. J.

Book of tickets for day-old bread, received by Anna Scutellaro on the day her husband was charged with killing the poormaster.
Courtesy of the Hudson County Prosecutor's Office.

She went about her chores, trying to distract herself. Around midday, she heard a loud rap on the door, followed by a few more, and the mingled voices of several men talking loudly. Anna opened the door to find more than twenty men pushing toward her, men dressed in heavy coats to protect themselves against the cold. Some were carrying boxy black cameras.

She must have let them in, though whether they had asked first was snuffed out by all that occurred after. The men barely crossed the threshold before barraging her with questions, each one rushing in when another had received his answer. She had responded to most of them, but it would have seemed as if she were speaking from a deep hole, sunk below the ground-floor room in which her interrogators stood. She had tumbled down unaware and had stood dazed, unable to break the rhythm of persistent questioning to ask a question of her own.[10]

One man asked how long they'd been living there. He was standing next to a photographer, who saw in Anna's bewildered compliance an invitation to begin taking pictures. His camera's flash interjected a burst of white light into the dim, plain kitchen—then another photographer followed, and another. Each sudden illumination was accompanied by the swift crackle of the bulbs' burning metal foil.

"We've been living at this address since we were married about seven years ago," Anna said. By this time she was holding Joseph in her arms. He blinked at the first jolts of light and laughed, but as more photographers joined in, he began to whimper. He turned his face away, seeking the comfort of his mother's shoulder. Marie edged Anna's hip, staring up woefully at the men who were pressing in on them.

A reporter asked how long her husband had been out of work.

"Joe lost his job about six months ago—he was a laborer for the General Electric Company," Anna replied. She did not mention that he had worked as a skilled carpenter's assistant when construction jobs were plentiful, nor that he had playfully acquired a chauffeur's license during their courtship. She did not declare his latest jobs digging ditches or report his backbreaking roadwork. The questions came too fast for her to give a full accounting of a thirty-six-year-old man's life, what kind of work he had done well, and the work he had taken on simply because it *was* work.[11]

Another reporter wanted to know how the family had been getting along. She told them about their bills, the borrowing, the small grocery order she had received from the poormaster weeks before, his retorts when Joe had told him that they would soon lose their electricity.

And how would you describe how Joe has been feeling lately? a voice questioned from somewhere within the crowd of newsmen.

Anna must have felt then that something bad had happened, for she said in a flat voice, "Joe's in some kind of trouble." She turned to the man closest to her, a man who was writing notes with a pencil on a small pad of paper, and implored, "Tell me—what has he done?" Her eyes focused on the one man, then cast around the room to others.

But no one answered. There was silence, then a resumption of the job at hand. One newsman later admitted, "Everybody evaded the subject—buried it under a new avalanche of questions."

A voice repeated the query about Joe.

"Since Joe's out of work, he's been sick," Anna replied haltingly. She explained how he had gone to the Jersey City Medical Center and had been told he had "a nervous condition." He was sick with worry. "He couldn't sleep. They gave him some medicine and told him to come back March 1," she explained. Again she left out details; she was not about to tell them that Joe had also told the doctor that he'd thought of committing suicide, that he'd imagined, in his despair, throwing himself in front of a trolley car. "He used to walk around all the time looking for a job," Anna said. He had left the house every morning at six or seven to look for work "but he could never get anything steady."[12]

And nothing from the poormaster for weeks? a reporter asked.

She had received a check that morning, for eight dollars, she said, and several reporters began to shout at once, asking her what time she had found it. When she told them that it had been around 10:15, a collective groan came from the crowd, and the reporters quickly scribbled this fact—that the killing had occurred just as the check was arriving at the Scutellaro home.

That must have been when three of her relatives rushed in to tell Anna that her husband had been arrested and charged with the slaying of Harry Barck, for the front pages of many metropolitan newspapers that evening and the next featured a photograph of Anna holding a handkerchief to her face in an attempt to staunch her flooding tears, and clinging to her was her little son, his face crumpled, weeping, as children do when they are ill and hungry and cold and frightened, and their mothers are grieving.[13]

Anna Scutellaro and her two children, after learning that her husband
has been charged with the murder of the poormaster.

New York *Daily News* Archive/Getty Images.

The local afternoon newspaper, the *Jersey Observer*, maintained an unusually cozy relationship with Hoboken's city hall. Located just across the
street, the daily's tendency to report the administration's point of view
had less to do with geographic proximity than with the publisher's enjoyment of a profitable side business selling stationery to the Hall and printing all of its election ballots and official publications. Nevertheless, the
paper could be counted on to publish the McFeely line whenever it was
called for.[14]

And so Harry Barck's clerk, Eleonore Hartmann, had immediately
talked to the *Observer* reporter she knew, allowing her tale to make the
deadline for the day's paper. She told her story even before she provided an official statement to the police. While her account was being

distributed on city streets, a Hoboken patrolman typed her statement and she signed it.[15]

Under a banner headline, the *Observer* laid out Eleonore Hartmann's version of the crime, an "eyewitness" account, the paper stated, of the slaying. For Hartmann claimed that she had actually *watched* the terrible deed take place. Indeed, she asserted, she was the sole witness, and in the days that followed, her version of the killing, and her description of her central role in assisting the dying poormaster and identifying the culprit, would take on a distinct shape and establish itself in the public imagination. The speed with which Hartmann's account had reached the *Observer*, and her unwillingness to alter it substantially, would later be cited as a sign of its truthfulness.[16]

Hartmann claimed she had been in her outer office when she heard her boss exchange a few words with Joe Scutellaro. She then heard "a loud grunt." She said she walked to the door of the poormaster's office. "The grunt I heard was Mr. Barck's as he was being pushed back against the steel file cabinet for medical supplies," she said. "Scutellaro then swung the steel-pointed file into Mr. Barck's chest and as the latter pushed the man away, he said, 'Oh my God, he got me, get an ambulance.'"

Hartmann described her boss stumbling from his desk. He had attempted to reach the pocket of his overcoat, which had been hanging near the partition that separated his office from the anteroom. It had been an effort, she said, "to apparently secure a police whistle he kept there." But as Barck reached for it, he had "crumpled up" and fallen to the floor. She tried to reach for the office phone to call for help, she said, but the poormaster had become entangled in the cord and had yanked it out of the wall as he fell. She cried out, and some of the relief clients still waiting in the reception room had hurried into the office and tried to rouse the fallen man. They had lifted him on to a settee. Dr. Lawrence Kelly, an intern at Hoboken's St. Mary Hospital, had arrived by then and, soon after, pronounced Harry Barck dead.

The following day, more New Jersey newspapers broadcast the news of the poormaster's killing. The *Hudson Dispatch* reported that Scutellaro had confessed after being questioned by Police Chief Edward J. McFeely, and it highlighted the arrival of the eight-dollar grocery check at the Scutellaro home just as he was entering the poormaster's office. "Had Scutellaro been a patient man and remained home," the reporter chastised, "he would have received the check by mail." Scutellaro was portrayed as "in a rage," then hurrying toward the street after his brutal crime.[17]

Eleonore Hartmann's story received some additional tweaking, too. She told the *Dispatch* how she'd hurried to Barck's aid and then "saw Scutellaro's hand leap out, saw him strike Barck on the chest." But in this new account—and in all future accounts given by this "witness"—Hartmann no longer claimed to have actually *seen* the long metal file in the alleged killer's hand. She only saw the blow. Now she stated that she had not known that Barck had actually been *stabbed* until much later. Otherwise she would have been seen as a woman who neglected to inform the arriving physician of the cause of her boss's injury, rather than as a tragic and loyal secretary. There had been no blood visible on Barck's shirt, and his chest wound had not been discovered until the doctor removed the injured man's clothing.

The following day, the *Observer* depicted on its cover a photograph of a primly attired Miss Hartmann—"who went to Barck's aid when attacked"—gazing thoughtfully at her boss's spindle-dotted desk. Placed alongside her picture were photographs of the "dazed but remorseless" slayer, Joe Scutellaro, and his tearful family, who had just been told the news of his arrest.[18]

Hartmann's account now included claims that she had heard Barck call to her as he was being threatened by the relief client, that she had tried to pull Scutellaro off, and that she had heard Barck repeatedly say "I'm done for" before he fell to the floor. Despite these embellishments, the *Observer* declared: "Out of the welter of conflicting stories originally surrounding the slaying, the version given by Miss Eleanor Hartmann, acting secretary to the poormaster, stands out clearly. She repeats the story without material deviation from its original form."

But at least one newspaper was not buying Hartmann's story, and with good reason. The *New York Post*, which was then preparing an exposé of Mayor Bernard McFeely's administration, held that the killing had been an accident—with Hoboken's own police chief, Edward J. McFeely, as the source. Just after Barck was killed, and before Scutellaro had spent hours in the police station—before the defendant had signed, with a shaky hand, a confession typed up by a police officer—the chief had spoken to a *Post* reporter. Scutellaro, he said, had told him, "I was asking Barck to give us more money for food. He wouldn't listen to me. He said, 'Dismissed, dismissed,' and I punched him in the face." After the poor-master reeled back, Scutellaro continued, "the next thing I saw there was a spike sticking in him. I pulled it out and dropped it on the floor."[19]

One aspect of the case was reported the same way in all the newspapers, including the *Post*. Reporters noted that when the spike was retrieved from the floor, several rejected applications from aid-seekers were still impaled upon it.[20]

5 | DEFENDERS

IT WAS ALREADY LATE Saturday morning when Joe Scutellaro, still dressed in the shabby green suit he had put on the day before, was led out of the city jail, through two sets of barred steel gates, and up a flight of stairs to be arraigned in the Recorder's Court on charges of premeditated murder and assault. His arraignment had been delayed while his attorney, Samuel S. Leibowitz, made his way to Hoboken from his home in Manhattan Beach, Brooklyn, to represent him.[1]

All Friday Anna had tried unsuccessfully to contact the New York lawyer and had finally made contact early Saturday morning, securing Leibowitz's services and commanding his swift departure for the western shores of the Hudson. By then she would have fully realized the monstrous threat—almost beyond imagining—that Joe, if convicted of murder, might receive a death sentence; and she would have found some relief in the anticipated arrival of a skilled defender who had kept so many from the electric chair.

Sam Leibowitz, like Clarence Darrow before him, was recognized as one of the country's top criminal defense lawyers. But while Darrow had inaugurated his career as a defender of labor, Leibowitz had not started out as a champion of *any* cause. The ambitious young lawyer had initially made his name by routinely winning acquittals for petty criminals and big-time gangsters like "Bugsy" Siegel and Al Capone.

But after accumulating such victories for a dozen years, Sam Leibowitz took on a groundbreaking case that "transcended his ambition": he became chief counsel for the defense of nine indigent defendants known as the "Scottsboro Boys," black youths who had been falsely accused in March 1931 of raping two southern white women. Based exclusively on Leibowitz's record of client acquittals, the lead organization supporting the youth's defense, the Communist Party–affiliated International Labor Defense (ILD), asked the headline-grabbing criminal defender to represent the "boys." Leibowitz, a mainstream Democrat, accepted the case after making it clear in the press that he was not in any way allied with the ILD or its politics.[2]

The Scottsboro case became a cause célèbre. Huge public rallies were held in major cities in the United States and internationally, as the defendants were tried and sentenced to death, then tried and sentenced again. Once committed to the case, Leibowitz worked for more than four years without pay and faced repeated death threats. He managed to win new trials for two of the defendants, following a successful appeal to the US Supreme Court, and made civil rights history when the court directed southern states to include black citizens on jury rolls after Leibowitz proved their deliberate exclusion. By the time of Joe Scutellaro's arrest, widespread national coverage of the lawyer's resolute defense of the Scottsboro nine, and the rallies in Harlem where the defender had been held aloft on the shoulders of supporters, had ensured the name Samuel S. Leibowitz would be recognizable to almost anyone who followed the news.[3]

But Anna Scutellaro had not been one to pay much attention to what was happening across the river, even when her family could still afford a daily newspaper. She had turned to a cousin who had always been on top of the news, and had gained his assistance in finding a lawyer to save Joe.[4]

Her cousin directed her well. He had surely known about Scottsboro—several months earlier there had been another burst of coverage, when four of the defendants were released by Alabama officials after evidence of the youths' innocence was grudgingly acknowledged—but Anna's relative had likely recommended Sam Leibowitz for the lawyer's growing, and well-publicized, practice among ordinary men and women. These clients had been indicted for the first time for a major crime— usually murder—and like Joe, they had faced the possibility of death if convicted. Anna's cousin would have known that not one of Leibowitz's "ordinary" clients had been executed, and that the defender had won outright acquittals for all but a few. "Everyone agreed," a historian would later note, that Sam Leibowitz "was the man to call if you were accused of a crime for which the jury might send you to the chair."[5]

Hoboken's city hall was packed with observers—jostling newsmen, piqued city workers, inquisitive neighbors—when the famous New York lawyer arrived. Just under six feet tall, stocky, with stooped shoulders and thinning, combed-over gray hair, forty-four-year-old Sam Leibowitz often made an unassuming first impression—if one ignored the finely tailored three-piece suit that bespoke comfortable success, the self-assured gait, and, most of all, the intent gaze that took in all that transpired before him.[6]

"Mr. Leibowitz!" one reporter called out to him. "Why this case?"

The lawyer broke stride briefly to reply. "I'm always interested in poor people," he responded, before making his way into the Recorder's Court.[7]

The courtroom Leibowitz entered was drab and musty, undecorated save for a large American flag hung vertically against the back wall. In front of the wooden rail that separated the desks of the judge and his clerk from the rows of benches stood a ragged line of local police reporters, correspondents from the wire services, and photographers from at least a dozen area dailies.[8]

The story of the poormaster's killing had already begun to appear in newspapers around the country, facilitated by wire services and newspaper syndicates. Except for local news, several thousand daily and weekly US newspapers regularly printed nearly identical reports from the Associated Press, United Press, or International News Service. By the time Leibowitz arrived in Hoboken, the slaying attributed to his client had been reported to readers well beyond the "metro area"—to cities as near as Gettysburg, Pennsylvania, and Dunkirk, New York, on the shores of Lake Erie, and others as distant as Abilene, Texas, and Ogden, Utah.[9]

Although there would later be coverage in several Italian-language newspapers, the residents of Hoboken's Italian quarter had not needed any publication to tell them what had happened in city hall and what was meant to occur that morning. Hundreds of downtown men and women had made their way to the courtroom, crowding in until there was no place left to stand. Many shared the Scutellaros' predicament, their poverty betrayed by their visibly mended, dusky coats, years out of style.

When the room could hold no more, the crowd spilled out into the corridor to wait, issuing a low rumble of sympathy for the alleged murderer, who, the papers claimed, had confessed. They knew nothing about the appearance of Sam Leibowitz, yet unannounced. They had rushed to city hall to catch a glimpse of *Joe Scutellaro*—the little man who had wreaked a kind of terrible justice for the city's poor, and for poor Italians, especially. They had felt most keenly the humiliations and slurs launched by the old poormaster and were undoubtedly a little awed by Joe's daring—or his desperation. They were afraid, too, on his behalf. They knew he could be sentenced to die.[10]

A neighborhood defense fund had been established as soon as word of Scutellaro's arrest had reached the downtown streets. Well over $1,000, most of it in small amounts, had been gathered before the arraignment. Donations from Italian American supporters would continue to pour in over the coming days, despite reports that Leibowitz was taking the case without compensation.[11]

Neighbors were looking after Anna and the children, too, for they had not only lost to prison a beloved husband, father, and family breadwinner, they had been stripped of the relief check and bread tickets Joe had so doggedly pursued. For after Joe was brought into custody, Police Chief Edward McFeely sent a sergeant to Monroe Street to escort Anna to the station. She was instructed to bring with her the aid she'd received from the poormaster. It was to be used as evidence at her husband's trial.[12]

Once in the courtroom, Sam Leibowitz had but a few moments to greet his new client, who stood near him, in the defendant's dock. Half a foot taller than Joe, Leibowitz leaned in to utter a few encouraging words before the proceedings began.

As always, Leibowitz was prepared to set the stage for his client's defense, to sway opinion, with his very first public statements. He knew he would be perceived as an interloper by the Hudson County prosecutors—a rogue New York lawyer coming to tell them how to handle their affairs—and that they would try to encourage potential jurors to see him that way, too. Although they would be unlikely to label him "this Jew from New York" as the county solicitor had done in Alabama, they would want to stoke the territoriality of Hudson County residents, which persisted despite the region's many ties to the vast metropolis across the river, despite easy access by ferry and a rapid transit link under the Hudson that could carry them, in just a few minutes, from Hoboken to Sam Leibowitz's lower Broadway offices in Manhattan. No jurors were being selected that day, or for many days, Leibowitz knew, but the minds of Hudson County residents were being shaped with each proceeding and with each new press account of the case.[13]

He began by politely asking the presiding judge, Frank Romano, a baby-faced young man with dark waves of fashionably brilliantined hair, to explain the anticipated proceeding, presenting himself as unfamiliar with local procedure. The judge sat at his desk, behind a row of bound statutes.[14]

When Romano finished his dissertation, Leibowitz requested a postponement. He had only been reached that morning by his client's family, he explained, and he had not been able to properly prepare: the little he knew about the case had been explained by Mrs. Scutellaro or had come from newspaper accounts, and he had had no opportunity to confer with his client. Romano denied his request, then nodded at Assistant Prosecutor Frank Schlosser, who was handling the early stages of the case for the state.[15]

Schlosser called Patrolman Thomas Carmody as the first witness. The assistant prosecutor had once held Romano's position, known as recorder of Hoboken's Police Court, and knew the process well.[16]

Before Carmody could stand, Leibowitz again addressed Romano, asking for a postponement in order to have a court stenographer in the courtroom.

"What would it avail you to have a stenographer?" Romano responded testily, his thick black eyebrows knitting together as he frowned. "It would make no difference as to the outcome, this arraignment being merely for the establishment of a prima facie case, and the defendant's commitment to jail."[17]

Leibowitz explained that he had found preliminary hearings in such cases were often the most important phase. In the brief period between his acceptance of the case and his crossing of the Hudson, Leibowitz had surely learned—if he had not already heard it through the legal grapevine—that the Hudson County Lawyers Guild was actively seeking passage of state legislation that would require official stenographers in all courtrooms for the best administration of justice. And he would have known that the guild had only recently approved a County Bar Association investigation into the "judicial and professional conduct" of Recorder Frank Romano—the very judge seated before him—for administering justice according to his "whim and fancy," for ignoring the rights and constitutional guarantees of defendants, and for allowing himself to be openly swayed by officers of the Hoboken Police Department.[18]

Romano's critics had further declared that the judge had "disgraced, debased, and degraded" a local lawyer who had attended his courtroom to represent another member of the bar. His client had alleged his receipt of a parking summons—followed by a disorderly conduct charge when he objected to the police officer—was an act of retribution by the McFeelys, for the ticketed counselor had dared to represent a former city employee who had had a disagreement with the mayor and had emerged from the Boss's office with a shiner below one eye. Mayor McFeely, it was reported in local newspapers, had sustained some slight bruising to his knuckles.[19]

The Bar Association might have been outraged by the mayor's actions, but they were most outraged by Recorder Romano's ill treatment of fellow attorneys. Those charges in particular, one member had asserted, warranted Romano's removal as recorder. But while a committee formed by the association investigated the charges against the judge, Romano continued to preside over the Recorder's Court in much the same way he had always done. He continued to be curt and offhand with defense attorneys—including the famous lawyer from New York.[20]

So when Sam Leibowitz persisted in his request for a postponement, Romano waved him aside. "Denied," he said sharply. He was eager to move on with the proceedings, to hear the testimony of Hoboken's police officers.

Patrolman Carmody was invited to take the stand. He was a stocky man with a soft schoolboy's face. Gently questioned by Schlosser, he spoke briefly about his post outside the poormaster's office, and his response to Eleonore Hartmann's call for help. When he entered the room, he said, he saw Barck lying on the floor and Joe Scutellaro standing at the official's desk.[21]

"Just what was the condition of the defendant?" Leibowitz then asked. "Did he look wild—frightened?" Reporters standing nearby were furiously scribbling his questions into their notebooks, already speculating that the defense attorney might launch an insanity defense.

"He appeared to be startled," Carmody replied, then added, "excited, and somewhat frightened."

Schlosser next called Dr. Lawrence Kelly, an intern at Hoboken's St. Mary Hospital. On the day of the killing, Kelly had been summoned to the poormaster's office to attend to Harry Barck. Leibowitz watched closely as Kelly began to speak. The lawyer's gray-green eyes scanned the young doctor's face for signs of deceit. A skillful reading of a man's face could help in deciphering what he was thinking—a talent Leibowitz believed was essential to a criminal lawyer's success. Kelly calmly explained how he had examined Barck's abdomen at first, believing that the poormaster had keeled over after being punched or kicked. He had not known that Barck had been stabbed, he said, until he saw a small, dark bloodstain on the elderly man's shirtfront and had opened it to find a puncture wound to the left side of Barck's chest. Kelly had been the one to pronounce the poormaster's death, believing a perforated lung had been the cause. The young doctor had not conducted the autopsy. Leibowitz studied Kelly's face for a few moments, then dismissed him.[22]

Police Chief Edward J. McFeely was called next. He was not an overly tall man, but he was blocky and commanded space. Dressed in a good suit and tie, gray-haired, jowly, with a thick neck and tightly fitting wire-frame glasses, the fifty-five-year-old chief could have been mistaken for a banker, though his barrel-chested swagger and self-satisfied smile suggested something of the neighborhood bully. He tilted his square chin up toward Recorder Romano in greeting, then began to explain how he had personally directed the investigation of the defendant. He had taken a signed statement from Scutellaro, he said, in which the defendant had admitted stabbing Barck with the desk file.[23]

"What did you say to him?" Leibowitz asked. The defense attorney had established himself early in his legal career as a "cop fighter." Employing what was then a new and highly effective defense, Leibowitz had used newspaper exposés of prisoner beatings and questionable interrogation techniques by New York City police officers to discredit his clients' signed confessions and to win acquittals—even when his clients were career criminals. His raised eyebrows while questioning McFeely would have implied that he would not have been surprised to learn that the Hoboken chief condoned rough treatment of prisoners.[24]

"I warned him about his rights," McFeely replied smoothly.

"Just exactly what did you say?" persisted Leibowitz.[25]

"I told him that any statements he made would be taken down in writing and used as evidence against him," McFeely responded. He knew Leibowitz's reputation, too, and he wasn't going to be baited.

"I'd like to see the signed confession," Leibowitz said.

Schlosser rose to object. The defense attorney, he asserted, had no legal standing to demand the confession, which had not even been introduced into evidence.

"All right, we'll get it another way," Leibowitz said, looking steadily at McFeely. The chief's mouth remained in a steady line.

The defense attorney continued his questioning, inquiring about who was present when the statement was made. In addition to himself, the chief said, two detectives and four policemen were present: *seven* members of the police force and Joseph Scutellaro. No other civilians were in the room. McFeely testified that Scutellaro had announced, "I will talk now," and then had admitted to picking up the file and stabbing the poormaster after being told his relief was in the mail.

Joe began to mutter a few words of objection, but Leibowitz raised his hand to quiet him.[26]

The chief continued. He said he'd shown Scutellaro the file that had been retrieved from the office floor. The defendant, he continued, had told him he would be unable to identify it because it had been straight when he picked it up, and the one McFeely held was bent.

Again Joe began to object, and again Leibowitz stopped him.

"You had no other conversation with the defendant at any time?" Leibowitz asked, turning toward the police chief. "There were no further statements—nothing has been left out?"

McFeely paused, and a contented smile spread across his big, fleshy face. "As far as I can recall, I have given the statement, substantially," he replied.

Assistant Prosecutor Schlosser stood and applied for commitment of Joseph Scutellaro, without bail, to the county jail. Recorder Romano ordered the defendant held for action by the grand jury. The arraignment was over.

In all, the hearing had taken about a half-hour, but Joe Scutellaro was exhausted. The shambling little man was led out of the prisoner's dock and returned to a heavily guarded cell in police headquarters, to await his transfer to the county jail. He sat listlessly on the cell's thinly covered metal bed, his back to the rank built-in toilet.

While Joe waited, Ralph Corrado, Nicholas Russo, and John Galdi Jr.—the clients who had been in the poormaster's waiting room when the alleged crime took place, and who had been held, until that morning, in the city jail—were booked as material witnesses and committed, without bail, to the county facility.

Several hundred supporters waited outside the door to the Recorder's Court, making the sidewalks of Newark Street impassible as they watched for Joe Scutellaro's removal to the county jail. They stood in the cold for nearly two hours, stamping their feet, calling out bits of news to each other in a mixture of English and Italian, until they saw him. Under guard of three detectives who towered over him, Joe was led from the Hall to a waiting police car. He did not seem to notice the mass of people who moved in closer as he neared the vehicle. His eyes were flat, and his face had become an ashen mask.

The waiting clique called out greetings, advice, encouragement—their hoarse cries overlapping so that they became indistinguishable, one from the other, culminating into a low roar of assent.

Joseph Scutellaro leaving the Hoboken jail in handcuffs.

New York *Daily News* Archive/Getty Images.

Then the car carrying the prisoner shifted into gear and pulled away from the crowd.

Sam Leibowitz made sure to speak to the reporters who called that night to inquire about the case. He had met with Scutellaro briefly at the Hoboken jail, he told them, but he and his client had had no privacy, as a number of policemen were around at all times. He would confer with his client to discuss defense plans on Monday—the same day, reporters later pointed out, that Harry L. Barck was to be buried. "The chances are," Sam Leibowitz told reporters, "that I am going to delve deeply into the way relief is distributed in Hoboken. I hope that other unfortunates are not driven to distraction as this man was."[27]

6 | TWO FUNERALS

LOCAL NEWSPAPERS ANNOUNCED TWO funeral services for Harry Ludwig Barck and advised the public that both were to be held at the Volk Mortuary Chapel on Washington Street in Hoboken. On Sunday night, February 27, they reported, members of Barck's Elks Lodge would perform a "ritualistic" rite; the following day a member of his Christian Science church would read from scripture before the poormaster's coffin was removed to the cemetery.[1]

The reporters who arrived at Volk's dutifully recorded the scene. They noted the twenty floral pieces sent by organizations. They observed the appearance of a delegation from the United Spanish War Veterans, in recognition of Barck's brief stateside service. And they decorously refrained from seeking comment from the poormaster's stunned survivors: his widow, Augusta Hoth Barck, with whom he had celebrated a golden wedding anniversary; his fifty-year-old son, US Army major William F. Barck, an engineer living in Washington, DC; and his two daughters, forty-six-year-old Eleanor Vanderwolf and thirty-seven-year-old Catharine Vanderwolf, who had married brothers and who were both living with their families in Dover, New Jersey.[2]

Ultimately, the newsmen were most interested in reporting on the parade of political notables who entered Volk's Chapel—a display some saw as befitting a powerful relief official who had served eight mayors and five political bosses during his forty-two-year tenure. "Many who knew and respected Mr. Barck for his administration of city relief—for his handling of the job as he thought it should be handled—were in attendance at his funeral service," a *Jersey Observer* reporter later proclaimed.[3]

More than two hundred of these friends and associates had bundled themselves against strong gusts and a sudden drop in temperature and had slowly filed past the mortuary's beveled and leaded glass window to enter the darkened chapel and pay their respects. At each service they formed a kind of *Who's Who* of Hudson County political life. "Prominent local folk" in attendance included octogenarian Michael Coyle, under whose local party leadership Barck had been appointed to the poormaster's post; several past and present county freeholders; former and incumbent state assemblymen, city attorneys, and commissioners; a district court judge; and, arriving with Mayor Bernard McFeely, six Hoboken policemen involved in the Scutellaro case. Along with the arresting patrolman Thomas Carmody, there was Captain Dennis D. Sullivan, who had led the defendant away in handcuffs; the lead detective, Inspector Thomas Garrick; and three top brass who were also related to the mayor: his brother Edward; his nephew Captain B. J. McFeely; and a lieutenant, J. Romeo Scott, whose son was married to a McFeely niece.[4]

These men—the assembled policemen and politicians—perceived the poormaster's killing as a crime against the established order, for Harry Barck had been one to follow the rules, both written and understood. He had been the oldest man in the city's employ—born in 1865, before electricity came to the city, before automobiles—and though industry and innovation had vastly changed city life during Barck's lifetime, Hoboken's views on bossism and aid to the poor had remained remarkably constant, and Harry Barck, the assembled mourners could agree, had given his all to ensure that continuity.[5]

Of those attending the services, perhaps only the aged pol Michael Coyle (still on the public payroll with an appointed county post) truly knew how the Hoboken of Harry Barck's youth both resembled and differed from the Depression-era city in which the poormaster had died. Barck had come of age during a period when German Americans still had power in the city. Voters of German and Irish ancestry had then totaled more than

60 percent of the county electorate, and up-and-coming Irish politicians had considered it prudent to court the self-interest of men of German heritage. Harry Barck would have had an opportunity to have a career rise out of his steadfast work for the county Democratic organization.[6]

Barck had no inherited wealth or advanced education, but he was a determined party man, and he offered the city and county bosses his unstinting loyalty. They, in turn, offered him a rare and coveted reward: secure employment. Working-class men who were similarly short of means and schooling but who lacked Barck's prospects would have been unlikely to ever gain the financial stability he enjoyed.[7]

Harry Barck had experienced some of that dead-end work in his twenties—when he had been employed as a shoe salesman—and even later, when he hustled liquor to local saloons. By the time he was offered the poormaster's position at age thirty-three, he must have been delighted in his transformation from working-class stiff to *executive*—the term he later chose to describe his occupation. Now, despite his position's demand that he insert himself into the lives of poor people, Barck's regular paycheck would separate him from the anxious reality of many in the city and—as the Depression would later reveal—from the chronic poverty of millions across the United States.[8]

Barck's aloofness from the material circumstances of the poor may have been reinforced by the teachings of his Christian Science church. He did not speak publicly about his faith and may have been a less-than-dedicated practitioner—followers were required to abstain completely from using tobacco, and the Hoboken poormaster was known to enjoy a cigar or two in his office—but at the very least, Harry Barck would not have found a conflict between his church's instruction and the long-standing ethos of local relief: that the poor produced their own misfortune. As one historian later explained, Christian Scientists held that "the mental or spiritual world was the true reality," not the physical plane. "As God created the universe through pure thought," the explanation continued, "so on a lesser scale did people *create their own world through their thought*." Accordingly, the Christian Science Church did not seek to alleviate human suffering by funding institutions of care, as some other Protestant churches did. Its followers recommended that the poor immerse themselves in the teachings of the church's founder, Mary

Baker Eddy. Believers, another scholar wrote, frequently claimed that poor people who followed the Scientists' path "quickly improved their economic standing."[9]

Harry Barck certainly knew the pleasure of a rise in station. His father, Harry Sr., had been a watchman. The older man's position had demanded honesty and a certain allegiance, but it would have been far less stable than a selected—and carefully maintained—position at city hall.[10]

The younger man had been especially fortunate that his entry into local partisan politics had dovetailed with the ascent of two political bosses with Irish roots: Hoboken's Mike Coyle, and *his* boss, Hudson County Democratic leader Robert Davis. After his 1888 induction as county boss, Davis became known as a "benevolent despot" who skillfully managed his political organization. Mindful of the German and Irish votes he needed to maintain power, Davis placed his emissaries where workingmen of both backgrounds congregated. Hotels, clubs, and saloons in Hoboken soon became centers for Democratic Party socializing and politicking, in much the same way such establishments had been used to build community and expand the reach of political machines in urban centers like New York and Chicago.[11]

Barck had attended some of those Hoboken venues, eager for political gamesmanship and comaraderie. Initially, he mingled with neighbors who shared his ethnic background. He frequented German cultural clubs and joined a local *schuetzen* corps for target shooting and equestrian parades. But once he made Davis's acquaintance, Barck made sure to join one of *his* clubs, too. Robert Davis had a paternal approach to young politicians in his camp, and he was known to direct his municipal bosses to clear a path for those he found deserving.[12]

At nearly six feet tall, with disarmingly pale blue eyes and black hair, Harry Barck stood out in those political gatherings, conveying authority as he strode into a hall. And given his eventual ascent, his fellows found him companionable, too. It would be unwise to install a man of uniformly sour temperament as a recurring city hall contact, and Barck's sardonic wit would likely have amused some.[13]

By the time he was thirty, Harry Barck had left the shoe store on First Street to become a liquor salesman. With hundreds of taverns in the city serving the dockworkers, seamen, railroaders, and shipyard workers, his shift in product promised a better income, and by then he had a wife and two young children to support. And it would have helped to know that saloon owners who were friendly to the county boss could pour all night, unaffected by legal restrictions, as Davis had also claimed the position of county sheriff.[14]

Within three years, Harry Barck had proved his usefulness and reliability to the county organization: he was appointed Hoboken's overseer of the poor. The prior poormaster had died in office, and a police captain had filled the position until Barck's selection, obligingly agreed to by city councilmen. The post gave Barck "exclusive charge of the poor" and required no exam, nor any prior experience with charitable work.[15]

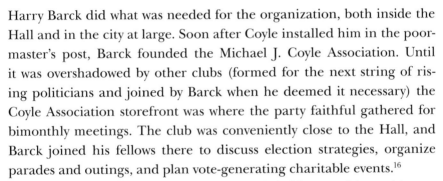

Harry Barck did what was needed for the organization, both inside the Hall and in the city at large. Soon after Coyle installed him in the poormaster's post, Barck founded the Michael J. Coyle Association. Until it was overshadowed by other clubs (formed for the next string of rising politicians and joined by Barck when he deemed it necessary) the Coyle Association storefront was where the party faithful gathered for bimonthly meetings. The club was conveniently close to the Hall, and Barck joined his fellows there to discuss election strategies, organize parades and outings, and plan vote-generating charitable events.[16]

By playing smart politics, Harry Barck held on to his position as Hoboken poormaster, pleasing first Davis and Coyle, then local bosses Jack Haggerty, Maurice Stack, Patrick Griffin, and finally, Bernard McFeely. He became known for expansive gestures of political support and for displays of generosity that cost him nothing. Over the years, banners and advertisements bearing the inscription CONTRIBUTED BY HARRY L. BARCK regularly appeared at political events, and the poormaster was expected to distribute Christmas gifts to "kiddies" during the annual giveaway sponsored by the *Jersey Observer*.[17]

But Barck's pleasures as a bureaucrat had been compromised early on. Even as he was establishing himself as the city's welfare chief, the state was whittling away the position's prestige. A year after he was placed in Hoboken's city hall, in 1897, the state of New Jersey began the gradual, decades-long process of taking control over several needy populations that had formerly been overseen exclusively by local poormasters. Widows with dependent children, abused or deserted children, the indigent blind, the elderly poor—these were groups commonly viewed as the "deserving poor," unlike the able-bodied unemployed. Decades later, when the Social Security Act of 1935 was passed, it followed a similar pattern: a provision allowed federal grants to states to provide direct relief to specified "unemployables"—the aged poor, the blind, and poor, fatherless children.[18]

The longer Harry Barck stayed in office, the more it must have rankled that the state (and later, the federal government) was limiting his supervision. Hadn't he put in years on the job? How could they possibly think they could do better? He had a set procedure for how to do this kind of work. He knew what he was doing. He had a well-earned place in the organization that was running the city.

The poormaster had used the same methods, day in and day out. He had pried into the embarrassing details of applicants' meager finances, their job layoffs, their personal crises. He had sought out past employers, talked to their priests, interviewed landlords—ostensibly to ferret out chiselers but also to publicly shame those who sought public aid. It had not been just a sign of his general lack of sympathy and his contempt (which were shared by many) for the jobless. By making the process so odious, Poormaster Barck would not only reduce the number of requests, he would drive some of the needy to seek assistance from the Boss's representatives. Aid-seekers might then avoid the indignity of the poormaster's investigation, but most important, the usefulness of Hall connections would be reinforced.[19]

And because politicians, including machine bosses, maintained power by assisting a broad base of constituents, the politically appointed poormaster would also make a show of sharing poor funds with the city's more comfortable classes. Harry Barck assigned relief orders to grocers and clothing retailers throughout the city, and when he deemed it necessary, he would engage the services of pharmacists and undertakers. Relief spending was controlled by the use of his orders, and merchants and professionals were reminded that the Hall was looking out for them.[20]

While the final service for Harry Barck was being held inside Volk's, a crowd was assembling outside its entrance at 631 Washington Street. At first it had appeared that a curious few had stopped to watch late-comers arrive at the mortuary, but that cluster of men and women had stalled and stayed, standing a few feet from the chapel's ornate window, which glinted blue-white in the shifting rays of afternoon sun. They huddled against the cold and mumbled assurances to one another that the wait would not be long. More came to stand with them, then still more. One hundred, five hundred, and still the number multiplied—until the sidewalk flanking Volk's was completely impassable and the west side of Washington Street, opposite the mortuary, was lined five- and six-deep for more than a half-block south of Seventh Street.[21]

As the throng gathered, it became clear that these men and women were the poormaster's former clients, easily distinguishable from the well-heeled mourners by their threadbare coats. Many more women than men were in the crowd—perhaps because it was a workday (for those who had work)—but perhaps they were in force for darker reasons, having to do with the comments the poormaster had so often directed to female clients.

Over the course of an hour the crowd had grown so large it must have seemed a threat to the poormaster's colleagues and family, still inside the building and readying themselves for the drive to the cemetery, just over the Hudson County border. A dozen patrolmen and plainclothesmen were swiftly dispatched to Washington Street, and Captain B. J. McFeely joined them outside, to keep order.

As the policemen patrolled the perimeter of the crowd on the east side of the street, the flag-draped, gray metal casket bearing Harry Barck's body was carried from the chapel on the shoulders of six dark-suited pallbearers. When they appeared, the crowd surged forward; a great mass of men and women pressed in as one. They strained to catch a glimpse of the overseer's glinting coffin, as if they would not believe the man who had long shamed them was truly dead. "It was at this particular point that certain of the crowd—men and women alike—betrayed their bitterness toward the dead man," a reporter later noted. They swore at the casket, loudly, bitterly. A few in the crowd, supporters of the poormaster, admonished the hecklers. "Shame!" one called out. But the cries of Barck's former clients seemed unstoppable, increasing in number and ferocity. They called out in fury for the crimes they believed Harry Barck had committed against them and drowned out the demand of others for respect of the dead.[22]

The women shouted at the casket as it was borne into the hearse. Barck's family emerged from the chapel to the sound of curses and the clicking shutters of newspaper cameras.

After the trauma of Harry Barck's murder and the terrible brutality of its execution came this shocking vituperation and the sudden awareness by Barck's family of the contempt with which this swarm held the man *they* had held most dear. He had only done what his job had demanded; and he had continued on for years and years—even after he had spoken of leaving—because Mayor McFeely had asked him to stay in office. Now this mob. They were not just displaying ingratitude, but hatred and disrespect. It was unspeakable.[23]

Augusta Barck, small, bent with grief, her old-fashioned topknot mostly covered by a hat and veil, stepped out of the chapel and was immediately shielded by her family. The men formed an outer wall of protection against the crowd, which seemed to swell toward them then subside as policemen approached. Her two sons-in-law had agreed with their wives earlier to look after Mrs. Barck in Dover once her son inevitably returned to Washington with his own family.[24]

The Vanderwolf brothers were not from Hoboken, but even if they had been, it was unlikely they would have been able to square their assessment of Mr. Barck with the perception held by his clients. The poormaster's sons-in-law and the people who had sought relief from him had all encountered the same man, but their views would have been so divergent, it would have been as if two separate men with the same name had lived in Hoboken, each with a larger-than-life presence. To Barck's sons-in-law, any claim that their elderly relative had done a disservice to Hoboken residents would have seemed outlandish, for they knew Harry Barck's attachment to the city to have been so complete, he had dubbed their vacation spot in Burlington, Vermont, "Camp Hoboken." Wherever he had traveled, he had taken Hoboken with him, its well-being upper-most in his mind.[25]

But the poormaster's clients were attached to that little patch of ground, too. Where else would they go? Their families had set root in the city, and now their destitution was so thorough, they could not afford relocation, could not conceive of it. Their minds were focused on their hunger, on how to quell it each day. They would not have been able to imagine the hardened poormaster, who had denied their children milk, with any kind of family. He was as depthless to them, as lacking in human dimension, as they had been to him.[26]

Eventually a cortege of twelve cars—including an open vehicle filled with flowers, the hearse, and a coach occupied by Mayor McFeely and his city commissioners—left Washington Street for Fairview Cemetery, where Harry Barck was interred in a family plot.[27]

The day after the funeral, Hoboken residents woke to learn that the city had a new poormaster. The city's Democratic leader, Mayor McFeely, had appointed Austin Tighe, a thirty-four-year-old clerk in the city's Department of Revenue and Finance, to the position. Like his predecessor, the new appointee lacked any prior experience in the administration of aid, and none was required.[28]

7 | TAKING ACCOUNT

AFTER THE HOBOKEN POORMASTER was killed, New Jersey governor A. Harry Moore announced he would assert his emergency powers and withdraw $1.5 million from general state funds to reimburse municipalities for their January relief payments. He did not mention the slaying.

Nevertheless, the *New York Times* easily united the two deeds when it reported Moore's announcement, and the leftist weekly the *Nation* declared in an editorial that the governor's action indicated state officials "realize that Scutellaro's act was not simple homicide but a fanatical gesture of misery long drawn out."[1]

Would Moore's act truly alleviate the misery of the city's jobless poor, or was it a kind of shell game? The governor clearly wished to prevent any future uprisings in his state, but his delayed initiative was intended only to return to municipalities what they had already spent. Under Harry Barck's tenure, Hoboken taxpayers had paid out little for poor relief, and the city would therefore be in line to receive a pittance—if it was to receive anything at all. The former Hoboken poormaster had refused to abide by the state's standards for relief, and because such compliance was required for a municipality to receive state funds, Barck's denial of aid might be perpetuated even after his death.[2]

But for Sam Leibowitz, there was bad news to contend with on a more intimate scale—an old police report had been released to the newspapers to buttress the public image of his Hoboken client as a vengeful assailant. Police Chief Edward McFeely informed reporters that the man accused of killing the poormaster had been arrested before. Joe Scutellaro had been charged with assaulting a state relief officer in October 1932, after his family had been denied aid.[3]

To some of the accused man's supporters, this revelation would seem to slam shut the death house door, with Joe inside. But Sam Leibowitz had been more cautious in his assessment. McFeely was using the newspapers as Leibowitz had always used them—to try to sway the opinion of future jurors. The resurrection of the six-year-old incident, which had resulted in a suspended sentence, was an attempt to predispose talesmen to the idea that the killing of the poormaster had been premeditated.[4]

The mere existence of a police record for his client would not have overly concerned Leibowitz anyway. His office had offered counsel to many clients with extensive rap sheets. During the early years of his practice, bootlegger and racketeer Al Capone had traveled to Leibowitz's home in a long lavender sedan to discuss representation on a triple-murder charge. Capone's prior crimes and reputation had not been issues to address then, his lawyer claimed; the facts of the case were what mattered.[5]

Leibowitz often remarked to reporters that a trial was not a fact-finding mission. He wanted to enter the courtroom knowing the answers to any questions that might arise there.[6] And so he had to find out what had happened in 1932, when the state of New Jersey had been temporarily involved in supplementing relief, and Harry Barck signed off on the decisions of a state employee named Harold Butler.

Sam Leibowitz was known in legal circles as a superb tactician. Although his court performances could seem spontaneous to jurors, the arguments he made before them were carefully prepared in advance. He was an inveterate note-taker and always had a small pad and pencil with him to record client comments and his own thoughts on strategy. Should an idea come to him in the middle of the night, his notebook awaited him on his bedside table.[7]

And so, when Sam visited Joe in jail to inquire about his past, and when he conferred with Anna and her in-laws in Anna's kitchen, he took out his notepad and patiently and methodically questioned them, adding to details he gathered from other sources.[8]

The bare facts of the October 18, 1932, incident had already been established through the arrest record and Hoboken court documents. On that day, Joe, his father Frank, and his brother-in-law Christy Angelo had approached state relief officer Harold Butler on the street as he was exiting his car. While Christy pinned the man's arms behind his back, Joe punched him in the face. Soon after, a police captain, a McFeely nephew, arrested Joe, who denied the assault and battery charge. He pleaded not guilty but then signed a waiver relinquishing the option of a jury trial and received a suspended sentence. He returned home to Monroe Street.[9]

Leibowitz must have wanted to speak with all the principals involved in the beating, but he would not be interviewing Anna's brother. Just a few weeks before Joe's arrest for the murder of Harry Barck, Christy Angelo had died. Alone in a small and spare rented room, the man who had once found seasonal work assisting the poormaster had succumbed to fumes from a gas heater.[10]

As for Joe and Frank, the two admitted straight away that Joe had struck Butler. And as they spoke about the assault, as Leibowitz came to understand the awful period that preceded it, he surely noted that the conditions the Scutellaros had endured in 1932 were distressingly similar to those they were to confront six years later. The most significant difference was that the official who refused them aid in 1932 had been hired by the state.[11]

Again, in 1932, Joe had been unemployed, along with twelve million men and women nationwide—nearly one-quarter of the workforce. Forty percent of American banks had collapsed. In Hoboken, the once-revered Steneck Trust Company had closed. Its shuttering was to leave thousands of downtown residents with no access to their savings for two years, while the bank president and vice president were indicted for fraud and their trial was repeatedly delayed. The bankers' lawyer claimed that an impartial jury could not be assembled "with 30,000 depositors of the closed bank inflamed against them."[12]

Almost immediately after the closing of Steneck Trust, nightmarish stories of depositors' legal limbo and suffering had circulated. An Italian grape dealer with a family of eight to support could not get credit to carry on his business even though the bank held $15,000 of his money. An elderly couple, with a passbook showing they had deposited $8,000, was reportedly living without gas, water, or electricity.[13]

Families were being dispossessed, and they were needy and frightened. And some were also burdened by the dishonor and stigma attached to poverty—so much so that they did not even *try* to get relief at first. Rather, they had sought to hide their decline. They suffered quietly, individually, and earnestly prayed their patched attire—shoes resoled with cardboard inserts and winter coats relined with old blankets—would not betray them to neighbors.[14]

Joe had sought to conceal his distress, too. As the economy bottomed out, he tried, at first, to hide from Anna the lack of incoming contracts for the family business. After he acknowledged their dismal financial situation, Joe Scutellaro—like so many faced with financial ruin during the Depression—had first turned to his extended family for support. By the time he approached state relief officer Harold Butler for assistance, he had surely reached a point where he could no longer tolerate living off the charity of his parents. He had wanted to apply for relief so he could pay them rent, as he had before the Depression.[15]

But the state employee had likely refused Joe's request based on a traditional reading of the old poor laws. For generations, the poormaster had the power to compel family members to support destitute kin. If they were unable, the overseer could then have the impoverished man or woman declared a pauper, stripped of the right to vote, and removed to the Hudson County Almshouse, known colloquially as "the poorhouse."[16]

Furthermore, the poor laws had long disallowed relief to homeowners. A year after Butler's refusal, the state circulated regulations specifically stating that home ownership was not a legal bar to relief, but that notification came too late for Joe. Butler refused to allow relief funds to go from Joe to Frank and Marie.[17]

And with that understanding of the impetus for the 1932 assault, Sam Leibowitz returned to the pressing case before him: a client charged with murder. He would not be quibbling in the courtroom over prior incidents or minor points of law. He would be taking on a system so incomprehensible and inhumane as to bring about a kind of madness.

As Leibowitz would later explain: "The troublesome problem confronting the court and jury is not so much *what the law is*, as *what happened*." The Scutellaro trial, he could predict, would mostly come down to one question: "Did he kill, and under what circumstances?' "[18]

In mid-March, a grand jury indicted Joe Scutellaro for the murder of Harry Barck. A few days later, supporters from Hoboken's downtown streets made their way to Jersey City for Joe's arraignment in the imposing Hudson County Courthouse. Many had never been inside the granite building before. They hesitated before fully entering the opulent great court, a mass of poor men in dun-colored coats, crowded at the perimeter of the glistening marble rotunda.[19]

Leibowitz, too, was on unfamiliar turf. He arrived at the courthouse with Thomas Tumulty, a former assistant US attorney general and well-established Jersey City lawyer, who could guide him on local matters and the finer points of Jersey law. The fifty-four-year-old Tumulty had been in the building countless times during his three decades as a practicing attorney, and he was unfazed by its grandeur. But Leibowitz, whose critical gaze had swept over the rotunda the first time he'd entered, had been taken aback by the contrast between the lavishly appointed county building and his client's impoverished state. Here he was defending a man who had gone to see the poormaster with just nine cents in his pockets, and the halls of justice where he was to be judged were fashioned out of pearl-gray marble and encircled by ornate balconies and painted scenes from storied battles. Under the lawyers' feet spread the great seal of the State of New Jersey, executed in bronze and inlaid into a tricolored marble floor.[20]

Leibowitz fished out his notebook and jotted down his observations, some of which would later appear in his closing argument. He likely wondered, as he looked around and considered future jurors who would decide his client's fate, how the average man would view this palace. And what would a taxpayer, struggling to support his family in a country with more than ten million yet unemployed, believe about justice for the poor?[21]

The two lawyers quickly climbed the wide, glossy stairs to the second floor, where the arraignment was to be held. The courtroom, Leibowitz would have noted, was a bit less grand than the rotunda, but only by degrees. It was also a soaring space, two stories high, and fitted with polished marble pilasters and bronze lighting fixtures capped with alabaster bowls. The judge's elevated platform overlooked the table behind which Leibowitz and his fellow defense attorney would sit. An identical table was reserved for the prosecution, to be represented once again by Assistant Prosecutor Frank G. Schlosser. Then came a series of long, polished wood benches, which were filled with jocular court reporters and Joe's murmuring neighbors, crushed in shoulder to shoulder. They quieted when the pallid, slight defendant was led in manacles into the courtroom.[22]

At the opening of the proceeding, Tumulty introduced Leibowitz to Thomas F. Meaney, the presiding judge of the Hudson County Court of Common Pleas, and asked "that the New York barrister be given the courtesy of the court." Tall and lean, the forty-nine-year-old judge bore a decidedly sour mien. He gruffly acknowledged the out-of-towner.[23]

In preparing for the arraignment, Leibowitz had surely heard quite a bit from his Jersey City colleague about Judge Meaney, and not only about his quirky habits, which included burning incense in his chambers and wearing a monocle as a self-declared act of "pure affectation." Tumulty, who stemmed from a well-connected political family that included a brother who had served as secretary to President Wilson, would have advised Leibowitz that Meaney was a devoted Hague man, an "obliging jurist" who could be called upon to do favors for the New Jersey boss. His background may have stirred in the New York lawyer some unease about Hudson County justice, but Meaney, fortunately, would only preside over this second arraignment.[24]

The presence of Assistant Prosecutor Schlosser, who stood to read the murder indictment, had already added a strange twist to the proceedings. In his former role as Hoboken's city recorder, then–municipal judge Schlosser had sentenced Joe Scutellaro for the 1932 assault and battery of Harold Butler.

Leibowitz rose to enter a plea of not guilty for his client. "This defendant was on relief, his children were starving, and his wife was in a very bad physical condition," he began softly, so that court reporters instinctively leaned forward to capture his words. "On this particular day, he was driven to distraction," he continued, raising his voice moderately. "Of course, what happened in Mr. Barck's office is a matter for the jury to decide, but I do not think the prosecutor can claim premeditation, or even that this was a murder in the second degree." The lawyer paused for effect. "It was one of those things people do," he declared, "in the heat of passion."[25]

Meaney turned to the defendant to inquire if he understood the charge against him. Joe stuttered his assent.

Next Leibowitz made a plea for bail he surely knew would be denied. But he was also intent upon shaping public perception of his client's case.

"Of course," he began, "if the court grants bail, it cannot be produced by the defendant because he is a pauper." The last, stinging term, Joe's lawyer surely knew, was one of reproach, freighted with a miserable history. For to be so designated had meant, for generations, that one had truly lost everything.

"Everyone in this case is working for charity," Leibowitz continued. "Any bail would have to be raised by the good neighbors and friends of the defendant."

Schlosser argued for the denial of bail. The prosecutor considered it a first-degree murder, he said, adding, "The matter of premeditation may be one of a second."

"What has the prosecutor to say about the fact that the letter file with which Mr. Barck was stabbed was not brought to the poormaster's office by the defendant?" Meaney asked helpfully.

Schlosser reiterated the prosecutor's view: this was a first-degree murder.

"I do not think that the prosecutor's viewpoint may be unreasonable," the judge sniffed. "And I will deny bail. But I will request the prosecutor to put the case down for an early trial."

An early trial did not come. Despite Leibowitz's best efforts to gain a speedy trial or to win his client's release on bail, despite the inscription above the courthouse door that proclaimed, "To Delay Justice Is to Deny

Justice," *State v. Joseph F. Scutellaro* was not going be heard before the court recessed for summer. No date was set.[26]

And so Scutellaro waited in the county jail, one of about 250 men held on several floors of the nine-story steel-and-cement structure. The sleeplessness that had plagued him at home continued there. He often had pounding headaches, and when the pain did abate for a while, he found he had no energy. He sat on the edge of his bed, staring without any focus at all. The solace of reading—even a simple prayer book—was no longer available to him, now that spots had begun to form before his eyes and paragraphs of type would double up when he tried to read a page.[27]

The doctor at the Jersey City Medical Center clinic had told him five years earlier that he had encephalitis, a kind of "sleeping sickness" brought about by swelling in the brain. The physician had given him medicine, but it didn't seem to do any good. The drowsiness and shaking had continued, and everything in him seemed to be slowing down. The illness had only compounded Joe's worries.[28]

He was still deeply depressed, as he had been before the fight with Barck and through its terrible aftermath, but he must have felt he was better off, now that he had left the Hoboken jail. Unlike the city lockup, which had been barely tended in the twenty-seven years since its opening, the county jail was just nine years old and smelled of disinfectant; its size assured a certain anonymity that could feel like safety. The Hoboken policemen Joe had known for so many years—the extended McFeely clan—would not be bullying him here. True, Joe had been forced, like all newly admitted county prisoners, to strip for a minute physical examination, but his clothes had then been returned, washed, and the exam had brought him to the jail's physician, who had treated a longstanding cut on his arm.[29]

Joe was not allowed to have family visits at the county jail, and that separation surely compounded his gloom. But he knew he was fortunate: he had Anna, resourceful and loving. She would make his isolation and waiting bearable. And so, every Sunday, no matter the weather, Anna traveled with little Marie and Joseph by trolley from Hoboken to Jersey City and stood outside the jail complex to wave at him, however fleetingly. Joe would go to the window in a common room and search the street below for their familiar forms. *There they were.* He'd lift his arm. And when his children spied him at the window, they would raise their arms excitedly and wave and wave and wave . . .[30]

On every other day, he subsisted within the jail's confines. He didn't gripe about conditions, didn't join in when prisoners complained about the biweekly change of linens that were returned with pockets of grime or caked with soap after fellow inmates botched the unfamiliar domestic chore. When he felt able, he wrote letters in his careful, curling script, using the soft-lead pencils allowed him. And though he felt his appetite was poor, Joe nevertheless found that the jail's regular meals were adding weight to his bony frame.[31]

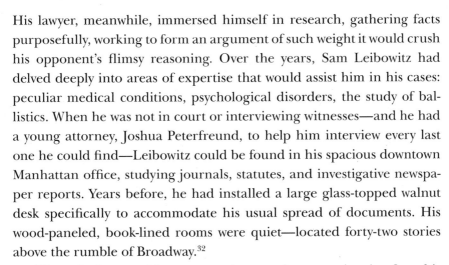

His lawyer, meanwhile, immersed himself in research, gathering facts purposefully, working to form an argument of such weight it would crush his opponent's flimsy reasoning. Over the years, Sam Leibowitz had delved deeply into areas of expertise that would assist him in his cases: peculiar medical conditions, psychological disorders, the study of ballistics. When he was not in court or interviewing witnesses—and he had a young attorney, Joshua Peterfreund, to help him interview every last one he could find—Leibowitz could be found in his spacious downtown Manhattan office, studying journals, statutes, and investigative newspaper reports. Years before, he had installed a large glass-topped walnut desk specifically to accommodate his usual spread of documents. His wood-paneled, book-lined rooms were quiet—located forty-two stories above the rumble of Broadway.[32]

The only threat to his concentration was the expansive view from his window—a stretch of crowded, lower Manhattan leading to New York Bay and to Liberty Island. Leibowitz had first seen the Statue of Liberty at age four, on the spring day in 1897 when he and his parents had risen out of steerage after a long ocean crossing. They had escaped second-class citizenship; Romanian Jews had then been forced into military service but denied the right to vote or to own land. Sam must have felt a certain satisfaction, to see from his law offices the whole of New York Harbor spread out before him. On clear mornings, his view might even encompass the slim edge of the state across the Hudson River, where his penniless client awaited trial.[33]

To develop Scutellaro's defense, Leibowitz had launched into a thorough review of Harry Barck's history as Hoboken poormaster, in all its appalling detail. When he encountered reporters, he suggested that in due time he might call any number of Hoboken relief clients to testify about what they had suffered at Barck's hands.[34]

He did not mention a less provocative but essential activity: the examination of state laws meant to guide Barck's decision-making. The defense attorney needed to be able to foresee how some of the evidence he would use to argue his client's innocence might be used by the prosecution to shape a far different conclusion. The prosecution might claim that the seemingly callous poormaster had merely followed established law and precedent—and there was something to this argument. State poor laws nationwide had long ensured that public relief would not be generous. And though Barck had helped to shape the current New Jersey statute as an advisor to a commission on the state's poor laws, Leibowitz would have been hard pressed to argue that state lawmakers had been persuaded by the Hoboken poormaster to override their deep commitment to the needy. Legislators had evinced their solidarity with the taxpaying electorate. Barck surely had this in mind when he routinely instructed his critics that boosting relief to the jobless poor would "undermine the will of the people," encoded in state statute.[35]

State legislators' understanding of the political underpinnings of the poor laws had ensured that the ancient system would persist into the twentieth century. At the beginning of the century, when the nonprofit organization that served as the state's primary assessor of local poor relief had declaimed against politicized appointments and advocated for a state-administered merit system, elected officials had refused to take action. And decades later, when the Depression stimulated calls to shift the administration of the poor laws away from local poormasters, compliant legislators had again declined to enact mandatory legislation.[36]

And so Hoboken's appointed poormaster had remained in office through the economic crisis, asserting with numbing regularity that "the city has no money for unemployment relief." Leibowitz would have questioned this claim from the start, but as he culled statistics from state relief surveys and reviewed newspaper reports, he likely began to wonder whether the mayor and his commissioners had simply *refused*, despite the yawning need, to increase the amount of public funds directed to the jobless poor. Newspapers had broadly reported that Hoboken, with a relief problem no greater than the other Hudson County municipalities, was the *only one* of the twelve, after the resumption of local responsibility, that did not continue relief on about the same scale as the state. How was it that Union City, a comparably sized Hudson County municipality (58,659 residents compared to Hoboken's 59,261) had spent $6.34 per capita on relief in 1937, while Hoboken had spent just 90 cents? Hoboken's ratables per capita, at $1,466, had *exceeded* Union City's $1,134.[37]

Where had Hoboken's money gone? Not to the poormaster. His budget had been less than $3,000 per month, with half admittedly going for office administration. And no one had accused Harry Barck of enriching himself from the public till—not since 1905, anyway, when he had been arrested on a bench warrant, accused with another city official of using public money "to satisfy political private debts." The charge had made the papers, but nothing had come of it in the end. Barck had kept his position. Now, in a city lush with knowing winks and whispering campaigns, there were none concerning the poormaster, who had even made a grotesque show of returning surpluses to the city after he had meted out minute sums to relief applicants.[38]

Tax dollars were obviously not going toward the maintenance of public buildings. One did not have to be an engineer or a building inspector to notice that the city's schools, its firemen's quarters—even city hall— were rotting. The lockup in the basement of city hall literally stank—a combination of a disintegrating sewer system and ancient washrooms that had not been upgraded since they were installed in the 1880s. The defense attorney had confronted this great stench when he had first visited the building.[39]

Now Leibowitz read in the *New York Post* that a day or two before Joe had gone to see the poormaster, Mayor Bernard McFeely had "spread upon the floor of his city hall office a new rug for which the city paid $750." Given the paltriness of Barck's average check, McFeely's decorative flourish had starved about a hundred families of even that meager relief.[40]

The defense attorney surely knew then he had to broaden his investigation. But before he covered his desk with a raft of damning news accounts and the published findings of a legislative examination of Boss McFeely's mysteriously gained wealth, Sam Leibowitz must have reflected on the fate of Poormaster Barck, whose sole "reward" had been his long-term employment. Perhaps only the poormaster's family would have cared to go further—to question whether he had zealously guarded the public purse only to have McFeely rob it, and then to ask: had Harry Barck died for that?

8 | THE NEPOTISTIC REPUBLIC

SAM LEIBOWITZ WANTED THE jurors at Scutellaro's trial to focus on the conditions his client had faced, not the brutal image of a spike driven through an old man's heart. If he could find out more about McFeely's wrongdoing and if the judge would allow its admission, the defense attorney might be able to shift jurors' attention to the corruption and cruelty that had closed in on Joe and trapped him.[1]

McFeely's grip on the city was palpable—and yet, the man himself, Leibowitz would discover, was elusive. Born in Hoboken to impoverished Irish immigrants, a grade school dropout after his father's death had forced him to work as a horse teamster, the hardened fifty-six-year-old boss rarely made public appearances. Some attributed his avoidance of public speaking to an unlikely self-consciousness about his poor grammar; others, to his rapidly retreating hairline. But it was certain that McFeely felt no obligation to attend community meetings or even to greet the electorate. The fine suits New York City tailors had fashioned to play up the bachelor boss's height and coiled boxer's build were not meant to impress voters during on-the-street glad-handing, and McFeely preferred to be chauffeured to and from the Hall in a sleek Cadillac notable for its uncommonly small and darkened windows.[2]

But the Boss *did* go to city hall—that could be affirmed, if only in repeated newspaper accounts of the vile temper he displayed in his office, when he turned his fists on any man who dared oppose him or pulled from his desktop objects he could employ as cudgels to beat dissenting city hires.[3]

Leibowitz could only imagine what McFeely would like to do to veteran *New York Post* reporter Vilas J. Boyle, given that the paper had published his ten-part exposé of the Boss's long career of "plunder, nepotism, and contract scandals." The series had appeared at just the right time for Leibowitz, who had tasked himself with linking Hoboken's impoverished relief coffers to the city's mysteriously missing tax dollars. The *Post* had laid out the treasure map for all to see.[4]

Vilas Boyle had discovered the channels McFeely had developed to siphon off taxpayer money. The city payroll, the journalist revealed, was but one of them, a source long tapped by Hoboken bosses to reward loyalists. Bernard McFeely had continued this tradition—but under *his* regime, the supporters he repaid were mostly named McFeely. Unrestricted by civil service or any requirement that his hires achieve a set level of competence, the Boss had installed over six dozen of his relatives in city posts. And with promotion a near certainty, the multiple McFeely paychecks had fattened nicely over time. The average annual income in New Jersey was less than $500, and *the entire 1937 budget* to aid the city's destitute thousands had been little more than $16,000, but Hoboken taxpayers, Boyle reported, were shelling out $39,000 annually for the salaries of just fifteen of the mayor's nearest kin.[5]

Boyle had not listed all the McFeely municipal payrollers "ranging in economic importance from city purchasing agent down to water-department clerk," but the newspaper had helpfully produced a diagram depicting the fifteen-branch "McFeely Plum Tree." Along with brother Edward ($5,000 annually as police chief—the same amount paid the mayor) and a pensioner sister and police lieutenant brother-in-law ($4,000), there were numerous McFeely nieces and nephews. Their gifted posts included police lieutenant, (two, totaling $6,000), police captain ($4,000), patrolman ($2,250), counselor in the Hoboken Law Department ($1,200), teacher ($1,800), school clerk (two, totaling an astonishing $6,800), city nurse ($1,500), city hall custodian ($2,000), fireman ($2,250), and fire department captain ($2,750).[6]

But even that stockpile had proved insufficient to meet McFeely's needs, Boyle reported. City employees were consequently obliged to hand over 2 or 3 percent of their salaries to the Democratic Party's "campaign fund." Never mind that McFeely deposited the cash in multiple bank accounts under his own name, or that he used but a small portion of what was collected to run for office. He piled up "donations" with impunity. Years before the *Post* exposé, when he had not yet acquired the mayoralty, McFeely had been queried by a New Jersey legislative commission investigating countywide political corruption: how had Bernard McFeely come to possess nearly $100,000 in his personal accounts, when his only claimed income was then a $4,500 annual salary as a city commissioner? Boss McFeely had grinned and replied, "I have no record of how I made the money."[7]

He would not account for his personal wealth, and the legislators, hampered by the "alleged loss, destruction, and theft of various records," had been stymied. But their investigation had made clear that Bernard McFeely was more single-minded in his pursuit of money and power, and more driven to consolidate both within his extended clan, than all the grasping pols who had ruled Hoboken before him. Political observers compared McFeely's take with the piles accumulated by his two political predecessors and determined that he had the older bosses "beat by a mile." County boss Davis had collected his bundle during thirty years of politicking, and Hoboken boss Patrick Griffin had become a millionaire in twenty-five; but Boss McFeely had amassed more than a quarter of a million dollars within three years of taking power. (In fact, McFeely's signal that he was to succeed Griffin as Hoboken boss came in the summer of 1925, when the older man began to dissipate his fortune by handing out ready money to bootblacks and news dealers he barely knew. The consequent physical examination determined Patrick Griffin was incurably insane.)[8]

The *Post* estimated McFeely's stash to be more than $3 million. And how had the boss achieved this princely sum? The answer, Boyle wrote, was to be found in Hoboken's garbage.[9]

Ten years earlier, McFeely's fellow commissioners had revised a local ordinance to give the city garbage contract, *in perpetuity*, to the McFeely family's cartage company—despite the company's exorbitant fee and the Boss's obvious self-dealing. Under the emended law, a bidder for the Hoboken contract was required to "own [or] have under lease" specifically defined plots of Hoboken land that just happened to be owned by the McFeelys. By the time the *Post* published its exposé, the family business—ostensibly run by the Boss's brother James—had pulled down nearly $1.5 million for a service the newspaper reckoned would have totaled $600,000 in another city of comparable size.[10]

To call what the McFeelys provided a "service" must have seemed preposterous to Sam Leibowitz anyway. When he first arrived in Hoboken to defend Joe Scutellaro, he would have noted its filthy streets. The anachronistic horse-drawn garbage wagons used by the McFeely company routinely showered roadways and sidewalks with debris—an insult felt most deeply in the Italian quarter of the city. Boyle's articles had revealed how the neighborhood's salvage men had repeatedly—and uselessly—submitted the lowest bids for carting, until the ordinance was rewritten. The Italian bidders had likely not imagined that city commissioners would blissfully ignore a New Jersey statute specifically forbidding elected or appointed officials from direct or indirect involvement with any city contracts.[11]

Nor could they have foreseen that the victorious boss would then claim dominion over all salvage in the city. He refused licenses to junk operators so that "salable refuse," left at curbs all over the city, would be collected exclusively by his family's company—for an additional profit. And when Italian contractors went to gain the required city approval to dig in the street—or sought permission to do just about any project—they discovered that they would have to use the McFeely company or be denied a permit.[12]

During the many days Joe's lawyer traveled to the Italian section to meet with Anna and her in-laws, he would have noticed the black-kerchiefed women who scoured their steps with scrubby brooms. He would have seen them set to work on the sidewalks, furiously trying to clear them of rot and ash.

Sam Leibowitz liked to arrive early at the Scutellaro home on the days he gathered information for Joe's defense. Neighbors were helping the family with milk for the children and with other supplies, and Anna made breakfast for everyone. She would serve the lawyer at her little kitchen table, seating him alongside her son and daughter, and often her in-laws as well.[13]

Her mother-in-law had never cared much for cooking, but for Anna, making and sharing food had long been a joy. In better times, she had prepared batches of homemade peach pie and lemonade to feed the devotional marchers who passed her home during saints' feast days. The attentive lawyer would have seen how pleased she was to again offer hospitality, and even though he had probably had his breakfast before he left the comfortable Brooklyn home he shared with his wife and their three children, he would have known that the Scutellaros would be most forthcoming if he joined them at their table.[14]

Now he would turn to them for background: about the way the city worked during the Depression years, about its residents' codes and biases and allegiances—anything that might guide him in understanding how Hudson County jurors might perceive Joe and his alleged crime, and how Sam might shape their conclusions.

Leibowitz was concerned about the role his client's heritage might play in jury selection. Hoboken neighborhoods were cut along ethnic lines, and uptown residents (of Irish or German ancestry) might dismiss the Italian district west of Willow Avenue with the pejorative "Guinea Town." Of course, that kind of facile prejudice and the general propensity for tribal skirmishes in congested cities would have been familiar to Leibowitz from a childhood spent first in Manhattan's fractious Lower East Side and then in more comfortably polyglot East Harlem. But the animosity in Hoboken was different, somehow—deeper.[15]

Sixty-four-year-old Frank Scutellaro, who sat across from Sam at Anna's kitchen table, would likely know something about the roots of that blatant frustration and bitterness. The lawyer studied him. The thick lenses of Frank's round eyeglasses were a concession to age, and his teeth betrayed his many years as a coffee drinker, but the elder Scutellaro had the upright carriage of a much younger man. Robust, with a carefully trimmed dark mustache, Frank still cut a dapper figure. The observant attorney would have noticed the finely made suits—now seven or eight years out of style—that the former contractor wore at his son's court appearances, and Sam would have detected the elder Scutellaro's wounded self-regard.[16]

Frank's anger flared occasionally while he spoke, in heavily accented English, about the family's losses. He had lived in Hoboken for fifty years and had come to know the vicissitudes of the city's political machine. He had worked hard to establish his family—that much was already certain from Leibowitz's conversations with Joe—but the lawyer learned, as Frank responded to his questions, that many of the city's Italians had once believed they would advance as other groups had before them and had then seen all opportunity snatched away.[17]

In the years before the Great War, Frank and his neighbors had been able to build for themselves what they needed. When prominent Irish Catholics had made them feel unwelcome at Our Lady of Grace—a colossal Willow Avenue church designed by the same architect who drew the plans for city hall—Italians had raised their own Roman Catholic churches, with parishes following regional affiliations from the Other Side. The modest St. Francis Italian Church on Third and Jefferson Streets had been founded by parishioners from Genoa; the more ornate St. Ann's, several blocks north, was organized by San Giacomese.[18]

The Great War shifted the perspective of these Italian immigrants. While Italy had slowly unified as a nation during the late nineteenth and early twentieth centuries, they had continued to identify themselves by their village or town of origin. But the war drew them together with new nationalistic pride. And when the United States entered the European conflict, becoming an ally of Italy in the Great War, many men of Italian heritage also experienced an unfamiliar sense of common cause with Irish Americans and other Hoboken residents who had previously reviled and stigmatized them. They did not then know that such feelings would be short-lived.[19]

Frank was already in his forties when the United States entered the conflict, but like thousands of local men, he was required to register for military service. The flurry of local enrollment, along with the influx of servicemen—Hoboken was selected as a port of embarkation for US soldiers leaving for military service in France—brought the war home to all city residents, as did the suppression and dispersion of the formerly large and influential German community.[20]

That population shift, Hoboken's inhabitants could see now, had created power-seizing opportunities for Irish American politicians like

Patrick Griffin and Bernard McFeely. But in 1917 they had only seen the government seizure of Hoboken's German-owned docks and the forced closure of over 250 nearby taverns to limit the availability of alcohol to American soldiers departing from the confiscated piers.[21]

Frank Scutellaro had surely reflected on the shuttering of so many local drinking establishments. Like many politically savvy and financially astute Hobokenites, he had tried his hand at running a corner saloon, where party alliances and contract offers could be generated along with additional income. He would have been able to predict that the prosperous booze trade along Hudson and River Streets, long cultivated by the regular visitation of merchant seamen, travelers, ticket agents, and longshoremen, was not about to be halted.[22]

And it wasn't—not in the least. Rather, Hoboken's Little Prohibition inaugurated a vigorous underground market for alcohol, which only grew larger when Prohibition was imposed nationwide from 1920 through 1933. The city became notorious as an "open" town and was labeled by Anti-Saloon Leaguers as the "Wettest Spot in the United States." Only three streets had no saloons. Patrolmen in full uniform could be spied bellying up to the bar for their whiskeys.[23]

Tavern owners soon learned they could practice the bootleggers' craft if they were generous with the police, who answered to Boss Griffin's protégé, Bernard McFeely. As the city commissioner charged with overseeing the police and fire departments, McFeely knew the city's uniformed hires lacked civil-service protections, unions, and contracts; they were vulnerable—as cops were all along the East Coast—to payoffs and coercion. They needed to curry favor with politicians in order to secure promotions. A few amenable Hoboken firefighters and patrolmen were found to serve as McFeely bagmen and to offer protection for bookmakers and other racketeers who proliferated during Prohibition.[24]

At first Frank and his Italian neighbors noticed that the homemade wine they stored in their sheds and basements was of little interest to McFeely—as it was, generally, to federal authorities. The National Prohibition Act disallowed the manufacture of distilled spirits and beer containing more than ½ percent of alcohol, but home brews of cider and wine, meant for home consumption, were outlawed only if they could be proved "intoxicating." If Hoboken police were not chasing down active bootleggers, surely residents of Italian heritage could keep a barrel close to the kitchen or parlor without fear, and wine could continue to be part of their Sunday meals or sipped after a crushing workday.[25]

The rare raid of a Hoboken speakeasy could almost always be traced to outside forces—coordinated by federal "Dry Squads." Raids made for great headlines, often accompanied by photos of government agents, revolvers tucked in their waistbands as they purposefully tipped beer into the gutter.[26]

But mostly, it was business as usual in Hoboken. It was understood, for a time, that unless a resident transgressed the order of things in some way, Prohibition would not reach into his home. If anything, the ban on booze offered a chance—a golden opportunity—to make a dollar.[27]

Those postwar Prohibition years had been lucrative ones for the Scutellaros, too, Frank told Leibowitz. There was a building boom then, with plenty of money available for fine carpentry or construction. His son had worked alongside him, and, Frank added proprietarily, Joe had earned sixty, maybe seventy dollars a week, just for *assisting*. They hadn't wanted for anything.[28]

Plus there had been all that city work—masoning, constructing bandstands—all set aside for Frank Scutellaro.

Frank leaned in to confide to Leibowitz that McFeely had even called upon him when he had needed a carpenter at his weekend retreat in Closter, New Jersey. That was where the Boss stabled several riding horses and polo ponies.[29]

Frank smiled, recalling his past rewards. He must have considered it only right that he had been favored for employment—and not only because of his recognized carpentry skills. He had played by the party's rules and benefited the machine. He should profit in return.

Few Hoboken Italians had actually been so favored—even as the demographics of the city had changed in their favor. Their prior division according to Old Country regional affiliations, and the designs of Irish political bosses like Griffin and McFeely, had held them back. In other cities—New York, Milwaukee, Providence—Italians from different

THE NEPOTISTIC REPUBLIC | 97

regions had been drawn together by wartime nationalism and had begun to unify around their shared experience of discrimination in the United States. Now Hoboken's Italian community began to do the same.[30]

By the late 1920s, dozens of the city's small clubs and regional societies, with a combined membership of five thousand, had merged into the United Italian-American Societies and Clubs of Hoboken, Inc. Their hub was a Fourth Street meeting hall owned by a member of the executive board, a young businessman named Frank Bartletta. The focused and self-confident thirty-year-old, who was positioning himself to publicly represent the city's large Italian population, also used the hall for meetings of the four-hundred-strong Frank J. Bartletta Association.[31]

Bartletta was just four years younger than Joe, but Frank Scutellaro was less likely to consider the gregarious political contender as a son than as a youthful version of himself. The two men shared many traits. Enterprising and aggressive, a former bar owner with a broad portfolio in banking, real estate, printing, and publishing, Frank Bartletta was known for his lavish gestures, as well as his business acumen and ambition. That Bartletta lived with his family uptown, on Hudson Street, would have impressed the elder Scutellaro as a singular achievement, but all would have noted that the young man's business and his political association were headquartered downtown.[32]

For a time, Bartletta had also been held in high regard by city hall, for his largesse to the machine's "election campaigns." But in the spring of 1928, when Bartletta asserted his leadership of the Italian community during a meeting in the Boss's office, McFeely had responded by tossing out the upstart. That did not fully satisfy the Hoboken boss. He must have already known what the newspapers reported soon after—that the United Italian-American Societies had gathered together "approximately 90 percent of the Italian manhood of Hoboken." If Italian American voters were directed to reject McFeely on a mass scale—especially if they shifted to the Republican Party—they might be able to bollix his efficient machine.[33]

Other politicians might have convened a new meeting with Bartletta, but the Hoboken boss was not about to negotiate with any challenger. He preferred force.

He unleashed the police into the homes of Bartletta followers.

Claiming prohibition enforcement, the police raids began at the uptown residence of Joseph Finizio, president of the Frank J. Bartletta Association. Soon after, squads of policemen armed with axes were tearing through cellars all over the city. When homemade wine was found, as it so often was, the officers seized the barrels or smashed them, then charged the winemakers with violating state laws.[34]

The raids continued through the spring and summer, outraging Italian American residents. While taverns with free-flowing rum and whiskey had been overlooked on almost every Hoboken street, policemen had rushed in to pour *their* wine into gutters—an affront to their heritage and their standing as Americans. Their wine had connected them to their forebears. But it had also been an expression of the kind of freedom and equality they had expected to have in the country their immigrant fathers and mothers had adopted.[35]

For those who had been soldiers in the Great War, especially, this was an old battle. They had returned from the front to their neighborhoods, convinced that they had finally proved themselves as *Americans*, equal to others, and entitled to the same rights. Watching their wine drain into city sewers, they must have known they would have to prove it to Boss McFeely, too.

The 1928 performance of the United Italian-American Societies' annual Columbus Day parade began in familiar fashion—with an extended barrage of fireworks. The October 12 pageant featured the usual bands playing patriotic and popular music, a float featuring a statue of Columbus, and the expected costumed marchers carrying Italian and American flags. Ten societies with over two thousand members assembled downtown to march through the streets of the city.

At first glance, the event would have seemed a reprise of parades past. But in this procession, no city commissioners marched, as they had in previous years. They had not been invited to participate.[36]

The parade leadership had changed, too. Yes, the procession was still headed by the Hoboken police band, but marching just behind them was an Italian American police detective who had reportedly been persecuted by the Hall for his allegiance to Bartletta. "His fellow coun-trymen knew why he was there," one reporter wrote, "and he was cheered at every street corner the parade passed." Frank Bartletta, as the parade's grand marshal, appeared next in line, to equal acclaim.[37]

In anticipation of the parade changes, the lineup on the Hall's reviewing stand had also been adjusted to boast a rare visitor. Bernard McFeely's tall, rigidly upright form could be easily distinguished from those of his doughier colleagues. Several fellow commissioners, a few state legislators, and then-mayor Gustav Bach (who had been hastily installed in 1925 following Griffin's illness) stood by McFeely's side.

Scowling and stern, the Hoboken boss watched as the marchers neared his elevated platform. He was surely anticipating a customary acknowledgement from the marchers—waving hands, a pause in the procession to hail the city leadership.[38]

But the orderly lines of marchers kept moving. They stared straight ahead, passing the reviewing stand and its bright, rippling flags without so much as a nod to McFeely and his cronies. First the police band, then the anti-McFeely detective, then Grand Marshal Bartletta . . . more than two thousand Italian Americans refused to turn toward the waiting city lead-ership. It was a demonstration so powerful one reporter declared that it signaled "the waning power of Leader 'Barney' McFeely and his machine."

The rebellious paraders turned off Washington Street and concluded their march in front of the Frank J. Bartletta Association. While "the bands played the Italian and American national anthems," a reporter observed, members of each society stepped forward to salute the associa-tion's namesake.[39]

Leibowitz would have known the outcome of the Italian Americans' protest even before Frank had finished offering his account. Hudson County lawyers had surely briefed the New Yorker on McFeely's temper, and the *Post* exposé that had contributed background on the mayor's fortune had filled him in still more, with testimony supplied by Joseph Clark, a police captain turned commissioner turned machine opponent. Clark had vividly recalled the order to break the unbowed Bartletta supporters. McFeely's rage had been so explosive, Clark said, his deputies had thought he "was losing his head." The Boss's thick neck had throbbed and bugled from his tight collar. "Don't permit them to do *anything!*" he'd spluttered. His meaty fists had clenched as he bellowed to his silent department heads: "Don't let them get away with *anything! Drive them off the street.*"[40]

Axe-bearing police had been at the ready, and the proliferation of McFeelys and their friends in public service gave the Boss eyes and ears to suss out every Bartletta supporter destined for punishment. And when Bartletta then dared—unsuccessfully—to initiate a political run against the machine, the Boss mobilized fully against the Italian American's campaigners.[41]

Frank Scutellaro was pulled down with those known to be in Bartletta's camp. The avenging force that swept in tore away Frank's city contracts, along with the security of his neighbors' wine cellars, the licenses fellow contractors required, and the permits Italian societies needed for public gatherings.[42]

McFeely bore down without letup until the Depression took over for him. The scarcity of jobs and the paucity of relief severely narrowed the energies of the majority of his opponents. Like the Scutellaros, most could only focus on the food they needed to secure each day. Now the Hoboken boss could turn the better part of his attention to the riches he might cull from the paychecks of residents able to work.[43]

9 | CIRCUS MAXIMUS

THE RECESSION OF 1937 had stretched miserably into the spring of 1938, prompting another federal turnabout on relief. On April 14, while Joe Scutellaro was still in the county jail awaiting trial, President Roosevelt proposed to Congress an increase in federal funding for relief programs and new appropriations for public projects that would generate jobs. Just a year before, despite warnings by WPA administrator Harry Hopkins and other advisors that Americans needed purchasing power to boost the economy, the president had championed federal deficit reduction and had called for cuts in relief spending. But now, in an evening "Fireside Chat" directed to the electorate, Roosevelt couched his request for $3 billion for additional relief funding in language meant to convey political, as well as economic, necessity. "In recommending this program, I am thinking not only of the immediate economic needs of the people of the nation, but also of their personal liberties," he said. "I am thinking of our democracy." Democracy had disappeared in other nations, he continued, not because the people of those nations opposed it, but because "in desperation, they chose to sacrifice liberty in the hope of getting something to eat."[1]

Listening to the president's radio address in the cramped Hoboken apartment he shared with his wife and six children, Herman Matson, sometime applicant for poor relief and a dogged seeker of WPA employment, must have been heartened by the promise of more aid and more jobs. Now thirty-seven years old, Herman had once been steadily

101

employed as a fireman on the S.S. *Leviathan*. Then the Depression had immobilized the loss-making passenger ship at her Hoboken pier, and he had gone to work as a coffee salesman in Brooklyn, until that job also ended. More recently, he'd been hired as a wood turner and, on WPA projects, as a general laborer.[2]

He closely followed the ever-evolving New Deal programs. From the start of the economic freefall, Herman had struggled to make sense of what was happening around the country, to respond as best he could to the conditions confronting his family and his good and hard-working neighbors. Hope, as much as family need and a sense of outrage, had propelled him. Herman had alerted state and federal officials to Harry Barck's miserable handling of relief and then began to organize Hoboken's jobless poor, focusing their attention on McFeely's exclusive power over the city and the continuing local administration of poor relief that had allowed the Boss and his poormaster to abandon them to starvation. At the very least, Herman wanted to push for changes in the city's aid practices, as committed groups had demanded and successfully accomplished elsewhere.[3]

Like so many who were made jobless and poor by the Depression, Herman Matson greatly admired Roosevelt, and he would have respectfully considered the president's comments about threats to democracy. But given his familiarity with Hoboken's handling of relief, Matson could be forgiven if he interpreted Roosevelt's remarks less as a caution about tyranny in Germany, or even as a warning about "Reds" fomenting rebellion in the United States, and more as an apt description of the surrender of rights, personal dignity, and cold cash that the McFeely administration had long demanded of the people of Hoboken in exchange for aid or jobs.[4]

Herman would have heard about Lena Fusco, the young woman who had argued with the poormaster the morning he was killed, and who had been sentenced to ninety days in the county jail for spitting on him. She had served five days. Published reports had casually mentioned that Fusco's husband and a number of neighbors had "appealed to Hoboken Mayor Bernard McFeely," and that Recorder Frank Romano had ordered her release. There had been no further reports concerning the debt Fusco might have incurred to bring about her reunion with her sickly children.[5]

Herman had his own history with the Hoboken poormaster. Harry Barck had been shifty, sometimes officious in his response, often impassive or brusque, growling refusals without looking up from his disordered desk. But Herman had been persistent. He wanted a WPA job, and he knew his first step was to apply for poor relief from the Hoboken poormaster.

The WPA was not strictly a jobs program, but one of "work relief." The federal agency required applicants to be certified as unemployed and eligible for work assignments prior to their consideration for WPA jobs. Essentially, they were to be declared able-bodied paupers, and that certification process, and consequent referral, was almost exclusively in the hands of local relief authorities.[6]

Certification procedures made it likely that Hoboken applicants would have to see Harry Barck more than once. If a certain period of time had passed between a worker's WPA jobs, or if a worker left the WPA to take on better-paying private employment, he or she would need to be recertified in order to become eligible again for a work-relief assignment. Or at least that had been true for Herman Matson. A local attorney later showed him a list of Hoboken men and women who were on the WPA, even though their families enjoyed city paychecks. They could not have been honestly declared destitute by the poormaster.[7]

But for Herman there had been a rigid process. He would be interviewed more than once by the poormaster's regular secretary and again by her replacement, Eleonore Hartmann. And each time Barck would check up on him as he said he did with all relief applicants, questioning former employers and landlords, prying into the records of local grocers and merchants, to determine if the applicant was both needy and worthy.[8]

Herman had first entered the WPA rolls in 1936 and had worked sporadically on local road and construction projects until May of the following year, when federal funds dried up. He was laid off with five hundred other workers. Until WPA money began to trickle in again, he had returned to the poormaster.[9]

Initially, Herman had tried to reason with Barck. After the poormaster made him return repeatedly to ask for milk for his children—then ranging in age from eighteen months to twelve years—Herman handed the official his dispossess notice, to prove his family's hardship. Barck eyed the document and retorted, "Go home and frame it."[10]

Herman had remained calm, though he had been galled by the scene, of the poormaster's implacability as applicants shuffled into his rooms to detail their misery. As a workman who had once had regular employment, he would have been unlikely to know firsthand that traditional poormasters had long argued that the distress caused by the application process would compel lazy applicants to go seek work.[11]

And so, for his next meeting with the poormaster, Herman had taken another approach: he'd introduced a letter from a state official that declared the Matson family's need and suitability for aid. Perhaps a directive from the state would persuade the Hoboken overseer to relinquish assistance.

But Barck had again refused, knowing the state had no power over his decision-making. "You're not bluffing me with that letter!" he shouted, and he directed Herman to leave his office.

That was when Matson had contacted the local newspapers. Six weeks before Barck's denial of aid and a possible slur set in motion his fateful struggle with Joe Scutellaro, the poormaster would dismiss Herman's documented need as the trumped-up ploy of a "radical" and a shirker. "I've been in this business 42 years and I can tell when they're chiseling and when they're worthy," the overseer had declared to the *Observer* reporter. "No worthy case is denied."[12]

That pretense of case-by-case consideration, Herman must have realized then, had to be confronted. The able-bodied unemployed were being denied subsistence *as a group*. They would have to organize and fight back as a group, too.

Herman had seen other attempts at organizing the city's jobless. In 1936 the severity of Barck's relief cuts had briefly mobilized area members of the New Jersey State Unemployed League, a local of a multistate "union of the unemployed." Initiated by socialists in the early days of the Depression, the Unemployed Leagues were best known for promoting self-help actions. A group from nearby Union City had arrived in Hoboken to feed the "starving unemployed" with donated canned goods. League members had vowed to investigate conditions in Hoboken and mentioned the possibility of staging street meetings in the city, "even at the risk of arrest." But the organization did not establish a strong presence in the city, and with conflicts to cover elsewhere, the press had also turned away.[13]

Now came the Scutellaro tragedy, with one man dead and another waiting for a trial that might conclude with his death sentence. The newspapers had seized upon the news of Barck's killing, but their coverage had not stirred reform. In the weeks since the new poormaster had been installed in city hall, the relief situation had improved little. The city's stinginess could no longer be blamed on the actions of one tight-fisted old man. Barck's replacement, Austin Tighe, was "a nice fellow," Herman ventured, "but he has to do what the McFeely machine tells him to do."[14]

Change was going to have to come from external pressure. Herman needed to figure out how to inform the unemployed—how to organize them—in a place where police thwarted any effort to distribute unsanctioned leaflets. He looked for guidance in Jersey City, and to the Workers Defense League.

By the spring of 1938, the Workers Defense League was often in the news, its active members pursuing a street campaign to challenge a Jersey City leafleting ban much like the one in neighboring Hoboken. The ordinance in "Haguetown" was being used by the sweatshop-friendly boss Frank Hague to block CIO organizing, and the resulting detention and deportation of union leafleteers was the kind of antiworker abuse the WDL had been created to challenge. Labor and Socialist party leaders had organized the WDL in 1936 specifically to offer legal aid to workers involved in civil liberties crises.[15]

In an acknowledgment of mutual concerns, the WDL had also allied early on with the Workers Alliance of America, a vigorous coalition of the organized unemployed and WPA hires. The Workers Alliance was itself a multistate merger of nonpartisan and left-leaning groups of employed and jobless workers, including those organized by Communists and Socialists.[16]

The Alliance's bold activism was well known—some would say notorious—at least in Herman's adopted home state. In the spring of 1936, the New Jersey branch had vividly highlighted the state legislature's inactivity on relief by occupying the assembly's chamber in the statehouse.[17]

The sit-in, which occurred just before spring recess and lasted for more than a week as lawmakers gingerly sought a politic outcome, deeply disturbed many of the state's staid and financially secure residents. Day after day they opened their newspapers to read about the unemployed protestors who refused to leave the "people's house" in Trenton, insisting that legislators take action and appropriate relief funds. Several hundred unemployed men and women camped out in the chamber and held mock legislative sessions, interspersing their oratory with occasional card games. They shared meals of cold meat, bread, and coffee and called for "frequent recesses." ("Just like the legislature," a Workers Alliance wit remarked to a *Times* reporter. "We are sitting here doing nothing.")[18]

Herman surely remembered that the statehouse occupiers were non-violent; nevertheless, they had inspired fears of revolution and anarchy. The protestors' accusations, presented in news reports without underlying facts, would have seemed extreme, as when one female protestor declared state legislators "murderers" because they were "letting people starve." Forces were mobilized to quash the outcry. Had the demonstrators not marched out of the assembly on their own, a waiting legion of state troopers and city police would have forcibly dislodged them. Many conservative New Jerseyans agreed with the assemblyman who denounced the jobless "legislators" as "a mob of occupation under Communist leaders."[19]

But something had to be done, and it could not be done alone. Herman Matson did not consider himself a Red, he would later explain, nor was he "a radical, a Socialist, [or] a Communist." He was a registered Democrat. But he was also dedicated to "fighting for free speech" and, as he put it, "fighting 'tooth and nail' for the poor and weak and defenseless of my community." The Workers Defense League was willing to battle over civil liberties in the streets and in court, and their members had also had the heart to supply money and food to the Scutellaro family after Joe was arrested and their hardships became known. Herman was moved to join the WDL. He would find in its members the fearless and savvy comrades-in-arms he needed for his Hoboken fight.[20]

Not long after, a group of Hoboken's unemployed gathered in the Matsons' Willow Avenue apartment, and Herman was elected "Chairman of the Hoboken Chapter of the Workers Defense League of New Jersey"—a lofty title that mostly established him as an open opponent of the McFeely administration and its handling of poor relief.[21]

His first public protest occurred several days before Roosevelt broadcast his radio address on democracy and relief. On April 5 Herman walked to city hall to distribute leaflets, accompanied by two out-of-town WDL "observers." They were to contact a lawyer affiliated with the WDL if Herman was detained or arrested.[22]

By midmorning, Herman had stationed himself at the First Street doorway reserved for relief applicants. The leaflets he carried pronounced Hoboken relief "inadequate and political" and held the city responsible for the death of Poormaster Harry Barck. At that time of day, the streets were usually crowded with aid-seekers, along with First Street shoppers and residents hurrying to do business in city hall. If he had been permitted to distribute freely, he would have had enough time to hand out a few thousand leaflets before clocking in for his afternoon job, a WPA position involving much-needed repairs to Washington Street.[23]

Though born in Manhattan, Herman had lived in Hoboken for over a decade, and he would have been familiar with the tactics used to curtail leafleting in his adopted city. But he had been emboldened by a new US Supreme Court decision, as well as a promise made to reporters by Hoboken police that they would abide by it. The WDL had filed an *amicus curiae* brief in the case, and it must have seemed only right to the new chair of the Hoboken chapter that he test its result.[24]

In *Lovell v. City of Griffin, Georgia*, the Supreme Court held that the Griffin city ordinance requiring a license for the distribution of "literature of any kind" was "invalid on its face." Liberty of circulating—pamphlets and leaflets as well as newspapers and periodicals—"is as essential to that freedom as liberty of publishing," the court stated. That seemed straightforward enough.

Still, Herman had been careful. The leaflet included a warning he may have hoped would aid in his own protection. Threats of the loss of relief or of WPA jobs, it read, "were being used to keep the unemployed and destitute people of Hoboken from demanding their rights."[25]

He managed to distribute a few of the leaflets before a patrolman approached. Herman handed a flyer to him. The policeman gripped Herman's arm and pulled him into the Hall, down to the basement, where police headquarters was located. He pushed Herman into the office of Inspector Thomas Garrick.

An old hand at city hall politics, Garrick had retained his position in the department for forty-eight years; his length of service had exceeded even the tenure of the late poormaster. By 1898, when thirty-three-year-old Harry Barck was installed in his post, the younger patrolman had already been wielding his stick for several years in the city's roughest waterfront district.[26]

Garrick had worked on the Scutellaro case. He read Herman's leaflet and its charge that the city had killed Harry Barck, then he telephoned the new poormaster to come down to his office.[27]

"What do you think we ought to do about this?" Poormaster Austin Tighe asked Garrick after he, too, had read the leaflet.

"We'll question him further," the inspector replied. While Tighe watched, Garrick grilled his detainee. Where was the local WDL office located? How many members did the organization have? Was it a "Red" organization? Was Matson a Communist? Herman refused to respond.

Then Garrick asked Herman if he was working on the WPA. He told the inspector he was on the afternoon shift.

"I'll find out about this," Garrick said. "And if you are not telling the truth, I'll have you kicked off the WPA."

Garrick made a phone call. The chief timekeeper for Hoboken's WPA projects confirmed Herman's schedule, but still Garrick refused to release him.

Nevertheless, Herman had not been charged with any crime, and when a WDL-affiliated attorney, alerted by the two WDL observers, arrived at Garrick's door, the detainee walked out. He immediately distributed the rest of his leaflets to the midday crowd surging past city hall.

As it turned out, Herman's first run-in with the Hoboken police coincided with the inauguration of the *New York Post* exposé, introduced with the front-page banner HOBOKEN: SYMBOL OF CIVIC SHAME.[28]

Perhaps predictably, and despite the comprehensiveness of the *Post*'s evidence, McFeely cronies swiftly rallied to support their leader. One of the city's larger Democratic clubs pledged "the faith and loyalty of its 600 members" to McFeely's leadership. The Hoboken Retail Merchants Association and the Lion's Club both issued resolutions praising the mayor for "the remarkable job he is doing."[29]

And who could be surprised at their expressions of fealty? As the WDL soon pointed out in leaflets—leaflets that Herman Matson distributed until he was again stopped by police—the McFeely champions were just ventriloquist dummies, "his Charlie McCarthies." Nearly all the spokesmen praising McFeely in newspaper reports were on the city payroll.

"You see the tie-up between the Mayor and the jobholders who get their organizations to act as stooges to support the Mayor in his policy of starving the unemployed," the new WDL flyer announced. "Their words don't mean anything, nor do those of the Mayor, unless they are backed up by deeds. For what the unemployed live on is FOOD—NOT WORDS.

"We speak for thousands of Hoboken citizens in demanding that the Hoboken city officials take immediate action to <u>END THE STARVA-TION WHICH CAUSED THE SCUTELLARO CASE</u>!!"[30]

On April 19 the foreman on Herman Matson's WPA job signed a complaint charging that Herman "disregarded orders," "does not put in a day's work," and "reports late." Accordingly, the letter continued, he was to be relieved of his duties on the WPA.

Herman approached the job foreman and asked him if he had signed the complaint. The accusations were untrue; he had even put in full days after he'd been transferred to the cement-mixing machine—a task one colleague later described as "one of the most punishing assignments that can be given out on the average WPA job." Herman had done the work. Perhaps someone had forged the foreman's signature. That simple signature on a mimeographed form was going to cause the destitution of Herman's family.[31]

"What could I do?" the foreman responded pleadingly. "I have to protect my job." He said a city employee who was on the WPA Personnel Advisory Committee had "told me to sign it and I signed it." That man was on the jobsite that very day.

Herman walked to the project tool house to return the tools he had taken up that morning for his day's work. When he turned around to leave, he saw the city employee had entered the tool house behind him. "Now get the hell out in the street," the man snarled.

Herman must have known his antagonist wanted to goad him into a fight. That would seal the deal. He would never work again on a federal project.

Herman could have taken on most any man and hurt him if he'd had a mind to do so. He wasn't very tall—about five foot seven, just about average for a man of his generation—but he was powerfully built, with a thick neck and strong upper torso, and large, capable hands. He was sure and steady on his feet.[32]

But unlike his opponents, Herman Matson did not solve his problems with his fists. He began to walk toward the door.

"I told you, you were fired," the city employee taunted, hurrying behind. Herman kept walking.

"You've got a family and don't want to work!" the city employee shouted, so near to Herman he must have felt the man's breath on his neck.

Herman turned around to face him and quietly asked, "What are you getting excited about?" He would have known immediately, when he saw the other man's sneering, reddened face, that he should not have given in to temptation. "You dirty son of a bitch!" the city employee shouted into Herman's face, as he grabbed the lapels on Herman's coat and shook him. "I've a good mind to drive you through the wall and knock you dead."

At this, Herman shook free and turned to leave the jobsite. "McFeely stooge," he muttered as he walked away.[33]

The B. N. McFeely Association held its Spring Ball a few weeks later, continuing a tradition that had been established under the more accommodating reigns of bosses Davis and Griffin. Generations of canny businessmen, ward heelers, and other grateful recipients of free-flowing patronage had once readily acknowledged the mutual benefit of attending this annual, publicly choreographed event. Now the occasion mostly signaled Boss McFeely's command.

During nearly thirteen years of bruising party leadership, McFeely's receiving lines had routinely taken hours to clear. The boss acknowledged his supplicants and accepted, along with handshakes and good wishes, rolls of cash barely disguised as "ticket proceeds."[34]

Many attendees of the spring 1938 ball, held in the vise of a recession, now rallied out of a mix of fear and reaction. "Recent attacks on the mayor by a New York newspaper were seen as the force which brought out the largest crowd ever to attend the McFeely ball," announced the *Jersey Journal*, which estimated attendance at eight thousand—a significant army in a city with fifty-nine thousand residents. "Observers hailed the turnout as the greatest demonstration of faith in the city administration ever accorded the mayor during his long term as chief executive."[35]

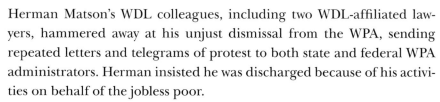

Herman Matson's WDL colleagues, including two WDL-affiliated lawyers, hammered away at his unjust dismissal from the WPA, sending repeated letters and telegrams of protest to both state and federal WPA administrators. Herman insisted he was discharged because of his activities on behalf of the jobless poor.

Finally word came that his dismissal, though avidly sought by Hoboken officials, would not go through. The WPA's State Labor Relations Section had determined "it would be better judgment to reinstate Mr. Matson to a project outside his municipality."[36]

He was transferred to a WPA project in Jersey City, which added the cost of transportation and an outside meal to his daily expenses. Still, he had work and was glad of it. Compared to the poormaster's puny relief allotments, the WPA's wages would have seemed generous. He was now taking in $60.50 a month.[37]

Many recipients of the WPA's comparative largesse would forget the poor reliefers they left behind, until they were forced to be among them once again. Herman Matson did not. Rather, he took his financial security as an opportunity to launch a broader public campaign to improve conditions for Hoboken's unemployed.

The new printing machine claimed most of the Matsons' small living room, but Herman—and the WDL members who tucked themselves around it at meetings—found the trade-off more than acceptable. The hand-cranked mimeograph used no electricity, was easy to operate, and required few supplies. With only a ribbonless typewriter to punch out messages on waxed paper stencils, and sufficient ink and paper, one person could crank out a thousand leaflets, or more, every night.

To the youngest Matson children, the appearance of the massive contraption was both strange and wonderful; it transformed their conventional living space into a little factory of news and outrage and announcements. Their father played every part in production, as needed. He became a daily newsman, a writer, composing his text with a pencil stuck in his dark, wavy hair; then a pressman, inking up the machine and wrapping a stencil to the cylinder, turning the hand crank to print sheet after sheet; and when he was done, his broad smile of satisfaction lifting the edges of his trim brown mustache, he would gather a sheaf of handbills and leave the apartment to hawk the news in the streets.[38]

Their mother, Elizabeth, brought up hard and poor in Pennsylvania coal country, would not have viewed the mimeograph machine with amusement, but she would have understood its worth. She believed in what Herman was doing and would fight alongside him, propelled by fury as much as a strong sense of commitment. While her husband could find humor as well as offense in the Hall's overt corruption, and could employ the power of public mockery, Elizabeth had a darker temperament. The humiliating and politicized handling of relief simply made her angry. She had fumed when Herman's nine-day suspension from his Hoboken WPA position had resulted in their eviction, but Herman had handled that event in his own way: when his work had resumed and they were again settled, he had trotted the kids down to the front of city hall and lined them up to sing "God Bless America," while he explained to reporters why he'd had to take a break from leafleting.[39]

Herman had purchased the duplicating machine as soon as he had money to spare. He had always been that way about money—not wasteful but viewing his paycheck as something to use, not hoard. Buying the mimeo machine meant that the Hoboken chapter of the Workers Defense League had its own inexpensive and discreet print shop.[40]

And Herman had immediately made use of it, printing flyers to announce a WDL-sponsored open-air meeting in early May, to be held at Church Square Park. Anticipating a large audience, he had taken care to apply for a permit for the early evening rally and had received one, after sending his request by registered mail.[41]

Church Square Park was the ideal spot to hold a meeting focused on the formation of a Hoboken union of the unemployed. It was centrally located, bordered by an uptown street to the east and skirting downtown to the west; and its benches and strips of lawn welcomed a range of residents, including students from neighboring high schools, parishioners of Our Lady of Grace Church, and—most congenial of all to the WDL—workers from the nearby pencil factory, recently unionized by the CIO.[42]

Even more, Herman had been offered the services of a native speaker of Italian, thereby broadening the meeting's reach to Hoboken's poorest—and most insular—residents. Barber Nicholas Piracci, an Italian émigré, had read one of Herman's leaflets and had resolved "to assist [the activist] in any way possible." Although English-language news syndicates would soon spread word of Herman's relief activism to readers across the country, the transmission of his critiques to Hoboken's Italian-speaking reliefers would have been impeded by police and by language. Now, with Piracci's bold offer, one of those barriers had been eliminated.[43]

Herman would recall the May meeting—one of the few public gatherings he managed to realize—as "fairly orderly." On that May evening, he remembered, about six hundred people had gathered around a portable speakers' stand to hear him speak, following short speeches by the national secretary of the Workers Defense League, Brendon Sexton, Piracci, and two New Jersey WDL representatives, Darrell O'Neill and Morris Milgram.

Herman had watched audience members nodding and murmuring their assent as the other speakers addressed them, but he had also noticed a man he recognized, a Hoboken fire captain, weaving his way through the crowd. The captain was known as one of McFeely's "collectors," assigned to gather from firemen an annual "tribute" to the Boss. At the park, the man had been carrying a small black bag. Herman later realized the fireman had been handing out rotted eggs to eager boys clustered at the group's edge. Periodically the boys had tossed their projectiles at the speakers, then disappeared into the crowd.[44]

It had seemed an infantile form of harassment at the time. The eggs had likely been distributed with the goal of inciting retaliation by the Hoboken WDL chairman and even to cause a wider public disturbance. He had not complied. Although he would add the incident to a growing list of insults and abuse he would later recall in great detail, Herman Matson would steadily refuse to be provoked.

The source of Herman's self-possession and optimism was something of a mystery, even to his wife and children. He did not talk much about his parents or his early childhood, and the little he did reveal would have left a listener marveling that Herman had not grown hardened and brutish from neglect. His mother, a French immigrant, was probably mentally ill; her instability had led to repeated hospitalizations. Herman's English father had abandoned her and their children. She married again and was again abandoned. For a time Herman lived on the streets of Manhattan's "Hell's Kitchen," when the area was notorious for roving gangs. His mother married a third time, to a German man, William Blumberg. This marriage, too, would fail. But the kindness William bestowed on his stepson was not lost on Herman. It was the one detail he readily shared with others.[45]

With little experience of constancy in his youth, Herman Matson had nevertheless proceeded to establish himself in adulthood as a capable and conscientious worker and, even more, as a good husband and father. When he met Elizabeth in New York, she already had two children from a prior marriage. But once Herman dedicated himself to her, *Elizabeth's* children became *his*, too—as dear to him as the four born later, in Hoboken. Herman always identified himself as "a father of six."[46]

At home, as in his public exchanges, Herman refused to argue, believing more could be resolved when levelheaded than in moments of fury. Elizabeth, fiery and resolute, was less inclined to wait for anger to pass. When she raged at times, Herman's response was routine: "Betty, I'm going for a walk." He would circle the block and return to take on the disagreement calmly.[47]

For a time, they agreed on the importance of speaking out against the inadequacy of relief in their city. Herman would brave the insults and the threats. He likely never allowed himself to imagine that harm might come to his family because he spoke up on behalf of the poor.

Joe Scutellaro still awaited trial, and Sam Leibowitz, with other clients requiring his services in New York courts, was called away from Hoboken. But as the New Jersey investigation was not yet complete, Leibowitz asked his young associate, Joshua Peterfreund, to continue in his absence, to gather information.[48]

Even with Peterfreund lightening his workload, Leibowitz was driving himself hard. When engaged in a courtroom battle, Sam would frequently work until dawn, then sleep two hours before returning to his papers. Finally, at the likely insistence of his wife, Belle, he had conceded his need for a break and had cleared his schedule to vacation with his family in Europe. The comfortable bourgeois life Leibowitz had secured for them during the 1920s had not been altered by the economic crisis; and now Sam took advantage of his earnings and booked their trans-Atlantic journey. Leibowitz left his eager colleague to follow through on the remaining interviews he sought for the Scutellaro case.[49]

Peterfreund was ready. He had studied the barely legible jottings on Barck's Relief Client form and assembled a list of men who had been in the poormaster's outer office the day of the alleged murder. He intended to interview them.

But first he was determined to find the poormaster's clerks—Misses Romayne Mullin, Adeline Cerutti, and Josephine Shea—and to gather their testimony. Perhaps their accounts of the morning of February 25 would be less polished than the frequently retold tale of their colleague, purported eyewitness Eleonore Hartmann.

His Hoboken mission was, at first, delayed by a late July heat wave. Then, on July 29, the dome of humid air that had slowed all city activity to a crawl burst open, releasing a thunderstorm that snapped branches in Hoboken parks and swiftly flooded low-lying and poorly drained downtown streets.[50]

When the storm ended, the temperature returned to a seasonable eighty-four degrees, with tolerable humidity, allowing the young lawyer to redouble his efforts to contact the poormaster's young employees. On the final days of July he visited lower Bloomfield Street in search of Cerutti, then traveled up to 807 Park Avenue for Shea, and finally reached the Eleventh Street address where Mullin lived. Often he looped back several times, trying to catch one of the women at home, or, when he did and his request for an interview was hurriedly refused, he would circle around to ask again.[51]

He must have thought that a night visit, and the partial cover darkness afforded, might make it easier for city hall payrollers to open their doors, for he returned to Romayne Mullin's residence after nightfall on August 1. He never spoke to her. Hoboken police lieutenant J. Romeo Scott was waiting outside her building, and he arrested the young lawyer as he approached.

Peterfreund was initially charged with disorderly conduct for "annoying witnesses"—despite the fact that Mullin had not even been at home that evening. His bail was set at $100, and he paid it with available funds. Then he was released—only to be rearrested, when a signed complaint from Mullin was introduced. Now he was charged with "obstruction of justice," and his bail had grown to $1,000. He was held overnight in Hoboken's lockup.[52]

In Leibowitz's absence, a new member of his firm, former Manhattan assistant district attorney Vincent R. Impellitteri, arrived in Hoboken the following morning to represent Joshua Peterfreund at a preliminary hearing. The two appeared before Recorder Frank Romano in the city's Police Court. Assistant Prosecutor Frank Schlosser was present to argue for the state.

After nine years in Manhattan's rough-and-tumble criminal justice system, thirty-eight-year-old Vincent Impellitteri had somehow retained a reputation for courtesy and an almost scholarly approach to the law. He was known for his sincerity. He had likely recalled with distaste some scuttlebutt about the Hoboken recorder that had appeared in the *Post* series: that Frank Romano was a tool of the city's police department and preferred to hold court with a high-ranking officer in attendance. "A nod or a headshake" by the officer was said to provide Romano with direction on the outcome of a case.[53]

Nevertheless, Impellitteri approached the Hoboken hearing as he would any other. He sought first to have the charge dismissed. He began by referring to Peterfreund's membership in the New York Bar, noting that the young man had never misrepresented himself and had carried a business card from Leibowitz's firm that proved his intent. And though the new lawyer had returned after some of the witnesses had pointedly refused to talk with him, Joshua Peterfreund, his defender insisted, had not browbeaten anyone. Impellitteri called for a dismissal, which Romano immediately denied.

Impellitteri then began to use the hearing to gather evidence, starting with his cross-examination of Edward McFeely, present to prop up the prosecutor's case. Even seated, the beefy chief of police would have seemed to dominate the trim defense attorney, but Impellitteri would not have been easily shaken from his deliberate questioning. He asked McFeely if he had ordered his men to watch the homes of all in the witnesses in the Barck murder case.[54]

Yes, McFeely replied casually. He had done so a few days earlier, after he'd been advised of Peterfreund's regular visits to the city. Leibowitz's assistant had been arrested, the chief asserted, because his effort to obtain testimony directly from the witnesses was "improper." When Impellitteri countered that the young lawyer was fully within his rights to seek statements from witnesses, McFeely responded that by contacting the prosecutor's office, Peterfreund could have availed himself of witness statements that had already been prepared at Hoboken's police headquarters.[55]

Romayne Mullin, too, was at the hearing. As she responded to Impellitteri's questions, her wide-set brown eyes alternately conveyed stubbornness and puzzlement. She admitted that Peterfreund had *not* intimidated her and that he had, in fact, "acted in a gentlemanly manner." Her statement had only charged that the lawyer's repeated visits had "annoyed" her.[56]

It would have seemed to the reporters present—and perhaps to Impellitteri, too—that the obstruction charge would be dismissed. Schlosser conceded he had presented "nothing to show any attempt at interfering with justice." But then, inexplicably, the assistant prosecutor reasserted the charge, and Romano upheld it, pending grand jury action.[57]

Vincent Impellitteri vowed, then, that he would conduct the required Hoboken interviews. "We will continue to interview every witness in this case," he declared at the close of the hearing, "and we mean to take the case to the United States Supreme Court, if necessary."[58]

Bond for Joshua Peterfreund was furnished through a surety company, and he was released in custody of his lawyer.

Some had predicted the beating. In the days prior to his September 15 open-air meeting, Herman Matson had been at the Hoboken piers distributing handbills denouncing waterfront "racketeering" and the city's fixed relief crisis.[59]

As Hoboken's WDL chairman, he had found it impossible to ignore the situation on the docks, which meshed the concerns of employed unionists with those of jobless workers. Men in both circumstances had quietly contacted Herman. They complained that the longshoremen's local was a labor union in name only—no meetings were held, no member votes were called for resolutions, and no organizational structure existed—and that workers who refused to capitulate to the "kickback racket" went unhired, forced onto the city's relief rolls. Working stevedores, covertly allied with the WDL, had informed Herman that Jimmy Nolan, the head of the Hoboken local and a delegate to the District Council of the International Longshoremen's Association, was shaking down dockworkers, demanding a kickback of 40 percent of all paychecks, which he then split with Boss McFeely.[60]

Even those who were willing to concede payment might end up on relief. Informants told the WDL that Nolan or McFeely had made an agreement with a Brooklyn personnel office that brought longshoremen across the Hudson every morning to take agreed-upon jobs along the Hoboken waterfront. They did not "shape up" like the men from Hoboken, who stood in line every working day, waiting to be chosen for different jobs by the dock boss. The Brooklyn longshoremen, the WDL supporters surmised, must not have objected to the kickbacks, but their concessions landed even more Hoboken dockworkers in the poormaster's office.

In a sign of what awaited him, Herman had found no local owners willing to rent their halls for his September 15 meeting, and he was refused a city permit to speak again at Church Square Park. He would only be able to receive the Hall's permission to set up a speaker's platform at uptown's Hudson Square Park, which sat between Fourth and Fifth Streets and bordered Hudson Street to the west and the Holland-America Piers to the east. Its proximity to the Fifth Street piers made it a thoroughfare for longshoremen making their way to and returning from the docks.[61]

Herman objected in writing and in person to the appointed meeting place. The commissioner in charge claimed he could not offer any other location. Herman finally acquiesced and continued with plans for the meeting; but when a supportive longshoreman came to the Matsons' apartment the day before the event to warn Herman that he would surely "get his skull cracked" at the waterfront park, the activist sought—and gained—assurances from the Hoboken police that he would have protection.[62]

The meeting was scheduled to begin at 8:30 PM. About 8:15 Elizabeth and Herman Matson joined fellow protesters at a WDL member's home on Fifth and Bloomfield Streets. "About ten of us," Elizabeth would later recall, walked together through the dark streets to Hudson Square Park. One of the men carried a collapsible wooden stand that would provide a three-foot-high platform for speakers, allowing them to be more visible to audience members. Herman held a large American flag that had been donated to the Hoboken WDL by a Paterson, New Jersey, member, who also walked with the group. Just behind them was Morris Milgram, New Jersey state secretary of the WDL, who was scheduled to address the meeting. Translator Nicholas Piracci and another planned speaker, national WDL secretary Brendon Sexton, were to meet them at the park.[63]

Herman must have been glad of Milgram's presence that night. Of the WDL participants, Herman relied most on Milgram's judgment, despite the disparity in their ages. Morris Milgram was then just twenty-two years old, but he was already a seasoned activist. While still in his teens, he had been expelled from New York's City College for protesting a party its administrators had organized for visiting Italian Fascists. Now a resident of Jersey City, Milgram had brought a mix of discipline and daring to WDL battles there. With his wife, Grace (she had been one of Herman's observers at city hall), he had become a reliable and dexterous supporter of the Hoboken chapter, especially its embattled chairman. Herman credited Milgram's letter-writing campaign with the reappraisal of his WPA status after his Hoboken dismissal. The younger man's commitment to his friend, and to their shared cause, would help sustain Matson in the difficult weeks and months to come.[64]

When the ten WDL members arrived at Hudson Square Park, they found a large crowd already assembled there. About five hundred people, highlighted by the street lamps' artificial brightness, were clustered near the center of the park, where the activists were to install their platform. As they set down their equipment, spectators began to draw closer. Space was cleared up front for a few women who were attending infants in carriages; some boys played at the fringes. Hundreds of people were streaming into the park, mostly in small groups but also in couples and singly.[65]

As Morris Milgram would later recall, he noticed a gang approaching three hundred men rallying at the edge of the park. He scanned the area to see if there were any police officers stationed in or around the square. He saw none. The closest patrolman was about two blocks away—too far to be of use if there was trouble.[66]

Milgram called out: Were there any reporters in the crowd? A few men shouted their assent, and Milgram asked them to come forward so he could give them a statement and put on record the group's complaint that the police had failed to stand by their pledge of protection.[67]

By now the WDL members had set up their stand. Herman planted the flag on top of it. It was 8:30 PM—time to start the meeting. With Elizabeth standing nearby, Herman climbed the three short risers to overlook the crowd, which had swelled to over fifteen hundred people. He, too, saw that the nearest policeman was two blocks away, and the officer seemed to be ignoring the growing swarm.[68]

Herman held out his arms, calling for the crowd to quiet for the meeting. His worn tweed jacket, made for a smaller, less muscular man, tugged across his chest. He had likely borrowed the suit he wore. As the crowd hushed, he began, politely, "Ladies and gentleman! We are here to talk about McFeely and the starvation in Hoboken."[69]

"Down with the speaker!" gurgled a drunken man standing in front of the platform. "I am going to sing a song in honor of Barney McFeely, our good mayor," he announced, and proceeded to sing a nonsensical jingle. He was shushed by others in the crowd, but in the minute it took him to finish his song, the gang of men that had been standing in stiff silence at the periphery of the park had hastened toward the assembled group.[70]

Nicholas Piracci had just arrived at the meeting with his three daughters and his son-in-law. He recognized the man who led the longshoremen into the park as one of Jimmy Nolan's cohorts on the docks and feared that the rumors he had heard about pending violence were about to unfold. Leaving his family behind in the square, Piracci raced out of the park to phone police headquarters. The lieutenant he spoke to assured him there were plenty of policemen around the park and hung up.[71]

Herman tried to begin the meeting again, but he felt the platform beneath him shudder from a forceful shove. Looking down, he saw Edward Florio, a stocky boss-loader on the Holland-America docks. "It's all right, Matson," Florio said. "Go right ahead and speak."[72]

Herman returned his gaze to the crowd and repeated his prior introduction. A barrage of catcalls followed—"a wave of sound," according to one reporter—and Herman's voice rose, straining to be heard above the clamor. "Hear me out!" he implored.[73]

The stand rocked forward. Florio now stood behind the platform, accompanied by a shorter, sharp-featured man Herman recognized as longshoreman Joseph McDonald. McDonald had both hands wrapped around one of the posts of the speaker's stand.[74]

Herman hastened to go on with his speech. "In justice and fairness," he called out, "at least hear what a man has to say! Let me tell you how we are suffering in Hoboken . . . how we are starving!"[75]

He had planned to protest relief standards, then to demand an immediate trial for longsuffering Joseph Scutellaro, but Herman's last shouted phrase became a plea, then a cry of alarm, as he was pitched forward from the stand on to the concrete walk below.[76]

"Let's give it to him," Milgram heard McDonald yell. It seemed to be a signal to the twenty or thirty men who rushed forward after the platform was torn away.[77]

Herman lay on the ground. The shoving, wrenching mass dragged him to the park's easternmost walkway and began to beat him. "He bent

Crowd overturning the temporary speaker's stand in Hudson Square Park, toppling Herman Matson and trampling an American flag.

AP Images/Harry Harris.

his head down, and bowed his head, and put his arms up, in order to ward off the blows, and to shield himself," Orestes Cerruti, the Paterson WDL member, would later recall. Moments after he saw Herman's attack, Cerruti, too, was knocked down and his vision obscured by blood. Milgram and others from their group were punched and chased by attackers.[78]

Through his latticed fingers, Herman could only see the work boots of the dozen or more men who were assaulting him. "They're killing me!" he shouted hoarsely as they kicked him. "My God, they'll kill me!"[79]

And then, among the workmen's boots he glimpsed Elizabeth's shoes. Though she was slightly built, and though she was then three months pregnant, Elizabeth had not paused before rushing into the crowd to try to help him.[80]

She struggled to get to Herman, scratching at pummeling arms, kicking the legs of the men bent over her husband's prone body. One man turned around to face her. Elizabeth swung her purse with as much force as she could muster. The glass bauble on her bag hit the side of the man's face and broke off, scratching his cheek. Swearing, he reared back and kicked her forcefully in the abdomen. She doubled over and fell to her knees.

Shaking and sobbing, Elizabeth tried to stand. She was shoved again before she fainted. A friend pushed his way into the crowd and managed to carry her to a park bench to keep her from being trampled.[81]

The men beat Herman for a few more long moments, the thudding of their fists and boots "plainly audible" to a reporter who would later describe the incident to readers.

Then they were done. The gang that had been so "grimly purposeful in their work" swiftly abandoned the park.[82]

Morris Milgram had steadied himself after a punch to the head. He found his friend still on the ground, bleeding from his eyes, nose, and mouth. It seemed they had broken Herman's nose, and his right eye was nearly black with pooled blood. Raw welts were already erupting on his face and neck. A later medical exam would find Herman's entire body slashed with cuts and stained with violet bruises.[83]

He struggled to stand. Milgram offered his arm to steady him. Herman could just barely make out Elizabeth, sitting on a park bench with other WDL members. "What a fine lot of men you are, hitting a woman," shouted Herman, likely believing the attackers were still in the park and could hear his retort. "Someone get a doctor for my wife," he said.[84]

Milgram intended to bring Herman back home or directly to a doctor. They walked haltingly down one of the park's concrete paths. Milgram thought they could pick up a bus or hail a cab on Washington Street, or make their way to a friend's car, parked a few blocks away.

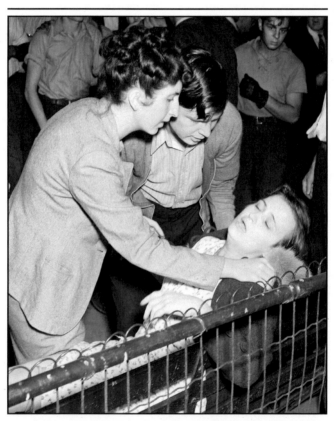

Two unidentified friends assist Elizabeth Matson after she was
knocked down trying to prevent a gang of men
from beating her husband.

AP Images/Harry Harris.

But when they reached the center of the park, they were approached by three plainclothes policemen, later identified to Milgram as Police Sergeant Arthur Marotta, Detective John McKenna, and Lieutenant J. Romeo Scott. One of the men seized Herman's free arm. "Come on, come on," he snapped, when Milgram refused to release his hold on his friend's other arm.

"Are we under arrest?" Herman asked. He recognized J. Romeo Scott and had heard Scott was related to Boss McFeely by marriage.[85]

"No," one of the other officers replied. "We're taking you home."

Milgram insisted *he* was taking his colleague home, but the policemen pushed in closer. They left the park together.

Herman Matson, left, holding a handkerchief to his face after he was beaten in Hudson Square Park. Fellow WDL member Morris Milgram, right, assists him.

Trailing the five men as they walked were about two hundred men and women, along with a large group of watchful little boys. Some would later give testimony on what they saw. The sudden flash of trailing newspaper photographers lent the odd night parade moments of eerie illumination.

When they reached the corner of Fourth and Washington Streets, it began to rain—lightly at first, and then harder, so that Herman's jacket and shirt clung heavily to his bruised frame. The crowd began to disperse, retreating from the downpour.

In a raspy voice Herman announced he was going home, to be tended by his doctor. One of the policemen countered that someone might attack him.[86]

Herman muttered to Lieutenant Scott that he had taken a beating already and the police had failed to protect him.

"We should have let them kill you," Scott retorted. "You didn't get enough."[87]

The two haggard, shuffling men and the three plainclothesmen came upon an idling police car. Scott pushed Herman inside. Shoving Milgram out of the way, the three officers climbed into the sedan and drove off.[88]

They took Herman directly to city hall, to its basement police headquarters. He heard Lieutenant Scott ask Inspector Thomas Garrick, "What will we do with him?" Herman was not yet under arrest. Garrick replied, "I guess send him home."

But Scott would not allow that to happen. Herman heard the lieutenant claim that the WDL activist had inflamed the crowd with rants about "starving or murdering babies." In that case, Garrick said, Herman should be charged with "inciting to riot."[89]

After he asked for and received permission to wash the blood off his face, Herman was locked in a cell. By the time he was allowed to see the two local lawyers the WDL had secured for his defense, it was nearly midnight. Shortly thereafter, his doctor, who had immediately left Newark after receiving a telegram from Morris Milgram, was admitted to examine Herman's wounds.

Herman was then led to the police identification room, where he was fingerprinted. After he was photographed in street clothes, he was made to undress for more photographs. This demand was not in itself out of the ordinary; visual documentation of the physical condition of newly arrested suspects had been standard procedure in urban police departments since the early 1920s. The public had become aware that officers were using violence to gain confessions, and juries, encouraged by defense attorneys like Sam Leibowitz, had begun to doubt the veracity of confessions obtained at police headquarters.[90]

But Herman later reported that Lieutenant Scott denied him his clothing for a half-hour after he'd been photographed. During that time, the activist said, the police officer alternately "reviled him" and plied him with questions. Herman would not reply.[91]

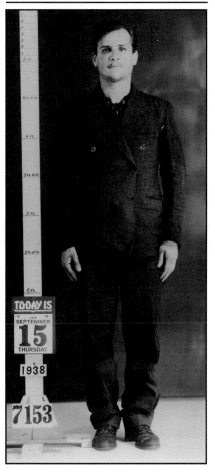

A clothed, full-length police mug shot of Herman Matson after he was arrested and charged with "using obscene language."

Courtesy of the Hoboken Historical Museum.

No one was apprehended for the attack on Herman Matson, and Lieutenant Scott would later admit he had made no attempt to arrest any of the assailants. They had their man. An unnamed police representative explained to local reporters that in their view, Matson's "inflammatory remarks were directly responsible for the riot."[92]

Accounts of the melee appeared in New York and New Jersey newspapers the following day—the day of Herman Matson's arraignment—and then spread to other states via syndication. Some articles included the comments of Jimmy Nolan, who had been among the crowd at Hudson Square Park and who told reporters he had attended the Hudson Square Park meeting "out of curiosity."

Representatives of International Longshoremen's Association Locals 86, 306, 881, 1064, 1198, 1247, and 1233 had been there, too, he acknowledged, but he denied any plan to attack Matson. "What happened," he said, "is proof that longshoremen are peaceable and happy, and do not want agitators to come among them."[93]

Herman Matson was arraigned before Hoboken recorder Frank Romano on September 16, charged with inciting to riot, and held on $5,000 bail, for a hearing on September 21. The amount of bail, a local lawyer would later recall, was "tremendous and quite unusual in such a case." Certainly a man who had recently been declared a pauper by the poormaster, and who had been certified for work relief, would not have that kind of money.[94]

But Milgram vowed he would secure bail for his friend before nightfall—and he did—though it would take another full day to get the Hoboken court to *accept* it. Judge Romano had unaccountably disappeared from the city and left in his position an "acting recorder" who claimed he was not authorized to accept bail. He refused to do so until Herman's defenders gained the intervention of a higher court judge.[95]

Herman might have been tempted to describe all that had transpired as a farce had the delay not meant his continued confinement in the Hoboken jail. While there, he later testified, Police Chief Edward McFeely had threatened to gouge out his eyes and "sweat" him until he revealed "who is in back of you."

He might have called it a farce even then. But his incarceration had meant that Elizabeth had been alone all that night and the following morning. She had been without him when her health spiraled down from her punishment in Hudson Square Park and when she miscarried.[96]

10 | THE MARBLE HALLS OF JUSTICE

FINALLY LIBERATED FROM THE Hoboken jail, Herman returned to the family's Willow Avenue apartment to tend Elizabeth. He was relieved to still have that safe place for her and the children: WDL lawyers had paid the Matsons' rent, forestalling their eviction.[1]

They were penniless. A few weeks before the Hudson Square Park meeting, Herman had managed to secure private employment in Hoboken, including a job painting the interior of a bakery on Sixth Street. He had enjoyed saving on carfare and other expenditures demanded by his previous, out-of-town assignment on the WPA; but when he was arrested, his local job had ended.[2]

Soon he would have to struggle to be reinstated on the WPA. In the past, when he'd been unable to find work, Elizabeth had sought employment as a housemaid, returning home at night to wrap her raw and ragged hands. They had done what was necessary. But for now, while Elizabeth was unwell, and while Herman prepared for his trial on the riot charge, their family would survive on the charity of friends and with the assistance of the WDL.[3]

Herman's lawyers were planning to request a trial delay, as Elizabeth, a principal witness, was still too weary to leave her bed. While she struggled to recuperate, a babysitter, hired by the WDL, looked after the Matson children. It would take a few weeks before Elizabeth would be strong enough to enter the Recorder's Court and describe the protracted hours of her decline, how she had been carried, finally, to a hospital, where she "had to submit to an operation."[4]

Elizabeth was not given to public speaking, but she had not shied away from making known her assault and consequent miscarriage. That ugly fact would, after all, follow other, awful details about wrongdoing and suffering in Hoboken—details she had circulated through WDL leaflets. Although Herman was the one who regularly voiced their beliefs and ideals, they had both been fighting all along for a decent quality of life for those with no choice but to seek relief.[5]

The Matsons may not have known it then—and if they had, it would not have changed the pressing need that propelled their campaign—but the general population was becoming increasingly hostile to reliefers who were openly critical of the administration of aid. The public would soon respond to anti–New Dealers' portrayals of reliefers as ungrateful and politically suspect. In fact, many were already inclined to view aid recipients as second-class citizens. In 1938 a "substantial minority" of Americans supported the idea of restricting the political rights of the unemployed on relief or the WPA. Nearly one in five Americans, according to a poll conducted that year by the American Institute of Public Opinion, favored disallowing reliefers the right to vote.[6]

Fourteen state constitutions, including New Jersey's, already contained a clause barring paupers from voting—a holdover from the old poor laws. Some said disenfranchisement was only applicable to persons who had taken "a pauper's oath" prior to permanent commitment to still-operative poorhouses. Nevertheless, during the Depression years, various public officials and anti–New Dealers sought the enforcement of existing "pauper exclusion laws" or called for new restrictions on the citizenship rights of relief recipients.[7]

Organizers of the jobless were now faced with a new kind of gag, created by the interweaving of the old poor law idea of surrendering rights for relief, with updated anti-Communist sentiment, seized upon by opponents of expanded public relief who surely feared the political mobilization of ten million men and women yet unemployed. Although the 1938 House Special Committee on Un-American Activities formally began its hearings just a month before Herman's disastrous Hudson Square Park meeting, the committee's well-publicized anticipative investigations into alleged Communist infiltration of the WPA and its chairman's accusations that the American Civil Liberties Union was part of a Communist "front" had already encouraged the casual censure of groups like the Hoboken chapter of the Workers Defense League.[8]

Herman Matson's urgent call to "at least hear what a man has to say" about the suffering in Hoboken was muffled in local news accounts by reporters' facile slurs suggesting that the speaker and his organization were fronting for Communists—accusations that were becoming the ready trade of the congressional committee, known by the name of its chairman, Texas congressman Martin Dies. The *Hudson Dispatch* would lazily appropriate the Dies Committee's popular descriptor "Communistic organization" to portray the Hoboken WDL when it reported on Herman's beating in the park; the *Jersey Journal* would label Herman as a "Red" who "tried to speak against Mayor McFeely."[9]

The idea that the poor did not really have the right to speak out about their conditions, and that those who did were Communist mouthpieces or dupes, had already been enthusiastically taken up by the Hoboken police. Chief Edward McFeely had simply not believed Herman when he had asserted during an interrogation on the second night of his detainment that he had his "own ideas and principles." The chief, Herman later recalled, had pulled out a sheet of WDL letterhead and read the names of members listed on it, concluding with the vituperative rejoinder that they were nothing but a "pack of dirty Jews and Communists."[10]

Herman would not have been surprised by McFeely's invective, but he must have been disheartened to learn that a congressional committee was attacking the WPA, and he would have likely been insulted, too, by the committee's allegations of Communist control over work-reliefers. No one could honestly argue that there were no Communists active in organizing the jobless in the United States or that those persons did not have a political agenda. They had been quite open about it. But there were also organizers like Herman, who were not, as he put it, members "of any of the so-called Red or Pink parties."[11]

Nevertheless, the very presence of Communists in organizations of the unemployed had made the Dies Committee's charges seem credible—a "basis in reality," as one historian would later put it. Now Herman would see Washington conservatives gaining the traction they needed to cast doubt on the loyalty of all work-reliefers. The anti–New Dealers were taking the first steps to limit the WPA, to make its workers fearful of any political engagement that might keep them off the rolls, and to return them to . . . nothing.[12]

At last, on September 19, came a sign that the Scutellaro case was going forward—but it was not a sign to Sam Leibowitz's liking. Assistant Prosecutor William George, who would be the state's lead attorney at trial, had applied for a "struck jury," a move that would, if successful, restrict jury selection to one hundred names culled by the court from prepared lists of past jurors. Both prosecution and defense would be permitted to "strike" a dozen of the selected names before choosing a jury from the remaining seventy-six.[13]

Prosecutors favored these "blue ribbon juries" because they claimed the men who served on them—often well-to-do businessmen and professionals—had been winnowed out for their intelligence and were thus better able to arrive at just verdicts in complicated cases. But criminal defense attorneys considered the special juries undemocratic and marred by class bias. Leibowitz had long believed that prosecutors packed them with "rope-pullers" who could be relied upon "to hand down a conviction." Just two days before his future Hoboken client would be charged with murder, he'd attended a public hearing convened by the New York State Assembly's Judiciary Committee and had asserted then that in his experience blue ribbon juries were never composed of men "from the ordinary strata of life. " Furthermore, Leibowitz had declared, "No Negroes or Italians are allowed to serve on such bodies."[14]

Now both Leibowitz and William George were in the grand Hudson County Courthouse, arguing their respective positions before Judge Robert V. Kinkead. The pale and tremulous defendant was also in attendance for the proceedings, as were the newspaper reporters who regularly covered the courts.

Leibowitz would have already delved into the legal backgrounds of George and Kinkead—as George had surely done from his own perspective—so as to understand their strengths and weaknesses. But there was much yet to learn firsthand. As Leibowitz faced the prosecutor and the jurist, he paid close attention to their expressions, looking for additional insight.[15]

Leibowitz knew the forty-eight-year-old first assistant prosecutor was an old hand at machine politics. William George had allied himself with Jersey City mayor Frank Hague early on and had, in turn, been advanced by the Boss. A second-generation American of Jewish heritage, George was a good public symbol for Hague, who liked to curry favor with the city's various ethnic populations by placing representatives from those groups in prominent (but limited) positions of public service. After gaining a state assembly seat with Hague's help in 1919, William George had returned to Jersey City four years later to serve in the county prosecutor's office. Over the next fifteen years, the lean and exacting assistant gained a reputation for fiery partisanship outside of the courtroom and for a certain cold calculation within it. His impassive oval face, capped by sleek, closely cropped brown hair, seemed almost machined.[16]

"This is a peculiar case," Leibowitz began when George had finished speaking. "It may involve political aspects—not through our choice, but by reason of circumstances. The McFeelys," he continued boldly, "may be involved. Also, a public official was killed." The politicized nature of the case, he argued, made a trial jury, chosen from the general panel, preferable to a blue ribbon jury.

The defense attorney paused for a moment to consider the judge, a tall, broad-shouldered man who had leaned forward as Leibowitz's voice rose and fell. Though the forty-six-year-old jurist had an unlined, open face, his brown, curly hair was rapidly turning gray.[17]

Robert Kinkead, like William George, had been recognized as "a Democratic lawyer" worthy of advancement. Although Hague-backed Democratic governor George Silzer had nominated Kinkead to serve on Hudson County's Court of Common Pleas, Kinkead's ties to Boss Hague would have seemed, at first, to be tenuous, at best. The two men had little in common save their Irish Catholic heritage. Each professed dedication to a distinctly different version of the Democratic Party. In fact, the jurist's appointment had been viewed by many as a way for the New Jersey boss to keep close his opponents within the party; Kinkead's older brother, Eugene, a former Democratic congressman and Hudson County sheriff, had vigorously opposed Hague.[18]

But any hope Leibowitz might have that the younger Kinkead shared his sibling's independence of mind would have been tempered by reports of the judge's harsh treatment of outspoken Hague opponents. Over the summer, civil libertarians had complained bitterly when Judge Kinkead had refused to release Hague critic James "Jeff" Burkitt on bail, despite the nonviolent nature of Burkitt's "crime": the alleged use of foul language during his arrest for protesting publicly in a Jersey City plaza.[19]

For now, Sam Leibowitz would focus on his objection to a struck jury, but his remarks would make clear his awareness of the politics underlying all too many court procedures. "The common talk," Leibowitz boldly asserted, "is that some of these lists are lists handed to the court by the prosecutor or other officials interested in a conviction." He quickly added, lest Kinkead bristle at the implication that the jurist would slavishly follow prosecutors' wishes, "However, we have faith in Your Honor's integrity, and so we want to strip the case of all possibility of criticism or bias, by having an ordinary jury."[20]

Leibowitz paused again, then came to the heart of his public argument. He knew reporters were busily taking down notes. "The defendant is a poor Italian," he declared. "He should be tried by a jury of his peers, by persons who understand what hunger means."

Joe Scutellaro's heart had likely quickened at the thought of such a panel. But it was not to be. Judge Kinkead granted the prosecution's application for a struck jury and said he would prepare the list during the next week or so, perhaps thereby allowing the accused to be tried by late October or early November.

On September 21, six days after Herman Matson was booked on the charge of inciting to riot, he appeared again, with his lawyers, before Recorder Romano. Now Herman faced an entirely different and previously unknown charge: disorderly conduct. Local lawyers Edward Stover and Harold Grouls had already made some preparations to defend their client against the riot charge, but they now saw a complaint that asserted that Herman had directed "indecent and offensive language" to the police on the night of the Hudson Square Park melee. Lieutenant J. Romeo Scott had signed the document just before the September 21 hearing.[21]

Herman's lawyers had been unable to secure a copy of the complaint beforehand—the clerk of the Recorder's Court claimed the judge had it; Romano referred them to the clerk—and now they knew why. When Romano was later asked to explain the six-day gap between the assertion of the old charge and bringing the new one, he had averred that it "was unusual but not irregular."[22]

Fortunately Herman's defenders had intended all along to request a postponement. The task of tracking down bystanders who could truthfully describe what Herman had said would fall to Harold Grouls, just six years out of law school and now counsel to the New Jersey WDL. The son of a longtime agent for the Stevens family development company, Grouls was familiar with some of the Hoboken WDL members who had been at the park, and he could also gather from them the names of additional witnesses not allied with the group.[23]

Stover, in contrast, had no links to WDL; prior to taking the case, he had known little about the organization. A lifelong resident who had practiced law in his hometown for thirty-two years, fifty-six-year-old Edward Stover was perhaps best known in the city for his reliable counsel to Hoboken's Independent Jitney Association. Although he was no fan of Boss McFeely, he had agreed to represent Herman not out of opposition to the mayor's repressive tactics but as a favor to a colleague, a WDL supporter who had become overwhelmed by the police runaround in the early stages of Herman's defense. After learning of his potential client's near destitution and about his large family, Stover had agreed to take on the Matson case. "My sympathy was aroused," he noted.[24]

Stover made a formal request for an adjournment until October 1, the earliest date, he said, that Mrs. Matson would be able to appear in court. He presented Recorder Romano with a signed medical certificate stating that Elizabeth Matson had been admitted to St. Mary Hospital in Hoboken after a stillbirth.

Romano postponed the trial until October 7. After continuing Matson's $5,000 bail, he concluded the hearing.[25]

News of Herman's beating had already traveled across the country via the newspaper syndicates, with articles and commentary appearing in small town and city newspapers such as the *Lowell Sun* (Massachusetts), *Mansfield News Journal* (Ohio), and the *Appleton Post Crescent* (Wisconsin.) The announcement of Elizabeth's miscarriage brought another round of news coverage, including more than a few articles bearing lurid headlines like BABY BORN DEAD TO BEATEN MOTHER.[26]

Elizabeth would have been too weak to summon much of a reaction to these articles, and she may even have considered the shock or revulsion they might provoke appropriate, but the WDL leadership in New York clearly concluded that such coverage was all to the good. The newspaper headlines were swiftly clipped, assembled, and reproduced for widespread distribution, as the national organization set out to solicit funds for Herman's defense and the support of his family and to seek greater public notice of WDL's civil rights advocacy.[27]

Socialist leader Norman Thomas, a national WDL committeeman, had already become involved in the case—privately and publicly. A former ordained minister who was radicalized by the horrors of World War I, Thomas was a pacifist committed to the pursuit of social justice. He was also a vigorous opponent of government censorship, having experienced firsthand its application to antiwar literature and activist speech. Thomas had joined with Roger Baldwin to found the organization that would later become the American Civil Liberties Union (ACLU).[28]

Thomas had failed in an earlier, behind-the-scenes attempt to raise Herman Matson's bail, but by working his extensive list of press and legal contacts, he had drawn support for Matson's defense and attention to the forthcoming Hoboken trial. Thomas's announcement that he had written to US attorney general Homer S. Cummings, urging the nation's top law enforcement officer to take note of the Hoboken case, had made the pages of the *New York Times*. The article further announced that leading civil liberties lawyer Arthur Garfield Hays had offered to defend Herman Matson at his trial.[29]

The focus of these two prominent men would soon direct the public's attention away from the relief crisis that had inspired the planned gathering. Commentary and subsequent reportage on the Matson case would increasingly focus on the city's suppression of speech, even though the substance of that halted oration continued to be of vital importance to Hoboken's poor—including their most vocal, and equally impoverished, spokesman. Just after the park incident, progressive journalist and *Post* columnist Dorothy Dunbar Bromley had interviewed Herman, and at the conclusion of their conversation, he had made his motivation plain. "If you can only expose relief conditions in Hoboken," he said, "I'm sure the people here will be thankful."[30]

But Hays and Thomas were not going to detail Hoboken's relief practices. Hays, especially, as defense strategist, meant to address the silencing of his client. That was, after all, his motivation for involvement. The day after the attack on Herman, Hays had sent Boss McFeely a telegram, noting the mayor's obligation to maintain the "right of free speech, even for your opponents." And though Thomas had a long history of advocacy for the unemployed, his focus now was almost entirely on Matson's thwarted speech.[31]

Both Hays and Thomas likely viewed the Hoboken case as another egregious example of civil liberties denial in Hudson County—a view shaped by their own widely publicized battles with Jersey City mayor Frank Hague. Arthur Garfield Hays had been hammering away at the intractable Boss Hague for four years by the time the Hoboken brawl occurred. As general counsel to the ACLU, Hays had initiated a campaign in 1934 to gain freedom of speech and assembly in Jersey City. Lawsuits had proliferated as Hague had refused CIO union organizers and their supporters the right to picket and to distribute their literature in his city—the protracted battle that had initially drawn Herman to the WDL.[32]

Speakers Hague deemed "communistic"—including Thomas, though he was an outspoken critic of Communism—had long been denied permits for public meetings. When they had challenged the ban, police had ejected them from the city, rather than arrest them and incur more lawsuits. Just a few months before the Hoboken incident, Norman Thomas had attempted to make a public speech there. When two policemen seized him and forced him onto a return ferry to New York—after first slugging his wife, Violet, in the tussle—he had brought charges of kidnapping.[33]

The Jersey City battles over civil rights had become national news, in part because of Hague's position as vice chairman of the Democratic National Committee. As Thomas noted in a radio speech, "Jersey City has acquired a symbolic significance. Other American cities may be actually or potentially as bad as Jersey City. But various factors, including the political prominence of Mayor Hague, have combined to give Jersey City a national importance."[34]

Reporters and editors, with their own interest in the exercise of free speech and the assurance of confrontational tactics and lively quotes from civil libertarians Hays and Thomas, had been eager to put the Jersey City conflict on the front pages. In preparing to cover the Hoboken trial, newspapers would again follow the lead of these two eloquent Hague opponents.

The *New York Times* began right away, giving prominence to the view, articulated by Thomas, that McFeely's administration was "but a part of the machine" operated by Mayor Hague—though it was, at most, a partial truth, extrapolated from knowledge of Hague's statewide political influence. If one focused exclusively on the suppression of civil rights, McFeely's rough treatment of protestors and unapproved union organizers did indeed mirror Hague's. But the suggestion that McFeely only did Hague's bidding implied a level of cooperation between them that simply did not exist: the two men hated each other. More than once during their long political careers McFeely had plotted to seize Hudson County from Hague's grasp and had been found out and thwarted. Their common ground was the primacy of stuffed ballot boxes. Hague's demand for large vote tallies had been matched by McFeely's need for the same, to ensure his family's pecuniary stranglehold on the city.[35]

McFeely's rule may have been limited to Hoboken, but as one close observer put it, his power was "virtually absolute within the mile-square limits of the city." The beating of Herman Matson now brought greater public scrutiny of this mile-square boss.[36]

In the weeks before the trial, press coverage about the Matson case and letters distributed by civil liberties advocates would stir civic, religious, and labor groups into action. Some issued resolutions stating their opposition to the violent "suppression of speech" in Hoboken. Copies of declarations made by the Young Men's Marion Improvement League of Jersey City, the New Orleans branch of the Socialist Party USA, a local of the United Electrical, Radio & Machine Workers of America, and an assembly of New Jersey's Methodist clergymen, made their way to Herman Matson, Mayor McFeely, New Jersey Governor Moore, US Attorney General Cummings, and even to President Roosevelt. The organizations did not protest relief conditions in the city.[37]

Herman's trial date arrived, and the Hoboken police court opened its doors to a rush of spectators. More than two hundred men and women jostled to gain seats in the small courtroom. Norman Thomas found a place on one of the court's long wooden benches, his tall frame and wispy gray hair familiar to readers who had seen his photo accompanying news accounts of his Jersey City skirmishes. A gaggle of newsmen spilled out into the hallway, including several photographers who jockeyed to take pictures of participants as they entered and left the court.[38]

Herman's defense team—Edward Stover, Arthur Garfield Hays, and young Harold Grouls—had agreed that the two seasoned attorneys would act as cocounsel at trial, with Hays, who was widely recognized as a brilliant debater and strategist, attending to the cross-examination of witnesses. As they stood together in the Hoboken court, the cocounselors must have seemed an odd pair. Both men were middle-aged, but they had little else in common physically. At six feet, Stover was at least a head taller and not much heavier than his stocky colleague. Even the two men's suits would have been evidence of dissimilar ways of life: Stover, a frugal bachelor, had likely thought little about his courtroom attire when dressing that morning, while Hays had surely chosen one of many finely tailored three-piece suits befitting a prominent man of means.[39]

Arthur Garfield Hays had become wealthy by representing the legal interests of Wall Streeters—a boon that allowed him to take on, without regard for remuneration, the civil liberties cases he valued most. Over the preceding dozen years or more he had traveled the country as general counsel for the ACLU, defending striking miners, trade unionists, and silenced activists. An eager press had followed. During more than one case, Hays had shared the spotlight with Clarence Darrow, most notably at the Scopes trial in Tennessee. The two had even been persuaded by the National Association for the Advancement of Colored People (NAACP) to represent the Scottsboro Boys—the aged Darrow would have come out of retirement to handle the case—but when the ILD became the lead organization supporting the youths' defense, Hays and Darrow were replaced by Sam Leibowitz.[40]

The Matson case did not offer Arthur Garfield Hays the kind of illustrious legal company he preferred, but it did not want for drama. After reviewing the case, Hays became convinced that the Hoboken police had resolved to arrest Matson the night of the meeting no matter what happened in the park and that they would even resort to framing him.[41]

Now that Hays stood in the city's police court, he must have recalled what Hoboken attorneys had said about its adjudicator. Lawyers had protested to the local bar association that Recorder Frank Romano took direction from the Hoboken Police Department. At sentencing, local counselors alleged, the judge would look to the highest-ranking officer in attendance. Should a guilty verdict be called for, the policeman would indicate the preferred ruling, holding either one finger up to his face (thirty days), two fingers (sixty days), or three (ninety days).[42]

Hays may have wondered what tricks he would witness that day, but he knew for sure that Edward McFeely, at least, would not be signaling the judge during Matson's trial. Although the defense team had subpoenaed the Hoboken police chief, McFeely had not deigned to attend. He was one of a dozen witnesses they had planned to call.[43]

The city's witness list had but three names. Sixty-eight-year-old corporation counsel Horace Allen, a twenty-year veteran of the city's law department, seemed to believe that the testimony of the three Hoboken police officers who had encountered Herman Matson in the park would be sufficient to find the defendant guilty under the Disorderly Persons Act. Allen began by calling Lieutenant J. Romeo Scott. Under the city attorney's gentle questioning, the tall, thick-bodied officer described police efforts to save a wounded Herman Matson from greater harm. The officers, too, had sustained blows and kicks from the mob, Scott said. The park had been thronged with people, and the three policemen had rushed to Matson's side to put him into protective custody. Just as they were leading him to safety, Scott claimed, Herman Matson had begun to curse them, calling the policemen "a pack of sons of bitches and bastards" and shouting, "Is this the kind of police protection I'm getting?"[44]

"At that time was he under arrest?" Horace Allen asked.

"No sir, he was not," Scott replied.

The city lawyer concluded questioning there.

Arthur Garfield Hays was now ready to cross-examine the witness. The change in pace was immediate. The defense attorney fired questions rapidly, homing in on the time and place of the defendant's alleged "vile" speech. He pushed Scott for increasingly specific details of the incident, trying to break down the officer's account. He gained an admission from Scott that he did not search for the men who beat Herman Matson and an acknowledgement that the other police officers said to be detailed to the park—Scott claimed there had been seventeen men on duty—did not find Matson's assailants either.

But as Hays queried his witness and began to unsettle him, city attorney Horace Allen began to launch objections, and as he did, Judge Romano sustained them.

In the course of an hour, Hays was prevented from questioning Scott about whether Inspector Garrick had informed the lieutenant that police protection had been requested for the park meeting; about the charge lodged against Herman Matson; about statements made by Scott to Inspector Garrick regarding the defendant's alleged offense; about how long Scott had been on the police force; about what had happened to the defendant while he was in the police station; about the date on which the "disorderly person" complaint against Matson was made; and about the charge originally entered against Matson in the police blotter.[45]

Hays asked for the police blotter to be produced, as it was under subpoena. Allen objected, contending that the defense team had improperly prepared the legal order. When Recorder Romano upheld Allen's objection, Hays lost his temper. In a move that no one could have predicted—and one that cocounsel would later privately describe as a kind of expedient showboating—the top-flight lawyer declared his immediate withdrawal as Herman Matson's counselor.

"I am withdrawing from this case because I cannot do justice to the defendant," Hays shouted. "I might have been of use in a court of law; I could have been of no use in a court of prejudice." There was a low rumble of observers expressing disbelief.[46]

Judge Romano did not trouble over Hays's exit. He readily, and perhaps with some pleasure, accepted the New York defender's departure—though Hays insisted on staying in the courtroom. The judge called for a brief recess. It would be left to Edward Stover, with the assistance of Harold Grouls, to defend Herman Matson.

As expected, when the hearing resumed, Sergeant Arthur Marotta and Detective John McKenna corroborated Lieutenant Scott's account of the incident in Hudson Square Park. Defense testimony was then initiated, with Herman Matson the first witness called.

Herman surely welcomed Edward Stover's first question—"Are you a Communist?"—and made his swift reply before the city attorney could object. His answer, when quoted by news reporters, would stand against the claims made by the Dies Committee about reliefers on the WPA. "No, I am not a Communist," replied Herman, "but a Democrat and a Roman Catholic."

Questioned steadily by Stover, the defendant proceeded to describe his attempts to secure police protection, the opening of the meeting, and his assault in the park. He spoke calmly during the initial spate of questions, but when he was asked if he would be able to identify his assailants, Herman's voice, though strong, shook a little with emotion. "I'd know their faces as long as I live," he declared.[47]

On cross by Horace Allen, Herman denied using the words attributed to him by the police, asserting that he was not one to use indecent language. He described how he stood in the park, bleeding from wounds to his face. He believed he had then cried out that he "would meet any one in single combat."[48]

"You didn't call any one a coward?" the city attorney asked, trying to get Herman to agree to one of the claims made by Lieutenant Scott.

"I probably did," Herman conceded.

"That's all," Allen said. "I'm through."

But Stover then posed a question he said was meant in rebuttal. He asked Herman if he was then placed under arrest.

Allen immediately objected, asserting that Stover's question was "not a rebuttal." Romano upheld him.[49]

Edward Stover then called numerous witnesses to the incident in the park, to testify in Matson's behalf. Most were not WDL members and had never met him before; none had heard him use the words ascribed to him by police.

Then the defense attorney called Elizabeth Matson to the witness stand. The chamber quieted as all watched the wan, dark-haired woman slowly make her way to the front of the room. Her left arm was in a sling, the result of an infection that had taken hold after she received intravenous fluids in the hospital.

Once she was seated, Elizabeth looked over at her husband. The defendant's chair was bunched close to the witness stand in the small courtroom, and she was now but a few feet from Herman's side. He would have been able to see that her dark eyes were dull with exhaustion, and he must have worried that she would faint, as she had earlier in the day.

Stover asked Elizabeth some opening questions to establish her identity, and she responded in a low, hurried voice. She spoke as if she were concerned that she might not complete her task, as if she were drawing on her last dregs of strength in order to testify.

She stated that she was thirty years old and the mother of six children. She had lived in Hoboken for eleven years.

Stover then asked, "Are you a Catholic?" but Horace Allen swiftly objected and was sustained.

Under Stover's mild questioning, Elizabeth described the attack on Herman and how she, too, had been kicked and knocked down. When she had regained consciousness, she said, she had heard Herman crying out, "Get a doctor for my wife!" Anguished by her collapse, she recalled, Herman had then shouted, "Cowards! I'll take you one at a time. Beating a woman! The protection we get from our cops." Her voice cracked as she described Herman's cries, and he reached out to touch her arm.[50]

Stover asked Elizabeth if her husband had said anything else. When she firmly stated "No," the defense lawyer announced he had no further questions for the witness and turned to Allen to proceed.

"No cross-examination," the city attorney said, and the spectators held their chatter as Elizabeth tentatively stood and left the stand.

Edward Stover next called Antoinette De L'Aquila, the twenty-four-year-old married daughter of WDL volunteer translator Nicholas Piracci. Mrs. De L'Aquila had attended the meeting with her husband and her two younger sisters.[51]

The defense attorney asked her if she was a member of the WDL. Before Horace Allen could object, she replied "No." Judge Romano instructed her not to reply until the court had ruled on an objection.

Stover plied her with questions about what she had seen and heard on September 15. After Elizabeth's vivid testimony, Antoinette De L'Aquila's description of the brawl she had witnessed did not cause much of a reaction among the trial's spectators—that is, until she stated that she could name one of the men who had taken part in the incident and "created a stir in court."[52]

"Who is that?" Stover asked, when the noise in the room had settled enough for him to be heard.

"That is Edward Florio," she replied, identifying the alleged attacker as a member of the Democratic Club on Fifth and Jackson Streets, a McFeely stronghold.[53]

Stover would not be able to press forward on this topic much longer—and not simply because of Horace Allen's readiness to object. No matter how stirring the witness's claimed identification, it would not assist with Herman Matson's defense on the disorderly person charge. Stover shifted his inquiry to the defendant's alleged use of obscene language.

De L'Aquila's reply evoked a pathetic scene. "He did not say anything like that," she said firmly. "He was just trying to say 'Please.' He was asking for help."[54]

The remaining witnesses for the defense testified similarly: they had not heard Herman Matson use any foul language.

Edward Stover was prepared to make his final argument, calling for an acquittal. After critiquing the testimony of the three police witnesses, the Hoboken defense attorney paused to gather himself for a summation that was to have more impact on his own fate than on the disposition of his client.

"This case cries for justice," Stover began. He looked squarely at the judge. Stover was prepared to bring out into the open what had been implied repeatedly during the course of the trial. "I know it is hard for you to judge this case," he continued, "because you have been elected to your exalted position by the same people who assaulted Mr. Matson—and also because you have your daily friends and associates to consider. But if we squelch this man, we have no more free speech here." A few spectators in the courtroom murmured their agreement.

"I ask you," Stover implored in closing, "to rally your mind and to acquit this man. He has suffered enough."[55]

Horace Allen's summation, in contrast, was casual, as if he had no need to assert points of law. The city attorney stressed his belief in the testimony of the police officers. He called for Herman Matson's conviction on the charge made against him—and then tempered his request. Using lighter terms to refer to the brutal beating of Herman Matson and to suggest its aftermath, Allen said he could "appreciate the excitement of that moment at the park and the provocation that was given there. Because of that, I ask that sentence be suspended."[56]

Recorder Frank Romano took but a moment to find Herman Matson guilty of being a "disorderly person," then followed the city attorney's suggestion and suspended Matson's sentence. The trial, which had drawn on for nearly five hours, was over. Romano stood to leave.

Arthur Garfield Hays, who had been sitting near to the bench, abruptly stood and called out to the judge. "A moment, Your Honor," he said, halting the jurist's stride. "If Your Honor pleases, you may hold me in contempt for what I am about to say," Hays said loudly, as reporters jotted down his words, "but I want it known that I shall inform the newspapers that my sole reason for withdrawing from this case is my belief that these proceedings are a travesty on justice." Romano did not reply, but glared at Hays before marching out of the courtroom.[57]

Herman and Elizabeth Matson returned to their Willow Avenue apartment. That night, Elizabeth fainted for a second time, and Herman called for an ambulance. When the hospital physician ordered bed rest, the WDL, in addition to paying the family's rent and food bills, set out to raise funds to send Elizabeth to a Caldwell, New Jersey, convalescent home to recuperate.[58]

After Antoinette De L'Aquila testified at Herman Matson's trial, her husband lost his job at the American Lead Pencil Company in Hoboken. The couple told Antoinette's father, Nicholas Piracci, that they were afraid something else would happen to them if Antoinette ever spoke again in a public forum about what she had seen at Hudson Square Park.[59]

Within a week of the trial, Edward Stover would write to the national office of the WDL, which had agreed to pay court costs. He wanted to wrap up his involvement in the Matson case. Although he would imply that there was trouble in Hoboken—"you must not have heard the latest development in regard to the reaction and retaliation that is now in progress," he wrote the WDL treasurer—Stover did not elaborate, and he did not request any assistance from the organization.[60]

But Herman Matson would investigate what had happened to the Hoboken attorney who had stood up for him. Herman would later recount how Edward Stover had been forced to resign his twelve-year position as counsel for the Independent Jitney Association. About a week after the Matson trial, Hoboken's city commissioners suddenly passed an ordinance restricting the idling time of buses operated by the association. Faced with the possibility of heavy fines when their busses waited for customers to load, as well as a substantial loss of income if they did not, the association well understood the impetus for the targeted ordinance and pressured Edward Stover to resign.[61]

At the end of October, Stover complied. The city ordinance was then revoked, and the association hired a new lawyer to replace him: City Attorney Horace Allen.[62]

Edward Stover was not one for self-pity, nor was he one for spectacle. He was clear-sighted on his participation in the Matson case—and also on the differing motives of those involved, including those who might, in their battle for individual rights, lose sight of one man.

"My object, of course, was different than yours," Stover explained to WDL treasurer David L. Clendennin in his letter summarizing the case.

"Namely, I did not want to fight this case for the advertisement or propaganda effects. My object was to see that poor Mr. Matson did not go to jail or pay an exorbitant fine." That object, Stover continued, "has been achieved. Mr. Matson was saved from jail and a large fine. True, it is, he was convicted, but this is only a technicality. He was let out a free man the second he was convicted."

Stover closed with his belief that Matson's advocates would win on appeal but that he saw such action as "an empty victory," as it would gain Herman Matson nothing. It would "simply mean glorification, advertising, and newspaper propaganda," the Hoboken lawyer concluded, "which will do Mr. Matson and his family no good."[63]

The hoopla surrounding his first trial had certainly done no good for Herman or his family. In a late October letter addressed to Harry Hopkins in Washington, DC, the indefatigable Morris Milgram urged the WPA administrator to intervene with local WPA officials on Herman's behalf. "Since the trial," Milgram wrote, "Matson has been unable to secure reinstatement on the WPA."[64]

11 | A JURY OF HIS PEERS

ALL THROUGH 1938, WHILE Herman Matson was clamoring for an end to the relief crisis that had led to the killing of the Hoboken poormaster, the man accused of the murder waited fitfully in a Hudson County jail cell. Joe Scutellaro, the warden said, was "a nervous prisoner." The forlorn defendant was surely dreading the trial to come and the still-open question as to whether he would, as one reporter put it, "have to battle for his life." And yet, Joe Scutellaro just as surely imagined that his ordeal would end swiftly, with a joyful return to his loved ones on Monroe Street.[1]

The possibility of a November 1938 trial, mentioned by Judge Kinkead, had disappeared when Sam Leibowitz had been called away to New York to defend another accused murderer. Leibowitz had been victorious there, but the delay had meant that his uneasy New Jersey client would wait still longer to learn his fate.[2]

Much had changed during Joe's ten-month incarceration, and Leibowitz would have taken note of every change in public opinion that might affect the trial. The nation's political ground, he knew, had shifted dramatically. A powerful rebuke of the New Deal had come just two years after Roosevelt's reelection with a massive Democratic majority. On Election Day 1938, in what the *New York Times* described as a nationwide taxpayers' "revolt" against spending by FDR, disgruntled voters had elected thirteen Republican governors, installed eight Republicans into the Senate, and doubled Republican representation in the House.

A new bipartisan coalition of congressional conservatives had emerged. They now wielded the power to block New Deal programs and pronounced their aim to shut down the WPA; but until they could, they pushed for an immediate decrease in federal spending on relief. Some proposed returning "the relief problem" to localities. The day before Christmas 1938, Senator Carter Glass, a Virginia Democrat, announced to the Associated Press that prior to federal involvement, the states and municipalities had done a fine job with relief. "They may not have done it on the luxurious scale of Harry Hopkins," Glass declared, referring to the WPA's first administrator, who had just resigned to become secretary of commerce, "but no one ever starved to death."[3]

In a grimly ironic twist for the impoverished Scutellaro family, Joe's defense fund had continued to grow during his prison stay. By January 1939, the sum had positively swelled. "Fellow relief clients," the *Daily News* claimed, had "contributed nickels and dimes" to raise $7,000 for Joe's legal defense. Though some newspapers put the figure at $10,000, all attributed the sizeable tally to a campaign by "local Italian residents, whose strong sympathy for the accused led them not only to canvas Hoboken for contributions, but also Jersey City and North Hudson." Eventually donations would come in from supporters residing well beyond Hudson County's borders.[4]

New York–based *Il Progresso Italo-Americano*, the most prominent Italian American newspaper in the country, had reported on Joe's case and alerted its readers to the family's need. "Any form of help will be greatly appreciated" by the Scutellaro family, an early article suggested to its readers, and the paper's owner, Generoso Pope, later authorized *Il Progresso*'s open solicitation and collection of funds. The "anti-red" daily, which was vigorously pro-Fascist when covering European politics but mostly favored the Democratic Party line in its take on the American scene, offered the case as a tragic story of a good Italian family man desperate to feed his children. It ran the dramatic story as a serial, often accompanying its installments with posed photographs of Joe's imploring, dark-eyed boy and girl. One cover featured the image of Marie and little Joseph kneeling in the family's apartment, their hands pressed together in prayer.[5]

Though it was by far the largest Italian-language publication to report on the Hoboken case, *Il Progresso* was not the only one. By the 1930s Italian Americans supported more than a dozen New York City–based Italian- and English-language dailies, weeklies, and trade newspapers of "all shades of political opinion." Smaller left-leaning and centrist publications closely followed the Scutellaro case, too. Some printed blistering editorials about the conditions the struggling relief client had faced. Their commentary, which had begun to appear soon after Joe had been charged, intensified now that his trial was about to begin, and editorialists argued the case's meaning and pointed out potential pitfalls at trial.[6]

Il Popolo, a weekly left-leaning newspaper, voiced a continuing fear of many Americans of Italian heritage—that "Giuseppe" Scutellaro would be subject to the ethnic bias of jurors and be put to death because of it. Its editors pointed out that local political conditions made it more likely that the jurors' verdict would be motivated by prejudice. "The eyes of Italians are turned toward Hoboken these days," an editorial began. "In a politically corrupt environment, the poverty-stricken Scutellaro runs the risk of being found guilty, not because, in a moment of exasperation, he killed a man who he saw as the cause of his young children's starvation, but more so because he is the US-born son of an Italian immigrant."[7]

Il Popolo editors speculated that Joseph Scutellaro might be affected by broader anti-relief reaction, stimulated by the Dies Committee investigations and confirmed in the November elections. "We cannot forget that the reactionaries try to divide people into Americans and Non-Americans," the newsweekly asserted. "The investigative committee headed by Dies is a reactionary effort directed against 'reds,' and, in essence, against Roosevelt's supporters, and in opposition to any progressive movement."[8]

Progressives outside of the Italian community weighed in on the Scutellaro case, too, with editorials appearing in publications like the *Nation* and the *Catholic Worker*. All had viewed Joe's predicament with an eye toward the politics of the day, though none could claim that Joe was himself a political man, of any stripe. Joe Scutellaro was not an activist. He had acceded to the demands of the Hoboken poormaster—gone home, filled out applications, waited, waited, waited—until he and his family were near starvation. He had not been an organizer, nor had he made demands for systemic change.[9]

Joe Scutellaro's very passivity, and his attempts to follow the poormaster's rules, may have moved some to pity him and to offer aid. But donors seemed stirred most of all by accounts of the deprivation faced by Marie and little Joe—the suffering of innocents. Poor, jobless adults could still be blamed for their lack and left without aid, but needy children were to be rescued. As news of the children's hardship spread from New York wire services and syndicates to English-language newspapers across the country, readers responded with donations just for them.[10]

News reports had surely alerted Bill "Bojangles" Robinson, renowned tap dancer and actor, to the conditions in Hoboken. A Broadway headliner whose fame had grown still more after he'd danced with child star Shirley Temple in three popular Hollywood films, Bill Robinson was, by the late 1930s, the "top-paid African American entertainer in the world." He was known as much for his unfailing generosity as he was for his fine clothes and fancy cars, afforded by stage engagements that paid him more than $3,500 per week. From the earliest days of the Depression, Robinson had supplied hard-up families with groceries, and had paid their bills for funerals and back rent. He had gone out of his way to help those with young children. The plight of the two Scutellaro children must have touched him, for as Marie Scutellaro would later recall in wonder, the celebrated entertainer simply arrived one day on Monroe Street and "put a hundred-dollar bill in my baby brother's hand."[11]

Much to Marie's delight, gifts from a Texas oilman had already been delivered to *her*: the executive had read about the family's misfortune and had sent a box packed with finery his young daughter had outgrown. Seven-year-old Marie would breathlessly pronounce the barely worn dresses "beautiful" and select the one she would wear for the first day of her father's trial.[12]

———— ✿ ————

Finally Joe's trial date was within sight—Monday, January 9, 1939—and the assistant prosecutor and the criminal defender began jousting in the press. Both seemed to enjoy the rough pretrial sport of molding public opinion, and they exchanged taunts unfettered by an umpire judge. Sam Leibowitz declaimed the "deplorable state" of relief in Hoboken, leading a *Jersey Journal* reporter to conclude that the New York lawyer intended to "put Barck's administration of relief . . . on trial along with Scutellaro," and for his part, Assistant Prosecutor William George reminded journalists that the defendant would be on trial for his life. "Not only do the facts support a first degree verdict," George told the *Hudson Dispatch*, "but Mr. Leibowitz, counsel for the defendant, when applying for bail at the courthouse, stated that his client did not get relief in time and left home in a savage mood. If that is true, the slaying of the poormaster was premeditated, wasn't it?"[13]

George's jab, implying that his call for a death sentence for Joe Scutellaro naturally followed remarks made by the accused man's lawyer, found an unusually vulnerable target that week. As William George well knew from news reports, one of Sam Leibowitz's former clients had been executed at Sing Sing prison just days before Scutellaro's scheduled trial. A parolee who had killed a policeman during a holdup, Salvatore Gati was the 140th defendant in a murder trial to be represented by Leibowitz and the first of Leibowitz's clients ever to be sentenced to death.[14]

Sam Leibowitz had for years built a reputation as an unvanquished legal gladiator. He had lined the walls of his office waiting room with framed newspaper photos of "climatic moments" in his biggest cases— what one approving reporter described as "the trophy room of the big game verdict hunter." Many reporters had kept score along with him. In its account of the Gati execution, the *New York Times* had invoked "the so-called record of Mr. Leibowitz that no person he had defended had died in the electric chair."[15]

To the record keepers, the execution of Salvatore Gati intimated a decline in Leibowitz's powers. It did not much matter to them that the assiduous and prideful lawyer had discovered, late in the process of defending his client, that Gati had lied to him about the murder, invalidating prior preparation. Nor did it concern those who were second-guessing him that Samuel Leibowitz had tried to withdraw as counsel to Salvatore Gati, and the judge had refused to allow it. The cornered lawyer had proceeded anyway and had pushed to save his client from execution by arguing for a jury recommendation of mercy. Under New York law, such a recommendation would have made mandatory for a guilty client a sentence of life imprisonment, rather than execution. And it had seemed, initially, that Leibowitz might succeed after all: the jury had deliberated for seventeen and a half hours before rejecting his compelling proposal.[16]

With Gati's execution, the tabloids stopped referring to Leibowitz as a courtroom "miracle man" and "a magician." Their reporters had to reckon with a man's death; they could no longer comfortably attribute Leibowitz's trial outcomes to supernatural guidance.

The defender would later admit to concern that he would be remembered "only for the Gati case"—for his failure. As he prepared to defend Joseph Scutellaro, Sam Leibowitz had his legal legacy, as well as a man's life, to protect. He was determined that a death sentence would never again be pronounced for one of his clients.[17]

Hudson County Court employees, hurrying to work on the morning of January 9, would have known right away that the two hundred men gathered on the granite steps were not the usual courthouse visitors. Lawyers and reporters did not wear such battered hats. True, nearly all of the assembled men were dressed in suits and ties befitting a visit to court, but the permanent stripe of sunburn at the back of their necks, and their jagged, enlarged hands, would have signaled the years they had spent toiling outdoors. As the court workers passed them, a few of the men averted their eyes and gazed instead at the building's marble façade and its bronze-lined windows. It had been a big job. During its many years of costly construction, the courthouse architect and its builders had cited as inspiration the great buildings of Europe.[18]

Just after 10:00 AM, the group drew out into several long lines. They moved past crisply attired lawyers paused before the bronze elevator grilles and slowly climbed the flight of marble stairs leading to the courtroom of Judge Robert Kinkead. When Joe's supporters were denied entry—seating had been reserved for attorneys, witnesses, reporters, and members of the accused man's family—the men assembled into two lines that traversed the length of the sleek corridor.[19]

At 10:40 the waiting crowd caught sight of Joe at the far end of the hallway—a small figure dressed in a neat gray suit, flanked by two officers. His hands were bound by manacles. At first the men watched Joe in silence, as if they were surprised to actually see the person they had come to affirm. But as the sheriff and court attaché shepherded Joe through the crowd, a great cheer rose up and traveled along the approving gauntlet—a response a *Daily News* reporter would describe as more befitting "a conquering hero than an accused murderer." Then the courtroom door closed behind the prisoner and his two keepers, and the men settled in to attend Joe's return.[20]

"The jury is the pivotal factor," Sam Leibowitz had once explained to a reporter who had wanted to know why the defender questioned potential jurors so extensively. "If my client is to have a fair trial, I must know the kind of men I'm talking to, trying to convince, entrusting with my client's fate." Now that Judge Kinkead had approved a struck jury for the Scutellaro trial and thus limited his candidates, Leibowitz's careful review of prospective jurors was all the more essential.[21]

To strike his first dozen names from the list, Leibowitz had reviewed a series of cards that bore basic facts about the possible selectees. Variously typed or scrawled in ink, the cards offered the candidate's age, occupation, residence, ethnic heritage, marital status, former jury service, and membership in any civic or religious organizations. Race was mentioned only to describe a would-be juror as "colored" or "Negro." All the nominees were men.[22]

Sam Leibowitz would later remark that he had been "eager to get a jury that isn't in Hoboken." The first four men he'd removed from consideration were Hoboken residents. A fifth had moved from Hoboken to Jersey City, but Leibowitz had cut him from the list because the man was a lawyer. Leibowitz routinely kept attorneys off panels because they deadlocked juries.[23]

The criminal defender also preferred young jurors. "They're still interested in people and they have a sense of brotherhood because of their fraternity ties," Leibowitz once told a reporter. "They're not set in their ways. They're tolerant. They're good listeners." He cut another group, ranging in age from fifty-one to fifty-eight, when he found no mitigating attributes—such as Italian American heritage or employment on the WPA—that might make them view his client more sympathetically.[24]

Assistant Prosecutor William George also reviewed the juror cards, seeking to remove anyone who might be inclined to favor the defendant. He cut from the list two men with Italian American surnames—an insurance salesman and a superintendent in a manufacturing plant. He declined consideration of several unemployed men. And he struck the names of four "colored" men: a clerk, a pharmacist, a trucker, and a funeral director. George knew that Sam Leibowitz had achieved international fame for his defense of the Scottsboro Boys and that Leibowitz's successful argument before the US Supreme Court was a landmark for African Americans in their long quest for equal justice. The prosecutor would not want to include on the jury any man who might consider his courtroom opponent a hero.[25]

Their first round of names struck, prosecution and defense now gathered in Judge Robert Kinkead's courtroom to finalize jury selection. Joe sat on the prisoner's bench, his masklike face unreadable.

Alert to public perception and the role ethnicity might play in the proceedings, the prosecutor's office had taken care to mirror, with its selection of lawyers, the ethnic composition of the defense team. Seated at the prosecutor's table were William George, the son of Jewish immigrants; his Italian American colleague Assistant Prosecutor Louis Messano; and their Irish American boss, Prosecutor Daniel T. O'Regan. Representing the defendant were Samuel Leibowitz, his associate Vincent R. Impellitteri, and counselor Thomas Tumulty.[26]

Behind the lawyers were ten or more reporters representing as many daily newspapers. They traded wisecracks and elbowed into position behind the rail that separated trial participants from the spectators' benches.

Court observers, dressed in their finest attire, crowded the benches; they were eager to observe the proceedings and were also fully aware that they were part of an unfolding drama that would be recorded in the press. In the second row, "careworn but comely," Anna Scutellaro sat with her children and a few members of her extended family. A small, peaked hat crowned Anna's dark curls; its oddly exuberant pheasant

quill indicated that it had been purchased during happier times. Little
Joe, dressed in clothes fit for church, sat in his mother's lap. He was fidg-
ety, but was soon distracted by a baby bottle filled with milk.[27]

Marie Scutellaro sat beside her mother, quiet and alert, keeping her
hands clasped in her lap, as she had been taught to do. She had carefully
lifted her ribbon-trimmed dress from its tissue-paper nest that morning
and put it on, along with a small brimmed hat. She had good shoes that
she wore with anklets; the recent springlike weather had freed her from
itchy stockings. She knew she was very well dressed for a poor girl. She
would have liked her father to see her.[28]

But her father's attention was fixed on the drum the court officer
was spinning. It contained the remaining names on the struck jury list.
Several dozen would be drawn to form a panel for final jury selection.[29]

The daylong selection process would later be described as the longest
local observers "could ever recall." Hudson County lawyers usually spent
an hour or so questioning prospective jurors. But to the methodical New
York defender, six hours was not very long; Sam Leibowitz had used a
week when he had needed it. "Frequently judges have tried to hurry me
in the selection of my juries, prodding me with the admonition, 'One
citizen is as good as another,' and seeking to inhibit me by limiting my
range of questioning," Leibowitz had once explained to a reporter. "I
refuse to be admonished or hurried."[30]

The defense attorney began his well-honed performance by questioning the Hudson County talesmen in a low, deliberate voice suited
to the occasion. A man's life was at stake—and so, too, was the lawyer's
reputation. Leibowitz would have wanted prospective jurors to realize
that no detail would pass unnoticed, but his manner suggested, too,
that they were there to work together; the jury would help him bring a
just result.

While questioning each candidate, Sam Leibowitz studied the man's
face. During his twenty-two years as a criminal defender, Leibowitz liked
to say, he had identified particular facial features he associated with
"hangers" and those he called "let-livers." He once explained to a journalist that men who were likely to convict signaled their closed-minded-
ness with tightly pressed mouths or pinched faces. "A criminal lawyer is a
failure unless he's a born psychologist," Leibowitz had asserted. "He has

to know and to feel human nature. He has to be able to tell from a man's face what's going on in his mind."[31]

Based on past experience, Leibowitz wanted certain types of men off his juries, too. He worked hard to keep off "self-made men of the assertive type," believing that such men compared their lofty status with the standing of the fallen defendant. "They have no sympathy for him," Leibowitz had complained. Such jurors would begin their service with the belief that the defendant was "a victim of his own weakness." That attitude was already all too familiar to his relief-seeking client, Joe Scutellaro.[32]

Now the defense attorney posed dozens of questions to his first candidate for the Scutellaro jury, an assistant bank auditor named Richard E. Van Horn. The majority were protested by William George and then disallowed by Kinkead, but Leibowitz surely knew the concerns he raised would be likely to linger in the minds of selected jurymen. And so he asked Van Horn, without receiving any reply, whether the potential juror would consider himself "duty bound to even it up because a life is gone," whether he might yield to a vote for a compromise verdict despite a belief that the defendant should be acquitted, or "if the testimony of a police officer would hold more weight for him than that of a private citizen." Leibowitz asked, "Do you know Mayor Bernard N. McFeely of Hoboken, who may be a witness in this case?" and was again overruled. Similarly, the defense attorney was permitted no response when he inquired about the prospective juror's knowledge of Police Chief Edward J. McFeely, Police Captain Bernard McFeely, Lieutenant Dennis McFeely, James L. McFeely of the family's cartage company, and Joseph M. McFeely of the Hoboken Law Department.[33]

But Leibowitz *was* able to receive a reply to his inquiry as to whether Van Horn was prejudiced against Italians. After the potential juror responded "no," the thirty-eight-year-old Jersey City resident was accepted for the jury and made foreman. He had been on the stand for thirty-five minutes.[34]

Undeterred by George's objections, Leibowitz continued to use his questioning to fix in the minds of future jurors the enforced supremacy of the McFeely family. The defense attorney asked William J. Lyon, a retired coal company clerk residing in Jersey City, if he had ever done business with the McFeelys of Hoboken. When George objected and was sustained, Leibowitz requested that he be allowed to pursue that line of questioning "in the interest of justice"—to gain a jury that was unconnected to the administration in Hoboken. Judge Kinkead then turned to the prospective juror and asked whether he had an association, past or present, which would prevent his "giving a just decision." "No," replied Lyon, and he was sworn in.[35]

The pattern of slow questioning by the defense, broken by the prosecution's objections, repeated through the morning and resumed after an hour's recess for lunch. Reporters listened for hints of future defense strategy; at least one newsman noted the introduction of "the relief angle" when Leibowitz challenged a WPA accountant—bringing about the prospective juror's removal—after the man admitted his findings in the case might affect his job.[36]

William George conducted interviews, too, but he was perfunctory, and journalists who reported the day's events found little mystery in his selection process. Even when he excused a potential juror "for cause"—the man had stated his opposition to capital punishment—longtime court observers understood that the assistant prosecutor was simply following up on his assertion that the state would likely seek the death penalty.

Overall, courtroom spectators were subdued. But as the selection process drew on, the voices of the Scutellaro children could occasionally be heard, reminding onlookers of the attendance of the defendant's little boy and girl. At one point, having caught her father's eye and received a smile in return, Marie Scutellaro called out to Joe, briefly piercing the steady bass murmuring of lawyers and prospective jurymen. "Daddy," she pleaded in a loud stage whisper and then repeated, more insistently, when Joe did not look her way again, "*Daddy.*" Anna reached over to draw her daughter closer to her on the polished wood bench, and Marie grew quiet.[37]

No further comments came from behind the railing until late afternoon, when the assistant prosecutor used one of his peremptory challenges (requiring no explanation) to remove thirty-five-year-old Kearny real estate dealer James B. Capobiano, the only man of Italian heritage called. An uneasy rumble went through the crowded courtroom. Anna exchanged looks with her in-laws. Was that it, then? They could not know if the man's presence would have helped their cause or if he would have served as a kind of amulet, focusing their prayers.[38]

———————— ✺ ————————

When the last juror was chosen just after 5:00 PM, courtroom observers contemplated the panel. Some found it easiest to describe the jury by pointing out what it lacked. None of the twelve men were from Hoboken. None seemed in any way connected to the city. None had Italian ancestry. And only one man on the jury—a former supervisor at a milk bottling plant—was jobless.[39]

Nevertheless, from the original "struck jury" list of well-established citizens, Sam Leibowitz had managed to select several employed jurors who might know something about staying just ahead of the poormaster. Four of the men, including coal company clerk Lyon, were industrial hires or shipyard workers: one worked for Standard Oil Company, one sold cement, and another was a supervisor at a boatyard. And even most of the remaining jurors, with larger, steadier incomes—two engineers, two accountants, a commercial bank clerk, a chemist, and assistant bank auditor Van Horn—might not have been as financially secure as their titles would suggest. All of the jurors but one were renters. Joe's home-owning parents had been property-rich compared to most of them.[40]

But the presence on the panel of that one homeowner, fifty-one-year-old mechanical engineer Harold D. Tompkins, would have puzzled many who remembered Leibowitz's earlier declaration that his poor client should be judged by his peers. For Tompkins's home was not in a "downtown" neighborhood like Hoboken's Monroe Street but was located on Bentley Avenue, one of Jersey City's finer blocks. Lined with stately single-family residences that sat comfortably on well-landscaped parcels, the western end of Bentley, where Tompkins lived, edged a large county park. The engineer's two-and-a-half-story shingled wood-frame home had been built around 1910. It was not the grandest building on the street, but it was spacious and solid and boasted the kind of wrap-around porch that only a few uptown Hobokenites enjoyed. It was the home of a well-to-do family, little affected by the nationwide economic crisis. Harold Tompkins had worked for twenty-five years for the same Jersey City manufacturer of iron cements, and his salary had remained generous enough to allow him to include in his household a live-in Irish maid and an Irish nanny for his three daughters.[41]

Tompkins could hardly be recognized as Joe's peer, even during the years when the Scutellaros had had a successful contracting business. The juror had more in common with the accused man's lawyer—including a shared alma mater, Cornell University. And Tompkins was also well placed socially. He had married a woman from a prominent Jersey City family: his father-in-law had variously been a Hudson County judge and a state assemblyman, widely recognized as the author of legislation that had brought about the construction of the Hudson County Courthouse, in all its marble splendor.[42]

But Harold Tompkins must have seemed to Leibowitz to be a reasonable choice in other respects. Perhaps the lawyer liked that Tompkins was married and had young children at home. Many of his fellow panelists were also fathers; they would be likely to reflect upon their own youngsters when hearing about the starving Scutellaro children. That was good for Joe.

Leibowitz had also sought jury members who had some recollection of their immigrant roots. Although every one of the selected jurors had been born in the United States, quite a few did not have to go too far back to identify immigrant ancestors. Henry A. F. Kelm's parents had left Germany for the United States; William Lindquist, married to a Finnish woman, was a second-generation Swedish American. Both of Robert Sinclair's in-laws were English; so was Thomas Hamilton's mother-in-law. Those jurors would be more likely to understand the struggle for security—financial, societal—waged by immigrants and their native-born children.

Ultimately it would be Sam Leibowitz's job to remind the jurymen that they were fundamentally not so very different from the defendant—and that they might have responded as he did, had they faced the vicious Hoboken poormaster. The criminal lawyer was going to make sure that Harry Barck, too, would be judged. "We intend to show what kind of man Barck was," Leibowitz promised.[43]

The twelve sworn jurors were to be sequestered at the seven-story Hotel Plaza on Sip Avenue in Jersey City. The local residents among them were already familiar with the ten-year-old hotel. Its banquet hall had been regularly used since its opening for meetings of the local Lions, Rotary Club, and Kiwanis; and Boss Hague had long enjoyed using it for rallies, during which he called for support of his Democratic organization and for the fight against Communists he said were trying to control organized labor, the press, and the courts.[44]

Some jurors had likely read news reports, just two weeks before the Scutellaro trial began, of Hague's annual New Year's Day reception. More than five thousand city hall dependents had lined up to shake the Boss's hand. The jurors would have discovered—as a disappointed and wary Sam Leibowitz surely did—that both Judge Robert Kinkead and Prosecutor Daniel O'Regan had "greeted" Hague that day "in his flower-banked office." Now Leibowitz would be on guard against potential coziness between the prosecutor and the jurist and any signs that Kinkead found boss rule acceptable.[45]

Before Judge Kinkead concluded the day's proceedings, he cautioned the jurors to refrain from discussing the case prior to deliberation. He would allow them daily newspapers but only after his court officers had clipped out references to the trial.[46]

With court adjourned, a deputy sheriff led the handcuffed defendant out of the room. The men who had lined the corridors all day cheered as Joseph Scutellaro was directed past them and returned to the county jail.[47]

12 | ON TRIAL: THE STATE'S CASE

THE FOLLOWING MORNING, TUESDAY, January 10, a band of reporters engulfed the accused man's family as they approached the courtroom doors. Photographers leaned in to take their shots, alarming and angering the Scutellaro relatives scrumming through the crowd with Anna and her children. Much to Marie's amazement and delight, one of her older female cousins shoved aside a photographer when he drew too near.[1]

There was a combative air inside the courtroom, too. After announcing that the state was abandoning the last count of the indictment against Joseph Scutellaro—assault and battery—William George offered an unusually withholding opening statement. Instead of mapping out his case, George stated curtly: "We will produce testimony and facts to support a first-degree murder charge. We will show that this defendant maliciously, feloniously, and premeditatedly slew Poormaster Barck." Then he stopped.

Sam Leibowitz's round face flushed in anger. "I have no reason to open my case, as the state has given me nothing to answer," the defender announced heatedly. It was the state's duty, he continued, to outline its case against the defendant. The assistant prosecutor retorted that the defense was also duty-bound to make an opening statement, and Leibowitz grudgingly complied. He turned to the jury and declared: "I will give you as many facts as he has given you. This man is innocent. We will produce testimony and facts to show the absolute and unqualified innocence of this defendant. We will show that he has committed no crime whatsoever."[2]

Leibowitz then asked that witnesses be excluded from the courtroom until they were called. He had seen the imposing wall of Hoboken police, all in uniform, standing near the prosecutor's table and had easily picked out Chief Edward McFeely's square, ruddy face among them. Any Hoboken witness called to testify would know the chief and his squad were watching.[3]

Judge Kinkead denied the defense's motion.

The assistant prosecutor began to establish the state's case. William George offered into evidence a floor plan of the Hoboken poormaster's office, along with a dozen photographs, which were to be passed to the jury for inspection and then pinned to a board so that the lawyers and witnesses might refer to them, as needed. Eight of the photographs depicted Harry Barck's desk from various angles or showed the waiting room and adjoining hallway. A pair of images depicted the dead man in his office, and two more documented his state prior to autopsy.

George called his first witness. Detective Rudolph Magnus Jr., a blocky middle-aged man of average height, seated himself heavily in the witness box. He explained that he was a photographer for the Hoboken Police Department, and when the assistant prosecutor inquired about the twelve photos placed in evidence, Magnus replied that he had taken them following the death of the poormaster.

Leibowitz asked the detective to look at a photo of Harry Barck, who was shown laid out on an office bench, and asked him to determine the poormaster's height and weight. Considering the length of the bench, Magnus noted, Barck was about six feet tall and would have been near to the photographer's own weight—about 210 pounds.[4]

Dr. William P. Braunstein followed next. The assistant county physician had performed the autopsy on Harry Barck's body with three other doctors. Braunstein testified that Barck had died of a "hemorrhage resulting from a puncture of the main artery leading from the heart." Starting from the puncture wound in the chest, he explained, the doctors had traced the damage to the sternum, which was perforated between the fourth and fifth ribs. On removing the sternum, they found

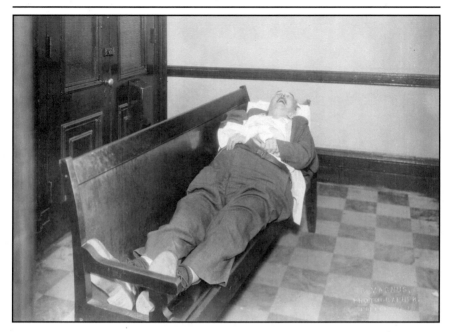

Detective Magnus's photograph of the deceased, Harry Barck,
laid out on a bench in the waiting room of his office.

From the case file *State v. Joseph F. Scutellaro*, 1939. Courtesy of the Hudson County Prosecutor's Office.

the sac surrounding the heart had also been perforated and had filled
with almost a pint of blood.[5]

On cross, Sam Leibowitz was brief. He asked the physician to describe
Harry Barck's physique. Braunstein said the poormaster had been just
under six feet tall and had weighed about 215 pounds. Directing the doctor's attention to the defendant, Leibowitz then asked him to describe
Joseph Scutellaro. He was probably five feet three inches tall and about
120 pounds, Braunstein replied.[6]

The assistant prosecutor called Eleonore Hartmann next. Harry
Barck's middle-aged secretary had long been identified as a "star witness," and reporters were prepared to record her every word. Hartmann
must have been conscious of all the eyes upon her, for as she approached
the witness box, she hurriedly tapped her temples, checking to see that

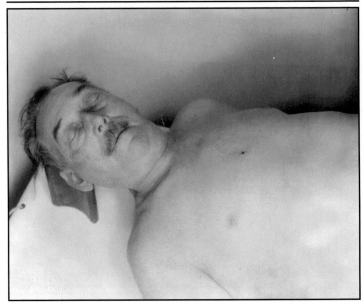

Forensic photograph of Poormaster Barck taken at Hoffman's
Morgue, showing the entry wound from the desk spindle.

From the case file *State v. Joseph F. Scutellaro*, 1939. Courtesy of the

Hudson County Prosecutor's Office.

only a few of her pressed, gray-blonde curls were peeking out from under
her dark toque. She would not be likely to learn that an Italian-language
newspaper would compare her "robust" build to Joe Scutellaro's gaunt
frame or that it would tell its readers that the green dress she wore accen-
tuated her girth.[7]

Eleonore Hartmann's eager account of the events of February 25,
1938, would have been familiar to any juror who had read a newspaper
after Harry Barck's death. She had been at her desk just outside the door
to her boss's office when she had heard Barck say, "Talk louder! I can't
hear you." Joe Scutellaro had demanded relief. Soon the voices of the two
men had become so loud, she said, she was roused from her work. When
she went to the doorway to investigate, she saw the poormaster backing
away from the relief client "with his hands in the air."

George was deferential toward his effusive witness. He asked her quietly what had happened next.

"With that," Hartmann said, lifting her chin as if she were a student proudly responding to a teacher's question, "I saw Mr. Scutellaro lunge at Mr. Barck and strike him a terrific blow."

"Where?" George asked, again in a soft tone of voice.

"Right here," Hartmann replied, placing her hand over her heart as she bowed her head a little. She said she hadn't seen what the alleged attacker had in his hand at the time, but she added that her boss had clutched his chest and told her to call an ambulance. "He said: 'He got me! He got me! I'm done for! I'm done for!'" Hartmann said.

Harry Barck had then reached for a police whistle he kept in the pocket of his coat, which was hanging on a hook along the wall. But when her boss found the whistle and blew on it, Hartmann said, "his breath left him and he crumpled at my feet, went down on his knees." She had been trying to telephone an ambulance when Barck fell to the ground, pulling the phone line out.

Hartmann had called out for help. "I was trying to pick Mr. Barck up from the floor," but he was too heavy for her to move alone, she said. Fortunately, three men who had been in the waiting room rushed in, she continued, and they lifted the poormaster onto a chair. By then, Joe Scutellaro was gone.

"Now Mrs. Hartmann—" William George began but was interrupted by the witness.

"*Miss* Hartmann," she corrected.

"Excuse me, please," George begged. "Forgive me, won't you?"

"Certainly," she said with a little nod.

The assistant prosecutor directed her attention to one of the exhibits, which she identified as a photograph of the poormaster's office. George asked Hartmann to describe the "pointed object" on the windowsill.

"That is one of those desk files," she replied, referring to a tool used to spike papers.

George held up a desk spindle he had marked for evidence. "And is it something like this one?" he asked. The device featured a six-inch pointed metal rod attached to a small hexagonal base. The assistant prosecutor wanted the jurors to have one of these sharp tools to hold, to imagine its use as a weapon.

"Yes, it is," Hartmann said.

"Did you ever see this before?" he asked, indicating the desk file he held in his hand.

"Mr. Barck had several on his desk," she replied obligingly.

"And were they like this one?" George asked.

"Yes, they were like that one."

"Is there any doubt in your mind, Miss Hartmann, that this was one of the spikes or spindles or files that was in that office?"

"There wouldn't be any doubt about it."

"I offer this in evidence," George announced.

Sam Leibowitz stood. He wanted to question the competency of the witness to make such an assertion and asked Judge Kinkead for permission. When it was granted, Leibowitz asked: "You say you recognize this spindle as being the spindle that was in Mr. Barck's office?"

"His spindles were all like that one," Hartmann said.

"You don't identify this one, do you?"

"It would be like the others," she said.

"Well," Leibowitz replied, "there are millions like it all over the country, aren't there?" A ripple of amusement went through the courtroom.

William George could see he was not going to be able to follow through on his plan. He withdrew his offer.

He would now attempt to establish his witness's caring response to her boss's distress. This was a role Hartmann took to readily. She added new flourishes to the story she had previously told. Now she said she had directed one of the office girls to get an ambulance for the poormaster; she claimed she had hastily fetched Harry Barck water and ammonia; and, she said, after noticing her boss's discomfort while seated in his office chair, she had cleverly directed the men, "Why not bring him out here on the settee and make him comfortable?" Soon after she offered this detail, the assistant prosecutor completed his questioning.

Sam Leibowitz stepped up to begin his cross-examination. "Mrs. Hartmann," he began.

"*Miss* Hartmann," William George called out.

Leibowitz corrected himself, but he did not apologize. He wanted his cross-examination of an untrustworthy witness to stand in opposition to William George's exaggerated solicitousness. He intended to disrupt Eleonore Hartmann's practiced story and destroy her credibility. One of the simplest methods he had employed over the years was to encourage derision by asking a witness: Have you ever told a lie in your life? "Invariably the witness blurts out, 'No,'" Leibowitz once explained, and "that calls for a laugh, for there isn't a man living who hasn't told a lie." He certainly believed it equally true of women.[8]

Leibowitz turned to Hartmann. "Now, you are under oath and I presume you want to tell the truth in this case," he said.

William George immediately objected. "The witness is under oath and it isn't a matter of choice," he protested.

"Oh, it is a matter of choice, Your Honor, with some people, whether they take an oath on fifty Bibles, or blanks," Leibowitz replied. "But it is not a matter of compulsion. An oath doesn't mean everything to everybody."

George repeated his objection, and Leibowitz began again: "Now you have no hesitation in telling the truth at any place—would you?"

"I always tell the truth," Eleonore Hartmann sniffed.

"You never lied in your life, have you?" Leibowitz asked, and again George objected.

Leibowitz rephrased. "Miss Hartmann," he asked, "you say you always tell the truth?"

"I was taught to tell the truth," Hartmann said.

"You always tell the truth?" Leibowitz asked again.

"I always tell the truth."

"You don't mind telling the truth—when it *is* the truth—to anybody, do you?"

"Certainly not," Eleonore Hartmann replied, her face coloring.[9]

Sam Leibowitz turned to his associate, Vincent Impellitteri, who was seated at the defense table, and asked his colleague to stand. After Leibowitz identified him for the record, Impellitteri returned to his seat.

"Did you ever see this man before?" Leibowitz asked Hartmann.

"I saw him in the office last week."

"You had a conversation with Mr. Impellitteri, did you not—a very brief conversation?"

Hartmann conceded that she had.

"Who was present at the time you spoke with Mr. Impellitteri?" Leibowitz asked.

"Mr. Tighe and Mr. Tumulty," Hartmann replied, referring to the new Hoboken poormaster and to Joe Scutellaro's New Jersey–based counselor, who was sitting at the defense table. After Leibowitz asked Thomas Tumulty to stand for the witness's identification, he asked, "Did Mr. Impellitteri or Mr. Tumulty ask you to tell them what happened on the day in question?"

Eleonore Hartmann said they had.

"Did they ask you to tell them what you knew about the case?"

"Yes, they asked me to tell them and I told them I didn't care to talk," Hartmann said.

Leibowitz continued to press her on her refusal to speak to defense counsel. "Who, if anyone, told you not to talk?" he asked. "Who instructed you that you were not to tell?"

"No one had to," Hartmann said, her mouth pulling in tightly after her assertion. "I knew that much myself."

Leibowitz wanted to know: Did she have prior experiences that would have led her to that understanding?

No, Hartmann said. She "just knew better."

"Well, how did you get that information?" Leibowitz continued. He now had his opening to introduce what would become a recurrent charge: that the McFeelys dominated Hoboken residents. "Where did you get that knowledge that you weren't to tell the truth to lawyers who were coming there, in the presence of your superior in a public office, in preparation of a case for trial, that you were to refuse to disclose what you knew about this case?" he asked. "Where did you ever get that information or that knowledge?"

"Well, I knew better than to talk to the other side of the case," Hartmann responded.

"What other side?" Leibowitz asked.

"Your side, the defense side."

Leibowitz began to corner her. "I am not quite clear what you mean, Miss Hartmann, by the word 'side.'"

"I am on the state's side," she said. "Why should I talk to the defense side?"

"You mean, why should you tell the truth to the defense?" Leibowitz said, and William George objected.

While the two lawyers sparred, Eleonore Hartmann sagged in the witness chair. Her long, beaky face had been tilted up at the start of the cross-examination, but now she was flagging. She must have been very uncomfortable with the turn in the proceedings, for she now turned to Judge Kinkead and implored, "May I talk to you, Judge, please?"[10]

"No, Miss Hartmann," Kinkead replied gently. "You see, you are a witness now, and you must answer the questions which are asked of you by counsel for the defense and by the prosecutor."

When Leibowitz resumed questioning, he focused on the witness's past friendship with Harry Barck and his family, which had been rekindled when she went to work for him.

"And you liked Mr. Barck, didn't you?" Leibowitz asked.

"Very much," Hartmann said.

"He was a very kindly old man, wasn't he?" the lawyer asked.

"He was."

"A civil, genial old man, wasn't he?" Leibowitz continued.

"He was."

"You never heard Mr. Barck abusing anybody?"

William George leapt up to object and was sustained by Judge Kinkead. But Sam Leibowitz had only begun to put Harry Barck's behavior on trial. "Was Mr. Barck in an angry mood that morning?" he asked. The witness replied "No" before George could object, but the assistant prosecutor was overruled anyway.

In response to Leibowitz's questions, Hartmann said that Harry Barck had been "friendly," not excited or angry, before he met with Scutellaro.

But "just a minute or two before that Mr. Barck had been in a fight with a woman, hadn't he?" Leibowitz asked. George now tried to block the defense from informing the jury of Lena Fusco's quarrel with the poormaster, but Kinkead allowed the question.

Hartmann elided it. "I wasn't in the room," she said.

"But did you hear Mr. Barck in an altercation with a woman just a few moments before you saw Scutellaro?" the defense attorney asked.

"I heard them talking in there," Hartmann replied. "I wasn't in that room, though."

"Talking loud enough for you to hear—yes or no?" Leibowitz pressed.

"Yes, they talked loud."

"Did you hear the conversation between Mr. Barck and the woman?"

"I was busy with my work; I didn't pay any attention," Hartmann replied.

After a few more exchanges, Leibowitz asked, with some exasperation: "You know, don't you, that the woman spat at Mr. Barck and Mr. Barck grabbed her and the policeman grabbed her and there was quite a scuffle in the place a moment or two before Mr. Scutellaro got into Mr. Barck's office? You know that, don't you?"

"I know that," Hartmann said.

"That is what happened—didn't it?"

"I know that," she repeated.

"Yes, and still you tell the learned Judge and this jury, citizens of this county, that a moment after, when you saw Scutellaro in the office, Mr. Barck was genial," Leibowitz said.

"He was," Hartmann replied.

As Leibowitz continued to question her, Eleonore Hartmann claimed that she was too busy with her work—"entering orders in the ledger and work like that"—to pay attention to the loud argument between Fusco and Barck in the next room; and yet, she also continued to insist that Barck's command—"Speak louder!"—and Joe Scutellaro's subsequent demand for relief had made her stop her work and go to her boss's door.

"Then there was loud talking?" Leibowitz asked about Joe's exchange with the poormaster.

"There wasn't much more loud talking after that," Hartmann admitted, though she would not admit much more. Further questioning revealed that she never went into Barck's office unless she was "on official business," but still she insisted the exchange between the two men had brought her to Barck's room.

Now Sam Leibowitz asked three men in the courtroom to stand and to identify themselves: Ralph Corrado, Nicholas Russo, and John Galdi Jr. They were there as witnesses for the state. When each man stood, Leibowitz asked Eleonore Hartmann if she recognized him. She did; they were the three men who were in the waiting room the day the poormaster was killed.

Leibowitz asked, "Isn't it a fact, Madam, that these three men entered Barck's office together with you?"

She denied it.

"Isn't it a fact, Madam, that Barck's whistle is the thing that attracted you into the room?"

"It did not," Hartmann insisted.

"And brought these three men and you into that room after the whole thing was over?"

"It did not," she said again; but she was shaken.

Sam Leibowitz was not finished with her yet. He wanted to know if she had spoken to anyone about the case. Her family, she said. Her friends. "The girls we work with" in the office. Newspaper reporters from the *Observer*. The police.

"What police did you talk to?" the defender asked.

"They all came up," Hartmann replied. "The chief came up."

"Chief McFeely, the man with the uniform and badge in his lapel standing up against the wall here? Is that who you mean?"

"That is the man," Hartmann said, again bowing her head.

Had she also spoken with Lieutenant J. Romeo Scott? Yes, she had. And Sergeant Charles Winters? Yes. And Patrolman Thomas Carmody, who had been stationed outside the poormaster's office? Yes. What about Chief McFeely's son, a lieutenant? "He was up there that day," Hartmann remembered.

"Did you talk to the mayor about the case, too?" Leibowitz asked.

"We saw the mayor, yes," she replied.

Now Leibowitz hoped to suggest what he would later describe as "the influence surrounding this woman." He asked: Wasn't it a fact that if she came to court and "even dared to say one word helpful to this defendant" that she would immediately lose her job?

The witness never got to respond. "That is objected to," William George called out, and the judge upheld his objection.

But Leibowitz was prepared to try another tactic. Over the years, he had learned that he could make jurors more responsive to his suggestions if the testimony he elicited from witnesses seemed less like a recitation of past events and more like a live drama happening before them. Sometimes, the defense attorney observed, he could excite the interest of jurors simply by having them anticipate something.[11]

Would His Honor allow a few minutes' recess? Leibowitz asked.

Kinkead hedged. Twenty minutes had elapsed since the start of cross-examination. The defense attorney hurriedly amended his request. He wanted "to go outside just for a minute," he said. With Kinkead's permission, Leibowitz left the court for the jury room.[12]

The defender's energetic return a minute later suggested he was newly armed with facts. *Now* he had the goods on Eleonore Hartmann—though he had surely known the details all along. Leibowitz questioned the witness briskly.

"Are you a stenographer, Miss Hartmann?" he asked.

"No, I am not."

"Do you typewrite?"

"Well, slightly."

"Can you read stenography?"

"No."

Leibowitz paused briefly, letting the expectant jurors mull over the loyal secretary's lack of secretarial skills. Then he confronted her again: "You say you are the person that asked that the body of Mr. Barck be moved into the anteroom and be placed on that bench?"

"Yes," she said.

"Are you sure?"

"Yes."

"Did you see an ambulance doctor there?" Leibowitz asked, pointing to Dr. Lawrence J. Kelly, who was waiting to be called as a defense witness. When Hartmann responded affirmatively, Leibowitz asked, "Wasn't the ambulance doctor the one that directed that Mr. Barck's body be brought out and put on the bench—wasn't it he?"

"He may have said that inside," she suggested. After repeated evasions and qualifications, she finally conceded her instruction had been an offhand suggestion to a woman standing with her outside the office door, as they both watched the life-saving efforts happening inside.

Leibowitz moved on to the poormaster's systematic denial of relief and Eleonore Hartmann's role as one of his emissaries. The defense lawyer asked: Joseph Scutellaro wasn't a friend of yours, was he?[13]

No, Hartmann replied, he was not.

"He was never a neighbor of yours, was he?" Leibowitz asked, and again received a negative reply. "Never an intimate or close associate of yours in any way, was he?"

Again, Hartmann responded no.

"Just a stranger, is that right?"

"That is so."

"Just a relief applicant—that is right, isn't it?"

"Just a relief applicant."

"Just another one of those people—is that right?" Leibowitz asked, but William George objected and was upheld.

Leibowitz shifted to Hartmann's claim that his diminutive client had backed the huge poormaster up against a file cabinet. After eliciting her description of Harry Barck as "tall," "large built," and "powerful," the defense attorney asked Joe Scutellaro to stand.

"He was easily twice the size of this man in weight, wasn't he?"

"Easily," Hartmann said.

"Mr. Barck could take this man and break him in half, couldn't he?" the defense lawyer ventured, but George objected before Hartmann could respond. Leibowitz asked his client to be seated.

He concluded his cross-examination the way he'd begun. "Before I sit down, Miss Hartmann, I just have one more question. Do you want to change your statement to me that you have never told a lie in your life?"

"I don't want to change it. I am not lying," Hartmann said.

Leibowitz persisted. "No, no, answer the question. You tell these twelve men in the jury box that in all your life you have never told one lie? Do you still say that?"

"I still say that."

"And you are telling the truth now when you say that?"

"I am telling the truth."

"That in all your life, you have never told even one lie," Leibowitz repeated, his voice expressing disbelief. "That is all."

The three other clerks who had worked for Harry Barck were now called in turn to testify for the state. Unlike their senior coworker, none had previously claimed to be eyewitnesses or rescuers, and their direct examination proceeded quickly. Under George's questioning, the testimony of twenty-four-year-old typist Adeline Cerutti, a stylish blonde, led to her discovery of the desk spindle on the floor of the poormaster's office. One of the men who had run in to help asked her to get Barck a glass of water. "I got a glass of water from a small sink in Mr. Barck's room," Cerutti said. "On my way to get water, I picked up his glasses, a [desk] file, a whistle, and the telephone" from the floor near his desk.

William George brought forward a desk spindle with a bent spike: Was this the one Cerutti had retrieved from floor of the poormaster's office? It was, Cerutti testified. The assistant prosecutor entered the desk file into evidence.[14]

Cerutti's dark-haired counterpart, Romayne Mullin, testified that when she had entered the poormaster's office, she'd seen three men. They had seated Mr. Barck in a chair and had opened his collar. "I went downstairs and got a bottle of ammonia and put it under his nose, and he was placed outside on a bench by three men," she said.[15]

Under cross-examination by the defense, Mullin said she could not recall if Eleonore Hartmann had been in Barck's office when she ran in. But under further questioning, the young typist revealed that she *had* seen Joseph Scutellaro in the office, sitting in a chair.

And how did he seem? Leibowitz asked.

"He didn't seem moved by what had just happened."

"He sat there like a dummy, didn't he?" Leibowitz said. He would develop this allusion later.

"Yes," Mullin agreed.

"And what did you say to him?"

"Why did you do it?"

And how had Joe Scutellaro replied? Leibowitz asked.

"I received no reply."[16]

Leibowitz then introduced a hint of his client's version of the morning's events. He asked Romayne Mullin if she had heard Joseph Scutellaro "tell police after his arrest that Barck fell over the spindle in a scuffle" with him. No, Mullin said, she had not. The journalists in the courtroom scribbled furiously. They now had their lead.[17]

Three of the poormaster's clerks, Adeline Cerutti, Romayne Mullin, and Eleonore Hartmann, leave the Hudson County Courthouse after testifying at the Scutellaro trial.

New York *Daily News* Archive/Getty Images.

The third clerk from the poormaster's office, Josephine Shea, had little to add to her colleagues' accounts. After she discovered her boss was in need of an ambulance, she raced down to police headquarters to summon one, she said. Before she stepped down, Leibowitz asked her "if she'd gone over the story with anyone." Shea replied that she'd discussed the case with her aunt. "You didn't tell it to Miss Hartmann?" he asked. No, Shea responded. To Romeo Scott? he asked. No, she said. Had she told her story to Lieutenant Dennis McFeely? he asked. Yes, she answered. "To Chief McFeely?" Leibowitz asked. Yes, she replied again.[18]

———————— ✦ ————————

The testimony of state's witness Ralph Corrado had once been happily anticipated by the prosecution: in his statement to the police, the unemployed baker had placed Hartmann in Barck's office before he'd rushed in, with two other men, to offer help. But since then, Corrado had agreed to talk to "the other side," and in the voluntary statement he gave to defense cocounsel Vincent Impellitteri, he had asserted that Hartmann and the three clients had run into the office *together*, in response to a whistle blast and a cry for help.[19]

As a result, when the assistant prosecutor called Ralph Corrado to the stand, he approached his witness with uncommon suspicion. "You know what it means to tell the truth . . . and swear by it?" George asked Corrado right away.[20]

Leibowitz rose to object, first pointing out that the state should not doubt the credibility of its own witness. After sustaining the defense's objection, Judge Kinkead concurred. "I must admit," he said, "it is a strange tactic the state is taking."

George softened his questioning a little and gained Corrado's detailed account of his early morning meeting with Joe, their wait in the poormaster's anteroom, and Barck's argument with Lena Fusco. But the relief client would not return to his former version of the race to Harry Barck's office, and George's irritation resurfaced. Scowling, the assistant prosecutor rattled his copy of Corrado's statement and paced back and forth before the witness box. He rephrased the same query over and over.

Finally Sam Leibowitz objected. "Don't try to bulldoze the witness," the defense lawyer called out. "After all, this *is* your witness," he continued. "And despite the fact that all the McFeelys are present," he could not help adding, "this isn't the Hoboken police station, you know." The laughter that followed was subdued by Judge Kinkead's call to order.

In his cross-examination, Leibowitz immediately sought Corrado's agreement that the witness's new statement had been made voluntarily. The defense attorney read portions of the document aloud. "Joe never said at any time that he was going to get Barck, never threatened him in any way, at any time," Leibowitz quoted with satisfaction. In fact, Corrado had avowed to Impellitteri that Joe had not gone to the office "with any intent towards any one."[21]

But Corrado would soon prove unreliable for defense purposes, too. He balked when Leibowitz tried to get him to repeat the recollection that would challenge Hartmann's purported "eyewitness" testimony. Exasperated, Leibowitz asked if Corrado felt the need to follow the state's evidence "to keep on the right side of the police."

No, responded Corrado, he did not.

Leibowitz knew some details of Corrado's troubled past. The defender would have withheld them had Corrado braved the consequences and reasserted what he'd recalled to Impellitteri. Do you admit, Leibowitz now challenged, to being incarcerated at a federal penitentiary for nine and a half months and to currently being on parole, so that you have to maintain a good relationship with the police?

William George stood to object, but Kinkead allowed the witness to reply. Yes, Corrado admitted, he had served time on a liquor charge. He was now on parole. Corrado tried again, belatedly, to salvage his standing with city hall. "You have nothing to fear from the police if you do nothing wrong," he said.[22]

But Leibowitz was ready to complete the picture of a man in step with the Hall's requirements. Holding Corrado's statement to Impellitteri in one hand, Leibowitz began to quote a new section, in which the witness explained to defense counsel that he had initially gained poor relief by getting "the okay" from Mayor McFeely and then announcing the mayor's approval to Poormaster Barck.

William George leapt up to object and was sustained.

Sam Leibowitz merely smiled. He informed the court he was likely to call Mr. Impellitteri at another time to testify about Corrado's statement. The defender would relish another opportunity to reassert to the jury that relief in Hoboken was politically controlled.[23]

By the following morning, Wednesday, January 11, the sequestered jurymen had received news of goings-on beyond the courtroom walls. Though their newspapers, as promised, had had all reference to the Scutellaro trial excised, the judge's assistants had left intact reports on the continuing nationwide need for relief and of federal and state legislators' increasing reluctance to appropriate funding for it. Headlines announced to jurors that congressional conservatives, bolstered by the November elections, were now agitating to cut the latest work-relief appropriation sought by President Roosevelt; and they proclaimed the resistance of the Republican-controlled New Jersey legislature to reimbursing municipalities for relief spending during the prior year. The state's general relief funds had been exhausted by July 1, 1938, but grocers in municipalities eligible for state aid had essentially kept their neighbors alive by continuing to honor food tickets. The tab had now grown to $9 million, and furious merchants were threatening a march on Trenton. They would march to the statehouse with their customers, the jobless poor.[24]

Perhaps mindful of this brewing dissent, police presence was increased outside of Judge Kinkead's court. On Wednesday morning, five county policemen were positioned next to the courtroom doors. The officers waved away more than a hundred down-and-out men who tried to enter the crowded chamber and watched apprehensively as the rejected spectators moved onto the courthouse balconies.[25]

The day's first prosecution witness was twenty-seven-year-old factory hand John Galdi Jr. He too had been waiting in the poormaster's anteroom that February morning. But unlike the others, Galdi had not been

Hudson County assistant prosecutor William George
and Police Captain James Murray, outside of the
courtroom on January 11, 1939.

New York *Daily News* Archive/Getty Images.

there in anticipation of relief. Rather, a court had ordered the young
man to pay three dollars each week in support of a child he had fathered
out of wedlock. Galdi was waiting that day to *give* money to the poormaster, for transfer to the child's mother.[26]

Such meetings were not unusual for Harry Barck. Though largely
unmentioned during the relief crisis, the poormaster's long reach into
the lives of impoverished residents had always gone well beyond prying
into their personal finances to determine fitness for assistance. Barck
had the power to force inquiries into the paternity of "bastard" children

whenever he reckoned those offspring might become poor-fund recipients. Legal scrutiny was meant to compel negligent fathers to care for their own, but it was also meant to punish frequently strapped laborers for their presumed apathy and irresponsibility. After just such an inquiry, John Galdi had begun seven years of meetings with the Hoboken poormaster.[27]

William George knew this biographical detail from Galdi's police statement, but he would not have been eager to dwell on it. That unsavory fact might taint the jurors' impression of a state witness and even their view of the deceased. Instead, after gaining an account of what Galdi had heard in the waiting room, the assistant prosecutor asked his witness to describe what had happened when he'd passed Joe Scutellaro at Harry Barck's door.[28]

"I heard him say '*That son of a bitch*,' as he came out," Galdi said—an assertion that supported the state's contention that Joe had been in a rage that morning. The growled remark set courtroom observers to whispering about the foul language used by the defendant.[29]

But the jurors would have seen that Sam Leibowitz remained unruffled. He had noticed this claim in Galdi's police statement and had likely concluded that once defense witnesses testified to Harry Barck's casual slurs, the jury would be unlikely to consider Joe's epithet extreme. The defender now focused on another section of Galdi's statement, again turning the words of a state's witness to his client's benefit. In the final moments of his cross-examination, Leibowitz had John Galdi affirm that he had run into the poormaster's office *just seconds* after Eleonore Hartmann.

Leibowitz picked up this refrain when he questioned the next prosecution witness, twenty-eight-year-old reliefer Nicholas Russo. "We went in all together; she was ahead of us," Russo told Joe's lawyer.[30]

And what about the incident between Lena Fusco and the poormaster?

Barck had been "mad and shaking" after the quarrel, Russo said.

When he was ready to call defense witnesses, Leibowitz planned to elicit from them a long list of Harry Barck's abuses. It was a tactic the defender had used with great success in countless murder trials—arguing that the person who had been killed had done great harm to others, including the defendant. Now he would have a state's witness initiate the record for him.[31]

And did he seem to you to be "a kindly, genial man?" Leibowitz asked Russo.

No, he did not, said the witness, who added that he'd met several times with Barck to gain relief.

And was he always calm? Leibowitz asked.

No, Russo replied, he was not.

A kindly gentleman?

No, Russo said again.

In a kindly mood that morning?

No, the witness repeated.

"Just the opposite?"

"Yes," Russo agreed.[32]

Sam Leibowitz did not challenge the testimony of the first Hoboken police officer called by the state, Patrolman Thomas Carmody, who had been posted outside of the poormaster's office that February morning. But William George would have known a sustained attack on the credibility of the Hoboken police was forthcoming from his famous legal opponent. In preparation for their contest, the assistant prosecutor had surely tracked down and studied the two-part profile of Leibowitz that had appeared in the *New Yorker* in 1932 and reviewed *Not Guilty! The Story of Samuel S. Leibowitz*, a hardcover published a year later. The authors of both had described the making of the Leibowitz legend. During his very first trial as a criminal defender, in 1919, Sam had argued that the confession made by his client, an accused thief, had been beaten out of him with a rubber hose. The man had been acquitted. Ever since, the claim of false confession had been a ready tool in Leibowitz's legal defense kit.[33]

And juries were highly receptive to this accusation. Leibowitz and other criminal defenders had been helped along by the public's increasing awareness of police brutality, which had flared during the postwar Red Scare and in the crime wave that accompanied Prohibition. New York newspapers had begun to document extensive police violence and evidence manufacturing, and by 1931, a presidential commission had released a report on police abuses in fifteen cities. Eight years later, as

William George was preparing to call police witnesses to Joe Scutellaro's alleged confession, both prosecutor and defender knew that terms like "frame-up" and "the third degree," lifted from the news by Hollywood screenwriters, had become familiar to any juror who went to the movies.[34]

George called Hoboken police lieutenant Joseph Romeo Scott. On hearing his name announced in the courtroom, the officer rose from his seat behind the prosecutor's table and lumbered over to the witness stand. Scott seated himself at the edge of the witness chair, leaning forward as if he were prepared to leave at any moment.

Again Leibowitz requested that officers waiting to testify be excluded from the room while the lieutenant gave his testimony; and now Judge Kinkead conceded, overruling George's objection. Chief McFeely, Sergeant Charles Winters, and Patrolman Bernard F. Walker turned in unison to leave the courtroom. Behind their broad backs followed two officers from the prosecutor's squad.[35]

George handed Scott a document to identify. That would be the voluntary statement Joseph Scutellaro made and signed after his arrest for the killing of Mr. Barck, Scott said. His overly formal manner was at odds with his accent, a regional version of the dialect associated with working-class New Yorkers. Scott said he had been one of three witnesses to Scutellaro's signing.

Leibowitz vigorously objected to the statement's admission into evidence. When he was overruled, he reserved the right to assert later that the statement was not voluntary. The row of reporters behind the railing busily took note.

In response to George's questioning, Scott described the procedure the police were said to have followed the morning Joe was arrested, beginning with Chief McFeely's explanation that the prisoner had the right to refuse to make a statement. But Joe had agreed to do so, Scott said, and Patrolman Walker, the chief's secretary, had then taken down Joe's words "in stenography." Walker had typed the final document, and when Joe had approved its wording, the accused man had signed his confession.

William George read the brief statement aloud, facing the jury. It began with Joe's request for aid and Barck's denial, then continued: " 'I said, "you're fooling me long enough and you've been fooling the poor people that is around here." ' " George paused for effect. " 'I said, "You can't get away with it,'" he read. The assistant prosecutor continued with Joe's alleged admission that he had spied the paper file on Barck's desk and "grabbed it," then "stabbed him in the right side of the chest." George's recitation concluded with Joe tossing the spindle to the floor and then realizing "what I had done," deciding to leave the office, only to be apprehended by the patrolman outside Barck's office.[36]

The confession seemed clear-cut. George handed over his witness for cross-examination by the defense.

With his opening sally Sam Leibowitz made clear that the document produced in Hoboken's police headquarters was anything but straightforward. Aren't you related to Chief McFeely by marriage, since your son married Frances McFeely? Leibowitz charged. Before Scott could reply, George immediately objected and was sustained.[37]

The defense attorney barely paused after the judge's ruling. Did you hear Scutellaro tell Chief McFeely it was an accident—that it had happened during a struggle? he asked, using a tone that suggested he believed the witness to be a practiced liar.

"I didn't hear any such statement," Scott said, pulling back sharply as if something offensive had been waved in front of him. The officer said he had been in the adjoining office when Scutellaro made his statement.[38]

And what were you doing in the anteroom? Leibowitz asked.

"I was standing there looking at the girls," Scott said. His admitted gawking, combined with his pronunciation of the last word—"goils"—brought loud guffaws from the spectator section of the courtroom. Scott's big face reddened. A few observers leaned forward to look at the poormaster's attractive young typists and tittered.[39]

Leibowitz took note of the witness's discomfort. Now the criminal defender goaded Scott by feigning an inability to understand him. The lieutenant's face tightened as he was forced to repeat the mirth-inducing remark.

And had you seen Joe Scutellaro in the chief's office? asked Leibowitz, after a second wave of laughter further rattled the police officer.

Scott replied that he had gone into the office "just to look at the prisoner, out of curiosity."

"What did you want to see him for?"

"To see him as everybody wants to see you."

186 | KILLING THE POORMASTER

"That isn't a wise crack, is it?" Leibowitz asked.

"I am a gentleman as well as you Mr. Leibowitz," Scott said.

"I'll not concede that," Leibowitz replied, "because I don't work in the Hoboken police station." After a pause, he continued with the same skeptical tone: "Did you go there to protect him?"

"From what?" Scott asked.

"I'll tell you later from what," Leibowitz said. "You were his friend?" Again his voice connoted doubt.

"Yes," Scott replied. "I wanted to help him. I always want to help everybody."

"In what way did you want to help him?"

"To tell the truth."

"It was a matter of slipping your lieutenant's coat on and your coat of friendship off, wasn't it?" Leibowitz remarked, without waiting for a response. He now pointed out that it had taken the police nearly five hours to obtain a 225-word statement from Joe Scutellaro. "Why did it take from ten o'clock in the morning until about four o'clock in the afternoon to get that confession?"[40]

"I don't know," Scott said.

It wasn't because Scutellaro was being "worked on" and "given the business" for five hours so that he would confess?

No, Scott said.

No one has ever been given the business in Hoboken? Leibowitz asked, an edge of mockery in his voice.

No, Scott said again, and spectators responded with a low rumble of disbelief. It was not the raucous laughter Leibowitz had once heard from a New York jury—the policeman Leibowitz had been questioning then had claimed that he had *never*, in decades of police work, seen a fellow officer beat a prisoner to gain a confession—but the defender must have been assured that Hudson County residents, too, were skeptical of police claims of fair treatment and honesty. His well-used strategy was still effective. Leibowitz would now tailor it for the Scutellaro case: he would argue that no force was needed to extract a confession from his client. Joe was so small and so timid he could be intimidated without blows.[41]

By now Scott was nervously mopping the back of his neck with a handkerchief. The weather had been unseasonably mild for two days, but Leibowitz surely knew the lieutenant was reacting to more than a fifty-degree day in January.

"Your Honor," Leibowitz called out mischievously, "it seems both the witness and I are hot. If it pleases the court, may we open a few windows?"[42]

But Scott's discomfort would be prolonged as Leibowitz quizzed him on the prisoner's removal from the basement police station to the poormaster's office. At first Scott denied any recollection of Joe Scutellaro's relocation, then suddenly remembered that the prosecutor's men had wanted the prisoner to show them the placement of the spindle on Barck's desk.

After pointing to his client, Leibowitz turned to face the witness he insisted on calling "Romeo Scott." "Who told you to take this little man upstairs?" he demanded.

"Chief McFeely," Scott replied without hesitation. All orders came from the chief of police.

"It was not because you have a job doing the bulldozing around that station, was it?" asked Leibowitz. William George immediately objected and was sustained.[43]

And what about the trip back down to the police station, when the other policemen left you to lead the prisoner through a darkened corridor, to help them get the confession Scutellaro had withheld for so many hours? Leibowitz asked. Did you get the confession by "threatening to knock the defendant's teeth down his throat?"

No, Scott said.

Reporters would later say that this was when they first heard Joe Scutellaro crying. Seated on the prisoner's bench, Joe issued gulping sobs as Leibowitz continued questioning Lieutenant Scott.

"Did you use your fists? There were fists weren't there?" Leibowitz asked. Joe's small, gray form was bent over, strangling his cries.

"No, there wasn't a hand laid on him," Scott replied.

"There *was!*" Joe suddenly wailed, now upright but shaking. A court officer came forward to subdue him, and Joe hid his face in a crumpled white handkerchief.[44]

Leibowitz continued, building a sinister image of intimidation, backgrounded by his client's muffled weeping. Wasn't the corridor leading from the upper level to the first floor "pitch dark"? Leibowitz asked. Without any illumination?

Yes, Scott hesitantly agreed.

Did you use handcuffs to lead the prisoner around? Leibowitz asked.

No, Scott said. But under further questioning, the lieutenant admitted that he had used another form of restraint, which Leibowitz asked him to explain. Scott described a type of single handcuff, with a chain and small handles that tightened around the prisoner's wrist.

And can the handles "be adjusted so they press into the flesh?" Leibowitz asked. He did not wait for a response but continued: Not something a "friend" would use, unless the friend wanted to gain a confession.[45]

Leibowitz walked over to Joe and placed his arm around the defendant's thin shoulders. Turning to Scott, he asked: "Didn't you go over to Scutellaro and pat him on the back and say '*Now you're my pal,*'" after he signed the confession? The lawyer's voice turned cloying when he imitated the false camaraderie Scott had offered his client.

"I might have asked him how he felt," Scott replied.[46]

Leibowitz shook his head before he began again. Did you know that Joe Scutellaro had been treated at the Jersey City Medical Center for sleeping sickness—for inflammation of the brain—on February 1? he asked, and again the front-row reporters took furious notes.

Although William George objected and the state's witness did not respond, the newsmen would now report that another line of defense had been advanced by Joe's famous lawyer. Tired and red-faced, Lieutenant Scott was released from the witness stand.

13 | ON TRIAL: THE DEFENSE

WHEN COURT RECONVENED ON Thursday, January 12, jurors may have noticed the men who had claimed several prime seats in the spectators' section. Local lawyers, some still wearing the fine camelhair coats they had put on that morning in response to winter's sudden return, had pulled rank to catch a few moments of the great Sam Leibowitz's presentation of his client's defense.[1]

The state had abruptly rested the night before, after the defender had dismantled the testimony of final witnesses Patrolman Walker and Martin Faber, a special investigator for the prosecutor's office. Again Leibowitz had reached for familiar tools: the lawyer had suggested the prisoner's coercion when Walker, Chief McFeely's longtime secretary, had claimed not to know why it had taken so long to jot down Scutellaro's 225-word statement; and Leibowitz had linked Investigator Faber's too-perfect testimony to the man's admitted court recess discussion of the case with his boss, Assistant Prosecutor George.[2]

Now Leibowitz was prepared to invert the jurors' perspective—to bring them close to the man they had been encouraged to view from a dispassionate and disbelieving distance. He called as his first witness Joe Scutellaro.

The courtroom grew quiet as the defendant rose from the prisoner's bench. He moved awkwardly; his small stature and stiff walk conjured the image of an unjointed wooden toy. A shaft of light from a courtroom window illuminated his long, chalky face. Joe shielded his eyes to search the second row for Anna, and when he saw her, he took a deep breath, as if he had been revived.[3]

Leibowitz began the direct examination slowly—calmly and purposefully drawing from his client a "tale of illness, privation, and grim poverty." The defense attorney took care to elicit precise, evocative details—the empty coal bin, the family living on coffee and stale bread—to fire the imagination of jurors and to stoke their sympathy. He mentioned Scutellaro's 1932 attack on the emergency relief officer to disallow the prosecution any element of surprise; and then he drew comparisons between those bleak early Depression years and the recession that was still punishing the nation's poorest families in February 1938. With this foundation, Leibowitz could return to the day Joe had argued with the poormaster.[4]

"On February 25, how much money was there between you and starvation?" Leibowitz asked.

"Fifteen cents," Joe replied, noting that he had even less after he bought three rolls for his family to share. As he described kissing his wife and children good-bye that morning, Joe again looked over at Anna and stopped speaking for a moment. He removed his glasses and wiped his eyes.[5]

Leibowitz waited while his client composed himself, then continued his questioning. Joe described walking to city hall with Corrado, waiting at the poormaster's office, and the argument between Fusco and Barck. After Barck had washed his face, Joe remembered, an aid-seeker named Romano had been called into the office, but the man came out half a minute later and signaled to the others "No relief." Corrado was supposed to go in next but told Joe to go before him.

Again Joe paused. He stared in front of him, as if suddenly lost in the bright room. Again Leibowitz drew him back with another question. Joe explained how he had told Barck that his children were sick. They were starving, Joe said. The gas and electric was going to be shut off. The soles of his children's shoes were worn through, he said, his voice quavering.[6]

And what are your children's names? Leibowitz asked, and Joe told him. "Are these the children?" his lawyer said, pointing to Marie and little Joe sitting by Anna's side.

Yes, Joe said.

And are these your daughter's shoes? Leibowitz asked, dangling from his long fingers a pair of worn leather flats.

Yes, Joe said.

The defense attorney announced his intention to enter Marie's shoes into evidence, but George objected and was sustained. As if to dispense with them, Leibowitz placed the husk-like little slippers on the defense table. He didn't mention the shoes again, but they remained there throughout the rest of the trial, where the jury could see them.

Leibowitz now turned to the subject of Joe's health, and his client's treatment for "sleeping sickness," mentioned briefly the day before. The defender would later call Joe's doctor to provide expert testimony on *encephalitis lethargica*, which in most patients developed into a form of Parkinson's disease, but he first wanted Joe to describe for the jurors what the illness had done to him. Under questioning, Joe portrayed himself as "drowsy, sleepy, and dopey all the time." He had headaches and double vision and sometimes trembled uncontrollably. In the weeks and days leading up to February 25, 1938, "I had funny ideas in my mind," he said, including thoughts of suicide. The suicidal thoughts were furthered along by his constant worries "about money and family troubles."[7]

And when was the last time your family received relief and for how much? Leibowitz asked.

On January 28, we received a check for $5.70, Joe replied. Then nothing more for four weeks. That trifling sum was sure to shock jurors. No family could survive for a month on that amount, never mind reach the minimum level for "health and decency" established years before by the federal government. In 1928 a *weekly* budget of forty dollars had been considered the bottom line for an American worker's family.[8]

Leibowitz walked Joe Scutellaro through his request for aid and the Hoboken poormaster's insulting reply. What did you take Mr. Barck's comment to mean? Leibowitz asked.

That my wife "should become a prostitute," Joe responded.[9]

You knew that "swing your bag" was one of Barck's favorite expressions, didn't you? Leibowitz asked. George's objection was overruled, and Joe responded affirmatively, after Leibowitz argued that had such a comment been new to Barck, if might have driven his client "into a blind rage, but if it was something widely known as a usual comment on many occasions, it might not be."[10]

Coaxed by his lawyer, Joe described his fight with Barck. He spoke with great difficulty, his speech blunted, as if his words were meeting some kind of physical impasse before he could utter them.[11]

"And why did you punch Barck?" Leibowitz asked.

"I was afraid of him," Joe said.[12]

Leibowitz paused to allow the jury to consider his client's comment, then announced that he would be calling upon Court Officer John Kuehn—later described by a reporter as "a husky six-footer about the size of Barck"—to assist with a demonstration.

The defender had long ago recognized the value of dramatic testimony in the courtroom and the need to bring abstractions to life. He was uncommonly suited to do both. While at law school, Sam Leibowitz had been an enthusiastic participant in both the Cornell Dramatic Society and the debate team. In the years since he'd joined the bar, he had often reflected that the practice of criminal law had allowed him to refine those talents and to develop still more. Listing the best-known theatrical impresario, actor, scientist, and politician of the day, he had once immodestly remarked to a reporter: "A criminal lawyer has to be a combination of a Belasco, a John Barrymore, an Einstein, and an Al Smith."[13]

Now, taking the courtroom as his stage, Leibowitz meant to use the stenographer's desk as a central prop, to have his client show the jurors what had happened to the poormaster and to show why Joe Scutellaro had every reason to fear Harry Barck.[14]

William George complained that the desk in the courtroom was not the same size as Barck's, but Judge Kinkead allowed the demonstration to go forward.

Joe stood in front of a rail that separated him from the stenographer's desk. On the other side, next to the stenographer, towered Court Officer Kuehn. Taking in the scene, jurors would have noted that Joe Scutellaro seemed the size of a child compared to Kuehn.

"Now show us what happened," Leibowitz instructed his client.

Joe took the officer's hands and placed them so they grasped his suit lapels. The large officer had to lean across the desk to do so, his shadow extending over the little man.

"Barck grabbed my coat," Joe began, "and I tried to pull away." He mimed attempts to draw back while Kuehn strained over the desk. The jury was taking in the image of a struggle between a giant and a little slip of a man. "I got very excited and punched at him. His face was very red," Joe continued.

Leibowitz asked Kuehn to let go. "How did he go down?" the lawyer asked.

Joe bent the officer over, with his arms edging his torso and his hands dangling beneath the desk. "He went down with a bang," Joe said. "He stood up with something sticking in his chest. It looked like a spindle. I pulled it out and threw it on the floor."[15]

That was all. The jury had seen the reenactment of a terrible accident. When Joe returned to the witness stand, his lawyer surely noticed the alert and troubled faces of the jurors.

Leibowitz moved on to question his client about his state of mind after the fight. Joe said he was not exactly sure what had happened. He could recall explaining to Chief McFeely that he had had an argument with the poormaster and that Barck had fallen on a spindle on his desk. But when the police officers brought him back up to Barck's office to re-create the scene, and Joe told them he didn't know where the spindle had been on the desktop, the chief had shouted, "Take him out! He's lying, boys."[16]

That's when all the other policemen went ahead, Joe continued. Lieutenant Scott took me down a dark corridor, and into a side room, alone—and then he threatened me. "You guinea bastard!" Joe said the lieutenant had shouted in his face. "If you don't tell us you stuck him, I'll knock your teeth down your throat!"[17]

And what was your reaction? Leibowitz asked.

"I was afraid," Joe said, his voice choked. Dizzy, frightened, and faint, he had been led back into the chief's office, where Chief McFeely had ordered: "*Now* tell us what happened."

And what did you say? Leibowitz asked.

"I told him, 'I stuck him,'" Joe said. He did not have his eyeglasses—the police had taken them from him—so he signed something he could not read.

Sam Leibowitz plucked from the defense table several letters Scutellaro had written to him while his client had been in prison awaiting trial. After Joe identified his own firmly written signatures, Leibowitz tore them from the letters and admitted the slips as evidence of Scutellaro's usual handwriting. The jurors would be able to compare them to the barely legible autograph Joe had affixed to a statement the Hoboken police said he had made voluntarily.[18]

William George would have none of it. He meant to dispel the view that Joe Scutellaro was to be pitied, that he was a victim, somehow unaccountable for his actions. No one was above the law. George intended to bring out that the defendant had been angry and, even more, ungrateful—a reliefer who had repeatedly refused to accept limits on his receipt of public charity.

At first George made some headway: he probed Joe about his association with parolee Ralph Corrado, even suggesting—until Leibowitz objected—that Joe was an ex-con, too, because of his 1932 suspended sentence in Hoboken's police court. And the assistant prosecutor bore down, as Leibowitz had expected, on Joe's attack on the emergency relief officer, Harold Butler. Hadn't Joe demanded relief from Butler and been denied? George asked. Wasn't he arrested on a charge of assault and battery of Harold Butler? Yes, Joe responded. Yes.[19]

George was cutting with the defendant, likely trying to anger Joe. When George handed him a copy of a legal document from the 1932 case, and Joe hesitated in identifying it, George interjected a little ethnic barb. "You read English, of course?" the assistant prosecutor asked. "I do," Joe replied, without taking offense, though the jurors, if they had looked out toward the spectators' benches, would have likely seen the defendant's father shaking his bowed head.[20]

As George hammered away at Joe's past conviction in the 1932 case, Leibowitz rose to object that George was "retrying this issue," and moved for a mistrial. "All this evidence is prejudicial and immaterial," he charged. But Judge Kinkead denied the motion, noting that Leibowitz himself had introduced the incident during direct examination.

Assistant Prosecutor George returned to his rapid-fire questioning, and Joe's replies became increasingly fitful. The defendant seemed to be hollowing out before the eyes of courtroom observers. Joe sagged in the witness box, staring blankly between queries. His eyes were rimmed red from rubbing them.

"You didn't like Barck when you went to his office that day, did you?" George asked.

"I had no grudge against him," Joe said. "I never had a dislike for him."

"Did you respect him as an official?"

Joe replied that he did.

"And did you respect, also, the problem he was dealing with in the matter of giving out relief?" George asked.

Joe stared ahead. "Yes," he said.[21]

"You knew it wasn't an easy job, didn't you?" George asked, and Joe said he knew.

"You just went there for relief and demanded it, didn't you?" George said.

"No, sir."[22]

George lifted from the prosecutor's desk the grocery check for eight dollars that Anna Scutellaro had received in the mail the morning the poormaster was killed. George entered it into evidence, along with the envelope Chief McFeely had made Anna sign when she had been forced to relinquish the relief.

Isn't this the relief that arrived at your home while you were in the poormaster's office that morning? George asked.

"I hadn't known about it then!" Joe protested, and began to sob. He was visibly trembling.

Sam Leibowitz jumped up and accused William George of "torturing Scutellaro with a lot of unnecessary questions to wear him down." Over the sounds of Joe Scutellaro's loud weeping, his lawyer requested a short recess.[23]

But after it was over, it soon became clear to both prosecution and defense that the break had changed nothing. When Joe returned to the witness box ten minutes later, he was not able to answer one question put to him by the prosecutor. Joe sat and cried and seemed unable to stop. After eleven minutes passed without a response to George's queries, the lawyers conferred with Judge Kinkead, and both agreed that Joe Scutellaro should be temporarily withdrawn as a witness, to regain his composure.[24]

————————— ✺ —————————

Leibowitz called Dr. Lawrence J. Kelly. The young doctor had been a hospital intern when he had been called the year before to assist Harry Barck. He was now a licensed physician.

Dr. Kelly's clarity and assurance on the stand made a striking contrast to Joe's opacity. Under Leibowitz's questioning, the doctor detailed his activities in the poormaster's office that February morning. As a further twit to the state's star witness, the criminal defender made sure that Kelly recalled his request that Barck be moved to a reclining position to allow for a better examination.[25]

Kelly had been prepared to leave Barck's office for the hospital, he testified, but Chief McFeely asked him to stay. While waiting in the poormaster's office, Kelly heard McFeely ask Joe Scutellaro what he'd done with the paper file. Scutellaro had explained that he'd pulled it out of the poormaster. Chief McFeely had responded, "You pulled it *out* of him? Who put it *in* him?" Joe had denied stabbing Harry Barck, Kelly said. The defendant—who the doctor described as "timid and meek and in a confused state of mind"—had told the police chief that Barck had "fallen over the desk and rammed his chest on the file."[26]

As Leibowitz continued with his questioning, Kelly confirmed that Joe had told McFeely that a fight had caused Barck to fall. But then Kelly added, "Scutellaro said that he had been coming for relief for some time and had been refused." Quoting Joe, the doctor testified: "Mr. Barck would say 'Next! Next!' and today, today it got so that I could not stand it anymore, and I took a punch at Mr. Barck."[27]

Not a fight caused by an offensive remark about the relief client's wife, but a punch thrown after a refusal of aid, after Joe Scutellaro "could not stand it anymore." Leibowitz quickly sought to gloss over the damning remark. He had Kelly repeat Joe's assertion that Barck had "stuck himself when he fell over the desk," then followed it with a question to establish Kelly's independence as a witness.[28]

"Did you ever know me personally?" Leibowitz asked.

"No sir," Kelly replied.

"Did you ever have any business with me?"

"No."

"Did you ever know this Italian man by the name of Scutellaro in your life before you saw him there in Barck's office?"

"No."

"Is there any reason under the sun, any interest that you have, any interest whatever, for you to come to court here and try to help this defendant unless you are telling the truth on the witness stand?"

"None," the doctor said.[29]

In his cross-examination, William George made it plain that he, too, believed Dr. Kelly's testimony—*all of it*. He had Kelly twice repeat his prior assertion that he had heard Joe Scutellaro tell Chief McFeely, "*Today it got so I could not stand it any longer, so I took a punch at Mr. Barck.*"[30]

And when Joe Scutellaro was again returned to the witness box after a lunch recess, George picked up his questioning of the defendant from that point. "What did you do or say after you told Barck that your wife is a decent woman?" George asked Joe.

The courtroom, which had been humming with the low chatter and rustling of trial observers, grew quiet. Joe drew his hand over his forehead as if he was clearing something away, but he said nothing.

"You still haven't answered me. Why?" George asked, after several minutes had passed.

Joe stared ahead. A *New York Times* reporter, seated by the rail with other journalists, observed that the defendant "seemed to be in a stupor" and was crying again.[31]

Finally, Joe said he was afraid. "You are afraid of me?" George repeated. "Please tell me—why?"

"Because you are the prosecutor," Joe said.

"You are afraid of me because I am the prosecutor, because you know I am trying to see to it that you tell the truth?"

"No, that you are trying to convict me," Joe said.

George's pointed reply—that he would convict Joe Scutellaro "upon the truth in this case," rather than the testimony calmly elicited by his defense lawyer—was stricken from the record.

"Mr. Scutellaro, is your desire that I ask you no more questions?" George asked, but Joe said nothing. "Is it?" George asked again, and received no reply.

Leibowitz came forward to ask Kinkead's permission to speak with his client privately, in the presence of the court. When the judge agreed, Leibowitz spoke softly to Joe, who held his head in his hands. Kinkead suggested that Leibowitz call another witness while the defendant recovered. As the defendant shuffled away from the stand, his lawyer called Reverend C. Robert Pedersen, pastor of the First Baptist Church of Hoboken—a man of moral authority—to recount Harry Barck's misdeeds.[32]

Sam Leibowitz had been as careful in his selection of witnesses as he had been in jury selection. Surely he had read about Herman Matson and knew the daring activist could have supplied him with vivid accounts of Harry Barck's denial of aid and also chilling details of the McFeelys' clenched domination of the city. But the defense attorney could not risk associating his client with an organizer of the jobless poor. Instead, through his research, Leibowitz had found Reverend Pedersen, the pastor who had publicly advocated on behalf of one poor, pleading family—the Hasties—and who could recall in detail his own unsavory encounters with the Hoboken poormaster. Tracing back issues of the local newspapers, Leibowitz had discovered that six weeks before Donald Hastie's death from starvation, the pastor of Hoboken's First Baptist Church had entered into a public war of words with Barck over the poormaster's unwillingness to provide enough aid to the boy's family. Leibowitz would have reckoned that jurors who had read about Donald's death would not have easily forgotten the awful news. By calling Pedersen to testify, the defense lawyer meant to call up memories of Harry Barck's most egregious offense.[33]

But before Leibowitz could begin, all attention was diverted to the horrible sound of Joe Scutellaro collapsing, tumbling head first so that "the thud of his head striking the marble floor could be heard through the crowded courtroom." Now motion and noise overwhelmed all courtroom decorum. Observers stood to watch, and newspaper reporters hustled to leave the room to call in the news. Anna Scutellaro's cries pierced through the buzzing chatter. Court matrons led Anna and her children, who clung to her hands, from the spectator's benches to the exit doors.

As the attendants led the way through the bronze doors, the white flash and crackle of camera bulbs seemed to rush toward the weeping family, like a lightning storm sweeping through the corridor.[34]

Inside Judge Kinkead's court, four officers lifted the unconscious defendant and, shouldering his rigid form, carried Joe into the jury room. Kinkead struggled to restore order. When the noise had ebbed sufficiently to allow him to be heard, the judge declared another recess to allow Joe's examination by a physician.[35]

Twenty minutes later, Dr. Murray Levin, a Jersey City Medical Center intern who had arrived by ambulance, announced to the court: "This man is not in shape to go on." Joe had regained consciousness but was to be returned to the county jail and placed under observation. Dr. Levin then left to see to Anna Scutellaro. She had been near collapse when she left court, and the attending matrons had taken her to another room.[36]

Kinkead recalled the jurors and had witnesses summoned to the courtroom. Sam Leibowitz cited Dr. Levin's conclusion and requested the trial be postponed for the evening because of "the shock" the defendant had suffered. William George concurred. With Judge Kinkead's apologies and his request for the forbearance of witnesses and the jury, court was adjourned until the following morning, Friday, January 13.[37]

Once again the defendant was led into court in handcuffs. Although he had received treatment at the jail's clinic, he would not be returned to the witness stand. With a guard beside him, Joe Scutellaro would sit out the rest of his trial on the prisoner's bench and stare at the parade of defense witnesses called to herald his good character—or to defame Harry Barck. Among the character witnesses were a priest from St. Ann's Church who described Joe as "honest and God-fearing"; a Franciscan brother who recalled performing Joe and Anna's marriage and noted that the Scutellaro's ten-year anniversary was but a few weeks away; and Joe's doctor from the Jersey City Medical Center clinic, who read from his patient's records and described the disquieting symptoms of *encephalitis lethargica*. The illness brought tremors and confusion and a strange flattening of expression; the face of a sufferer might appear unresponsive, the doctor said—even when that person was fully aware of what was going on around him.[38]

William George was gentle with these witnesses. He would not challenge testimony on Joe's faith, his loving marriage, or his ill health. But when Leibowitz had completed his direct examination of Joseph Vincent, the district supervisor of the New Jersey State Employment Service, the assistant prosecutor became confrontational. Vincent had testified to his own unpleasant exchanges with Harry Barck and to the bitter complaints of hundreds of Hoboken job seekers. The poormaster had always been "vicious, quarrelsome, and irascible," Vincent said, and had even been known to shove people out of his office after denying them aid.[39]

George hammered away at Vincent's assertions, what he claimed to have heard from "hundreds" of clients. He meant to challenge Leibowitz's implication that Barck's insults were an outrage equal to a deadly attack. And in all your conversations with Hoboken job seekers, George asked the witness, had Barck's reputation included inflicting bodily injuries on *any* person?

The defense objected, but Judge Kinkead allowed the question. "To my knowledge, it did not," Vincent admitted.[40]

But Leibowitz was determined to establish Barck's bad character. He had greater success when he again called Reverend Pedersen to the witness stand. Under Leibowitz's questioning, the minister recalled his repeated attempts to obtain public aid for the Hastie family.

Pedersen said he had only recently arrived in Hoboken, when the Hasties' troubles became severe. At first, he sought no municipal aid for them, but marshaled his parishioners to provide charity directly. James Hastie had lost his job at a local battery factory, and after initially receiving assistance through the state program, he had been cut off when Barck purged the Hoboken relief rolls in April 1936. First Baptist congregants agreed to pay the Hastie family's modest rent—James exchanged janitorial services for the rent reduction—and supplied food parcels and milk for the three boys. Nevertheless, by mid-May, the pastor recalled, the church's stopgap measures were failing. The family had lost its electricity and gas because of nonpayment, and they had run out of the oil they'd been burning for light.[41]

James had begged the pastor to intervene. Maybe Barck would listen to a clergyman. But Pedersen learned that Barck would *not*—no matter how many times he confronted the overseer. Citing the municipal budget, Harry Barck had bluntly refused to assist the Hasties and, in dismissing Pedersen, had suggested that freeloaders had taken in the gullible minister.

Not long after, Barck responded publicly to mounting criticism of the cuts he had made in relief—cuts that had abandoned thousands of Hoboken children to hunger. The press release Barck issued to defend his policies must have been haunting for the minister to recall. "Nobody is starving in Hoboken," Harry Barck had declared.[42]

William George allowed the minister to step down without further questioning. With Pedersen's testimony, Leibowitz had revealed to jurors an all-powerful bureaucrat who could blithely deny, based on his false "understanding" of the jobless poor, what was readily apparent to a politically neutral newcomer: that a Hoboken family was starving and needed public relief to survive.

But who had given Harry Barck such powers? Leibowitz would now call to the stand Joseph Clark, the former Hoboken commissioner whose recollections of Boss-directed attacks on his Italian political opponents had been featured in the notorious *Post* exposé of the McFeely tribe. Leibowitz was going to try to advance his claim that the McFeelys commanded the city and every person employed in the Hall.

Joseph Clark had been a police officer for twenty years prior to his ascension to city commissioner, and he had the requisite height and heavy build of a Hoboken cop. But he also had a sad, hangdog face that would have registered hurt when trial observers snickered at his current occupation: caretaker of seven children. Court spectators only learned later, through Leibowitz's continued questioning, that Clark had become a widower in the early years of the Depression and that he had been unable to find new employment since his forced resignation, in 1934, from his Hoboken commissioner's post.[43]

Clark had once been considered McFeely's "closest friend," but the two had split violently when Commissioner Clark, as overseer of the police department, had tried to press charges against the mayor's brother for lounging at home, drunk, instead of reporting for duty as the chief of police. Clark had feared he would be "thrown out of the window" for challenging the mayor. Instead, the former commissioner had been crushed by job loss.[44]

William George knew very well why Leibowitz had called Joseph Clark as a defense witness. The assistant prosecutor vigorously blocked every question the defender asked that would have allowed testimony on Boss McFeely's rule. Twenty-five times George objected, and twenty-five times Judge Kinkead upheld him. Finally Leibowitz limited his queries to Clark's knowledge of Harry Barck. Clark said he had known the poormaster for thirty years and that Harry Barck's reputation was really "very bad." The poormaster, he testified, had a reputation for insulting women.[45]

In a sense, trial testimony ended there. The late-afternoon session, devoted to the examination of rebuttal witnesses, introduced little of value to prosecution or defense, and so often devolved into verbal sparring between the lead attorneys that Judge Kinkead issued an exasperated scolding to both. By then trial spectators could also see snow falling outside the courtroom window, and the attention of the restless among them had likely wandered during the proceeding's more tedious moments, to thoughts of traffic conditions for their return journey home.

After rebuttals and counter-rebuttals, testimony came to a close with Leibowitz's curt declaration, "That is all." Judge Kinkead adjourned court until 10:00 AM the next morning, when the two lawyers were to make their final arguments before the jury.[46]

14 | THE HAND OF GOD

OVERNIGHT, WINTER RETURNED. A steady snowfall buried the crocuses that had blossomed in uptown gardens during the preceding false spring. Saturday morning, January 14, emerged with a cloud-thickened sky and the lows of Hudson River ships carrying across Hoboken.

Eight inches of snow now covered the city's pocked streets, temporarily erasing evidence of debris scattered by the McFeely Company's open horse carts. At daybreak, before footprints and shovels unearthed the familiar, the streets and yards of downtown were dizzying to behold, with sudden sweeps of white replacing steps and clothesline stakes recast as sugared steeples. The accumulation would, in the end, turn too slushy for a full weekend of sledding or for packing the best snowballs; but on first viewing, Sixth and Monroe Streets, and every other block in Hoboken, would have seemed transformed.[1]

Little Joe Scutellaro was too young to know the particular delights of a "snow day" or to understand the disappointment of a Friday night snowfall to the city's schoolchildren. But neither he nor his more knowledgeable sister would be playing outside, anyway. Instead, the Scutellaro children were bundled into their well-worn woolens and too-small winter coats and readied to travel to the Hudson County Courthouse. They knew they would see their father there, but they did not know much more.

Traffic moved slowly out of the city that morning—everything and everyone slowed by the snow. The glittering blanket draped over every

ordinary house and gate and walkway had made Hoboken unreal—
starry and soft-edged, where it was not.

———————— ⚓ ————————

The morning papers announced that state troopers would be stationed
outside the chambers of the New Jersey Assembly on Monday, to block
the Newark grocers and relief clients who planned to arrive that evening by the busload. Under the state formula, Newark, as New Jersey's
largest city, was owed about $2 million for the preceding year's relief
outlay. Protestors would demand their repayment and also insist that
legislators come up with a plan to meet current relief needs. But in
calling for state troopers, Assembly Speaker Herbert J. Pascoe seemed
determined to treat the planned statehouse march as a threat to legislators' dignity, rather than a sign of frustration with legislative inaction.
"There will be no sit-in strikes such as disgraced the session several
years ago," Pascoe announced. The troopers, the speaker vowed, would
keep dissenters from the assembly's galleries, to prevent "any undue
demonstration."[2]

Scutellaro trial jurors read the newspapers that morning, and some
might have been alarmed by the thought of the poor clamoring at the
statehouse doors. But the papers had not even hinted at the true depth
of New Jersey's relief crisis—the untold numbers receiving no federal or
state assistance and little, if any, aid on the local level. No reports mentioned that in the preceding year, nearly half of New Jersey's 567 municipalities had received no state payments at all for general relief.[3]

———————— ⚓ ————————

Leibowitz arrived in court ten minutes late and apologized to Judge
Kinkead and the jury. Although he had rushed to get to the courtroom,
the criminal defender would have noticed the adjoining hall and balconies were empty. Fearing demonstrations and disorder, the judge had
relegated Joe's supporters to the icy steps outside the building.[4]

"Please forgive me for appearing tired in pleading for this man's life,"
Leibowitz began, after Kinkead acknowledged the defense attorney's

readiness to offer a summation. The half-moons under Leibowitz's eyes were deeper and more pronounced than usual, and his face was unshaved. His eyes had the gleam of too little sleep and too much coffee.

He explained to the jury that he had not slept, as another murder case had demanded his attention. He would not go into the details—Leibowitz had been retained to defend a Bronx milliner, Louis Greenfield, for the "mercy killing" of his severely handicapped son—but the lawyer let them know that he had worked through the night.[5]

Leibowitz's rough appearance that morning was likely a matter of choice, for he surely could have taken a few moments to shave before court, had he wanted to. But he had seized upon an opportunity for a bit of theater, a demonstration of his dedication: Leibowitz's stubble could be read as a sign of the demands made upon him as a famous defender, or it could portray an image more familiar to the jurors—the look of an ordinary man, straggling in after a hard day's work.[6]

Leibowitz pushed forward with his client's defense, beginning his summation in a calm, measured voice. "Although the law says the burden is on the state, the burden is on Joseph F. Scutellaro in proving he is innocent," Leibowitz said. His client had been paraded into court each day in manacles, as though Joe were a savage in need of containment. But the case before the jury was not about a brute, Leibowitz insisted, nor was it even about the act of murder. "This is not by the widest stretch of the imagination a murder case," he said.

Picking up the desk spindle the state's attorney had entered into evidence, Leibowitz acknowledged "there is no question that Barck died on February 25, 1938, from a wound, as testified by Dr. Braunstein—a wound inflicted by an implement." The lawyer plainly described the spindle piercing the poormaster's body. "The main issue in this case," Leibowitz announced—using a familiar refrain—"is what happened in that room," between the man who had died and the man accused of killing him.

The defender briefly addressed—and just as quickly dismissed—the testimony of Barck secretaries Shea, Mullin, and Cerutti, "who did not see what happened." And so "we come to the alleged eyewitness, Miss Eleonore Hartmann," Leibowitz continued. A hint of sarcasm had edged into his voice. He would spend much longer taking apart the secretary's false claims than the assertions of her peers, pointing out portions of Hartmann's testimony that were illogical or, to his mind, coached. He had not been able to fully unmask her on the stand, but he intended to do so now.

What had Miss Hartmann claimed she had seen? Leibowitz asked. He read her testimony about Joe's "lunge" at the poormaster. "She said she didn't see *anything* in Mr. Scutellaro's hand," Leibowitz pointed out. "I'll tell you why—because if you get a witness like that and she is telling the truth, a jury would think she had seen too much. A very clever woman made that up. That is better drama, better stagecraft. This story has been gone over many times, and this lady knew exactly what she was to tell on the witness stand." The testimony of Miss Eleonore Hartmann, he asserted, had been "gone over with a fine comb—not once but many times."

"This woman lied for a reason," Leibowitz continued. "Who is this woman? Just see what her interests are in this case. Is she a disinterested witness? First of all, Barck had known her since she was a little baby. They were neighbors. She used to pal with Barck's daughters. Barck was her employer. Barck was a man who gave her her bread and butter, her boss, her superior. She worked with him day after day, so you see the close relationship there." The lawyer's speech turned cloying. "A kindly, charitable, genial man," he said, paraphrasing Hartmann's testimony.

"Look at the axe she has to grind," Leibowitz suggested, his voice rising in indignation. "Well, it pays to be on the side of the administration that hired her. I don't need any evidence to establish that. It pays to be on the side of the state, and Hoboken is part of the state. She is not a civil service employee—she is hired. That may have something to do with it. She may not want to offend someone in Hoboken. That is a natural impulse."

But Eleonore Hartmann had not simply been *reluctant* to speak. "'I knew better than to talk to the other side of the case,' was her response to a question," Leibowitz pointed out. "Disinterested witness? She's in a camp, she's on a *team!* A witness is a witness, and many may be questioned by 'the other side.' She was like a politician rooting for his party." Leibowitz reminded the jurors of Miss Hartmann's refusal to talk to defense cocounsel about the case. "Imagine anyone trying to bulldoze anyone in city hall!" Leibowitz said, feigning the disbelief of a Hoboken ward heeler.

The defense attorney reminded the jurymen that important trials brought a certain amount of notoriety to those involved, elevating in stature even the most minor figures who had little to do with the events detailed in the courtroom. Eleonore Hartmann's tale had grown larger and more important, as needed. "She had a little talk with someone in city hall and she became an eyewitness," Leibowitz asserted. Never mind the truth. "It's only a little wop—only a nobody," he said. But "who bears the cross?" the lawyer asked. "Who is the martyr? This poor, unhappy man, who can barely find the energy to stand."

Leibowitz pointed to his ghostly client. "If you are going to crucify a man on stuff that came from sources of that kind—go ahead and do it, but stop calling it America!" he exclaimed. There would be no justice then. "To convict a man on stuff and nonsense!" Leibowitz continued. "Would you bank your life on that woman's story? How sure are you? I submit to you that she was not in the room at all when it happened. She is contradicted by every other state witness."

He reminded them of the testimony of Nick Russo and John Galdi. If Hartmann's claims are "just a fabrication, a figment of her imagination," he said, "then the state's case fails." And surely her testimony was false. "Why would Barck want to blow the whistle if the policeman and Miss Hartmann were there?" Leibowitz asked. "Barck blew the whistle because there was no one in the room."

The defender asked the jurymen to question how they could convict a man who may have been railroaded, to imagine "getting into a corner" and having the authorities decide, "This Italian, we ought to make an example of him; if we don't convict him, there will be murder in Hoboken."

Joe Scutellaro had been visibly trembling throughout the first part of his lawyer's summation, and now he slumped forward. While Leibowitz paused for a moment and the jurors watched, a court attendant leaned in close and whispered to the defendant, and Joe seemed to revive.

Leibowitz directed their attention to Anna Scutellaro and her children, seated in the same seats they had occupied throughout the trial. "What about the two little kiddies and the woman who are waiting to see what twelve men are going to do—whether they are going to break up a family and send him to the electric chair?" Leibowitz's voice was soft and pleading. Anna's sobs could be heard throughout the courtroom, though she tried to muffle them. Her son had climbed into her lap, and she pressed her face against him. From their position at the front of the room, reporters noted a few jurymen sweeping aside tears with their fingers.

"The one thing George is interested in is getting a conviction," Leibowitz now declared, deftly launching an attack on the assistant prosecutor's motives for threatening the death penalty, while diverting attention away from the defense's own need for a restorative victory. "If it's glory he wants, let him have it," Leibowitz said with a weary sigh. "I am tired of glory, tired of publicity. I am getting along in years. I am tired of getting out of bed in the middle of the night. If I could give the glory I have to George in exchange for this defendant, I'd gladly do it."

Assistant Prosecutor George, as the local lawyer, had been unfair, Leibowitz insisted. There had been rumors and innuendo about out-of-town counsel. "Counsel is a rogue, he is from New York," Leibowitz said. "I heard 'the lawyer from New York' coming a thousand miles away from here. I heard it in the 'Dark Belt,'" he said—an allusion to the Scottsboro case. "That is not honesty. It is prejudice of the refined sort, calculated to make men say, 'Well, that fellow from New York, where criminals live and men are rogues.' I have heard it when things were not so good, and I have heard it in this courtroom. Well, I am not ashamed of coming from New York. Many of you men travel across the river to earn your livelihood there." But William George, Leibowitz suggested, had interjected this prejudice into the proceedings, intimating, "You've got to show that lawyer he can't win in Hudson County with a local boy." The defender added, "I wonder if that got across to the jury."

The prejudice against his client, as a man on relief, would be harder for Leibowitz to combat. Although the Depression had upended the beliefs of many, the veteran defender surely knew that the "blue ribbon" jurymen he now addressed were not likely to challenge the status quo. Leibowitz would steer clear of anything that would remind the jury of organized radicals. Instead, he would call upon the jurors' conservative notions of charity and their sense of fairness and right behavior toward their fellow man. Joe Scutellaro, Leibowitz insisted, was not one to *demand* his rights. His client had faithfully followed Barck's arbitrary rules, and still his family had been denied enough to eat.

Leibowitz again detailed the privation of the Scutellaro family. Joe's father, he said, had once owned property, "but the property now owns the father." The defender described the meager breakfast Joe, Anna, and their children had shared the morning of February 25. "It's a hard thing for a person with a full stomach to define hunger. Have you ever tried to feed four persons on twenty-five cents a day?" Leibowitz asked. "Do you wonder that people are driven to desperation?" Leibowitz shook his head in disbelief. "I'm disappointed not so much with Mr. Barck, but at a system that permits poor people to starve on $5.70 a month for four. There is something rotten there somewhere." Now the lawyer's disparaging tone became a plea. "Good God, how can such things exist among us when we pride ourselves as being the best nation in the world?" he implored. "It was no pleasure for this man to go to Barck's office. . . . When hunger calls and children cry, you put your pride in your pocket and go."[7]

But Harry Barck, Leibowitz insisted, was "a man inured to suffering, treating people not like human beings but like cheap objects, who had the poor in the palm of his dirty hand and crushed them like eggshells." Of course, he hastened to add, "Barck could have been the worst creature that was ever made—bad though he was, he had a right to live. The fact that a man's character is bad, that he is a wretch, is not just cause to violate a law." Nevertheless, the poormaster's bad character had to be discussed. Multiple defense witnesses had described Barck as "heartless, vicious, quarrelsome, and abusive of the poor over whom he had jurisdiction," Leibowitz said. But harsh as they were, those words did not fully convey Barck's dissociation from the poor. In preparing for his summation, the criminal defender had conjured various "word pictures" to describe the poormaster. At first Leibowitz had likened Harry Barck to a piece of machinery. But the lawyer finally settled on a metaphor that would not only recall the tyranny his parents had escaped when they left Romania but would also bring to mind the many tyrants that had emerged since. The Hoboken poormaster, Leibowitz declared, was a kind of "imperious czar," an autocrat "who became a Hitler, a Mussolini, a Stalin."[8]

What had happened when the poormaster, a ruler of "his own little world," had heard the pleas of weak and needy Joe Scutellaro? "Barck boiled to have a poor, little unfortunate coming in there who couldn't speak above a whisper," Leibowitz said. How could Scutellaro be the kind of man who would go there to start trouble? "Why even Miss Hartmann said that the man spoke so low that Barck had to say to him, 'Speak louder.'" Scutellaro had gone to the poormaster because his children were starving. "Did he go there with malice in his heart?" Leibowitz asked. "If he did, wouldn't he have gone prepared? He knew there was a cop at the door, that he couldn't escape. If he was going there to attack that man, wouldn't he have gone prepared with a knife, a stiletto, or something?"

"There was no malice in Scutellaro's heart when he went to Barck's office," Leibowitz asserted. "He carried no weapons of any kind in his pockets." The two men had scuffled in the office following Barck's suggestion that Anna Scutellaro work the streets as a prostitute. "Ask any American to take that from a no-good dog like that, who brought his own death on his shoulders. If you had a club handy, you'd have batted his brains out," Leibowitz declared. And yet Joe Scutellaro had done nothing of the sort, the defense lawyer insisted; Barck had accidentally been impaled on the spike during the struggle between the two men.

Now Leibowitz reached for an unlikely defense: he would attribute the killing of Harry Barck to the hand of a vengeful God. He had used this argument at nearly a dozen trials, always with great success. The defense seemed to work because so many jurors, even if they did not attend a house of worship, believed human actions were overseen by a higher power or were fated. Or maybe those jurors simply did not want to send to the chair an ordinary person who, in extremis, had made a fatal mistake.

"It is my belief that the culprit responsible for Barck's death is not Joseph Scutellaro. It is not even Barck," Leibowitz began. "The responsibility rests with a system which expects a man to live in this great democracy under such shameful circumstances. If Barck had not pushed this man aside and had been mindful of his misery and suffering, this would not have happened! It was the hand of God that struck down Harry L. Barck, for all the misery he had brought on the poor and unfortunate. It was the hand of God that struck down Harry Barck."[9]

And Harry Barck, Leibowitz was quick to remind the jury, was a McFeely stalwart. The poormaster's death would not be ruled an accident when the political machine wanted Joe Scutellaro to go down for murder. Dr. Kelly had testified that Chief McFeely had been present when Scutellaro said it was an accident. "If that *isn't* what he told McFeely, why didn't McFeely take the stand?" the defender asked. Chief McFeely had been readily available throughout the trial. "He has been sitting in a chair of honor all week, smiling complacently," Leibowitz declared, pointing to the chief of police. "He didn't dare testify. If Dr. Kelly is telling the truth, their whole case is a miserable frame-up." The doctor—"that man Kelly"—Leibowitz said, is "like a bone in the throat" to the state.[10]

The defender now turned his wrath on Lieutenant Scott, who eyed Leibowitz warily. "Romeo Scott is a man who has never beaten a prisoner," Leibowitz said. "Just look at that face, just look at that face," the lawyer instructed, and the jurors turned to stare at the jowly, frowning officer. "He's a tough man—he showed it on the witness stand by his behavior. Just figure what he looks like down there where he is boss in his own station house."

Courtroom spectators leaned forward in a rapt state, hanging on Leibowitz's "every word," a *Times* reporter later wrote. Certainly observers from Hoboken would have been astonished by the defender's audacity. Sam Leibowitz was publicly confronting some of the city's most powerful and vengeful men.

Scott "didn't have to lay a hand on him," Leibowitz continued. "He didn't have to strike him in the condition that he was in at that time." Just look at Scutellaro's alleged confession, the defender added. Look at the defendant's shaky signature. It was a confession that had been coerced. "I don't care what is written on that paper. If Romeo Scott took the defendant into the room and"—Leibowitz now raised a clenched fist—"*threatened* him, this confession is worthless." He walked over to where Scott was sitting and cooed, "My pal, my nice little pal." Then the defender turned and approached his client. Putting his arm around Joe's slight shoulders, Leibowitz nodded in Scott's direction and repeated, "*My pal.*"

Leibowitz paused, perhaps to gather strength: he had been speaking for nearly three hours. But his voice betrayed no fatigue as he neared his conclusion. The defender challenged, then entreated the twelve jurors to acquit his client. "You may as well send him to the electric chair as behind gray prison walls," Leibowitz announced, disparaging the idea of prison as an acceptable middle ground between freedom and a death sentence. The lawyer circled around the defense table and picked up a

212 | KILLING THE POORMASTER

paper cup. It was "smart business," he said, to buy one cup for a nickel and then to ask a dollar for it, making a later compromise seem reasonable. It was smart business, too, Leibowitz continued, for the state to ask for "any kind of conviction."

But the man before them, Joe Scutellaro, "is either guilty or not guilty," Leibowitz declared, returning the flimsy cup to the table. "I am praying to Almighty God that when you get in there, you will agree with the defense and let him walk out of here a free man after almost a year in prison for something he didn't do."

Leibowitz's voice was now accompanied by the "audible sobs" of Joe's relatives. Jurors dabbed at their eyes, perhaps responding as strongly to the Scutellaro family's raw distress as to the theatrical power of Joe's defender. "I am going to pray to God Almighty that men are not weak enough to sell their souls and their own consciences when one man says 'guilty' and ten or eleven say he is not—to compromise," Leibowitz said. "While you're in there, I will die a thousand deaths waiting for your verdict, but what I want is a just verdict, based on the evidence. Send this man home to his family."

At 3:00 PM, after a recess, court reconvened. The assistant prosecutor would have to follow a summation at least one reporter described as "the most masterful ever heard in the courthouse." But William George would have betrayed no uncertainty. He had years of experience with Hudson County jurors, and he was not about to be undermined on his own turf.[11]

George began with praise for Leibowitz's skilled summation, then doubled back to condemn it. The famous Sam Leibowitz, George said, had used his legendary eloquence to vilify "the whole prosecution." The defender had insinuated that the state's attorneys sought only a conviction, not justice, George charged, and Leibowitz had accused *him* of being a glory-seeker. "If there is anyone in this box, who, because he may know me and decide to further my ambitions, and for that reason and only that reason convict this defendant, let him speak up," George announced, "because I want to sleep the sleep of a babe tonight." He challenged jurors to refuse the defender's disreputable charge that the prosecutor's office, in cahoots with Hoboken police, would stop at nothing—perjury, threats, a false confession—to convict Joseph Scutellaro.[12]

The jurors should follow the evidence, George said. Much had been made of Harry Barck's insulting remark about Anna Scutellaro, for example, but Mrs. Scutellaro, the assistant prosecutor pointed out, had failed to testify.

An angry Sam Leibowitz called out an objection. When it was denied, he asked for an exception. Mrs. Scutellaro, the defense attorney announced when his request was granted, was not present when she was insulted by the poormaster, so there was no need to call her.

The assistant prosecutor continued, seemingly unperturbed by Leibowitz's interruption. George defended the state's witnesses, paying special attention to the ridiculed Hoboken police lieutenant J. Romeo Scott. "Scott is not a graduate of Yale University," George said, implying that the famous defense attorney was a coddled elitist. "Scott's childhood was not protected and nurtured by a French governess." The Hoboken cop, the assistant prosecutor continued, was "just a fellow like you and me."

George paused, perhaps considering that some jurors might know that Sam Leibowitz had come up from the streets of New York's Lower East Side. "Every one of us here has sprung from the common people," the assistant prosecutor continued, "but some of us have had better opportunities. J. Romeo Scott became an ordinary cop twenty-three years ago." Surely Scott had not used "the finest of language," George conceded, but the officer was a plainspoken man. The assistant prosecutor asked the jurors to credit the Hoboken police officer with honesty.[13]

William George returned again to Leibowitz's fancy oratory, which the prosecutor had studied in preparation for their legal contest. Sam Leibowitz so savored his own rhetoric, George charged, that the phrases the defender favored resurfaced in trial after trial. And indeed they did. "I have been around and I have heard summations before," George chided. "I have heard summations similar to [the one we heard today,] by the same man, almost word for word. It is the result of a legal philosophy which has padded the career of this celebrated lawyer, which has given him a reputation [that] causes the various news agencies to follow him around the country. Gentlemen of the jury, if your families have saved the newspapers containing stories of this trial, you will see what I mean. He is news. He is Sam Leibowitz. He has a big reputation." The jurors, George warned, should be wary of Leibowitz's "stock-in-trade" manner of preying on their sympathies.

To make his point memorable, George stole a page from Leibowitz's book and offered the jurors a visual reference: the worn slippers, belonging to Scutellaro's daughter, that Leibowitz had tried—and failed—to introduce into evidence. The little scuffed shoes had remained on the counsel table all day, George said, so the jury could see them. "If this case is based only on sympathy, I say to you, 'Acquit him,'" George declared. "But in doing so you will prostitute your oath, and you will violate the integrity which this disinterested judge believes you have."

Similarly, George insisted the jurors not be swayed by the defendant's gaunt appearance, nor should they reflect upon his hunger. Those conditions did not make his actions acceptable. Remember Harry Barck's difficult line of work, George cautioned the jury. Remember that Barck was a public relief official working with a scant budget. "If a man hasn't got the money to pass out in the quantities someone believes he should have," George asked, his voice rising, "should he be murdered?"

Leibowitz immediately rose to complain that the assistant prosecutor's comment was inflammatory, and Kinkead ordered it stricken from the record. "If Mr. Scutellaro asked me for relief, and I could give it to him, I'd give it to him just as quickly as Mr. Leibowitz," George said. Again he shifted his attack to encompass the defender and his client. "One's heart can bleed profusely for a client who pays him to prevent his conviction of a proper charge of murder," George said.

Again Leibowitz objected. There is no evidence in the case that I am being paid, the defense attorney protested. "These are some of the hitting-below-the-belt tactics I complained of," he grumbled to the judge. Kinkead agreed that the comment was unfortunate, but the jurist was less concerned about Leibowitz's reputation than he was about Scutellaro's. He didn't think it fair, he said, for George "to intimate that this man, who was on relief, had sufficient funds to bring over counsel and create the impression that he was a fakir."

"There are many cases in which I have not received a nickel," Leibowitz continued, still fuming over the assistant prosecutor's remark. "I'm for the underdog," he said, "and it's not fair for Mr. George to assume anything but the evidence."

"I'm willing to leave that to the understanding of any twelve intelligent men who understand what is going on in this country," George retorted. Leibowitz again objected and was again sustained.

When George resumed speaking, his voice was thick with tamped anger. "If the time comes when you will be permitted to take by law what you want, even if it is necessary to take what man can't create—a human life—it will be bad," he warned, shaking his head. "This defendant is a schemer," he announced. "He is not so innocent as he would like us to believe." Yes, George admitted, they had all witnessed Joseph Scutellaro's blank stares and his inability to respond to questions in court. The defendant's afflictions, the assistant prosecutor could not help but notice, had been most pronounced when Scutellaro was being cross-examined by the prosecution. But Joseph Scutellaro had not been "in a stupor on February 25," George asserted. On that day, the defendant "was alert. He reeked with venom." Joseph Scutellaro had stabbed Harry Barck on that day, George declared, because the relief claimant had been enraged that Poormaster Barck had not rushed a check to him when Scutellaro had demanded one.

Now, George said, the jurors were witnessing Scutellaro's genuine distress at the horror his rage had wrought. Scutellaro's faltering testimony was not "phony," George assured the jury, but the "result of strain. For eleven months, the ghost of Barck has haunted and plagued Scutellaro. He saw the blood of Barck on his hands. That's why he was nervous."[14]

And what about the testimony of Dr. Kelly? George asked, his voice now calm, almost casual. The doctor, he said, "is no bone in my throat, but a dagger to the side of Mr. Leibowitz." After all, George continued, it was Dr. Kelly, a *defense* witness, who had recalled Scutellaro's words: "Today it got so I could not stand it any longer, so I took a punch at Mr. Barck." Dr. Kelly "told the truth," George said, and the doctor's testimony contradicted the defendant's claim that the fight with the Hoboken poormaster had been sparked by an insulting comment about Mrs. Scutellaro.

George also found suspect Scutellaro's description of Harry Barck's fall onto the desk spindle. "We can't violate the laws of gravity," the assistant prosecutor declared. "We fall *back*." George now called upon one of his colleagues, Louis Messano, to help him with a demonstration—again imitating one of Leibowitz's techniques. The criminal defender must have been furious to see Messano and George reenact the demonstration *he* had previously directed, though now it would have a different outcome. Messano was heavyset, but as the shorter man, he played the role of Joe Scutellaro in the prosecutors' performance. There was no struggle between the two men, no grasping of lapels. Messano mimed a blow to his colleague's face, and George fell back.[15]

George next took the desk spindle and measured its length on a pad of paper, which he handed to Messano. "This defendant, in giving us a reenactment of the crime, was asked how Mr. Barck fell forward after he had been punched," the assistant prosecutor said. Joe Scutellaro, he continued, answered, "With his arms under him." But that posture would have made it impossible for the spindle to pierce his chest, George said. Leaning over the table with his arms under him, the assistant prosecutor demonstrated to the jury that the pillow formed by his arms kept his chest from touching the tip of the spindle, as marked on the pad held by his colleague.

"When Mr. Barck stood up, that instrument was pulled from his body," George continued. "Did *Mr. Barck* pull it out? He was still standing up. He was on the other side of the desk, and Scutellaro was on the far side." George paused for a moment. "What is the first normal reaction to pain?" he asked. "For Mr. Barck, as quickly as he felt the prick of his skin, to pull it out?" George ventured that if *he* were accidentally stabbed, he would certainly call for a doctor, instead of reaching for a police whistle. "You don't call doctors by police whistles. You call the police. You don't call police when you only want a doctor," he said. "Gentlemen of the jury," he continued, "I have asked you to believe the normal, reasonable properties of the mind of that human being, in those circumstances. If you do, there can be no altercation," he concluded, and therefore, there can be no accidental death.

George called upon the jury to find the defendant guilty as charged. "If I did not ask that, you would be the first to clamor for my dismissal from office," he said, and cautioned that if he called for anything less, "we would have a dangerous situation in this county and in the country." George encouraged the jurors to view their verdict as a bulwark against rebellious reliefers. Consider the "sit-down relief strike" in Trenton, he began.[16]

But Leibowitz jumped up to object, calling the assistant prosecutor's remark "highly inflammatory." Judge Kinkead upheld the defender's objection.[17]

George swiftly moved on to attack another defense claim: that politics played a role in the Scutellaro case. Although George well understood the sway a political boss could hold over a city's government and its population, he argued away defense suggestions that Bernard McFeely, and his family's many officeholders, were responsible for the desperation evinced in the Hoboken poormaster's office. Sam Leibowitz "read a long list of McFeelys for the same reason that Joe Clark was called here as a witness," George said. The former McFeely ally, now unemployed, was "called here for one purpose—to spit political venom." Again George insisted the jury consider the evidence alone. He asked them to find the defendant guilty, as indicted, of the "willful, deliberate" murder of Harry Barck.[18]

But Joe Scutellaro had been indicted for murder in the first degree. A jury verdict, "as indicted," would ordinarily result in a death sentence, though a recommendation of mercy could substitute death by electrocution with a life sentence at hard labor. Now, as Leibowitz had predicted, Assistant Prosecutor George withdrew his earlier call for the defendant's execution. "I do not ask that this defendant be electrocuted," George said. "God knows I do not want that." He opened the way for a "compromise" verdict of second-degree murder, bringing with it a maximum of thirty years imprisonment, or even manslaughter, with a maximum of ten—though he did not mention these alternatives. He only said he would "leave the rest of it to this great judge for whatever sentence is to be imposed," a statement Leibowitz called highly improper.[19]

The assistant prosecutor was prepared to close. "Tonight I will sleep the sleep of a child," he announced. "I will be able to look my God in the face. I have done my duty." William George raised his voice, overwhelming the sound of Joe Scutellaro's broken sobs. "I have given you implicitly, honestly, every aspect of this case," he declared, "and I know that you will find from the evidence a verdict of guilty as indicted."[20]

Both prosecution and defense would later praise Robert Kinkead for his courtesy and fairness during the trial and for the extreme care with which he charged the jury. If Sam Leibowitz had once questioned Kinkead's New Year's Day hobnobbing with Boss Hague, the defender would, at the close of the trial, reveal no concern over the judge's potential political bias. Leibowitz had observed Kinkead's gentle approach to Joe Scutellaro throughout the proceeding and had determined that the judge was "an upright man."[21]

Leibowitz's favorable view of Robert Kinkead would have been helped along by the jurist's ready incorporation of defense arguments into his thirty-five-minute charge to the jury. After explaining the different verdicts, the judge referred to the confession and to the defense's contention that it had been coerced. "If you believe the defendant's version of how Barck met his death, you must acquit," Kinkead said, noting that even if the jurors disregarded the claim of an accidental killing, they might still consider Scutellaro's right of self-defense if he was in a position that caused him to fear bodily harm—whether or not he was actually in danger.

Here, too, the judge followed Leibowitz's lead, inviting jurors to put Barck's character on trial. Kinkead asked the jury to carefully weigh witness testimony describing the Hoboken poormaster as "vicious, quarrelsome, irascible, and offensive." Consider the weight and stature of the two men, the judge urged the jurors. Consider Barck's frame of mind, knowing that Lena Fusco had spat on him prior to his meeting with the defendant.[22]

Kinkead also returned to Scutellaro's admission that he had been convicted of assault on a state relief officer and explained that Leibowitz had asked about it to test the defendant's credibility as a witness. That conviction, the judge warned, was not to be considered part of the trial.

By 6:30 PM Kinkead was done. The jurors were to be kept in session until they reached an agreement or were ready to report a disagreement, the judge said. "May Almighty God guide you in your deliberation in the jury room" so that the verdict you return will "serve the cause of justice, justice to the State of New Jersey, and justice to Joseph Scutellaro."

As the twelve men filed out of the courtroom to begin their deliberations, a squad of county police officers swept through the courthouse halls to evict any lingering spectators. Then the police locked the courthouse doors.[23]

During the first two hours of jury deliberation, Marie Scutellaro and her brother distracted themselves with play. The marble halls outside the Court of Oyer and Terminer, cleared now of their father's supporters, became their temporary playground. While their weary mother waited in court, Marie and little Joe took up a game of tag, sliding on the marble floors as they rounded the railing of the center well. After Marie tired of the diversion and returned to her mother's side, her little brother found several newsmen and photographers more than willing to pass the time pitching pennies.

Around 9 PM the jurors returned to the courtroom. When they asked the judge to clarify the circumstances required for acquittal, Joe's family must have felt its thrilling possibility—that Joe might soon be returned to them. But by midnight, no verdict had been returned. While Anna sat upright, knowing Joe would search for her as soon the officers returned him to court, Marie and little Joe stretched out on a court bench, falling asleep on thick "improvised beds made of overcoats."[24]

William George and his colleague Louis Messano left the courthouse just after midnight. Sam Leibowitz remained; but on the urging of his associates, he left Kinkead's court for another section of the building, where a couch was available. He had not slept for almost forty-eight hours.

Nevertheless, the defense lawyer found that he could not rest, and walked the courthouse corridors instead, stopping occasionally to chat with cocounsels Vincent Impellitteri and Thomas Tumulty or to smoke with newsmen waiting to report the outcome of the trial.

Just before 4 AM on Sunday, January 15, Judge Kinkead left for his Jersey City home. He would have to be called back to the courthouse when a verdict was announced. Leibowitz and his colleagues prepared to leave, too. The lawyers shrugged on their heavy winter coats. As they descended into the marble rotunda, a man called out to Leibowitz from the balcony. In the dimly lit great hall, the defense attorney tilted his head back to catch sight of the man who had shouted his name.

Wait! the court officer called out. *A verdict is expected.*[25]

Marie Scutellaro awakened abruptly at the sound of the judge's gavel. The tired girl sat up just long enough to climb from her makeshift bed into her mother's lap, then she returned to sleep.

It was 4:45 AM. The twelve jurors had filed back to announce their verdict to the trial participants and to the few observers permitted in court. Most were newspaper reporters and photographers.

All turned to watch as the pallid, gray-suited prisoner, moving "like a robot," was led into the room. Anna Scutellaro, seated in the same spot she had held throughout the trial, met her husband's gaze and smiled. But the strain behind that smile was great; when Joe shuffled past and could no longer see her face, Anna began to cry. Little Joe stirred and awakened from his slumber. *I'm hungry,* he wailed several times before Anna wiped her tears and settled the toddler with a bottle he had already drained of milk.[26]

Now came the jury's verdict. Joe did not react when the young foreman, Richard Van Horn, announced it: *manslaughter.* After a six-day trial and ten hours of deliberation, the jurors had determined that Joseph F. Scutellaro had killed Harry Barck "in a sudden transport of passion, in the heat of blood, or with reasonable provocation and without malice."[27]

How had they decided? Although one of the jurors later told the *Hudson Dispatch* that the panel had "agreed at the outset not to reveal to anyone what transpired in the jury room," several newspapers quickly printed accounts of the jury's deliberations, perhaps based on tips received from court employees. *Il Progresso Italo-Americano* described the verdict as a compromise reached in response to "the pig-headedness" of a single juror. The eleven other men were said to have given in to the dissenter in order to avoid a mistrial. "A well informed source" identified the holdout to the Italian-language newspaper as Harold Tompkins, the prosperous mechanical engineer who was the jury's sole homeowner and the only juror to ask Kinkead to review the portion of his charge explaining first- and second-degree murder. The New York *Daily News* matched *Il Progresso's* account, announcing a compromise forced by Tompkins, "who for more than ten hours, held out against the eleven others, who favored outright acquittal."[28]

The verdict, though not completely unexpected, stunned Joe's relatives. At first, they were silent. Then came Frank Scutellaro's repeated gasps, as if he had been leveled a physical blow, and the high keening of his wife and daughter-in-law.

As court matrons tried to calm the distraught family, Joe's defense team asked that the jurors be polled. "Several of the jurors appeared on the verge of tears when they were polled for their individual verdicts," the *Daily News* reporter later wrote. The jurors "replied hesitatingly, their eyes averted from the seemingly-stupefied defendant, as if they regretted their decision and still wished to change it." Maybe so, but the twelve men had made no request that the judge be merciful, which they could have done. Joe Scutellaro, they determined, had killed Harry Barck. They left Joe's fate to Judge Kinkead, as William George had directed them. That pronouncement was to wait for a sentencing hearing yet to come.[29]

The trial was over. Leibowitz had expended his great reserve of energy on his summation, and now his shoulders sagged with exhaustion. He had kept Joe Scutellaro from the electric chair, but he had not persuaded the jury to acquit. Leibowitz would try to secure his client's release through other means—on appeal, possibly, or through a persuasive argument put before Kinkead at sentencing—but first he needed rest. He could do little more now than encourage the judge to give him a sympathetic hearing in the future.

After the jurors were discharged with the thanks of the court, the famous orator turned his charm on Judge Kinkead. "Counsel for the defense," Leibowitz announced, "very deeply appreciates the extreme courtesy, gentleness, and fairness—of the conduct of Your Honor—during this trial. We want the whole world to know," Leibowitz enthused, "that never a fairer judge" has "ever graced the bench."

Robert Kinkead must have been well pleased. "Don't think I'm fulsome in saying that your reputation precedes you as one of the foremost lawyers of this country," the judge responded. "A tribute from you is deeply appreciated by this court."

And that was all. The tired lawyers and newsmen abandoned the courthouse to meet other obligations. Leibowitz would spend time with Anna and her relatives before heading home to Brooklyn. Impellitteri was to confer with Joe after he was returned to his cell in the Hudson County Jail.[30]

The men who had been ejected from the courthouse had crowded its top steps until midnight, waiting in the bitter air for the jury's verdict. Their number had dwindled through the early hours. By sunrise, when the verdict was declared, only the hardiest among them—or the most determined—remained on the frost-crazed steps to hear the news. Their verbal response, if there was any, was not recorded. The demonstration that Judge Kinkead had feared did not occur.

When they were ready, the poorest men walked the mile and a half back to Hoboken. A few lingered on the granite steps long enough to hear Vincent Impellitteri make a statement to the Italian-language press. Given the evidence presented by the state, Impellitteri announced, Joe Scutellaro should have been acquitted. But in this case, the defense associate said, "prejudice" had taken "an upper hand to justice." Harry Barck "was a politician," he charged, "while the accused was an Italian," a powerless man in a city that conceded nothing to Italian Americans, never mind those who were on relief. Nevertheless, the associate observed, the verdict was lighter than it could have been. "A few months ago," Impellitteri announced, "the opinion of the political circles in Hudson County was that Scutellaro should receive the electric chair."[31]

Certainly Joe's supporters were relieved that the former relief client would not be executed by the state. But in the days to come, at least one editorial would note that the poor man's sympathizers were not the only ones pleased by his evasion of the death house. "The Hoboken authorities are mainly interested in drawing the curtain, which the trial momentarily pulled back, over the terrible realities of the lives of men and women on relief in New Jersey," the *Nation* asserted. "A death sentence would have had the opposite effect. The jury's verdict, carrying a maximum penalty of ten years, has the advantage, for Hoboken, of putting the bewildered little man back behind the bars."[32]

The publication urged its readers to remember what the Scutellaro trial had revealed about the lives of the jobless poor and to take that knowledge into future battles over relief. A *Nation* contributor, McAlister Coleman, later declared: "I commend study of the full record of the Scutellaro case to those who would take one million Americans off the WPA rolls and turn them back to the mercies of the local authorities."[33]

Anna went back to Monroe Street and put Marie and little Joe to bed. Accosted by reporters waiting outside her home, she refused to be questioned or photographed. She was now far too savvy to allow newsmen inside the apartment. But her refusal did not prevent a local paper from reusing an image of her and her children, taken eleven months earlier, when they'd finally learned of Joe's arrest. Under the photograph of the sobbing family, the *Hudson Dispatch* inserted a caption claiming the picture expressed "the feelings of the wife and children of Joseph Scutellaro" on hearing the jury's verdict.[34]

The *Dispatch* also sought reaction from Harry Barck's widow, Augusta, who had moved out of her upper Hudson Street apartment to stay near her daughters, in Dover, New Jersey. One of Mrs. Barck's sons-in-law, Peter Vanderwolf, spoke to reporters just long enough to inform them that the family was shielding the widow from all mention of the case.[35]

Twice postponed, the sentencing of Joseph Scutellaro was finally set for February 2, 1939, the day before the Scutellaros' tenth wedding anniversary. On that morning, the prisoner's father-in-law, John Angelo, and Joe's father Frank, accompanied Anna to the hearing. She did not bring her children, who stayed at home, in a neighbor's care.

A dozen or more newsmen, including at least one reporter from the Italian-language press, also returned to Judge Kinkead's court, to record the final disposition of the case. The reporter for *Il Progresso Italo-Americano* took careful notes for the paper's dedicated readers, detailing Joe's entrance into court, his handcuffs, his immediate search for Anna in her usual spot. When Joe's eyes met hers, he smiled reassuringly, perhaps noticing, as the reporter had, that Anna's eyes were rimmed red

224 | KILLING THE POORMASTER

from sleeplessness and worry. Sam Leibowitz then approached his client and, putting a hand on the little man's shoulder, whispered a few words in his ear before advancing to the defense table.[36]

For a time, the defender would have had some hope that Kinkead would release Scutellaro on sentencing day, elating Joe and his family, of course, but also turning the case into another clear Leibowitz victory. Area newspapers had highlighted a remark Kinkead had made at a church convocation not long after the trial's conclusion, that "the main duty of a jurist was to dispense justice, which did not necessarily mean that every person convicted of a crime should go to jail." The judge may have floated the option to test political reaction. Governor A. Harry Moore, a Hague ally, had proposed Kinkead's promotion to the New Jersey Circuit Court, and the judge's backers would not have wanted the relief claimant's tale of near-starvation to cling to their nominee.[37]

Response to Kinkead's suggestion of clemency—at least from those charged with dispensing relief—had not been favorable, Leibowitz now knew. *Il Progresso* would later cite the displeasure of "various relief agencies" and the "strong pressure" they had exerted on the judge, "so that the crime that was committed [would] not go unpunished." Relief employees, the newspaper reported, feared that a show of leniency for Joe Scutellaro "could provoke a wave of rebellion amongst relief applicants, who are often denied assistance." Now, after denying the defense's two motions—for an arrest of judgment and for a stay of sentence on the grounds of alleged errors in the case and a conviction against the weight of evidence—Judge Kinkead allowed Leibowitz one final go at a plea for mercy for his client.[38]

By all accounts the criminal defender's forty-five-minute appeal was passionate. His round face flushed, Leibowitz challenged and declaimed, drawing upon older themes he invested with immediacy by linking them to current events. "Scutellaro is not responsible for this crime," the criminal defender declared, "but the conditions in this state, which permit relief at the rate of a penny a day to be paid out by a poormaster to a starving family, while billions are spent for roads and bridges." Leibowitz had surely read that the New Jersey State Legislature was considering a bill that would offset the City of Newark's $2 million claim for relief reimbursement with its $2 million debt to the state for highway construction.

Some were calling it a hardhearted tradeoff. And indeed, when the bill later passed, Newark's mayor, Meyer C. Ellenstein, declared: "The unemployed of the city of Newark have asked for bread and the legislature has said: 'Let them eat State Highway Route 21.' "[39]

But the defense attorney, adjusting his rhetoric, did not want to suggest that his client was anything like those Workers Alliance picketers, the reliefers and unpaid grocers who had continued to protest at the New Jersey Statehouse while Joe had awaited sentencing. The demonstrators had refused Assembly Speaker Pascoe's offer to allow a few of their number into the chamber, because the offer came with the requirement that they remain silent while there. Citing their unwillingness "to barter away their constitutional right of free speech," the Workers Alliance members had returned to the street and continued their protest.[40]

"I do not feel I am pleading the cause of a criminal who has committed a crime against society for gain or advantage," Leibowitz now said. "Scutellaro had always been a quiet citizen, not an agitator as are so many these days and whom the country would be well rid." Leibowitz may have been swept into rallies during his defense of the Scottsboro Boys, but he could never be confused with a comrade-in-arms. He had taken on the Scutellaro and the Scottsboro cases to *win*. Now, in arguing for Joe's release, Leibowitz drew a line between vocal protestors and his passive client. It would be a "great injustice," the lawyer insisted, to make Joe Scutellaro "a scapegoat, so his sentence would serve as an example to others."[41]

In closing, Leibowitz suggested that the judge satisfy the wishes of the greater community, the struggling, proud families of Hudson County, to whom the defender attributed a desire for leniency for his client. "This is a case where the court would be justified before God and the people of this community in erring on the side of mercy," Leibowitz announced. "I dare to say the good women of Hudson County, had they been able to come here, would have voted 99 percent in favor of having this man go back to his wife and children. I ask Your Honor to do the same."[42]

Kinkead, at least one reporter noted, was moved by Leibowitz's plea. He took a few moments to compose himself before speaking. But when the judge began his response, he delivered a speech he had prepared well in advance. Rather than responding to the defense arguments made just moments before, Kinkead launched into a reply to absent critics, who had lamented his performance at trial. It is "unfortunate," Kinkead opined, that some had the impression that in the charge to the jury, the court had attacked Barck's character, when the court had only referred to testimony by defense witnesses.[43]

Harry Barck, the judge continued, "was an earnest public official, doing the best he could for the city. If he had only displayed sympathy and understanding of the circumstances, he would not have made the short answer he made to Scutellaro but would have advised him to go home, where he would have found his relief check." Instead, Kinkead said, "Mr. Barck, in a rage because of treatment just received from a woman client before Scutellaro entered, ordered Scutellaro out of his office."

In Kinkead's telling of the events of February 25, 1938, Barck's rage had then been matched by the rage of Joe Scutellaro. Holding the desk spindle that had been placed into evidence, Judge Kinkead asserted that the furious relief client had "picked up this desk spindle and plunged it into Barck's body." He declared the court in accord with the jury verdict of manslaughter and added: "The court cannot overlook the fact that human life has been taken."[44]

Kinkead now called the blank-eyed defendant by name, as if to awaken him. "Scutellaro," the judge declared, "I can't let you go home today, but I am keeping in mind the extenuating, mitigating circumstances." He mentioned that several priests had spoken on Joe's behalf. Then, drawing himself up, Kinkead made an announcement. "Mayor Bernard McFeely of Hoboken appealed to me yesterday for leniency," the judge revealed, as newsmen bowed their heads to scrawl the judge's unexpected statement. "I consider Mayor McFeely a big man for his act, despite adverse criticism of himself and his administration," Kinkead said. "The mayor told me he knew you and your family and that you were not a relief chiseler or a troublemaker."[45]

The judge then pronounced his sentence: *Two to five years in state prison.*[46]

Joe Scutellaro bent his head as he was led out of the courtroom to the county jail, to await removal to Trenton. He looked up once as he was shuttled past the gleaming benches, to find Anna. A reporter noted that she was "seated in the same spot she [had] faithfully held every day," and there, she wept without restraint.[47]

On that same day, February 2, 1939, Herman and Elizabeth Matson received stirring news that they hoped would bring change to Hoboken—maybe even topple Boss McFeely. The office of the United States Attorney General had telegrammed to confirm a meeting with a delegation from the Workers Defense League of New Jersey. In ten days Herman would be one of nine WDL representatives traveling to Washington, DC, to discuss the "flagrant violation of civil rights" in Hudson County. The Justice Department was about to begin an investigation into Herman's assault in a Hoboken park, after he had tried to speak out against political corruption and the inadequacy of public relief.[48]

Anna Scutellaro leaving the courtroom with defense attorney Samuel Leibowitz after her husband's sentencing.

New York *Daily News* Archive/Getty Images.

EPILOGUE

Human patience is a beautiful and terrible thing.

—Lorena Hickok, in a letter to federal relief
administrator Harry L. Hopkins, September 9, 1934

FOR SOME, THE CLOSE of the Scutellaro case allowed for a new start. Two days after sentencing the Hoboken relief client to state prison, Robert V. Kinkead was sworn in as a New Jersey circuit court judge. Joe's trial was the last Kinkead would hear in the Hudson County Courthouse.

Two months later, on April 2, 1939, Joe's father stood before fifteen hundred cheering McFeely supporters, at a reelection fundraiser in the fashionable uptown Union Club. Knowing all eyes would be upon him when he took to center stage, Frank Scutellaro had surely dressed for the evening with tremendous care. He would want the gala's attendees to recognize him as a man of consequence. Among the ward heelers and Hall employees were seated some of the city's most powerful men, names familiar to anyone who wanted to get ahead in Hoboken. Mayor McFeely was there, of course, along with his slate of commissioners, including a recent addition, Frank Romano. The former Hoboken judge had been invited to join the McFeely ticket after another commissioner had died in office. Seated nearby were Edward Florio, the boss-loader who headed the Third Ward Democratic Club, and ILA delegate Jimmy Nolan.

A *Hudson Dispatch* report later relayed the message Frank Scutellaro had wanted the assembled guests to understand. He had "sought the opportunity to tell the Italian people of Hoboken that he does not regard Mayor McFeely as his enemy," the paper noted, "and he is aware that the mayor, during his trouble, was his friend." To rousing applause, the elderly contractor had then announced his wish: "That his friendly attitude toward the mayor be conveyed to all Italian residents of Hoboken."[1]

Sometime after he made his speech, Frank Scutellaro's contracts with the City of Hoboken were restored.[2]

Others linked to the case withdrew from public scrutiny. Even before Joe Scutellaro had been sentenced, the Barck family had retreated. They never again resided in Hoboken. Harry's widow, Augusta, lived out the rest of her days with her daughters and their families in Dover, New Jersey. She was buried alongside her husband in Fairview Cemetery.[3]

Several Hoboken residents continued on trajectories launched by the Scutellaro case. Herman Matson's decision to speak publicly against starvation and corruption in Hoboken in September 1938, and the beating he endured, led to a series of legal actions, extended over two years. Although Arthur Garfield Hays had withdrawn after the first hour from Herman's trial for the use of "vile and indecent language," the master strategist had drawn legal prescriptions for future actions, to be filled by other attorneys. One of Hays's colleagues would lead the couple's civil action against the city for failure to protect them, and WDL lawyer Harold Grouls, who had assisted Edward Stover with Herman's first case, would help lodge complaints against two men Herman had identified as his assailants, a longshoreman, Joseph McDonald, and McFeely stalwart Edward Florio.[4]

The hearing on Herman's assault and battery allegations was held first, before Judge Romano, in October 1938. (Romano's exit from the bench was still several months away.) After repeatedly asking the judge for a hearing, Herman said Romano told him: "Well, I know you, Matson, if I don't do this, you'll get that Communistic Workers Defense League to publicize it, so I'd better do it." No warrants were issued. Romano chose a date and promised that McDonald and Florio would appear.[5]

Florio packed the Recorder's Court with waterfront allies, though only a few took the stand to testify on his behalf. Each said it was Florio's habit to go to the Third Ward Club every night, though none could say for sure that he had actually *seen* Florio at the club on the evening of the brawl. An alibi witness for Joseph McDonald arrived in court drunk; he testified that McDonald had been drinking at a Ninth Street bar at the time of Matson's beating. For their part, Herman, Elizabeth, and WDL colleague Morris Milgram positively identified McDonald and Florio as Herman's attackers. The hearing took four hours. At its close, Judge Romano determined that Herman "could not possibly know who beat him." Florio and McDonald, he added, could now sue Herman for civil damages "for false prosecution." He then dismissed the case.[6]

The Matsons' suit against the City of Hoboken took far longer to conclude. While waiting for the case to come to trial, both the ACLU and the WDL made sure that Herman's beating was not forgotten. The ACLU highlighted the Hoboken "mob attack" in its literature, and the WDL invited the Hoboken chairman to speak at mass meetings along-side trade unionists and other civil libertarians. Herman's speech at a November 1938 rally in New York City "to commemorate the death of Joseph Shoemaker" linked Herman's activism and its violent reception in Hoboken to a broader history of machine-sanctioned brutality against labor organizers and political progressives. Shoemaker, an organizer of the unemployed in Tampa, Florida, and a leader of a new local party that had challenged that southern city's corrupt administration, had died three years earlier, after he and two fellow activists were illegally seized from a private home by city police, then flogged, tarred, and feathered by a gang awaiting their release from police headquarters. By the time the WDL held its mass meeting in New York, the men who had been tried for Shoemaker's murder had all been acquitted.[7]

Herman's presence at this large memorial gathering, and at other meetings of political progressives, could instill some hope, and maybe courage, in the gathered crowds. He had been beaten bloody but he had not been silenced. His fingers remained ink-stained from his nighttime printing sessions. All through 1939, protest flyers, including a weekly series attributed to a new Hoboken political group, the Independent

Citizens Committee, tumbled off Herman's mimeograph machine and into the hands of covert supporters.[8]

By then law enforcement officials in Washington, DC, were finally looking into McFeely's undemocratic rule, as well as repressive tactics in Jersey City. After Herman and his WDL colleagues traveled to Washington, the director of the Justice Department's new Civil Liberties Division, Henry Schweinhaut, began a probe into Hudson County civil rights violations. FBI agents from the Newark bureau arrived in Hoboken to gather documentation of infractions. Herman's accusatory flyers were added to Justice Department files thick with reports of speaking venues denied to machine challengers; the ruination of opponents' businesses; beatings, threats, and election day brawls; the detention of pamphleteers; and in-depth agent interviews with civil rights victims and their alleged victimizers. As news spread of the Civil Liberties Division investigation, some Hoboken residents sent complaints directly to Schweinhaut. Letter-writers often included a plea that they not be identified. "Please don't let my name [be] known or that I wrote to you because McFeely will ruin me," one downtown woman begged.[9]

Justice Department officials were watching, but the Boss's thugs still roamed the streets. On May 8, 1939, the day before Hoboken's mayoral election, Herman and his fourteen-year-old son Bill were on the street distributing opposition-ticket pamphlets when three men jumped from a car to pummel them. In an unnerving replay of the 1938 park incident, the Hoboken police did not detain the Matsons' assailants but arrested Herman, charging him again with the use of bad language.[10]

Eventually the arresting officer would withdraw his charge against Herman. But before that happened, a WDL leader wrote to the director of the Justice Department's Civil Liberties Division about the second beating and declared his hope that, with the feds' help, "we really will be able to work out, before it's too late, some way of dealing with these petty politicians, whose notion of civil liberties ends with their hip-pocket: wallet and gun."[11]

That day would not come soon enough for Joseph Clark. The former McFeely commissioner, who had testified at the Scutellaro trial, had since announced himself as an opposition candidate in the 1939 mayoral election. Clark was beaten in a Jefferson Street polling station on Election

Day. According to one witness, Clark had protested the placement of city employees "to cajole, threaten, and force citizens to vote for the McFeely machine," and a fight had ensued. There was only one arrest: Joseph Clark, battered and bleeding from a deep gash to his face, was charged with disorderly conduct and assault and battery.[12]

But neither Joe Clark nor Herman Matson would back down. Clark fought the charges against him. And Herman upped his public protests, holding several demonstrations right in front of city hall. During the summer of 1939, while a line of uniformed officers stood guard by the front door, and the mayor likely fumed inside, Herman marched in front of the building wearing a sandwich board that read, WE REFUSE TO STARVE QUIETLY. He gathered on the Hall's steps with Morris Milgram and Italian-language translator Nicholas Piracci, explaining to large crowds how the city's poor were organizing.[13]

A June 22 speech by the US Attorney General, in which the nation's top law enforcement officer pointedly denounced political interference with civil liberties, surely encouraged the activists all the more, as the speech was delivered at a college commencement in Hague's own Jersey City. Maybe President Roosevelt was finally turning against the New Jersey powerbroker who had delivered him so many votes. After all, the attorney general's complaints had been issued within weeks of the removal from power of another big city boss, Tom Pendergast. The Kansas City Democrat had been sentenced in late May to serve fifteen months in a federal penitentiary for tax evasion. At least one commentator surmised that "the days of the old-time boss" were finally coming to an end.[14]

Elizabeth and Herman Matson's suit against the City of Hoboken, for police failure to protect them from mob violence, finally went to trial in June 1940. But Edward Stover's prediction—that the Matsons would gain nothing out of future legal actions—proved correct. The jury rejected the evidence presented by the couple's witnesses—including the testimony of two news reporters, who supported their assertions with enlarged news photographs of the incident—and favored the testimony of Hoboken police officers, including Lieutenant J. Romeo Scott. A dozen or more policemen claimed they had not seen Herman Matson with a black eye and bloody nose after the melee. Scott recalled only Herman's use of "obscene language" when the police arrived to rescue him.

After forty-five minutes of deliberation, the jury returned a verdict of "no cause of action."[15]

Exhausted, hard-pressed for work, and disheartened by the outcome of the court case and the feds' inaction against McFeely or Hague, Elizabeth and Herman reluctantly decided to leave Hoboken. Some of their children would later remember that the beating of their brother Bill had convinced Elizabeth that their life in the city was untenable. She likely shared the perspective offered by Joe Clark, when he, too, moved out of Hoboken in October 1940, to live in North Bergen, New Jersey. Although he had lived all his life in Hoboken, Clark told a reporter, it was not "a proper place any more to raise my children."[16]

The Matsons moved to the Bronx, and Herman easily found work as a boilermaker in the Brooklyn Navy Yard, readying vast iron ships for service in World War II. He stopped his nighttime printing and daytime leafleting. Now, every weekday morning, Herman rose in the near dark to travel to the waterfront, pleased that after years of uncertainty and struggle, he could support Elizabeth and their six children—and later, a seventh, Daniel.[17]

Bronx-born Daniel Matson would be the only one of Herman and Elizabeth's children who would have no direct knowledge of the conditions in Hoboken. But he would sometimes hear his father and one of his brothers, Raymond, telling stories about their time there. Herman would laugh, recalling the McFeely crimes he'd uncovered and then revealed in his mimeographed pages. There had always been people who wanted the truth to come out, Herman remembered. Some had fought alongside him, insisting that the poor were citizens, too—that jobless men and women, and working stiffs, had a right to speak out and to organize and to vote freely. They were the ones who finally defeated McFeely—aided by tamper-resistant voting machines, supervised by state police—seven long years after the Matsons left Hoboken.[18]

The mayor's defeat was made possible, too, by an unlikely set of new dissenters: disgruntled Hoboken police officers had vowed to break the machine hold on city hires after their own effort to gain contractual protections had been brutally opposed by their chief and his brother. The rebel officers' charges—of a McFeely-directed campaign of intimidation, harassment, and beatings—had a familiar ring. It was meant to force their silence and their resignations. Instead, the embattled officers followed the route taken by street protestors like Herman Matson: they went public. And when they formed a "good government" alliance with other machine opponents, they, too, helped to topple Bernard McFeely.[19]

An Italian American, former McFeely supporter Fred DeSapio, gained the mayor's seat. "We have only started on Barney [McFeely]," the Boss's old nemesis, Frank Bartletta, had announced in 1928, when Hoboken's Italians had tried, and failed, to secure representation in the Hall. "We have the goods on him," Bartletta declared then, "and he will go the way they all go. It may be days, weeks, or months. But the forces of decency will drive Barney McFeely and his tribe of plunderers from Hoboken." Nearly twenty years later, Hoboken's downtown residents cheered and waved flashlights as the returns came in from the city's fifty election districts, heralding a landslide for a "good government" ticket and McFeely's eviction from city hall. In the days after the election, one reporter observed, "a Mardi Gras gaiety spread throughout most of Hoboken." More than ten thousand residents swarmed Washington Street to watch their new representatives take their oaths of office in a May 19 ceremony in front of city hall.[20]

The new administration made one symbolic—and urgently needed— change right away: they hired an out-of-town cartage company to carry away the city's garbage, in closed trucks.[21]

———— ✦ ————

Two days after his brother's ouster, Edward McFeely retired his position as chief of police. Hoboken poormaster Austin Tighe, Harry Barck's successor and Mayor McFeely's occasional secretary, also left his post after the Boss's Election Day loss. A year after taking office, the new administration retired the public relief officer's medieval-sounding title. Hoboken would never have another poormaster. The "director of welfare" would now head the city's "Department of Public Welfare."[22]

———— ✦ ————

At Hoboken's city hall, crowds hail the swearing in of a new administration led by representatives of Italian American heritage, on May 19, 1948.

Courtesy of the Historical Collection of the Hoboken Public Library.

Sam Leibowitz lost no more clients to the electric chair. Not long after the close of the Scutellaro case, the once-eager defender conceded his weariness with criminal defense work and ceased private practice. But the masterful courtroom performer was by no means tired of the law or of being a public figure. Leibowitz was keen to try his hand as a prosecutor or to rise to the bench. In 1940 he was elected judge for Kings County Court, chosen to command one of the most active criminal courts in the country. (His initial term was for fourteen years, but Leibowitz's tenure as a judge—almost thirty years, including eight as a justice of the New York State Supreme Court for Kings County—eventually exceeded his twenty-odd years as a criminal defender.)[23]

Although some might have imagined that the former criminal defender would go easy on convicted felons, Judge Leibowitz soon gained the moniker "Sentencing Sam" for his toughness in sentencing. And, in keeping with the laws of New York State, Judge Leibowitz also sentenced convicted murderers to die in the electric chair—forty men, according to one account. Although the death penalty was then mandatory in New York State for first-degree murder—unless a jury recommended life in prison—Leibowitz did not enforce the law under protest: he argued that fear of capital punishment could be an effective deterrent.[24]

Joe Scutellaro served eighteen months in state prison, mostly at a work farm in Bordentown, New Jersey, sixty miles south of Hoboken. Every Sunday during his incarceration, Anna hired a car and driver and packed up the children for a long journey and a brief reunion with Joe.[25]

Anna had found work as a waitress in a Hoboken luncheonette. Although the travel expense strained her budget, and the family ate more potatoes than she would have liked, she no longer had to explain her decisions to an overseer. The Scutellaros would not go on relief again.

When Joe finally returned to their family in August 1940—he was released early on good behavior—he had been away from Monroe Street for nearly two and a half years, including the eleven months he'd spent waiting for trial in the Hudson County Jail. In many ways, the life he'd left behind was waiting for him upon his return: Hoboken would continue to be dominated by Boss McFeely for another seven years, and the city's jobless poor, like so many across the country, were still struggling. Economic recovery would take a few more years, advanced by US entry into World War II and the consequent boom in military-related industries.

In the summer of 1940, in all but a few of the largest cities, the able-bodied unemployed were still scrounging to meet basic needs. Five years after the federal government had withdrawn from "this business of relief," eight states were refusing all relief to the able-bodied unemployed, six states offered them "practically no relief," and thirteen more allowed "limited funds" for "employable persons." One health commissioner described its city's relief program as "an experiment in malnutrition."[26]

As in years past, work was hard to come by—and now, work *relief* was diminishing, too. While Joe was in prison, congressional conservatives had taken aim at the WPA program, adding a provision to the Appropri-ation Acts of 1939 and 1940 that mandated a worker's removal from the WPA rolls after eighteen months of continuous employment and then required the furloughed worker to wait sixty days before attempting rein-statement. Although legislators insisted the rule would force work-reliefers to seek private employment and would open limited WPA positions to new hires, later studies showed that the provision effectively made jobless the vast majority of those who were furloughed.[27]

For the able-bodied who were unable to find work, the federal gov-ernment would now do less, even as it moved to provide greater economic security to the steadily employed. The Social Security Act of 1935 had established unemployment and "old age" insurance programs for work-ers in covered industries, but only if those eligible workers, upon job loss or on retirement, had contributed enough to the system through their sustained employment. When the act was amended in 1939, the old-age insurance program was broadened to include the retired worker's wife and children and to allow them survivors' benefits should the covered worker die prematurely. The amendments essentially transformed Social Security from an individual retirement program into an economic secu-rity plan for *families*—or, rather, for a certain *type* of family, as the 1939 provisions favored households headed by a wage-earning husband and a full-time homemaker wife.[28]

Joe Scutellaro had returned from prison weak and disoriented, but he tried, even so, to earn money for his family—and he often failed. There were few jobs in Hoboken for a frail man. During his first six months back in the city, Joe earned just $100 from pickup work. Anna was at odds as to how she might help her husband without wounding his pride.[29]

In March 1941 reporters for the *New York Times* and the *Jersey Journal* somehow got wind of the unlikely solution Anna had fashioned: Mrs. Scutellaro, the newspapers reported, had purchased a five-story building in Hoboken. After putting down $2,300 in cash for 600–02 Adams Street, the reports stated, Anna had received a $20,070 five-year mortgage from Hoboken Bank for Savings. When the two reporters questioned her, Anna explained that her husband had been without sustained work since his return from prison. Now, with their purchase of the building, he could be a maintenance man.[30]

The reporters surely knew that a rental building in Hoboken could not be described as a vast moneymaker for the Scutellaros—the city was in obvious decline, as was its population—but both journalists wanted to know: *How did she pay for it?*[31]

"It's no one's business but my own," Anna responded, surely trying to hold on to the little bit of privacy she had regained at the trial's end. She vigorously denied that she had used the defense fund, raised in Joe's behalf, to make the down payment. "I'll be glad to return any donation that anyone made to the fund, if they now regret they helped us," Anna said.

So where did the money go? the reporters must have asked, for both newspapers reported Anna's assertion, that of $5,300 raised in donations—not $7,000 or $10,000 as previously reported—$3,000 had been paid to Samuel Leibowitz after all. The criminal defender's fee had been $5,000, Anna said, but Leibowitz had returned $2,000 to her.[32]

Even after the family purchased the Adams Street building, and even as the symptoms of his encephalitis worsened, Joe Scutellaro continued to look for paying work. He would have felt it was not right for a married man, a father of two, to be unemployed. And so, he had searched, and as the economy improved during the war years, he had sometimes landed employment, for a while. When Hoboken's Bethlehem Steel Shipyard needed thousands of workers, during the war years, for round-the-clock shifts converting passenger ships to troopships, Joe gained a position there, as a helper. But his illness guaranteed he would not hold that job—or any job—for very long. After four months, Joe was fired from Bethlehem Steel. "Lethargia" was the reason cited on Joe's work card. Beneath that, a supervisor wrote: "DO NOT REHIRE."[33]

Anna held the family together. They went out to eat celebratory dinners whenever Joe landed a new job; she comforted her husband when he was, inevitably, let go. She kept on. Anna made sure her children and her husband were well fed and that the family's bills were paid. She continued to work as a waitress until she was fifty-six years old, when crippling arthritis forced her to retire.[34]

In the years after, Joe and Anna Scutellaro kept to their simple morning routine. While Anna slept in, Joe prepared their coffee. Then he would leave the house, just as he did on the morning of February 25, 1938, to buy a few rolls for his family's breakfast.

ACKNOWLEDGMENTS

MY SEARCH FOR THE lived history of Hoboken's poorest Depression-era residents lead me to many offices, collections, and libraries in my home state, and to archives in New York, Massachusetts, Maryland, Michigan, and Washington, DC. Thickets of paper awaited me. Without the resourceful guides I encountered along the way, I would probably be searching still.

When I needed court records, Hudson County prosecutor Edward J. DeFazio and first assistant prosecutor Gaetano T. Gregory were exceptionally generous with their time and expertise. They located decades-old case files, advised me on the finer points of law, and encouraged me at every turn.

The reference librarians at the main branch of the Jersey City Public Library patiently retrieved hundreds of reels of microfilm for my intensive review of area newspapers. The excellent staff at that library's New Jersey Room—especially the late Charlie Markey, Bruce Brandt (now retired), and current staffer John Beekman—secured facts, pulled public documents, and made bound copies of old newspapers available when microfilm copies were unreadable. Currently directed by Cynthia Harris, the New Jersey Room is an indispensable resource for historians of Hudson County.

Peggy Ann Brown, PhD, was my sherpa of the stacks at the National Archives in College Park, Maryland. Much of Herman Matson's activism would still be unknown were it not for Peggy's diligence and finesse. William LeFevre, reference archivist at the Walter P. Reuther Library, Wayne State University, also located vital Workers Defense League files and put me in touch with researcher Sandy Eklund, who found documents relating to WDL members Herman and Elizabeth Matson.

Several archivists and librarians tracked down records that deepened my understanding of the poormasters' long history. Special thanks go to Sean A. Curry and Bette M. Epstein of the New Jersey State Archives and to Robert Heym (Jerseyana), Tom O'Malley (Law), and Teri Taylor (US Documents) at the New Jersey State Library. Doris Oliver, librarian at the Stevens Institute of Technology's S. C. Williams Library, and David Webster, archivist at the Hoboken Historical Museum, supplied much-needed Hoboken records and images. Archivists at Fairview Cemetery, Fairview, New Jersey, and at the Department of Veterans Affairs in Washington, DC, located biographical material on the Barck and Vanderwolf families, as did Marilyn Stearns at the Local History and Genealogy Department of the Morristown and Morris Township Library, Morristown, New Jersey.

Keri Long and Pat Cummings kindly pulled records for me at the Hudson County Administration Building; Bill LaRosa opened courthouse doors. Thanks go to the staff at the Property Assessor's Office of Jersey City, the Schlesinger Library at Radcliffe, the Brooklyn Historical Society, the Cambridge Public Library, and the New York Public Library's Rare Books and Manuscripts Division. The Hoboken Public Library staff graciously fulfilled numerous interlibrary loan requests and made their Historical Photographs Collection fully available. I also received help from Adriane Hanson, project archivist of the Seeley G. Mudd Manuscript Library, Princeton University; Matthew Hanson, archives technician, Franklin D. Roosevelt Presidential Library; Shawn O'Sullivan, photo researcher at the New York *Daily News*; Pete B. Asch, graduate student, New York University Archives, the Elmer Holmes Bobst Library; and Tim Engels, senior library specialist, scholarly resources—manuscripts, Brown University Library. New York State Library loaned microfilm containing *Il Progresso Italo-Americano*'s coverage of the Scutellaro trial, which was ably translated from Italian into English by Elisa Varano.

I was very fortunate to receive financial support to research the history of the Hoboken poormaster. The New Jersey Historical Commission, a division of the Department of State, provided me with two grants to forward this work. Special thanks go to former NJHC grants director Mary Murrin for her dry wit, clarity, and outstanding advice over the years, and to current acting executive director Sara Cureton for her enthusiastic support of this project.

Preparing grant proposals required me to outline the direction my research would take, but I did not know whether I would meet the children or grandchildren of the relief recipients I encountered in reports and documents. Much to my delight, Marie Scutellaro Werts contacted *me*, after learning of my research into the history of the Hoboken poormaster. During my visit to her home, she recalled her family members with candor and compassion. She shared her experience of her father's trial, brought out newspaper clippings and family photos, and made a delicious lunch, to boot. I am especially grateful for her account of Anna's remarkable fortitude during that dreadful time and for allowing me to quote lines from a brief autobiographical sketch her mother prepared with an unknown ghostwriter.

When I tracked down members of the Matson family, I learned that the open and generous spirit attributed to Herman Matson by his contemporaries was bequeathed to his children and grandchildren. Conversations with sons Raymond and Daniel, daughter Evelyn Olsen, and grandsons Scott and Raymond Jr. were a great joy and brought Herman and his wife Elizabeth near. Sadly, Ray Sr. and Evelyn passed away before this book (and its record of their parents' bravery and activism) was published. I hope they would have approved of the final result.

Talented and insightful colleagues—including residents and staff at Blue Mountain Center—helped shape my thinking and gave me strength and direction. Thanks to Howard Green and Sada Fretz for flagging errors in my manuscript and for suggesting improvements; to Robert Sullivan for editing a proposal; to Mari Coates and Chris Gregory for sharing my manuscript with associates; and to James H. Clark for worrying about the people in these pages. The Writers Room made a New York City workspace affordable; fellows of the Social Justice Writers Group in Cambridge were boon companions during the months I lived and wrote in their city. My great thanks go to my agents, Michael Carr and Katherine Boyle of Veritas Literary, for championing my work; and to senior editor Jerome Pohlen, project editor Devon Freeny, and the Chicago Review Press team for ushering it into print.

During this book's long genesis, I've been very fortunate to have generous people care for me and about the history I sought to recover. Hank Forrest and Stella Strazdas offered a quiet space in Hoboken; Nora Jacobson and David Ferm gave respite in Vermont. Laura Alexander encouraged me to dare time and again. Michelle McMillian, Diane Oltarzewski, and Lucy Honig puzzled out problems over homemade feasts. Nell Hunt and Alice Searle shared all manner of stories, with links and books and dispatches from across the United States and across the Atlantic. Robert Foster read the manuscript with an eye for Hobokenalia and went the extra mile. And well before Occupy took to Wall Street, Jennifer Oman Payne assured me the activist spirit described in these pages lives on.

There are two friends I hardly know how to thank, for I owe so much to them. When Helen Fremont and Donna Thagard opened their home in Cambridge to me, they gave me a place where I could build a manuscript from notes and drafts and thousands of pages of documents. There, on the first floor of their late-nineteenth-century cottage, I set out two long tables and, for the first time, laid out my work in its entirety. And then, during a ten-month remove from my beloved, adopted hometown, I wrote.

Grateful acknowledgment is also made to the following publishers and holders of copyright for permission to quote from and/or reprint the following copyrighted material:

Evening Journal Association: "Scutellaro Takes the Stand," *Jersey Observer*, January 12, 1939. *Jersey Observer* copyright 1939 by Evening Journal Association. Reproduced with permission of Evening Journal Association via Copyright Clearance Center. "Defense Hints Death of Barck Accidental," *Jersey Observer*, January 11, 1939. *Jersey Observer* copyright 1939 by Evening Journal Association. Reproduced with permission of Evening Journal Association via Copyright Clearance Center. "Slayer's Wife Tells of Fight Against Poverty," *Jersey Observer*, February 26, 1938. *Jersey Observer* copyright 1938 by Evening Journal Association. Reproduced with permission of Evening Journal Association via Copyright Clearance Center. "Mother Says Dead Child Ate Paint," *Jersey Journal*, July 16, 1936. *Jersey*

Journal copyright 1936 by Evening Journal Association. Reproduced with permission of Evening Journal Association via Copyright Clearance Center. "Defense Fund Reported Under Way for Slayer," *Jersey Observer,* February 28, 1938. *Jersey Observer* copyright 1938 by Evening Journal Association. Reproduced with permission of Evening Journal Association via Copyright Clearance Center. "Leibowitz Makes Three-Hour Appeal to Save Scutellaro," *Jersey Observer,* January 16, 1939. *Jersey Observer* copyright 1939 by Evening Journal Association. Reproduced with permission of Evening Journal Association via Copyright Clearance Center. "Barck Slayer Arraigned; Is Refused Bail, Samuel Leibowitz Makes Earnest Plea to Court," *Jersey Observer,* March 25, 1938. *Jersey Observer* copyright 1938 by Evening Journal Association. Reproduced with permission of Evening Journal Association via Copyright Clearance Center. "Struck Jury in Barck Slaying," *Jersey Observer,* September 19, 1938. *Jersey Observer* copyright 1938 by Evening Journal Association. Reproduced with permission of Evening Journal Association via Copyright Clearance Center. "Matson to Appeal Conviction," *Jersey Observer,* October 9, 1938. *Jersey Observer* copyright 1938 by Evening Journal Association. Reproduced with permission of Evening Journal Association via Copyright Clearance Center. "State Summation Strikes at Accident Defense in Killing," *Jersey Observer,* January 16, 1939. *Jersey Observer* copyright 1939 by Evening Journal Association. Reproduced with permission of Evening Journal Association via Copyright Clearance Center. "Scutellaro Faces 10-Year Prison Term," *Jersey Journal,* January 16, 1939. *Jersey Journal* copyright 1939 by Evening Journal Association. Reproduced with permission of Evening Journal Association via Copyright Clearance Center. "Convict Scutellaro of Manslaughter," *Hudson Dispatch,* January 16, 1939. *Hudson Dispatch* copyright 1939 by Evening Journal Association. Reproduced with permission of Evening Journal Association via Copyright Clearance Center. "Scutellaro Gets 2 To 5 Years," *Jersey Journal,* February 2, 1939. *Jersey Journal* copyright 1939 by Evening Journal Association. Reproduced with permission of Evening Journal Association via Copyright Clearance Center. "Man Convicted in Poormaster Slaying Buys Apartment," *Jersey Journal,* March 10, 1941. *Jersey Journal* copyright 1941 by Evening Journal Association. Reproduced with permission of Evening Journal Association via Copyright Clearance Center.

The Nation: "The Shape of Things (excerpt)," by Freda Kirchwey. Reprinted with permission from the January 21, 1939 issue of the *Nation*. For subscription information, call 1-800-333-8536. Portions of each week's *Nation* magazine can be accessed at www.thenation.com.

The New York Times: "Hoboken Slashes Its Relief Cases from 2,000 to 90 in a Few Weeks," by Russell Porter. From *The New York Times*, May 24, 1936 © 1936 The New York Times. All rights reserved. Used by permission and protected by the Copyright Laws of the United States. The printing, copying, redistribution, or retransmission of this Content without express written permission is prohibited. "Jury Is Long Out in Barck Slaying." From *The New York Times*, January 15, 1939 © 1939 The New York Times. All rights reserved. Used by permission and protected by the Copyright Laws of the United States. The printing, copying, redistribution, or retransmission of this Content without express written permission is prohibited. "Jobless Man Kills Hoboken Overseer." From *The New York Times*, February 26, 1938 © 1938 The New York Times. All rights reserved. Used by permission and protected by the Copyright Laws of the United States. The printing, copying, redistribution, or retransmission of this Content without express written permission is prohibited. www.nytimes.com.

Workers Defense League Collection, Walter P. Reuther Library, Wayne State University, Detroit, Michigan: Unpublished materials of the WDL, used by permission.

NOTES

The following abbreviations are used for frequently cited sources:

AS   An unpublished, undated, typed, autobiographical sketch produced by Anna Scutellaro with the help of an unknown "ghost writer"; quoted with permission of Marie Scutellaro Werts

DN   *Daily News* (New York)

DOJ   Department of Justice

HD   *Hudson Dispatch*

HOB   *Hudson Observer*

JJ   *Jersey Journal*

JO   *Jersey Observer*

NACP   National Archives at College Park, Maryland

NYP   *New York Post*

NYT   *New York Times*

PIA   *Il Progresso Italo-Americano*

SVJS   *State v. Joseph F. Scutellaro,* indictment 313, December term 1937, Hudson County Court of Oyer & Terminer, case file, courtesy Hudson County Prosecutor's Office, Jersey City, New Jersey

Map of Hoboken

1. The map of Hoboken appeared in Federal Writers' Project of the Works Progress Administration for the State of New Jersey, *New Jersey: A Guide to Its Present and Past* (New York: The Viking Press, June 1939), 267. The book was later reprinted in a revised edition as *The WPA Guide to 1930s New Jersey* (New Brunswick, NJ: Rutgers University Press, 1986).

February 25, 1938

1. Autopsy performed at Hoffman's Morgue, Hoboken, NJ, February 25, 1938, by Doctors Arthur P. Hasking, William P. Braunstein, Manuel Hernandez, and

Thomas S. Brady on the body of Harry Ludwig Barck Jr., who died at city hall, Hoboken, NJ, on February 25, 1938, *SVJS*.

1. Waiting for Nothing

1. Relief Client List prepared by Harry Barck, February 25, 1938, Hoboken, NJ, in *SVJS*. Newspaper accounts differ on number of waiting aid applicants; Barck's list indicates twenty-three. Nineteen were noted prior to Scutellaro, who is not listed. Three men were waiting outside when Scutellaro entered the office. Estimated number of destitute Americans in 1933 varies from twelve to eighteen million; see Richard Lowitt and Maurine Hoffman Beasley, eds., *One Third of a Nation: Lorena Hickok Reports on the Great Depression* (Urbana: University of Illinois Press, 1981), xvii. For comparison of "the first month of 1938" and "the depths of 1933": Nick Taylor, *American-Made: The Enduring Legacy of the WPA; When FDR Put the Nation to Work* (New York: Bantam Books, 2008), 318. For background on "Roosevelt recession" 1937–38: Alan Brinkley, *The End of Reform: New Deal Liberalism in Recession and War* (New York: Alfred A. Knopf, 1995), passim.
2. Relief Client List prepared by Harry Barck, February 25, 1938.
3. "Jobless Man Kills Hoboken Overseer," *NYT*, February 26, 1938, regarding Barck's "usual way of dismissing one client and summoning another" and stationing of Carmody. "Confession Introduced in Evidence at Trial Here," *JJ*, January 11, 1939, reporting trial testimony of Ralph Corrado. Statement of Ralph Corrado to Hoboken Police, February 25, 1938, *SVJS*.
4. Barck's appearance, actions, and remark, trial testimony of Nicholas Russo: "Scutellaro Takes the Stand," *JO*, January 12, 1939. See also "Confession Introduced." I have added the word "bread" for greater comprehension, as in today's usage "tickets" might suggest a parking violation or entertainment admission.
5. Politician extolling a poormaster's cuts, example: Hoboken Mayor George Gonzales's message to council, January 1, 1911, *Council Minutes: City of Hoboken 1911–12* (Hoboken, NJ: n.d.), 8. Hopkins remarks from his book: Harry Hopkins, *Spending to Save: The Complete Story of Relief* (New York: W. W. Norton & Company, 1936), 100. Attitudes of poormasters prior to Great Depression: Michael B. Katz, *In the Shadow of the Poorhouse: A Social History of Welfare in America* (New York: Basic Books, 1986), 148–49; Paul Tutt Stafford, *Government and the Needy: A Study of Public Assistance* (Princeton, NJ: Princeton University Press, 1941), 3. See also Frances Fox Piven and Richard A. Cloward, in *Regulating the Poor: The Functions of Public Welfare* (New York: Vintage Books, 1993), 47–48.
6. Millions jobless, see *Historical Statistics of the United States, Colonial Times to 1970, Part 1* (Washington: US Department of Commerce, September 1975), section D, 6. Unemployment estimates were prepared by a number of organizations. For partial list of organizations and varying estimates: Hopkins, *Spending to Save*, 13–14. Hickok remarks: Lowitt and Beasley, eds., *One Third of a Nation*, 37, 67.
7. Forms used by Barck: New Jersey Commission on Defective, Delinquent and Dependent Children and Their Care, 1908, Exhibits, 1308–9, collection of the New Jersey State Archives. Few soup kitchens: "Franciscan Sisters Feeding Hoboken's Unfortunates," editorial, *HOB*, January 10, 1929, and James A. Weschler, "Hoboken: Story of a Sick City," *PM*, vol. 1, no. 40 (August 12, 1940): 16, on continuing shortages.

Fusco's encounter with Barck and her family's circumstances: "Relief Client Kills Poormaster," *NYP*, February 25, 1938.

8. On working-class Americans' overwhelmingly positive view of President Roosevelt until "well into 1934": Robert S. McElvaine, ed., *Down & Out in the Great Depression: Letters from the "Forgotten Man"* (Chapel Hill, NC: University of North Carolina Press, 1983), 13. Overwhelmed aid offices: Irving Bernstein, *The Lean Years: A History of the American Worker, 1920–1933* (Boston: Houghton Mifflin Co., 1966), 301. Piven and Cloward, *Regulating the Poor*, 74–75, note that twenty million "were on the dole" by winter 1934, about one-sixth of the population.

9. Piven and Cloward, *Regulating the Poor*, 94.

10. McElvaine, *Down & Out*, 25: "at its peak in 1936," the Works Progress Administration "gave jobs to only about one-fourth of those counted as unemployed." Piven and Cloward, *Regulating the Poor*, 109: "some 7 or 8 million" were still without jobs when work relief was at its height. On work relief, see: Katz, *In the Shadow*, 235–36. Donald S. Howard, *The WPA and Federal Relief Policy* (New York: Russell Sage Foundation, 1943), 622, cites November 1937 census of New Jersey relief cases indicating just over 74 percent of the total were considered "employable" but did not receive WPA jobs. Conditions in other states: ibid., 73–85.

11. New Jersey's abolition of its direct relief program: Stafford, *Government and the Needy*, 111. The federal government withdrew from direct relief in 1935 and 1936. Without federal finances, New Jersey's Emergency Relief Program was reconsidered. The state legislature enacted a law in 1936 that abolished the New Jersey State Emergency Relief Administration and returned control of emergency relief to municipalities. On New Jersey poormasters, see Douglas H. MacNeil, *Seven Years of Unemployment Relief in New Jersey, 1930–1936* (Washington: Committee on Social Security, Social Science Research Council, 1938), 100–103, and "Plight of N.J. Idle Stressed in New Report," *JJ*, July 3, 1936. Federal Writers' Project of the Works Progress Administration for the State of New Jersey, "New Jersey: The General View, History" in *New Jersey: A Guide to Its Present and Past* (New York: The Viking Press, June 1939), 53, on study that determined the average New Jersey family on relief lived on an amount nearly half the minimum standard for subsistence. "Chiselers" and number of people cut from relief by Barck: Russell B. Porter, "Hoboken Slashes Its Relief Cases from 2,000 to 90 in a Few Weeks," *NYT*, May 24, 1936.

12. On New York's and New Jersey's emergency relief administrations: Josephine C. Brown, *Public Relief, 1929–1939* (New York: Henry Holt and Company, 1940), 89–94. New Jersey's post-FERA plan: James Leiby, *Charity and Correction in New Jersey: A History of State Welfare Institutions* (New Brunswick, NJ: Rutgers University Press, 1967), 280–82. Hudson County Supervisor's comments: "Says Nobody 'Is Starving in Hoboken,'" *HD*, May 26, 1936.

13. Porter, "Hoboken Slashes Its Relief Cases."

14. Piven and Cloward, *Regulating the Poor*, 63–64.

15. Mauritz A. Hallgren, *Seeds of Revolt: A Study of American Life and the Temper of the American People During the Depression* (New York: Alfred A. Knopf, 1933), passim, and MacNeil, *Seven Years*, passim, detail organized actions by unemployed in Washington, DC, Trenton, and other locations. See also Helen Seymour, *When Clients Organize* (Chicago: American Public Welfare Association, 1937), passim. For a

description of nonviolent action by protestors during Hunger March to Washington: Dorothy Day, *The Long Loneliness: An Autobiography* (San Francisco, CA: Harper & Row, 1952) 162–66. Day uses the word "jeering" to describe the policemen.

16. MacNeil, *Seven Years*, 216, compares relief authorities and nineteenth-century industrialists. See also Marilynn S. Johnson, *Street Justice: A History of Police Violence in New York City* (Boston: Beacon Press, 2003), 149–80. "Bleeding heads": Bernstein, *The Lean Years*, 427. Role of political unrest in government's decision to expand aid: Piven and Cloward, *Regulating the Poor*, 45–79. See also Hallgren, *Seeds of Revolt*, 192–95, and Seymour, *When Clients Organize*, passim, for background on organizing by leftists.

17. Power of Edward McFeely during his brother's mayoralty: Paul Samperi, interview by Pat Samperi, April 27, 2006, transcript, Hoboken Oral History Project, Hoboken History Collection, Hoboken Public Library, Hoboken, NJ. On urban bosses: Blaine A. Brownell and Warren E. Stickle, eds., *Bosses and Reformers: Urban Politics in America, 1880–1920* (Boston: Houghton Mifflin Company, 1973), 56. See also Vilas J. Boyle, "Hoboken: A Look at McFeely, the Man," *NYP*, April 9, 1938.

18. Alfred Steinberg, *The Bosses* (New York: Macmillan Publishing Co., 1972), 1–9.

19. "Arrest Distributors of Circulars Laying Couple's Death to Hoboken Mayor," *JJ*, December 29, 1932.

20. See chapter 9 for detailed accounts of harassment and violence by McFeely supporters against Herman Matson and members of the Workers Defense League.

21. Observations about being watched and jobs lost for speaking up, from author interview with Marie Scutellaro Werts in Toms River, NJ, September 17, 2008. For example of McFeely administration's retribution against opponents, see chapter 10, regarding Herman Matson's lawyer, Edward Stover. For details of a McFeely campaign to cause the collapse of an opponent's business, see John T. Madigan, FBI agent, Newark, NJ, office, report "Regarding Bernard N. McFeely, Alias Barney McFeely; Edward McFeely; Frank Romano, Civil Rights and Domestic Violence," filed June 6, 1939, box 17313, 4th folder (1/25/39–7/26/39), DOJ Central Files, Classified Subject Files, Correspondence, Records of the DOJ (RG 60), NACP; and Ann Harper to Attorney General Frank Murphy, February 10, 1939, box 4402, folder section 1 (1/2/39–2/15/39 236400), Records of the DOJ (RG 60), NACP. For additional allegations of McFeely administration refusal to allow political opponents to speak in public parks, and allegations by his political opponents of false charges and arrests, see telegram from Jean Louis D'Esque, campaign manager, Fusion Commission Government League, Hoboken, to Hon. Frank Murphy, Attorney General, DOJ, April 21, 1938, box 17593, folder 144-48-0, section 1 (4/5/39–9/5/39), DOJ Subject File 144-48-0, Records of DOJ (RG 60), NACP.

22. "Scutellaro Takes the Stand," reporting trial testimony of Thomas Carmody. Thomas H. Reed and Doris D. Reed, *The Government of Hoboken: A Report of an Administrative and Financial Survey of the City of Hoboken, New Jersey* (New York: National Municipal League, January 1948), 3–7, describes disrepair of public buildings under McFeely reign.

23. "Scutellaro Held Without Bail to the Grand Jury," *JO*, February 26, 1938.

24. Relief Client List prepared by Harry Barck, February 25, 1938, and typed statements to Hoboken Police signed by Galdi, Russo, Corrado, and Scutellaro, *SVJS*.

25. Hoboken city directory listings for Frank Scutellaro, 1899–1911, change from carpenter to contractor. Frank's prior position as a "prosperous building contractor

and owner of real estate" described in "Relief Check Arrived Hour After Scutellaro Left, Wife Reveals," *JJ*, February 25, 1938. New Jersey's construction boom
and bust: Douglas H. MacNeil, *Supplementary Relief Study* (Trenton, NJ: New Jersey
Emergency Relief Administration, May 1936), 19. Joseph Scutellaro's role in his
father's company: author interview with Marie Scutellaro Werts. See also "When
Barck Slain, $8 Reaches Wife as He Stabs File into Heart," *HD*, February 26, 1938,
and Vilas J. Boyle, "Leibowitz Takes Relief Murder," *NYP*, February 26, 1938. Background on Frank's work for city and McFeely's reaction to his support of Bartletta:
author's interview with Marie Scutellaro Werts; see also Quentin Reynolds, *Courtroom: The Story of Samuel S. Leibowitz* (Farrar, Straus and Giroux, New York: 1950),
163–64. For distress among workers in building trades: MacNeil, *Seven Years of
Unemployment Relief in New Jersey*, 35; and Lowitt and Beasley, eds., *One Third of a
Nation*, 354.

26. Multiple newspaper reports stress Joseph Scutellaro's small stature, pallor, frailty,
and glazed expression. See, for example: "M'Feelys Kept Off Record at Slaying
Trial," *NYP*, January 9, 1939; and "Scutellaro Takes the Stand."

27. "Scutellaro Says Death Was Accident," *JJ*, January 12, 1939, includes Scutellaro's
trial testimony as to Corrado's comment.

28. "Relief Client Kills Poormaster," for description of Scutellaro's suit; see also front
page *JJ* photo (February 25, 1938). Regarding death of Harry L. Barck: statement
of Dr. Lawrence J. Kelly of St. Mary Hospital, Hoboken, New Jersey, as provided to
Hoboken Police, February 26, 1938, *SVJS*.

2. A City Divided

1. Judge Charles DeFazio Jr. interviews by Nora Jacobson, 1988 and 1992, as collected
in: Charles DeFazio, *Hoboken: Circus Maximus at All Times; Recollections of Judge
Charles DeFazio, Jr.* (Hoboken, NJ: Hoboken Historical Museum and Friends of the
Hoboken Public Library, 2002), 6, 13.

2. Photograph Hoboken Meadows, ca. 1890, Historical Photographs Collection,
Hoboken Public Library, Hoboken, NJ.

3. G. Waring, comp., *The Tenth Census of the United States, Report on the Social Statistics
of Cities*, part 1 (Washington, 1886), 690; Geoffrey W. Clark, "An Interpretation of
Hoboken's Population Trends, 1856–1970," in *Hoboken: A Collection of Essays*, ed.
Edward Halsey Foster and Geoffrey W. Clark (New York: Irvington Publishers,
1975), 47–62.

4. Irish population: Clark, "An Interpretation of Hoboken's Population Trends," 50.
The phrase "near-subsistence wages" is Clark's. Dangerous trades: Federal Writers'
Project of the Works Progress Administration for the State of New Jersey, "New
Jersey: The General View, Racial and National Groups," in *New Jersey: A Guide to Its
Present and Past* (New York: The Viking Press, June 1939), 120. "The Men Who Per-
ished in the Hudson Tunnel Disaster," *Evening Journal*, July 21–23, 1880, describes
worksite disaster that claimed the lives of many Irish American workers.

5. Christoph Lohmann, trans., *Radical Passion: Ottilie Assing's Reports from America and
Letters to Frederick Douglass* (New York: Peter Lang Publishing, 1999), 90–93.

6. Selling the docks: Geoffrey W. Clark, *History of Stevens Institute of Technology, A Record
of Broad-Based Curricula and Technologies* (Jersey City, NJ: Jensen/Daniels, 2000),
18–19. John Maxtone-Graham, *The Only Way to Cross* (New York: The MacMillan

Company, 1972), passim, describes North German Lloyd and Hamburg America's ocean liners. Michael La Sorte, *La Merica, Images of Italian Greenhorn Experience* (Philadelphia: Temple University Press, 1985), 37, 50–54, describes Castle Garden and debarking in Hoboken to be loaded into barges destined for Ellis Island.

7. Clark, "An Interpretation of Hoboken's Population Trends," 50; La Sorte, *La Merica*, 117; and Pete Hamill, *Why Sinatra Matters* (Boston: Little, Brown and Company, 1998), 37–39.

8. Clark, "An Interpretation of Hoboken's Population Trends," 51; "immobilized" is Clark's phrase. German ships seizure and outcome: Howard B. Furer, "Heaven, Hell or Hoboken," *Hoboken History* (1994): 3–10.

9. In "An Interpretation of Hoboken's Population Trends," 60, Clark points out that "census criteria for categorizing the foreign born and their offspring differed with every decennial census," making it difficult to precisely state Hoboken's ethnic changes. However, he does cite 1920 figures regarding the three largest "foreign white stock" groups (either "foreign-born" or native whites with both parents or one parent foreign-born): Italian 16,007, German 13,230, and Irish 8,744, from the *Fourteenth Census of the United States Taken in 1920, Population* (Washington, 1923), 952–53. Italians were therefore the city's largest ethnic group by war's end.

10. Needlework: James A. Weschler, "Hoboken: Story of a Sick City," *PM*, vol. 1, no. 40 (August 12, 1940): 12–19.

11. 1930 U.S. Federal Census Index for Hoboken, on Ancestry.com CD. Neumann Leathers, 1939 company records and photographs, Hoboken Historical Museum collection, Hoboken, NJ; and Philip S. Foner, *The Fur and Leather Workers Union: A Story of Dramatic Struggles and Achievements* (Newark, NJ: Nordan Press, 1950), 537–38, 562, for background on 1930s-era work conditions and brief mention of the Neumann Leathers strike in 1939. Ferry Street was later renamed Observer Highway.

12. Federal Writers' Project of the Works Progress Administration for the State of New Jersey, *New Jersey: A Guide to Its Present and Past*, 262, lists all ten lines that docked in Hoboken. Seven were devoted exclusively to freight; the others carried passengers as well as freight. Day labor: see Marjory Collins and Wilfrid Zogbaum, "Hoboken: The Photographers' Forbidden Paradise," *U.S. Camera* (August 1941): 39–54. List of Italian villages is based on predominant origins of populations that built three Hoboken churches: St. Francis Italian Church (Genoa), St. Ann's Roman Catholic Church (Monte San Giacomo), and the private chapel built by the Societá di Mutuo Soccorso Santa Febronia Patti e Circondario (Patti). For background on St. Francis, see www.stfrancishoboken.com; for St. Ann's, www.st-annchurch.com, and Santa Febronia, Margo Nash, "Retaining Devotion to a Saint and Her Private Chapel," *NYT*, August 27, 2000.

13. Downtown markets: "With Thousands in Closed Bank, Steneck Depositors Have to Beg," *JJ*, October 15, 1932, and 1926 Hoboken city directory listing Italian poultry market owners. At least half, located downtown, carry Italian American surnames. "Poor Box Will Feed Starving: Hoboken Grocers, Faced by Too Many Demands, to Ask Customers' Aid," *JO*, May 29, 1936.

14. Goats: Vilas J. Boyle, "Hoboken: City Could Be Rich; It's Held Down Now," *NYP*, April 12, 1938; and Collins and Zogbaum, "Photographers' Forbidden Paradise," 39–54. On architecture: Federal Writers' Project of the WPA for the State of New Jersey, *New Jersey, A Guide to Its Present and Past*, 262–64.

15. Carrying beer: Albert Hegetschweiler, interview by Jane Steuerwald and Robert Foster, January 31, 1989, reproduced in Albert Hegetschweiler, *Everybody Seems to Know Me by the Paper Hat* (Hoboken, NJ: Hoboken Historical Museum and Friends of the Hoboken Public Library, 2003), 4–5.

16. Blaine A. Brownell and Warren E. Stickle, eds., *Bosses and Reformers: Urban Politics in America, 1880–1920* (Boston: Houghton Mifflin Company, 1973), x, 2.

17. David M. Kennedy, *The American People in the Great Depression: Freedom from Fear,* pt. 1 (New York: Oxford University Press, 1999), 145.

18. Ibid., 253. For a complete analysis of Roosevelt's bolstering of preferred city bosses through federal patronage: Lyle W. Dorsett, *Franklin D. Roosevelt and the City Bosses* (Port Washington, NY: Kennikat Press, 1977), passim. Not only Democrats were favored. Independent Republican Fiorello LaGuardia was one of Roosevelt's preferred city powerbrokers—and Tammany, the out-of-power Democratic Party organization of New York County, was left with nothing.

19. Get-out-the-vote efforts or tithes: Kennedy, *American People in the Great Depression,* 253. Jobs on city payroll: Thomas H. Reed and Doris D. Reed, *The Government of Hoboken: A Report of an Administrative and Financial Survey of the City of Hoboken, New Jersey* (New York: National Municipal League, January 1948), 3–7.

20. Regarding starved budget: Russell B. Porter, "Hoboken Slashes Its Relief Cases from 2,000 to 90 in a Few Weeks," *NYT,* May 24, 1936, which notes Hoboken was *only one* of twelve Hudson County municipalities that had not continued relief on about the same scale as under ERA, and Vilas J. Boyle, "Hoboken: McFeely Tottering; Citizenry Aroused," *NYP,* April 15, 1938, estimating Hoboken's per-capita relief expenditures at less than thirty cents. The workings of Hoboken's relief budget are discussed in detail later in this text. "E. McF" on Relief Client List prepared by Harry Barck, February 25, 1938, *SVJS.*

21. Joseph Scutellaro's date of birth, February 18, 1902: *Social Security Death Index,* accessed via Ancestry.com. On political dynasties: Reed and Reed, *The Government of Hoboken,* passim.

22. Elmer E. Cornwell Jr., "Bosses, Machines, and Ethnic Groups," in *Bosses and Reformers: Urban Politics in America, 1880–1920,* ed. Blaine A. Brownell and Warren E. Stickle (Boston: Houghton Mifflin Company, 1973), 6–22.

23. "Defense Hints Death of Barck Accidental," *JO,* January 11, 1939, notes statement by Ralph Corrado to Scutellaro's counsel regarding their meeting on February 25, 1938; it was read into the trial record. Insufficient funding for WPA jobs: Paul Tutt Stafford, *Government and the Needy: A Study of Public Assistance* (Princeton, NJ: Princeton University Press, 1941), passim.

24. Scutellaro's job history: "Investigation for Out Door Relief," application by Joe Scutellaro, February 1, 1938, *SVJS.* The General Electric Vapor Lamp Company operated its Grand Street plant in Hoboken from 1911 to 1939. Scutellaro's physical and psychological complaints: Jersey City Medical Center records, January 1938, included in case file. Scutellaro's view of WPA as "almost shameful": AS, 8–9. "Pampered poverty rats": James T. Patterson, *America's Struggle Against Poverty in the Twentieth Century* (Cambridge, MA: Harvard University Press, 2000), 45.

25. Joe and Anna Scutellaro's meeting with Harry Barck: "Scutellaro Says Death Was Accident," *JJ,* January 12, 1939, and "Scutellaro Quits Stand," *HD,* January 13, 1939.

26. "Scutellaro Quits Stand."

27. Jumble of papers depicted in crime scene photographs, *SVJS*.

28. Rarity of home ownership in Hoboken: Boyle, "Hoboken: City Could Be Rich," citing WPA survey. Thirty dollars rent listed for Joseph Scutellaro, *Fifteenth Census of the United States, 1930, Population Schedule*, Hoboken, Hudson County, NJ, enumeration district 272, sheet 7A.

29. On begging for aid: "Scutellaro Hits Stand, Collapses," *HD*, January 13, 1939.

30. "Slayer's Wife Tells of Fight Against Poverty," *JO*, February 26, 1938; "Scutellaro Says Death Was Accident"; "Scutellaro Takes the Stand," *JO*, January 12, 1939; John R. Bott, "Scutellaro on Stand Tells Story of Killing, *NYP*, January 12, 1939; and "Scutellaro Quits Stand" offer accounts of Joseph Scutellaro's morning preparation.

31. Walk to city hall: "Confession Introduced in Evidence at Trial Here," *JJ*, January 11, 1939; "Scutellaro Says Death Was Accident"; Bott, "Scutellaro on Stand"; "Scutellaro Quits Stand"; "Jury Hearing Scutellaro Case," *JJ*, January 13, 1939; "Scutellaro Collapses," *JO*, January 13, 1939; and Ralph Corrado, statement to Hoboken Police, February 25, 1938, *SVJS*, provide background on Corrado and their meeting. See "Jury Hearing Scutellaro Case" for Scutellaro's testimony regarding Corrado, his criminal record, and the prospect of their partnership: "when a person is down and out, he'll do anything to make a dollar," and, when asked by the prosecutor what he meant by "anything," his response, which I have paraphrased here: "To get something to eat for my family."

32. Fallen prices: David E. Kyvig, *Daily Life in the United States, 1920–1940* (Chicago: Ivan R. Dee, 2002), 227.

33. Streetcar fare, buildings, and layout of Washington Street: Federal Writers' Project of the WPA for the State of New Jersey, *New Jersey: A Guide to Its Present and Past*, 262–63. Proliferation of FOR RENT signs: Collins and Zogbaum, "Photographers' Forbidden Paradise," 45–46.

34. Established poormaster office hours: Robert L. Stevens Fund for Municipal Research in Hoboken, *Directory of Public Officials, Education, Civic and Charitable Organizations, Churches and Religious Congregations of the City of Hoboken* (Hoboken, NJ: 1911). On Cerutti: "Saw Barck Slain, Woman Asserts," *NYP*, January 10, 1939; "Confession Introduced"; photo caption, front page, *JO*, January 11, 1939, describes Cerutti and her job. Office workers' conversations with policemen: "Barck Jurors Get Confession of Death Blow," *NYP*, January 11, 1939; and "Scutellaro Takes the Stand." The *Fifteenth Census of the United States, 1930, Population Schedule*, Ward 5, Hoboken, Hudson County, NJ, block 161, sheet 3B, lists Josephine Shea as twenty-six years old; in 1938 she would have been thirty-four years old. She had no occupation listed in 1930. Hiring dates of Barck's secretaries: see statements of Josephine Shea, Romayne Mullin, and Adeline Cerutti to the Police Department, City of Hoboken, February 25, 1938, *SVJS*. "Mother Says Dead Child Ate Paint Because of Lack of Food in Home" *JJ*, July 16, 1936, includes Barck's claims he had "no need for trained social workers in this business" and a high school education was all that was needed.

35. For Hickok quotes: Richard Lowitt and Maurine Hoffman Beasley, eds., *One Third of a Nation: Lorena Hickok Reports on the Great Depression* (Urbana: University of Illinois Press, 1981), 8, 47–48. Kennedy, *American People in the Great Depression*, 253, notes New York Mayor LaGuardia's receipt of Washington largesse. See also Dorsett, *Roosevelt and the City Bosses*, 58–59, detailing patronage in New York.

36. Donald S. Howard, *The WPA and Federal Relief Policy* (New York: Russell Sage Foundation, 1943), 82–83, from findings of 1938 survey of "43 representative areas in 28 states," which concluded that such practices were found "throughout the country, different only in degrees."

37. Porter, "Hoboken Slashes Its Relief Cases."

38. The spelling of Eleonore Hartmann's name varies on official documents and in newspaper accounts. Partial trial transcripts for *State v. Joseph F. Scutellaro* spell her name Eleonore Hartmann, and I have used that spelling. Per *Social Security Death Index*, Eleonore Hartmann was born July 26, 1892; she would have been forty-five in February 1938. The *Hoboken City Directory 1910–1911* lists Harry L. Barck Jr., overseer, at 621 Bloomfield Street. Eleonore Hartmann's address, 631 Bloomfield Street, appears on her statement to Hoboken Police, February 25, 1938, *SVJS*.

39. "Poormasters for Uniformity of Laws for Them," *HOB*, December 16, 1912; "Poormasters of State Decide," *HD*, December 16, 1912; "Hoboken May Out for Charity Job," *Trenton Evening Times*, January 15, 1915. "Barck Veteran of War of 1898," *HD*, February 26, 1938, describes Harry Barck's career and his activities as "a staunch Democrat," including regular reelection as president of the Hoboken Rumson Club. For society page references, see, for example, "Gossip of Long Branch," *NYT*, May 10, 1903. For a history, see "Rumson Country Club," *Rumson Borough Bulletin* (Summer 2008): 1–4. For Hartmann's descriptions of her boss: "State Hopes to Complete Side Tonight," *JJ*, late edition, January 11, 1939. Autopsy report, February 25, 1938, performed at Hoffman's Morgue in Hoboken by Doctors Arthur P. Hasking, William P. Braunstein, Manuel Hernandez, and Thomas S. Brady, *SVJS*, states Barck's body was seventy-one and a half inches in length (five feet, eleven and a half inches) and weighed more than 215 pounds.

40. "Saw Barck Slain" and photographs published on front pages of *HOB* and *HD*, January 11, 1939; *JJ*, January 14, 1939. Hartmann's view of Barck and her lack of secretarial skills: "Eye-Witness Gives Story of Murder," *JJ*, January 10, 1939. *Polk's Jersey City and Hoboken Directory, 1925–1926* lists Hartmann's occupation as "artist." Hartmann's work at No. 7 School: statement by Eleonore Hartmann to Hoboken Police, February 25, 1938, *SVJS*. Regarding Barck's regular secretary: "Harry Barck Stabbed by Relief Client, Seize Slayer of Hoboken Official at the City Hall," *JO*, February 25, 1938. Handwritten notes by interviewer: Joseph Scutellaro, Investigation for Out Door Relief, application, February 1, 1938, *SVJS*. Barck sometimes chose to see clients himself: *SVJS*, partial trial transcript, January 10, 1939, testimony of Eleonore Hartmann, 37.

41. Barck excused Hartmann: "Harry Barck Stabbed." "Relief trust" comment: "No One Goes Hungry, Says Poormaster," *HOB*, January 10, 1938.

42. New Jersey poormasters blocking change and doing what taxpayers demanded: Stafford, *Government and the Needy*, 100, 162. On the latter, he quotes *Child Welfare in New Jersey, Part 4* (US Department of Labor, Children's Bureau, publication no. 180, 1927), 22.

43. "Barck's Death Violently Ends Relief Storm," *HD*, February 26, 1938, quoting remarks Barck made at meeting of State Association of Overseers of the Poor. See also Josephine C. Brown, *Public Relief, 1929–1939* (New York: Henry Holt and Company, 1940), 277, regarding development of social-work personnel standards under New Jersey's Emergency Relief Administration.

44. Barck often criticized New Jersey ERA; see, for example, Porter, "Hoboken Slashes Its Relief Cases." After Barck regained control over local aid and publicly criticized the federally financed state program, the former director for Hudson County Emergency Relief, John F. O'Neil, countered that Barck had been the one to sign off on Hoboken aid under the program.

45. Ibid., and Harry Hopkins, *Spending to Save: The Complete Story of Relief* (New York: W. W. Norton & Company, 1936), 101–2.

46. On Barck's attitude toward Herman Matson: "No One Goes Hungry"; on his attitude toward "foreigners," see Porter, "Hoboken Slashes Its Relief Cases."

47. "Poormaster Barck Punched by Relief Client," *JJ*, February 7, 1938; "Is Jailed for Barck Assault," *HOB*, February 8, 1938.

48. See "Is Jailed for Barck Assault" for Barck's use of the word "spitfire" to describe Rose Zitani. This article also refers to her as "slender" and a "comely young matron."

49. "Zitani Offers Apology, Freed," *HOB*, February 12, 1938; "Zitani Released on Parole in Attack on Poormaster, *HD*, February 12, 1938; and "Attacker of Poormaster Is Released," *JJ*, February 12, 1938.

50. Scutellaro's account of what happened in the poormaster's office: "Scutellaro Says Death Was Accident"; "Scutellaro Takes the Stand." See also Bott, "Scutellaro on Stand"; "Barck Trial Halts as Prisoner Faints," *NYT*, January 13, 1939; and "Scutellaro Quits Stand."

51. Report prepared by Dr. Laurence M. Collins for Prosecutor's Office, November 5, 1938, *SVJS*, states Scutellaro was five feet, five and a half inches in height and, after gaining weight during nine months of incarceration, weighed 127 pounds. Appearance of poormaster's office from forensic photographs, *SVJS*.

3. Suffer the Little Children

1. Condition of Hoboken Jail cells: Thomas H. Reed and Doris D. Reed, *The Government of Hoboken: A Report of an Administrative and Financial Survey of the City of Hoboken, New Jersey* (New York: National Municipal League, January 1948), 3–7; Building Conservation Associates, *Hoboken City Hall, Exterior Preservation Plan, Appendix D: Jail Documentation* (New York: January 2003), 69–73, History Collection, Hoboken Public Library.

2. Lack of glasses: "Scutellaro Says Death Was Accident," *JJ*, January 12, 1939. "That son of a bitch": statement of John Galdi to Hoboken Police, February 25, 1938, *SVJS*. Galdi claimed Joe muttered the phrase as he left Barck's office.

3. "Scutellaro Trial Gets Underway," *JJ*, January 10, 1939 and "Scutellaro Takes the Stand," *JO*, January 12, 1939, are among numerous accounts of Joe being moved to tears at the mere mention of his children.

4. The Italian family as "a stronghold in a hostile land": Luigi Barzini, *The Italians* (New York: Athenaeum, 1964), 190. Years Joe knew Anna before they married, and date of their anniversary, February 3, 1939: report prepared by Dr. Laurence M. Collins for Prosecutor's Office, November 5, 1938, *SVJS*.

5. Author's interview with Marie Scutellaro Werts in Toms River, NJ, September 17, 2008.

6. AS, 2.

7. Barck as "a big politician": AS, 3. Barck role in supervising Christmas gift giving: Vilas J. Boyle, "Leibowitz Takes Relief Murder," *NYP*, February 26, 1938. See "McFeely Flayed for Blocking Christmas Charity in Hoboken," *JJ*, November 24, 1928, for complaint by United Italian-American Societies and Clubs of Hoboken that City distribution of Christmas baskets was politically based, did not "reach the poor," and did not include necessities like food.

8. "The vote-winning generosity of politicians": AS, 3.

9. See David M. Kennedy, *The American People in the Great Depression: Freedom from Fear*, pt. 1 (New York: Oxford University Press, 1999), 24–25, for discussion of Robert S. and Helen Merrell Lynds' 1925 study of Muncie, Indiana (later published as *Middletown: A Study in Modern American Culture*), which showed employment insecurity demarcated one's position as "working class." Caroline Bird, *The Invisible Scar* (New York: David McKay Company, 1966), 40, notes there were always more poor people in America than recognized. The Depression made them visible.

10. Biographical background on Frank Scutellaro: *Fifteenth Census of the United States, 1930, Population Schedule*, Ward 3, Hoboken, Hudson County, NJ, block 75, sheet 7A, line 12; the 1899–1900 *Hoboken City Directory*, and the following: "Relief Check Arrived Hour After Scutellaro Left, Wife Reveals," *JJ*, February 25, 1938; and "When Barck Slain, $8 Reaches Wife as He Stabs File into Heart," *HD*, February 26, 1938. Leaving on his bicycle: Author interview with Marie Scutellaro Werts. Hereafter, biographical details about the Scutellaro family, unless otherwise noted, are from this source. Biographical background on Marie (Thomas) Scutellaro: *Fifteenth Census of the United States, 1930, Population Schedule*, Ward 3, Hoboken, Hudson County, NJ, block 75, sheet 7A, line 12, which notes she arrived in America in 1887, at age four.

11. For vivid accounts of the vicious treatment of Italian immigrants arriving on the Hoboken piers, see Michael La Sorte, *La Merica, Images of Italian Greenhorn Experience* (Philadelphia: Temple University Press, 1985), 50–52.

12. Ibid., 63, on majority untrained Italian immigrants; on Italian and Irish conflict, 148–52. La Sorte notes: "Some eight of every ten Italians who came to the United States between 1871 and 1910 were from the rural and urban laboring classes, and had no job specialties."

13. For images of downtown Hoboken celebrations in the early twentieth century, see Hoboken Historical Museum collections, www.hobokenmuseum.org. For descriptions, see also Pete Hamill, *Why Sinatra Matters* (Boston: Little, Brown and Company, 1998), 49–50. Description of backyard communal table based on Hoboken photographs from 1920s, author's collection.

14. In 1900 the most common household size in the United States was seven or more people: Frank Hobbs and Nicole Stoops, *Demographic Trends in the 20th Century*, US Census Bureau, Census 2000 Special Reports, CENSR-4 (Washington, DC: US Government Printing Office, November 2002), 137.

15. "Harold Lloyd": AS, 1. Joe's courting of Anna: author's interview with Marie Scutellaro Werts.

16. "Sunny little smile": AS, 8; Joe Jr.'s small size and sickliness are noted on pp. 9 & 10 of same.

17. See Irving Bernstein, *The Lean Years: A History of the American Worker, 1920–1933* (Boston: Houghton Mifflin Co., 1966), 331, for references to multiple reports of

deaths by starvation in 1931 and 1932, and "Hoboken Child Dies of Starvation: Family of 5 Stricken Off Relief in April; Have Existed on $5 Food Order Every Two Weeks Since," *HD*, July 15, 1936.

18. "Hoboken Child Dies of Starvation." See also front-page photos, *JJ* and *HOB*, July 16, 1936, depicting the grieving parents and others beside Donald's coffin. Bird, *The Invisible Scar*, 38, on inability of poor to afford newspapers during the Depression.

19. Author interview with Marie Scutellaro Werts.

20. The Hastie story dominated front pages of local newspapers, *Observer*, *HD*, and *JJ*, from July 15 to July 17, 1936, and involved persons in city hall (including the poormaster's office), the local hospital, police, and at least one church congregation. Quote from First Baptist minister C. Robert Pedersen: "Hoboken Child, Suffering from Lead Poison, Dies," *JJ*, July 15, 1936.

21. "Mother Says Dead Child Ate Paint Because of Lack of Food in Home" *JJ*, July 16, 1936.

22. From caption under photo, front page *JJ*, July 16, 1936.

23. See Douglas H. MacNeil, *Seven Years of Unemployment Relief in New Jersey, 1930–1936* (Washington: Committee on Social Security, Social Science Research Council, 1938), 113, regarding municipalities' payment of indigents' hospital bills, as authorized under state's poor relief law. Surviving City records indicate longstanding City appropriations to St. Mary Hospital for care of the poor. See, for example, *Financial Statement of the City of Hoboken*, May 1, 1911 to May 6, 1912, noting payment of $25,000. Police report is no longer available; references appear in "Hoboken Child Dies of Starvation"; "Mother Says Dead Child Ate Paint"; and "Boy's Funeral Draws Crowd to Tenement," *HD*, July 17, 1936. The report's content was never contested, though the final "cause of death" differed.

24. "Hoboken Child, Suffering from Lead Poison, Dies."

25. See "Mother Says Dead Child Ate Paint."

26. "Simple Service for Dead Child," *JO*, July 17, 1936.

27. "Mother Lays Child's Fatal Paint Eating to Starvation," *HD*, July 16, 1936.

28. "Mother Lays Child's Fatal Paint Eating to Starvation" and "Child's Death Causes Storm," *JO*, July 16, 1936.

29. "Boy's Funeral Draws Crowd." See also front-page photograph, *JO*, July 16, 1936, captioned "Destitute Parents Near Collapse at Child's Casket."

30. More than a dozen journalists: "Boy's Funeral Draws Crowd." "Widespread publicity" in "Child's Death Causes Storm."

31. "Relief in Hoboken Found Deplorable," *NYT*, January 8, 1938. Also, see *State of New Jersey Financial Assistance Commission, 1937 Relief Report* (Trenton, NJ: 1937). Hoboken is included in charts indicating inadequate relief allowances; the city is not mentioned specifically in the text.

32. "We did all we humanly could": "Jobless Man Kills Hoboken Overseer," *NYT*, February 26, 1938. "Poormaster Barck Murdered," *JJ*, February 25, 1938. "Administration is a local matter": "Relief Check Arrived."

4. In the Dark

1. Anna had stayed in bed: "Scutellaro Takes the Stand," *JO*, January 12, 1939, and John R. Bott, "Scutellaro on Stand Tells Story of Killing," *NYP*, January 12, 1939.

On learning to stay in bed to stay warm: Caroline Bird, *The Invisible Scar* (New York: David McKay Company, 1966), 38.

2. Nick Taylor, *American-Made: The Enduring Legacy of the WPA; When FDR Put the Nation to Work* (New York: Bantam Books, 2008), 29; Richard Lowitt and Maurine Hoffman Beasley, eds., *One Third of a Nation: Lorena Hickok Reports on the Great Depression* (Urbana: University of Illinois Press, 1981), 10.

3. "Barck Slayer to Face Court," *Newark Evening News*, February 26, 1938.

4. Descriptions of Anna, Marie, and Joseph Scutellaro Jr.'s physical appearance and attire from newspaper photographs accompanying "Figures in Hoboken Tragedy," *Newark Evening News*, February 26, 1938; "Principals in Hoboken Relief Tragedy," *HD*, February 26, 1938; and "Husband Held as Slayer," *NYP*, February 25, 1938.

5. Author interview with Marie Scutellaro Werts in Toms River, NJ, September 17, 2008.

6. David E. Kyvig, *Daily Life in the United States, 1920–1940* (Chicago: Ivan R. Dee, 2002), 57, 64.

7. *SVJS* includes postmarked envelope and its contents. Three short typed statements are on the reverse; each statement closes with the signature of Edward J. McFeely, chief of police. The first statement, signed by Anna Scutellaro, attests to her receipt of the letter from her mother-in-law "about 10:15AM, Friday, Feb. 25, 1938." The second statement, signed by Adeline Cerutti, certifies that the typist mailed the letter "about lunch time" the previous day. The final statement details the receipt of the letter by Edward J. McFeely and notes the envelope contained a grocery order and a book of bread coupons. Additional letter in *SVJS* from Hoboken Post Office city carrier 12, Allen Brusco, dated February 25, 1938, certifies he delivered the letter "some time between 10.00 and 10.20 AM" on that day. Brusco stated he placed the letter "on top of the mail box in the vestibule at 611 Monroe Street at the request of Mrs. Marie Scutellaro, due to the fact that the mail boxes were out of order."

8. "Relief Check Arrived Hour After Scutellaro Left, Wife Reveals," *JJ*, February 25, 1938, quotes Anna: "My husband used to go all the time [. . .] and Barck told him to fill out an application. We didn't want applications, we wanted food. How can anyone live on $5.70 for five weeks?" As the first check was received on January 28, 1938, and the second on February 25, 1938, and I have not presented the information as a direct quote, I have changed the number of weeks from five to four. Reference to candles is a direct quote from Anna: "Barck Slayer to Face Court."

9. From a comment attributed to Anna, as reported in "Slayer's Wife Tells of Fight Against Poverty," *JO*, February 26, 1938.

10. Unless otherwise noted, Anna's encounter with reporters, their use of flash, and failure to explain what had happened to Joe comes from "Slayer's Wife Tells of Fight." The reporter notes "over a score [twenty] of reporters and news photographers." AP photographs show Anna and her children, sometimes weeping, inside the house, so she must have allowed them entry.

11. 1922 Hoboken city directory notes Joseph Scutellaro's acquisition of a license, listing his occupation as "chauffeur." Digging ditches: author interview with Marie Scutellaro Werts.

12. Anna's comments about Joe's "nervous condition" and treatment at Jersey City Medical Center: "Relief Check Arrived." See also trial testimony of Dr. John J. Mackin, who saw Scutellaro on January 3 and February 1, 1938: "Jury Gets Scutellaro Case

This Afternoon," *HD*, January 14, 1939. In "Out of Work, Two Children Ill," *HD*, February 26, 1938, Anna explains Joe left every day between 6 and 7 AM to look for work.

13. Three relatives identified as Anna's father-in-law, a cousin, and an aunt: AS, 16.

14. According to the *Manual of the Legislature of New Jersey*, 1938, the *Jersey Observer*, with offices at 111 Newark Street, was published every afternoon in Hoboken. From 1911 to 1924, it was called the *Hudson Observer*; from January 31, 1924 to November 16, 1951, the *Jersey Observer*. Numerous city reports during the 1920s to 1940s bear the *Observer*'s imprint. Its espousal of the administration's point of view becomes clear when its coverage is compared to articles published in other area dailies, including the *Jersey Journal* (which had its own bloody contest with Jersey City mayor Frank Hague) and the Union City–based *Hudson Dispatch*. The *Observer*'s reliance on its printing contract: Vilas J. Boyle, "Hoboken: McFeely Tottering; Citizenry Aroused," *NYP*, April 15, 1938.

15. Report of Hartmann's testimony at Scutellaro trial, "Accident May Be Defense in Barck Slaying," *JO*, January 11, 1939: "She had talked with those men [relief clients], she added, and also with one *Jersey Observer* reporter who she knew, immediately after the fatal stabbing." Signed statement of Eleonore A. Hartmann, cosigned by typist/patrolman 16, Bernard Walker, February 25, 1938, 4:40 PM, *SVJS*.

16. The *Observer*'s first article, "Harry Barck Stabbed by Relief Client, Seize Slayer of Hoboken Official at the City Hall," *JO*, February 25, 1938, introduces Eleonore Hartmann (misidentified as Mrs. Eleanor Hartmann) as a relief worker who "witnessed the actual killing of her superior, and went to his aid as Scutellaro sought to escape." There was another "eye-witness" claim much later: In his 1955 self-published memoir, *Halo over Hoboken: The Memories of John Perkins Field as Told to John Leroy Bailey* (New York: Exposition Press, 1955), 86–87, Field claimed he'd been first on the scene after hearing noises in Barck's office. Field worked nearby in the Water Department. His name, however, does not appear on any witness lists prepared by police, defense, or prosecution.

17. See: "When Barck Slain, $8 Reaches Wife as He Stabs File into Heart," *HD*, February 26, 1938.

18. Photographs appeared in *JO*, February 26, 1938. Article describing Hartmann's adjusted account of the crime, "Scutellaro Held Without Bail to the Grand Jury," begins p. 1

19. "Relief Client Kills Poormaster," *NYP*, February 25, 1938, 1. *NYP* exposé appeared in April 1938.

20. Ibid.

5. Defenders

1. Jail description: Building Conservation Associates, *Hoboken City Hall, Exterior Preservation Plan, Appendix D: Jail Documentation* (New York: January 2003), passim, History Collection, Hoboken Public Library. "Leibowitz to Defend Barck Killer, Plans Probe of Relief," *HD*, February 28, 1938.

2. Leibowitz's early cases: Diana Klebanow and Franklin L. Jonas, *People's Lawyers: Crusaders for Justice in American History* (Armonk, NY: M. E. Sharpe, 2003), 159, 176. An entire chapter in their book is devoted to Leibowitz's career, 155–201; Jonas cited as chapter's author. See also Robert Leibowitz, *The Defender: The Life*

and Career of Samuel S. Leibowitz, 1893–1933 (Englewood Cliffs, NJ: Prentice Hall, 1981), passim; *New Yorker* magazine's two-part profile by Alva Johnston, "Let Freedom Ring," pt. 1, June 4, 1932, 21–24, and "Let Freedom Ring," pt. 2, June 11, 1932, 18–23; and Fred D. Pasley, *Not Guilty! The Story of Samuel S. Leibowitz* (New York: G. P. Putnam's Sons, 1933), 118–20. On Scottsboro: James Goodman, *Stories of Scottsboro* (New York: Vintage Books, 1995), 103–4, 152.

3. For synopsis of Scottsboro case with Leibowitz as chief counsel, see Klebanow and Jonas, *People's Lawyers*, 173–85.

4. Author interview with Marie Scutellaro Werts in Toms River, NJ, September 17, 2008.

5. "Grudging release": Klebanow and Jonas, *People's Lawyers*, 184. Was "the man to call": Goodman, *Stories of Scottsboro*, 101.

6. Leibowitz, physical appearance: Pasley, *Not Guilty!*, 120–21; Leibowitz, *The Defender*, 5, 22. Photographs of Leibowitz from late 1920s and 1930s, inset in *The Defender*, invariably show him wearing a three-piece suit. Quentin Reynolds, *Courtroom: The Story of Samuel S. Leibowitz* (New York: Farrar, Straus and Giroux: 1950), 155 ("a relentless eye," noted by a *Bridgeport Herald* reporter). Murray Schumach, "Samuel S. Leibowitz, 84, Jurist and Scottsboro Case Lawyer, Dies," *NYT*, January 12, 1978, cites Leibowitz's birth date, August 14, 1893.

7. "Italians Raise Barck Slayer Defense Fund," *JJ*, February 28, 1938.

8. From photograph of Recorder's Court taken May 27, 1920, Hoboken Historical Photographs Collection, Hoboken Public Library, Hoboken, NJ.

9. Identical reports: David E. Kyvig, *Daily Life in the United States, 1920–1940* (Chicago: Ivan R. Dee, 2002), 190. See Ancestry.com database; newspapers carrying the story on February 25, 1938, included *Dunkirk Evening Observer* (Dunkirk, New York), *The Gettysburg Times* (Gettysburg, Pennsylvania), *Abilene Reporter News* (Abilene, Texas), *Ogden Standard Examiner* (Ogden, Utah); on February 26, 1938, publications included *Albuquerque Journal*, *Gazette Bulletin* (Williamsport, Pennsylvania), *Kokomo Tribune* (Kokomo, Indiana), *North Adams Transcript* (North Adams, Massachusetts), *San Antonio Light*, and *Hammond Times* (Hammond, Indiana).

10. "Italians Raise Barck Slayer Defense Fund." See also "Il Capo Del Relief non era che l'oppressore dei poveri," *PIA*, February 28, 1938, in which a neighbor speculates anti-Italian feeling may have contributed to Barck's hostility toward Scutellaro, translated for author by Elisa Varano.

11. "Defense Fund Reported Under Way for Slayer," *JO*, February 28, 1938; "Leibowitz to Defend Barck Killer."

12. Supporters helped the Scutellaros with fuel and electric bills and bought milk for the children: "Speeds Defense of Barck Slayer, Leibowitz Visits Scutellaro—1,000 Attend Funeral," *HD*, March 1, 1938. *SVJS* includes postmarked envelope from the poormaster's office and its contents. Three short typed statements are on the reverse; each statement closes with the signature of Edward J. McFeely, chief of police. The final statement details the return of the letter to Edward J. McFeely and the following note on its contents: "Contents order No. 7546-E185 dated Feb. 24, 38. book containing 30 salmon color cupons [sic] for bread, Continental Baking Co."

13. Set the stage: Klebanow and Jonas, *People's Lawyers*, 171. "Leibowitz Makes Three-Hour Appeal to Save Scutellaro," *JO*, January 16, 1939, includes references to attempts to curry anti–New York feeling. "Jew from New York": F. Raymond Daniell, "New York Attacked in Scottsboro Trial," *NYT*, April 8, 1933. Leibowitz's office

was at 225 Broadway, next to the Woolworth Building and within a few blocks of a station for "the Tubes" connecting New York and New Jersey by commuter rail. Ferries also ran from downtown Manhattan to Hoboken, and motorists could drive from Manhattan, through the Holland Tunnel, to reach Hoboken.

14. *Fifteenth Census of the United States, 1930, Population Schedule*, Hoboken, Hudson County, NJ, roll 1349, p. 5B, enumeration district 288, image 771.0, estimates Frank Romano's date of birth as 1907, which would make him around 31 in 1938. Physical description of Romano derived from a photograph accompanying "Romano Made Hoboken Judge," *JJ*, May 21, 1935. Photograph of Recorder's Court, History Collection, Hoboken Public Library.

15. Accounts of arraignment: "Defense Fund Reported Under Way"; "Italians Raise Barck Slayer Defense Fund"; and "Leibowitz to Defend Barck Killer."

16. Frank Schlosser was Judge Recorder of Hoboken from 1930 to 1934, when he became Prosecutor of Pleas for Hudson County. See A. N. Marquis, ed., *Who's Who in New Jersey 1939* (Chicago: A. N. Marquis Co., 1939), 777.

17. Photograph accompanying "Romano Made Hoboken Judge." "Defense Fund Reported Under Way."

18. "Lawyer Guild in Hague Slap," *JJ*, December 10, 1937. The Guild's Judiciary Committee recommended placing stenographers in all courts.

19. "Recorder of Hoboken Under Lawyers' Fire," *JJ*, November 19, 1937. On McFeely's disagreement with former employee: "McFeely Battler Fails to Appear in Court," *JJ*, October 25, 1937, and "Mayor McFeely's Sparring Partner Still Missing as Police Search," *JJ*, October 26, 1937.

20. "Recorder of Hoboken Under Lawyers' Fire."

21. See "Second Police Group" photograph accompanying "Hoboken's Finest Has Proud History," *JO*, February 7, 1942.

22. Gray-green eyes: Leibowitz, *The Defender*, 5. Skillful reading: Pasley, *Not Guilty!*, 127–28, quoting Leibowitz.

23. Physical description and age from Edward John McFeely, *U.S. World War II Draft Registration Cards, 1942*, roll WWII_2372200, Hudson County, NJ, via Ancestry.com. All but the swagger is depicted in a photograph of Edward McFeely in "End of a Boss," *Life*, May 26, 1947, 40. See also photographs accompanying "PBA Cheers McFeely as It Honors 12 Retired Men," *JO*, April 25, 1939, and "Hoboken's Finest Has Proud History."

24. "Cop-fighter" from Johnston, "Let Freedom Ring," pt. 2, 22. Discrediting police: Marilynn S. Johnson, *Street Justice: A History of Police Violence in New York City* (Boston: Beacon Press, 2003), 3, 114, 122, 125, and Johnston, "Let Freedom Ring," pt. 1, 21.

25. Exchange reported in "Defense Fund Reported Under Way."

26. Ibid.; "Overseer's Slayer Maps His Defense, Jobless Man Who Stabbed Hoboken Relief Official May Plead Temporary Insanity," *NYT*, February 27, 1938.

27. "The chances are": "Leibowitz to Defend Barck Killer" and "Service Held for Barck," *NYT*, February 28, 1938.

6. Two Funerals

1. "Throng Present at Barck Rites," *JO*, March 1, 1938; "Service Held for Barck," *NYT*, February 28, 1938; "Hundreds at Services Held by Hoboken Elks for Barck," *HD*, 28 February 1938; "Speed Barck Murder Case," *JJ*, March 1, 1938.

2. Pension File, Harry L. Barck Jr. Spanish American/Philippine Insurrection, 4 Regiment, NJ Infantry Co. M, volunteer, shows he mustered-in July 11, 1898, Jersey City, and was stationed in Sea Girt, New Jersey, and Greenville, South Carolina, until October 18, 1898, when his resignation was accepted and he was honorably discharged. *Fifteenth Census of the United States, 1930, Population Schedule*, Ward 2, Hoboken, Hudson County, New Jersey, sheet 11B, lines 60 & 61, for Harry and Augusta Barck, cites 1887 as year they married; "Client Kills Relief Head at Hoboken," *Daily Record*, February 25, 1938, noted they "celebrated their golden wedding anniversary recently." However, photostatic copy of marriage certificate of Harry Barck and Augusta Hoth, First Methodist Episcopal Church of Hoboken (appended to an April 2, 1938 Veterans Administration application for widow's benefits) states they married December 31, 1886. For birth dates of Barck's children, see *Thirteenth Census of the United States, 1910, Population Schedule*, Ward 2, Hoboken, Hudson County, NJ, sheet 1B; and information from Ancestry.com, including *Social Security Death Index, Master File* listing for William (October 15, 1887), Eleanor (April 19, 1891 in California Death Index), and Catharine (December 26, 1900).

3. "Throng Present at Barck Rites."

4. Architectural walking tour, www.hobokenmuseum.org, provides background on glass window, imported from Europe in 1913. "Throng Present at Barck Rites."

5. Oldest man: "Today's News in Pictures," *JJ*, February 26, 1938.

6. Coyle's position as boulevard superintendent: "Coyle, Maloney Killed in Crash," *JJ*, February 13, 1941. Appointment by commissioners: Free Public Library of Jersey City, *A Brief Outline of the Government of Hudson County* (Jersey City, NJ: Free Public Library, 1914), 9. More than 60 percent of county electorate: George C. Rapport, *The Statesman and the Boss: A Study of American Political Leadership Exemplified by Woodrow Wilson and Frank Hague* (New York: Vantage Press, 1961), 74–75. The birthplace of Harry Barck's parents was variously recorded in censuses as the United States or Germany. Barck's death record, issued by the Board of Health and Vital Statistics of the City of Hoboken, lists Germany as the birthplace of his father and mother (the former Katherine Brandenburg).

7. David M. Kennedy, *The American People in the Great Depression: Freedom from Fear*, pt. 1 (New York: Oxford University Press, 1999), 24, referring to pre–Depression era findings on role of employment insecurity in lives of working-class people.

8. *Jersey City–Hoboken Directory*, 1889–90 and 1891–93, list Harry L. Barck Jr. as a shoe salesman, 67 First Street; also mentioned in his obituary, *HD*, February 28, 1938. Barck's identification as liquor salesman: *Jersey City–Hoboken Directory*, 1893–94 and 1894–95. Barck listing as "Executive": *Fifteenth Census of the United States, 1930, Population Schedule*, Ward 2, Hoboken, Hudson County, NJ, sheet 11B, line 60. Chronic poverty: Harry Hopkins, *Spending to Save: The Complete Story of Relief* (New York: W. W. Norton & Company, 1936), 111.

9. Abstaining from alcohol and tobacco: Stephen Gottschalk, *The Emergence of Christian Science in American Religious Life* (Berkeley: University of California Press, 1973), 241. Barck's enjoyment of a cigar in his office: "Check in Mail as Man Kills Relief Official," *Newark Evening News*, February 25, 1938. Christian Science belief that people create their own world through thought: Beryl Satter, *American Women, Sexual Purity, and the New Thought Movement, 1875–1920* (Berkeley: University of California Press, 1999), 3 (my italics). Critics' charges that Christian Scientists

were unconcerned with social problems, did not spend money on orphanages, and were focused on "quickly improved . . . economic standing": Gottschalk, *Emergence of Christian Science*, 219, 269–70. Depression-era editorials in the *Christian Science Monitor* make clear, however, that the church did not oppose publicly funded work relief or direct cash relief. See, for example, "Meeting the Relief Need," *Christian Science Monitor*, February 10, 1938.

10. *Twelfth Census of the United States, 1900, Population Schedule*, Ward 1, Hoboken, Hudson County, NJ, sheet 231A, linc 3.

11. Irish roots of Coyle and Davis: T. F. Fitzgerald, Legislative Reporter, *Legislative Manual, State of New Jersey, 1892* (Trenton, NJ: T. F. Fitzgerald, 1892), 235–36. "Benevolent despot": Ransom E. Noble Jr., *New Jersey Progressivism Before Wilson* (Princeton, NJ: Princeton University Press, 1946), 10. See also Rapport, *Statesman and the Boss*, 29–31. Saloons and political machines: Madelon Powers, *Faces Along the Bar: Lore and Order in the Workingman's Saloon* (Chicago: University of Chicago Press, 1998), 3.

12. German clubs: "Barck Veteran of War of 1898," *HD*, February 26, 1938, and "Barck Murder," *JJ*, February 26, 1938. Davis's paternal approach: Rapport, *Statesman and the Boss*, 31.

13. Description of young Harry Barck: Pension File, Harry L. Barck Jr., Company Muster-in Roll for 1898, when he was 33. Review of Barck family photos, circa 1923–35. For two examples of Harry Barck's way with words and sarcasm, see "Minister Challenges Statement That No One Is Starving," *JO*, May 27, 1936, and "Barck Claims Cleric Erred," *JO*, May 28, 1936.

14. Barck's occupations: *Jersey City–Hoboken Directory*, 1893–94 and 1894–95. Precise figures on number of bars in Hoboken during that period are unavailable. For a later story on Hoboken bars: "284 of Hoboken's 328 Saloons Are Under U.S. Ban," *JJ*, October 1, 1917. Davis as permissive county sheriff: Rapport, *Statesman and the Boss*, 31.

15. "Hundreds at Services"; Robert L. Stevens Fund for Municipal Research in Hoboken, *Directory of Public Officials, Education, Civic and Charitable Organizations, Churches and Religious Congregations of the City of Hoboken* (Hoboken, NJ: 1911), notes that "according to statute" the overseer of the poor has "exclusive charge of the poor."

16. *The Evening Journal (Jersey City) Almanac* (Evening Journal, 1900), n.p., lists members of executive committee of the Michael J. Coyle Association, including Harry L. Barck. Coyle Association: Alfred Steinberg, *The Bosses* (New York: Macmillan Publishing Co., 1972), 40–41.

17. "Smart politics": Vilas J. Boyle, "Leibowitz Takes Relief Murder," *NYP*, February 26, 1938. See *Souvenir, 50th Anniversary of the Exempt Fireman, 1860–1910* (April 9, 1910), History Collection, Hoboken Public Library, Hoboken, for example of Barck's political ads.

18. "Deserving poor": Paul Tutt Stafford, *Government and the Needy: A Study of Public Assistance* (Princeton, NJ: Princeton University Press, 1941), 83–85. Text of 1935 Social Security Act, www.ssa.gov/history/35actinx.html; Frances Fox Piven and Richard A. Cloward, in *Regulating the Poor: The Functions of Public Welfare* (New York: Vintage Books, 1993), 92, 116.

19. See "Resents Barck Statement Says the United Aid, Declares Poormaster Reflected on Society's Work," *JO*, December 13, 1928, for statement issued by president of private local charities association protesting "arbitrary and unsympathetic attitude"

of the poormaster's office; she pointedly noted *her* organization extended aid to persons "without consideration of their political affiliation." Poor people's preference for machine representatives over welfare officials: Stephen Pimpare, *A People's History of Poverty in America* (New York: New Press, 2008), 152.

20. Lyle W. Dorsett, *Franklin D. Roosevelt and the City Bosses* (Port Washington, NY: Kennikat Press, 1977), 6. New Jersey Commission on Defective, Delinquent and Dependent Children and Their Care, Public Hearing Transcripts, 1908, testimony of Harry L. Barck, 1303, in collection of New Jersey State Archives, Trenton; Douglas H. MacNeil, *Seven Years of Unemployment Relief in New Jersey, 1930–1936* (Washington: Committee on Social Security, Social Science Research Council, 1938), 85, 86–89.

21. "Speed Barck Murder Case"; "Throng Present at Barck Rights"; "Speeds Defense of Barck Slayer, Leibowitz Visits Scutellaro—1,000 Attend Funeral," *HD*, March 1, 1938.

22. "Throng Present at Barck Rights" includes phrase "demand of others for respect of the dead."

23. "Check in Mail as Man Kills Relief Official," *Newark Evening News*, February 25, 1938, includes portions of a January 11, 1938, interview, during which Barck discussed retirement.

24. "Two Women Can't Forget Poor Office Slaying Tragedy, Relatives Shield Barck Widow in Dover: Mrs. Scutellaro Won't Reveal Feelings," *HD*, January 16, 1939.

25. *Fourteenth Census of the United States, 1920, Population Schedule*, Ward 2, Dover, Morris County, NJ, sheet 3B, indicates Peter Vanderwolf (Eleanor's husband) was born in Holland, immigrated to the United States in 1915, and was naturalized in 1919. The author was unable to locate records for his brother, who married Catharine. Both described as Dover, New Jersey, residents in "Barck Veteran of War" and "Throng Present at Barck Rites." "Camp Hoboken" reference from an undated family photo postcard, ca. 1925–35.

26. Author interview with Marie Scutellaro Werts in Toms River, NJ, September 17, 2008.

27. "Speeds Defense of Barck Slayer," and Fairview Cemetery, Fairview, New Jersey, regarding Harry L. Barck's purchase of plot 21, block 22, section E on April 13, 1911. As of 2005, seven family members had been buried there, including Harry L. Barck Jr. and, in 1945, his wife, Augusta.

28. "Barck's Successor Named," *JJ*, February 28, 1938, and "Tighe Appointed as Poormaster, Expected to Open Office for Relief Clients Today," *HD*, March 1, 1938. *Report of Commission Appointed to Investigate, Codify and Revise the Laws Relating to the Settlement and Relief of the Poor, Pursuant to Joint Resolution, No. 3, Approved March 11th, 1922, to the Legislature, Session of 1923* (Trenton, NJ: MacCrellish & Quigley, Co., State Printers, 1923), 9, and Stafford, *Government and the Needy*, 162.

7. Taking Account

1. "Jobless Man Kills Hoboken Overseer," *NYT*, February 26, 1938; "The Shape of Things," *Nation*, March 5, 1938, 258–59.

2. "Relief in Hoboken Found Deplorable," *NYT*, January 8, 1938; "Hoboken Relief Is Flayed Again," *JO*, January 8, 1938; "Hoboken Relief Is 'Deplorable' Says State Aid," *HD*, January 8, 1938; "Hoboken Poor Chief Is Scored," *JJ*, January 8, 1938.

3. "When Barck Slain, $8 Reaches Wife as He Stabs File into Heart," *HD*, February 26, 1938.

4. Diana Klebanow and Franklin L. Jonas, *People's Lawyers: Crusaders for Justice in American History* (Armonk, NY: M. E. Sharpe, 2003), 171.

5. Defense of mobsters: Alva Johnston, "Let Freedom Ring," pt. 1, *New Yorker*, June 4, 1932, 21; Alva Johnston, "Let Freedom Ring," pt. 2, *New Yorker*, June 11, 1932, 19. "Long lavender sedan": Robert Leibowitz, preface to *The Defender: The Life and Career of Samuel S. Leibowitz, 1893–1933* (Englewood Cliffs, NJ: Prentice Hall, 1981).

6. Fred D. Pasley, *Not Guilty! The Story of Samuel S. Leibowitz* (New York: G. P. Putnam's Sons, 1933), 122.

7. Leibowitz as super tactician: Klebanow and Jonas, *People's Lawyers*, 159. Seemingly spontaneous: Johnston, "Let Freedom Ring," pt. 2, 18. Use of notebook: Leibowitz, *The Defender*, 16.

8. Author interview with Marie Scutellaro Werts in Toms River, NJ, September 17, 2008.

9. Signed statement by 1932 relief officer, Harold J. Butler, produced February 26, 1938, for Hoboken Police Department, *SVJS*, included: typed "Record of Arrest" form stating, "Prisoner is charged with striking the complainant [Harold Butler] about the face with his hands"; October 19, 1932, waiver signed by Joseph Scutellaro and recorder Frank Schlosser allowing Scutellaro to be tried immediately (waiving indictment and trial by jury); and a complaint for assault and battery with handwritten notes ("Pleads not guilty—signs waiver. 90 days County Jail. October 19—Recons. & sp."). See also *SVJS*, partial trial transcript, January 12, 1939, testimony of Joseph Scutellaro, 7, 9, 14, 26.

10. AS, 14.

11. Ibid., 9.

12. US Bureau of the Census, *Historical Statistics of the United States, Colonial Times to 1970* (Washington, DC: US Government Printing Office, 1975), 126, reports in 1932, 12,060,000 Americans were unemployed, or 24.1 percent. Bank collapse: Tracy Brown Collins, ed., *Living Through the Great Depression* (Farmington Hills, MI: Greenhaven Press, 2004), 8. On Steneck Bank closure: "State Officials and Hudson Bank Men Confer 7 Hours Before Course Is Determined," *JJ*, June 27, 1931, and "With Thousands in Closed Bank, Steneck Depositors Have to Beg," *JJ*, October 15, 1932. The City of Hoboken was a depositor at Steneck, too, but it was able to borrow to make payroll. "Mitchell Acquittal Blow to Steneck Delay Pleas: N.Y. Verdict Gainsays Defense's Contention That 'No Banker Could Get a Fair Trial Now'—Review of Case Continued," *JJ*, June 24, 1933.

13. "With Thousands in Closed Bank."

14. Caroline Bird, *The Invisible Scar* (New York: David McKay Company, 1966), 38; David E. Kyvig, *Daily Life in the United States, 1920–1940* (Chicago: Ivan R. Dee, 2002), 221.

15. Joe hiding lack of income from Anna: AS, 7. Joe's application for relief to pay rent: *SVJS*, partial trial transcript, testimony of Joseph Scutellaro, 9, 14, 26.

16. Paul Tutt Stafford, *Government and the Needy: A Study of Public Assistance* (Princeton, NJ: Princeton University Press, 1941), 164.

17. Douglas H. MacNeil, *Seven Years of Unemployment Relief in New Jersey, 1930–1936* (Washington: Committee on Social Security, Social Science Research Council,

1938), 66–67, notes professionally trained social workers usually claimed possession of limited capital assets was not a barrier to relief if one needed it to maintain the family. New Jersey poormasters traditionally declined to give aid to those who owned real estate or an automobile, even after passage of a 1924 poor law that allowed one to own a home and to receive $200 per annum. The law applied to the person in whose name the title was held. MacNeil, *Seven Years*, 75, notes 1933 Emergency Relief Administration announcement that home/auto ownership was not a legal bar to relief. The bank actually held the mortgage to the Scutellaro home, but they had paid down some of it. See *SVJS*, partial trial transcript, testimony of Joseph Scutellaro, 12.

18. Both quotes: Quentin Reynolds, *Courtroom: The Story of Samuel S. Leibowitz* (New York: Farrar, Straus and Giroux, 1950), 409. Italics in original.

19. Author interview with Marie Scutellaro Werts. Courthouse description: "Tour Notes: The Hudson County Courthouse, Jersey City, N.J., May 9–10, 1975," in collection of the New Jersey Room, Jersey City Public Library, and the Hudson Vicinage, "Brennan Court House" section of www.njcourtsonline.com, New Jersey Judiciary's website.

20. "Thomas F. Tumulty," obituary, *NYT*, December 29, 1953, and details in biographical note about Tumulty's son: Josephine A. Fitzgerald, *Fitzgerald's Legislative Manual, State of New Jersey, 1944* (Trenton, NJ: J. A. Fitzgerald, 1944), 291. Comments on lavish Courthouse versus poverty, see "Leibowitz Makes Three-Hour Appeal to Save Scutellaro," *JO*, January 16, 1939. Marble floor: "Brennan Court House" section of www.njcourtsonline.com.

21. Closing argument: "Leibowitz Makes Three-Hour Appeal." Number unemployed: US Bureau of the Census, *Historical Statistics*, 126.

22. "Barck Slayer Arraigned: Is Refused Bail, Samuel Leibowitz Makes Earnest Plea to Court," *JO*, March 25, 1938. See also William G. McLoughlin, *Court Houses and Court Rooms, United States and New Jersey: Their History and Architecture* (Jersey City, NJ: John Marshall College, 1937), 16; "Hudson County's New Court House: Handsome Building to Be Formally Opened Tomorrow," *JJ*, September 19, 1910.

23. "Courtesy of the court": "Barck Slayer Arraigned"; "Thomas F. Tumulty," obituary; background on Meaney derived from "Thomas Meaney, Ex-Judge, Is Dead," *NYT*, May 18, 1968.

24. "Thomas Meaney, Ex-Judge, Is Dead"; "Meaney Rejection Is Urged by Edison," *NYT*, May 19, 1942.

25. "Barck Slayer Arraigned." All other quotes from Leibowitz at second arraignment are from this source.

26. "Counsel to Ask Early Trial for Barck's Slayer," *JJ*, May 12, 1938.

27. There were six floors to the jail, but several were two stories high, with ceiling heights that allowed for mezzanines: "Visitors Impressed with Features of New Jail," *JJ*, January 4, 1929. Two hundred and fifty was the maximum number of men the jail was designed to hold. Joseph Scutellaro's mental and physical state while in the county jail: report prepared by Dr. Laurence M. Collins for Prosecutor's Office, November 5, 1938, *SVJS*.

28. "Jury Gets Scutellaro Case This Afternoon," *HD*, January 14, 1939; report prepared by Dr. Collins, *SVJS*.

29. Report prepared by Dr. Collins, *SVJS*.

30. Interview with Marie Scutellaro Werts.
31. See Jon Byrne, "A Trip Through the County Jail," *JJ*, January 10, 1941. Samples of Joe's penciled letters to his lawyer, *SVJS*.
32. On Leibowitz's deep research: See Alva Johnston, "Let Freedom Ring," pt. 2, *New Yorker*, June 11, 1932, 22; Pasley, *Not Guilty!*, 34, 118–26; Klebanow and Jonas, *People's Lawyers*, 171; and Leibowitz, *The Defender*, 182.
33. Klebanow and Jonas, *People's Lawyers*, 159–60.
34. See "Defense Fund Reported Under Way for Slayer," *JO*, February 28, 1938, in which the reporter (unnamed) asserts Leibowitz planned to call "many of the city's poor who claimed they had suffered at Barck's hands."
35. *Report of Commission Appointed to Investigate, Codify and Revise the Laws Relating to the Settlement and Relief of the Poor, Pursuant to Joint Resolution, No. 3, Approved March 11th, 1922, to the Legislature, Session of 1923* (Trenton, NJ: MacCrellish & Quigley, Co., State Printers, 1923), 9. Barck's fellow commissioners acknowledged his influence in their final report. "No One Goes Hungry, Says Poormaster," *HOB*, January 10, 1938.
36. See Stafford, *Government and the Needy*, 81, 94–95.
37. "No money for unemployment relief": "Pastor Claims Hoboken Poor Are Starving," *HD*, May 27, 1936. Hoboken only Hudson County municipality that did not continue relief on the same scale as the state: Stafford, *Government and the Needy*, 106–11; "Relief in Hoboken Found Deplorable." There are no precise figures on the number of poor persons in Hoboken during this period. But see "Death of Child, 3, Stirs Relief Row," *NYT*, July 16, 1936, which estimates the number of Hoboken residents who had previously received relief as "almost 10,000." This is an increase from 7,870 cited in Russell B. Porter, "Hoboken Slashes Its Relief Cases from 2,000 to 90 in a Few Weeks," *NYT*, May 24, 1936. Earlier figures based on number of Hoboken residents receiving aid from the state in April 1936. See Emergency Relief Administration, *Emergency Relief in New Jersey, October 13, 1931–April 15, 1936: Final Report to the Governor and to the Senate and General Assembly, State of New Jersey* (Trenton, NJ, July 31, 1936), Appendix A–Z, Municipalities in Hudson County, Total Persons Receiving Relief, Hoboken, March 1936. Records indicate the state counted an entire family as a "case." The 7,870 figure is likely an estimate based on actual number of cases (2,308) multiplied by an "average" family of four, with some reduction to reflect individual relief recipients. The average family was likely larger than four, however, and the later *Times* article may have increased the figure to reflect that understanding. *State of New Jersey Financial Assistance Commission Relief Report* (Trenton, NJ: 1937), 38.
38. "To satisfy political private debts": "Serious Charges Made Against Hudson Officials," *Trenton Times*, October 3, 1905. No one accusing Barck of enriching himself during the 1930s: Reynolds, *Courtroom*, 163. Returning surpluses: "Mother Says Dead Child Ate Paint Because of Lack of Food in Home" *JJ*, July 16, 1936.
39. Rotting buildings: Alexander L. Crosby, "The Bosses Leave Town," *New Republic*, March 22, 1948, 18; Thomas H. Reed and Doris D. Reed, *The Government of Hoboken: A Report of an Administrative and Financial Survey of the City of Hoboken, New Jersey* (New York: National Municipal League, January 1948), 3–7.
40. Rug quote: Vilas J. Boyle, "Hoboken: McFeely Tottering; Citizenry Aroused, *NYP*, April 15, 1938; author telephone interview with Daniel Matson, April 8, 2009, indicating Herman may have been the source for the rug revelation, received from an outraged McFeely secretary.

8. The Nepotistic Republic

1. On alleged McFeely wrongdoing, see, for example, Vilas J. Boyle, "Hoboken: Symbol of Civic Shame; A City Rots as Its Mayor Waxes Rich," *NYP*, April 5, 1938. Leibowitz's strategy, see, for example, Quentin Reynolds, *Courtroom: The Story of Samuel S. Leibowitz* (New York: Farrar, Straus and Giroux, 1950), 165–69.
2. "Barney McFeely's Death Recalls an Earlier Hoboken," editorial, *JJ*, August 10, 1949. McFeely's appearance and background, see "End of a Boss," *Life*, May 26, 1947, 40; Vilas J. Boyle, "Hoboken: A Look at McFeely, the Man," *NYP*, April 9, 1938; "The McFeely," *Time*, May 26, 1947, www.time.com/time/magazine/article/0,9171,793712,00.html.
3. McFeely's alleged beating of a school janitor with an ashtray: "McFeely Battler Fails to Appear in Court," *JJ*, October 25, 1937. McFeely's use of "physical force" to eject opponent Frank Bartletta from his office, with resulting cuts to the mayor's hands: "The Rise and Fall of Ambition," *HD*, February 11, 1928.
4. Boyle, "Hoboken: Symbol of Civic Shame." The *NYP* series was introduced on April 5, 1938, and concluded on April 15, 1938.
5. Absence of civil service protections on the East Coast: George C. Rapport, *The Statesman and the Boss: A Study of American Political Leadership Exemplified by Woodrow Wilson and Frank Hague* (New York: Vantage Press, 1961), 186. Hoboken voters did not approve the civil service system until November 1946; see Alexander L. Crosby, "The Bosses Leave Town," *New Republic*, March 22, 1948, 18. Mark Wasserman, "Great Depression," *Encyclopedia of New Jersey*, ed. Maxine N. Lurie and Mark Mappen (New Brunswick, NJ: Rutgers University Press, 2004). Comparison of relief budget and City pay to McFeely kin: Vilas J. Boyle, "Hoboken: McFeely Tottering; Citizenry Aroused, *NYP*, April 15, 1938. See also Boyle, "Hoboken: Symbol of Civic Shame," reporting that as many as seventy-nine of "the McFeely kin" were being supported by Hoboken taxpayers.
6. Amounts paid to McFeely kin listed in: Crosby, "The Bosses Leave Town"; Boyle, "Hoboken: Symbol of Civic Shame."
7. Thomas H. Reed and Doris D. Reed, *The Government of Hoboken: A Report of an Administrative and Financial Survey of the City of Hoboken, New Jersey* (New York: National Municipal League, January 1948), 3. The legislative committee that investigated countywide political corruption was named after its first chair, New Jersey State Senator Clarence E. Case. Final report: *Journal of the Eighty-fifth Senate of the State of New Jersey* (Trenton, NJ: MacCrellish & Quigley, Co., 1929), 1098–1151. Page 1117 refers to collection of at least 3 percent of the annual salary of Hoboken's public employees; the demand did not cover law department employees—probably because they could be disbarred, as the system was in violation of the Election Law—and was said to exclude all those "holding appointive offices." McFeely's bank accounts: "Boss Rich in 3 Years," *JJ*, September 21, 1928.
8. "Alleged loss": *Journal of the Eighty-fifth Senate of the State of New Jersey*, 1145. "Milton Also to Be Quizzed," *JJ*, July 13, 1928, on Case Committee findings. "Griffin Dead," *JJ*, January 15, 1931, states courts valued Griffin's fortune in 1927 at more than $1 million. McFeely's fortune: "The McFeelys as 'Go-Getters,'" editorial, *JJ*, September 21, 1928. See "With McFeely New Leader, Griffin to Stay Out of Hoboken," *JJ*, September 30, 1925; "P.R. Griffin to Be Buried on Saturday," *JJ*, January 15, 1931; and "Milton Also to Be Quizzed," regarding Griffin's illness and permanent

institutionalization in an asylum, which also put him out of the reach of the state legislative commission's investigation into county corruption.

9. Estimate of McFeely's wealth: Boyle, "Hoboken: Symbol of Civic Shame." Article about garbage contracts: Vilas J. Boyle, "Hoboken: There's Gold in That Garbage," *NYP*, April 6, 1938.

10. Ibid. Boyle cites mandated dimensions for the plot: "The bidder must own, have under lease, the right to control or possess the contract for the purchase of . . . a plot of ground of the dimensions of 100 by 200 feet located with the city of Hoboken, west of Harrison Street, between Second and Sixth Streets, or west of Jackson Street, between Fifth and Ninth Streets, or west of Madison Street, between Ninth and Jackson Streets." See "Milton Also to Be Quizzed," citing the Walsh Act, Chapter 221 of the Laws of 1911, which prohibits official self-dealing on city contracts.

11. Horse-drawn garbage wagons: Reed and Reed, *The Government of Hoboken*, 137. Details of 1923 bidding war for City of Hoboken garbage contract: *Journal of the Eighty-fifth Senate of the State of New Jersey*, 1136–38; Boyle quotes this source in "Hoboken: There's Gold in That Garbage." See also "Milton Also to Be Quizzed."

12. "Story of Hoboken—Truck Racket, Too," *NYP*, April 7, 1938. See also "Commissioner Clark and Mayor McFeely in Break," *JJ*, May 3, 1934.

13. "Speeds Defense of Barck Slayer, Leibowitz Visits Scutellaro—1,000 Attend Funeral," *HD*, March 1, 1938; interview with Marie Scutellaro Werts in Toms River, NJ, September 17, 2008.

14. Author interview with Marie Scutellaro Werts. Leibowitz at home: Fred D. Pasley, *Not Guilty! The Story of Samuel S. Leibowitz* (New York: G. P. Putnam's Sons, 1933), 215; Robert Leibowitz, *The Defender: The Life and Career of Samuel S. Leibowitz, 1893–1933* (Englewood Cliffs, NJ: Prentice Hall, 1981), 51.

15. Leibowitz's concerns about jury bias: "Tilts Mark Selection of Barck Jurors," *JO*, January 10, 1939. Ethnic animosity was common in Hoboken prior to World War II; see Louis LaRusso II interview by Chris O'Connor, as collected in *The Simple Dialogue of My People: Recollections of Hoboken Playwright Louis LaRusso II* (Hoboken, NJ: Hoboken Historical Museum and the Friends of the Hoboken Public Library, 2006), 3. "Guinea town" reference: Agnes Carney Hannigan, quoted in Kitty Kelley, *His Way: The Unauthorized Biography of Frank Sinatra* (New York: Bantam Books, 1986), 23. Leibowitz's familiarity with ethnic sparring: Pasley, *Not Guilty!*, 64.

16. Background on Frank Scutellaro derived from author interview with Marie Scutellaro Werts and family photographs she shared. See also photographs in *Daily News* archive (www.dailynewspix.com).

17. Testimony during 1928 Case Commission investigation revealed McFeely thwarted Italians out of political pique and economic rivalry; they were competing with him for the City garbage contract. See *Journal of the Eighty-fifth Senate of the State of New Jersey*, 1098–1151; and Vilas Boyle, "Hoboken: The Rackets Bloom in the McFeely Garden," *NYP*, April 8, 1938, which quotes from commission findings. See also copies of "The Hoboken Citizen," circa 1938–39, a weekly newsletter, in English and Italian, distributed by the Hoboken Independent Citizens Committee, which negatively compares McFeely's rule with the "live and let live" philosophy of his predecessor, Patrick Griffin, box 17594, folder 144-48-1, DOJ Subject File 144-48-1, Records of the DOJ (RG 60), NACP.

18. See transcript of interview by author and Robert Foster with Jack O'Brien for Hoboken Oral History Project, July 15, 2004, p. 5, in which he describes Our Lady

of Grace as "an Irish parish," transcript in history collection, Hoboken Public Library. St. Francis Italian Church was completed in 1889 and St. Ann's Church (originally St. Anna) in 1900–1903. Online histories of St. Francis Church (www .stfrancishoboken.com) and St. Ann's (www.st-annchurch.com/history.asp) cite Italians' need for their own churches.

19. See, generally, Stefano Luconi, "Forging an Ethnic Identity: The Case of Italian Americans," *Revue francaise d'etudes americaines*, vol. 2, no. 96 (2003): 89–101, www .cairn.info/revue-francaise-d-etudes-americaines-2003-2-page-89.htm.

20. Draft registration card, Frank Scutellaro, *World War I Draft Registration Cards, 1917– 1918*, roll 1712109, Hudson County, NJ, draft board 2, via Ancestry.com. Frank, born on December 20, 1874, registered on September 12, 1918; this last of three waves of registration included men born between September 11, 1872 and September 12, 1900. Regarding effect of World War I on Hoboken's German community, see generally, Howard B. Furer, "Heaven, Hell or Hoboken: The Effects of World War I on a New Jersey City," *New Jersey History*, vol. 92 (1974): 147–69.

21. "284 of Hoboken's 328 Saloons Are Under U.S. Ban," *JJ*, October 1, 1917; "Uncle Sam Closes 385 Hoboken Saloons," *JJ*, November 21, 1917; "Army Raiders Find Whiskey in 'Tea' Pots," *JJ*, March 30, 1918.

22. Author interview with Marie Scutellaro Werts. Location of Scutellaro's bar and dates of operation could not be confirmed. According to *City Council Minutes* for May 26, 1909, Frank was then a petitioner for a retail liquor license.

23. "Hoboken 'Wettest Spot in the U.S.' Anti-Saloon League Superintendent Slams Gov. Larson," *JJ*, March 17, 1930. "Hoboken Police Seen Drinking at Bar," *JJ*, April 26, 1930.

24. Vulnerable East Coast cops: Rapport, *Statesman and the Boss*, 186. Hoboken firefighters and patrolmen who served McFeely: Boyle, "Hoboken: The Rackets Bloom," which draws upon Case Commission reports.

25. David E. Kyvig, *Daily Life in the United States, 1920–1940* (Chicago: Ivan R. Dee, 2002), 20; "Allows Home Brew over Half Per Cent," *NYT*, July 25, 1920.

26. See, for example, "120 Agents in Dry Army Make Raid on Hoboken," *JJ*, June 12, 1930. Mark Edward Lender and James Kirby Martin, *Drinking in America: A History, The Revised and Expanded Edition* (New York: The Free Press, 1987), 154, notes many states were unwilling to pay the bill for enforcement and "were inclined to surrender their enforcement responsibilities to the federal Prohibition unit." The author has found no published statements revealing Griffin's or McFeely's position on enforcement responsibilities.

27. See Charles DeFazio, *Hoboken: Circus Maximus at All Times; Recollections of Judge Charles DeFazio, Jr.* (Hoboken, NJ: Hoboken Historical Museum and Friends of the Hoboken Public Library, 2002), 11–12.

28. Douglas H. MacNeil, *Supplementary Relief Study* (Trenton, NJ: New Jersey Emergency Relief Administration, May 1936), 19, regarding 1920s building boom in New Jersey and "the entire country," with attendant employment. Amount Joe made: AS, 5.

29. Author interview with Marie Scutellaro Werts; Boyle, "A Look at McFeely."

30. Luconi, "Forging an Ethnic Identity," www.cairn.info/revue-francaise-d-etudes -americaines-2003-2-page-89.htm.

31. Joseph A. J. Dear, ed. *The Book of New Jersey* (Jersey City, NJ: Jersey City Printing Co., 1929), 180; "McFeely in Panic over Desertion of 6,000 Italians," *JJ*, October 25,

1928; and *Social Security Death Index*, citing Frank Bartletta's date of birth, August 20, 1898, via Ancestry.com. "Hoboken Police Continuing Lottery Probe," *HD*, February 13, 1928.

32. Bartletta's home address, 913 Hudson Street, and work history: Dear, ed., *The Book of New Jersey*, 180. Address of Bartletta's Association, 508 Fourth Street, appears in numerous articles, including "McFeely Flayed for Blocking Christmas Charity in Hoboken," *JJ*, November 24, 1928. Additional background on Bartletta: "The Rise and Fall of Ambition"; "Bartletta Enjoins Police," *JO*, February 15, 1928; "Bartletta 'Alias Luke Adams,'" *JO*, February 11, 1938. See also Kelley, *His Way*, 26, regarding surreptitious support of Bartletta, a Republican, by Frank Sinatra's mother, Dolly, then a ward heeler for McFeely: "He [Bartletta] was an Italian, and that was more important to Dolly than his political affiliation."

33. "The Rise and Fall of Ambition"; "Boss Rich in 3 Years." On United Italian-American Societies: "McFeely in Panic over Desertion of 6,000 Italians."

34. On raids: "Bartletta Aide Raided in Hoboken," *HD*, February 15, 1928; "Bartletta Expected to Visit Prosecutor," *JO*, February 27, 1928; "Wine Seizure Case Taken to Higher Court," *JJ*, March 29, 1928; "McFeely Slings Mud as Italians Plan Suit to Get Bazaar Permit," *JJ*, December 4, 1928; "Testimony Taken in Fight for Dance Hall Permit, *HD*, December 21, 1929; and Vilas J. Boyle, "Hoboken: The Police Are Disgusted," *NYP*, April 8, 1938, citing Joseph Clark's testimony before a Supreme Court commissioner. During their raid of Finizio's home, police seized three barrels of wine: "Bartletta Aide Raided in Hoboken."

35. Pete Hamill, *Why Sinatra Matters* (Boston: Little, Brown and Company, 1998), 75–76, regarding Hoboken Italian Americans' belief, after their participation in the World War, that they "had earned the right to be called Americans," and also regarding their views on wine and Prohibition.

36. "Parade Features Celebration of Columbus Day in Hoboken," *HD*, October 13, 1928.

37. "Italian Parade Is McFeely Bolt," *JJ*, October 12, 1928.

38. "Parade Features Celebration"; for descriptions of McFeely's general demeanor: "The McFeely," *Time*.

39. "The waning power of Leader 'Barney' McFeely and his machine" and "the bands played the Italian and American national anthems": "Italian Parade Is McFeely Bolt."

40. Biographical background on Clark: "Joseph A. Clark Dead," *NYT*, October 11, 1960. See Boyle, "Hoboken: The Police Are Disgusted," for a reprinted portion of Clark's testimony before a Supreme Court commissioner, after he was removed without cause or compensation from his city hall position. Clark viewed this as punishment for breaking politically with McFeely. Italics added by author. See also "Clark's Bolt Causes Change In 1935 Lineup," *HD*, May 4, 1934; "Ouster Witness Charges Drinking Impeded Clark," *JJ*, July 26, 1934; and "Clark Trial Adjourned After Lively Session," *JJ*, July 30, 1934.

41. Author interview with Marie Scutellaro Werts.

42. "McFeely Flayed"; "Ask High Court to Stop McFeely War on Italians," *JJ*, December 19, 1928.

43. Caroline Bird, *The Invisible Scar* (New York: David McKay Company, 1966), 28.

9. Circus Maximus

1. Recommendations to increase funding for WPA and other relief agencies and to provide new funding for public works projects were two items on a longer list Roosevelt presented to Congress. See "The Text of President Roosevelt's Recovery Program Message to Congress," *NYT*, April 15, 1938. Despite warnings: Nick Taylor, *American-Made: The Enduring Legacy of the WPA; When FDR Put the Nation to Work* (New York: Bantam Books, 2008), 346. Roosevelt received this advice from Hopkins, economic advisor Leon Henderson, and, most strongly, from Federal Reserve Board chairman Marriner Eccles. By early 1938, other advisors joined in support of public spending increases to "stimulate mass consumption"; see Alan Brinkley, *The End of Reform: New Deal Liberalism in Recession and War* (New York: Alfred A. Knopf, 1995), 24–28, 82–101. "Address of the President Delivered by Radio from the White House, Thursday, April 14, 1938, (about 10:30 PM)," www.mhric.org/fdr/chat12.html. The request for new relief-related expenditures totaled $2.062 billion; $950 million was requested in federal loans: see also Brinkley, *End of Reform*, 100–101.

2. Herman Matson was born on July 10, 1900; he was three months shy of his thirty-eighth birthday when he heard the April 1938 radio address. See Herman Matson, Connecticut Department of Health, *Connecticut Death Index, 1949–2001*, Ancestry.com. Further background: Morris Milgram, statement to John T. Madigan, FBI agent, Newark, NJ, office, report dated May 4, 1939, file 7-77, p. 22, box 15205, folder 109-286, section 1 (3/25/39–5/4/39), DOJ Central Files, Classified Subject Files, Correspondence, Records of the DOJ (RG 60), NACP. On the *Leviathan*, formerly the *Vaterland*, see www.atlanticliners.com/vaterland_home.htm. On Matson's work: Herman Matson, statement to John T. Madigan, FBI agent, Newark, NJ, office, report dated June 30, 1939, file 44-2, p. 12, box 17593, folder 144-48-0, section 1 (4/5/39–9/5/39), DOJ Subject File, Records of the DOJ (RG 60), NACP. "Relief in Hoboken Found Deplorable," *NYT*, January 8, 1938; "No One Goes Hungry, Says Poormaster," *HOB*, January 10, 1938. During this period the Matsons resided at 812 Willow Avenue. Description of apartment's close quarters from author's telephone interview with Herman's daughter, Evelyn Olsen, April 1, 2009. Recollection of Herman listening to Roosevelt's "Fireside Chats" on the family radio from author's telephone interview with one of his sons, Raymond Matson, April 15, 2009.

3. Background on Matson's positive outlook and focus on the well-being of others from author telephone interviews with his son Daniel Matson, March 31, 2009; grandson Scott Matson, April 13, 2009; son Raymond Matson, April 15, 2009; and daughter Evelyn Olsen, April 1, 2009. See also Dorothy Dunbar Bromley, "Strike a Balance," *NYP*, September 22, 1938. For background on and successes of organizations of able-bodied unemployed, see Frances Fox Piven and Richard A. Cloward, in *Regulating the Poor: The Functions of Public Welfare* (New York: Vintage Books, 1993), 64, 104–11; Mauritz A. Hallgren, *Seeds of Revolt: A Study of American Life and the Temper of the American People During the Depression* (New York: Alfred A. Knopf, 1933), 192–95; and Franklin Folsom, *Impatient Armies of the Poor: The Story of Collective Action of the Unemployed, 1808–1942* (Niwot, CO: University Press of Colorado, 1991), 341–87. On hope, along with desperation and fury, as driving forces for

some Depression-era protestors, see T. H. Watkins, *The Great Depression: America in the 1930s* (Boston: Little, Brown & Co., 1993), 15.

4. Poor's support of Roosevelt: Richard Lowitt and Maurine Hoffman Beasley, eds., *One Third of a Nation: Lorena Hickok Reports on the Great Depression* (Urbana: University of Illinois Press, 1981), 10. Matson's admiration for Roosevelt from author interview with Evelyn Olsen.

5. "Woman Who Spat at Barck Is Free from County Jail," *JJ*, March 3, 1938.

6. Donald S. Howard, *The WPA and Federal Relief Policy* (New York: Russell Sage Foundation, 1943), 247. On WPA employment as an uneasy "hybrid" of "public relief and public employment," see especially, Chad Alan Goldberg, *Citizens and Paupers: Relief, Rights, and Race, from the Freedmen's Bureau to Workfare* (Chicago: University of Chicago Press, 2007), 109–14.

7. Certification process and reapplication: Howard, *WPA and Federal Relief*, 368–72. List shared with Matson: Herman Matson, statement to John T. Madigan, FBI agent, Newark, NJ, office, report dated May 4, 1939, file 7-77, p. 43, box 15205, folder 109-286, section 1 (3/25/39–5/4/39), DOJ Central Files, Classified Subject Files, Correspondence, DOJ (RG 60), NACP.

8. Local variability regarding determinants for eligibility: Howard, *WPA and Federal Relief*, 271.

9. "Employment Record of Mr. Herman Matson, 812 Willow Avenue, Hoboken, New Jersey," produced by the WPA, box 1878 (NJ I–R 1937–38), folder 641 (NJ Ma–Mc), Central Files, State 1935–1944, Records of the Works Project Administration 1922–1944 (RG 69), NACP. Also, Herman Matson, statement to Madigan, May 4, 1939, file 7-77, p. 43.

10. "Relief in Hoboken Found Deplorable"; "Hoboken Relief Is Flayed Again," *JO*, January 8, 1938.

11. Author interviews with Raymond Matson and Evelyn Olsen. See also Bromley, "Strike a Balance." On traditional poormaster's view that disagreeableness and inadequacy of public aid was "good," see Lowitt and Beasley, eds., *One Third of a Nation*, 36.

12. "No One Goes Hungry."

13. Lowitt and Beasley, eds., *One Third of a Nation*, 5, quoting Hickok about the Unemployed League she encountered in Pennsylvania, "a sort of union of the unemployed." On Unemployed Leagues: Frances Fox Piven and Richard A. Cloward, in *Regulating the Poor: The Functions of Public Welfare* (New York: Vintage Books, 1993), 105–8. During this period the Leagues had about 450,000 supporters in eight states, including New Jersey, New York, and Pennsylvania. See Matt Perry, *Bread and Work: Social Policy and the Experience of Unemployment, 1918–39* (London: Pluto Press, 2000), 155. "Unemployed Hit Hoboken Relief," *JO*, June 3, 1936, states county headquarters for New Jersey State Unemployed League was 630 Palisade Avenue, Union City. "Even at the risk of arrest": "Jobless Unit for Hoboken Is Their Aim," *JO*, June 5, 1936.

14. "Nice fellow" quote in Bromley, "Strike a Balance."

15. On the CIO's and WDL's early 1938 battles to distribute circulars in Jersey City, see: "No License Needed to Pass Circulars," *NYT*, March 29, 1938; "Jersey City Ends Ban on Circulars," *NYT*, April 1, 1938; and "Limitless Leaflets," *Time*, April 11, 1938. "Haguetown": McAlister Coleman, "Hague's Army Falls Back," *Nation*, November 26, 1938, 557. On formation of Workers Defense League: Harry

Fleischman, *Norman Thomas: A Biography* (New York: W. W. Norton & Co., 1964), 159. Norman Thomas, national chairman of the Socialist Party, was one of WDL's founders, along with friends in the labor movement.

16. Joseph Shaplen, "Socialists Move to Restore Unity," *NYT*, May 28, 1936, regarding WDL and WAA's formation of a joint committee. On WAA's activities on behalf of WPA workers: Goldberg, *Citizens and Paupers*, 107–52; Piven and Cloward, *Regulating the Poor*, 106–10.

17. Piven and Cloward, *Regulating the Poor*, 108n64.

18. Lauren D. Lyman, "Jobless Assembly in Trenton Votes State of 'Revolt,'" *NYT*, April 26, 1936.

19. Ibid.; see also "Jobless to Picket Assembly Members," *JJ*, April 23, 1936; "Jobless Force Assembly Meet Tomorrow," *JJ*, April 24, 1936; "Jobless, in Uproar, Start New Party," *JJ*, April 28, 1936; "Jobless Army Ousted," *JJ*, April 30, 1936.

20. Registered Democrat: Matson, statement to Madigan, June 30, 1939. "Fighting for free speech": "Matson Denies Red, Criminal Accusations," *JJ*, October 18, 1940. WDL assistance to Scutellaro family: "Barck Murder Trial Postponed to Nov. 14," Workers Defense League of New Jersey *News Bulletin*, October 1938, in the Workers Defense League Collection, box 130, folder 7, Archives of Labor and Urban Affairs, Wayne State University, and "Speeds Defense of Barck Slayer," *HD*, March 1, 1938. Matson's membership in WDL: "Matson Denies Red." Hague's bare-knuckles campaign, beginning in late 1937, to suppress a Congress of Industrial Organizations' drive to organize workers in Jersey City and to prevent circulation of literature for same: Alfred Steinberg, *The Bosses* (New York: Macmillan Publishing Co., 1972), 55–58; Coleman, "Hague's Army Falls Back." In 1939, the US Supreme Court affirmed, in *Hague v. Congress of Industrial Organizations*, that parks and streets were public forums protected by the First Amendment. ACLU counsel Morris L. Ernst successfully argued for the respondent. Matson's initial contact with WDL: Morris Milgram, WDL of NJ state secretary, statement to John T. Madigan, FBI agent, Newark, NJ, office, report dated June 30, 1939, file 44-2, p. 6, box 17593, folder 144-48-0, section 1 (4/5/39–9/5/39), DOJ Subject File, Records of the DOJ (RG 60), NACP.

21. Matsons' apartment, 812 Willow Avenue: Herman Matson, statement to Madigan, June 30, 1939, file 44-2, p. 12.

22. Ibid.

23. "Distributor of Circulars Shifts to Hoboken," *JJ*, April 5, 1938. See also "Employment Record of Mr. Herman Matson," produced by the WPA, box 1878 (NJ I–R 1937–38), folder 641 (NJ Ma–Mc), Central Files, State 1935–1944, Records of the WPA 1922–1944 (RG 69), NACP.

24. Background on Matson's birthplace: Author interview with Raymond Matson, and Connecticut Department of Health, *Connecticut Death Index, 1949–2001*. Searches for a birth certificate have been fruitless. References to length of Matsons' residency in Hoboken vary, but see "Now Matson's Counsel Queries Him on His Belief in God," *JJ*, June 5, 1940, in which Matson describes himself as "a resident of Hoboken for more than 12 years." US Supreme Court decision and Hoboken police promise to abide by it: Herman Matson, statement to Madigan, June 30, 1939, file 44-2, p. 21. Regarding 1938 Supreme Court decision, *Lovell v. City of Griffin, Georgia*, see "No License Needed" and "Limitless Leaflets," *Time Magazine*, April 11, 1938. The WDL filed an amicus curiae brief in the case.

25. "Distributor of Circulars Shifts to Hoboken."
26. Joseph A. Clark to John T. Madigan, FBI agent, Newark, NJ, office, report dated June 2, 1939, file 7-77, p. 82, box 15205, folder 109-286, section 2 (6/2/39), DOJ Central Files, Classified Subject Files, Correspondence, Records of the DOJ (RG 60), NACP; and "On Hoboken Police Force 43 Years," *NYT*, March 13, 1933.
27. Description of Matson's interrogation: Herman Matson, statement to Madigan, June 30, 1939, file 44-2, pp. 22–23.
28. Vilas J. Boyle, "Hoboken: Symbol of Civic Shame; A City Rots as Its Mayor Waxes Rich," *NYP*, April 5, 1938.
29. See "Fifth Warders Uphold McFeely," *JJ*, April 13, 1938, and "Hoboken Groups Assail the Post," *NYP*, April 7, 1938. Fred M. DeSapio, a McFeely club founder and later head of the Good Government ticket that unseated McFeely, offered the Lion's Club resolution. Charles DeFazio Jr., then a city payroller and later a DeSapio campaigner, seconded the resolution.
30. WDL flyer, "Mayor McFeely and His Charlie McCarthies," box 1877 (NJ C–H 1937–38), folder 641 (NJ He–Hz), Central Files, State 1935–1944, Records of the Works Progress Administration 1922–1944 (RG 69), NACP.
31. "Punishing assignments": letter from Pierson Ostrow, Elizabeth, New Jersey, to David K. Niles, Assistant Administrator, WPA, Washington, DC, May 17, 1938, arguing for an investigation into Herman Matson's layoff from the WPA, box 1878 (New Jersey I–R 1937–38), folder 641 (NJ Ma–Mc), Central Files, State 1935–1944, Records of the Works Progress Administration 1922–1944 (RG 69), NACP.
32. Herman Matson's appearance: author interviews with Raymond Matson and Scott Matson; and a full-length mugshot taken by the Hoboken Police Department on September 15, 1938, now in the Hoboken Historical Museum archives, Hoboken, NJ, Hoboken Police Collection, 2002.0008.2000. The average height of a native-born American man, who was born in 1900 (as Matson was), was 66.9 inches: Richard H. Steckel, "A History of the Standard of Living in the United States," EH.net Encyclopedia, Robert Whaples, ed., July 21, 2002. http://eh.net/encyclopedia /article/steckel.standard.living.us. Matson described himself as five feet, eight inches tall, a slight exaggeration: Herman Matson to the Editor of *Time* Magazine, October 31, 1938, The Workers Defense League Collection, box 130, folder 19, Archives of Labor and Urban Affairs, Wayne State University.
33. Tool house incident: Harold Grouls, WDL attorney and counsel to Herman Matson, statement to John T. Madigan, FBI agent, Newark, NJ, office, report dated June 30, 1939, file 44-2, pp. 2–3, box 17593, folder 144-48-0, section 1 (4/5/39–9/5/39), DOJ Subject File, Records of the DOJ (RG 60), NACP.
34. See, for example, "Giant Tribute Paid McFeely," *JJ*, November 4, 1935, and "Mayor M'Feely Hailed by 5,000," *JJ*, May 4, 1936.
35. Federal Writers' Project of the Works Progress Administration for the State of New Jersey, *New Jersey: A Guide to Its Present and Past* (New York: The Viking Press, June 1939), 262, cites a population of 59,261 in Hoboken; "McFeely Hailed by 8,000 at Ball," *JJ*, May 3, 1938.
36. Protests sent on Matson's behalf include: letter from Harold Grouls, attorney, to Nels Anderson, Deputy Administrator for Labor Relations, WPA, Washington, DC, May 4, 1938; letter from Channa Tanz, attorney, to Nels Anderson, May 12, 1938; and Western Union telegram from Morris Milgram, secretary, Workers Defense League of New Jersey, to Nels Anderson, May 4, 1938. Decision to reinstate Matson

on a Jersey City WPA project: letter to David K. Niles, Assistant Administrator, Works Progress Administration, Washington, DC, from Robert W. Allan, acting state administrator, Newark, NJ, October 27, 1938. All in box 1878 (New Jersey I–R 1937–38), folder 641 (NJ Ma–Mc), Central Files, State 1925–1944; Records of the Works Progress Administration 1922–1944 (RG 69), NACP.

37. Amount of Matson's WPA wages: Bromley, "Strike a Balance."

38. Author interview with Evelyn Olsen.

39. Elizabeth Matson biographical details: author interviews with Raymond Matson and Evelyn Olsen; listing in the Connecticut Department of Health, *Connecticut Death Index, 1949–2001*, Ancestry.com. Elizabeth's support of Herman's activism: Elizabeth Matson, typed statement to John T. Madigan, FBI agent, Newark, NJ, office, report dated June 30, 1939, file 44-2, pp. 30–34, box 17593, folder 144-48-0, section 1 (4/5/39–9/5/39), DOJ Subject File, Records of the DOJ (RG 60), NACP. "Picketing Resumed," *Corpus Christi Times*, May 17, 1938 (a syndicated article carried in papers nationwide), via Ancestry.com.

40. Author interview with Evelyn Olsen.

41. Matson's recollection of Church Square Park meeting (except imprecise dates): Herman Matson, statement to Madigan, May 4, 1939, file 7-77, pp. 26–27. The meeting was held May 10, 1938; see "Eggs Thrown as Hoboken Relief System Is Scored," *JJ*, May 11, 1938.

42. Demarest High School and Hoboken Stevens Academy, a grade and high school, bordered the park. American Lead Pencil Company's Hoboken union: "Pencil Company Stays Closed," *NYT*, June 29, 1937, and "Pencil Concern Signs with C.I.O.," *NYT*, July 8, 1937.

43. Nicholas Piracci, statement to John T. Madigan, FBI agent, Newark, NJ, office, report dated June 30, 1939, file 44-2, p. 37, box 17593, folder 144-48-0, section 1 (4/5/39–9/5/39), DOJ Subject File, Records of the DOJ (RG 60), NACP. "Eggs Thrown as Hoboken Relief System Is Scored." Nicholas Piracci is incorrectly identified as Viracci in this article.

44. Known as "one of McFeely's 'collectors'": Clark to Madigan, June 2, 1939, file 7-77, p. 82. See also "Eggs Thrown as Hoboken Relief System Is Scored"; and Herman Matson, statement to Madigan, May 4, 1939, file 7-77, p. 26.

45. Author interviews with Raymond Matson, Evelyn Olsen, and Daniel Matson. Herman Matson, statement to Madigan, June 30, 1939, file 44-2, p. 12. New York's "Hell's Kitchen": Norval White and Elliot Wilensky, eds., *AIA Guide to New York City* (London: Collier-MacMillan Ltd., 1969), 100–101, and Richard O'Connor, *Hell's Kitchen* (Philadelphia: J. B. Lippincott Company, 1958), 55.

46. Author interview with Evelyn Olsen. Elizabeth and Herman's last child, Daniel Matson, was born in 1946, after they had moved from Hoboken to the Bronx. Herman's identification as "a father of six": See, for example, "WPA in Hoboken Accused," *NYT*, October 24, 1938.

47. Author interview with Evelyn Olsen.

48. "Barck Trial Lawyer Is Put Under Arrest," *HD*, August 2, 1938.

49. "Two Thugs Guilty in Police Killing," *NYT*, June 30, 1938, regarding the trial that would command Leibowitz's attention until early July 1938. Leibowitz's sleep patterns during trials: Diana Klebanow and Franklin L. Jonas, *People's Lawyers: Crusaders for Justice in American History* (Armonk, NY: M. E. Sharpe, 2003) 171. Belle's initiation of outings: Robert Leibowitz, *The Defender: The Life and Career of Samuel S.*

Leibowitz, 1893–1933 (Englewood Cliffs, NJ: Prentice Hall, 1981), 154. The names of Sam Leibowitz, his wife, Belle, and 18-year-old twin sons Robert and Lawrence appear on the passenger list for the S.S. *Vulcania*, sailing from Trieste on August 22, 1938, and arriving at the Port of New York on September 5, 1938; *New York Passenger Lists 1820–1957*, microfilm serial T715, microfilm roll T715_6211, line 26, via Ancestry.com. Leibowitz's comfortable home life: Fred D. Pasley, *Not Guilty! The Story of Samuel S. Leibowitz* (New York: G. P. Putnam's Sons, 1933), 215.

50. New York City and Northern New Jersey weather during the final days of July: "Lightning Kills Farmer During Storm in Jersey," *NYT*, July 28, 1938; "Freak Storm Halts Subway Line," *NYT*, July 29, 1938; "Mercury Hits 90 degrees, Record for Year," *NYT*, July 30, 1938.

51. "Weather Nearer Normal with Temperature at 84 degrees," *NYT*, July 31, 1938.

52. "Barck Murder Trial Lawyer Held for Jury," *HD*, August 3, 1938; "Lawyer Held for Talking to Witness, New York Bar Member Is Under Bail in Quest of Barck Case Proof," *JO*, August 3, 1938.

53. Impellitteri biographical facts: Robert D. McFadden, "Vincent Impellitteri Is Dead: Mayor of New York in 1950s," *NYT*, January 30, 1987. On Impellitteri's association with New York's local Democratic Party organization: Warren Moscow, *The Last of the Big-Time Bosses: The Life and Times of Carmine DeSapio and the Decline and Fall of Tammany Hall* (New York: Stein and Day, 1971), 91–93. "A nod or a handshake": Bernard Glick, attorney, Hoboken, NJ, statement to John T. Madigan, FBI agent, Newark, NJ, office, report dated May 4, 1939, file 7-77, p. 72, box 15205, folder 109-286, section 1 (3/25/39–5/4/39), DOJ Central Files, Classified Subject Files, Correspondence, Records of DOJ (RG 60), NACP.

54. "Leibowitz Aide Held for Jury in Barck Case," *JJ*, August 3, 1938.

55. "Barck Trial Lawyer Is Put Under Arrest."

56. "Lawyer Held for Talking to Witness"; see also photo of Romayne Mullin and Eleonore Hartmann on the cover of the *JJ*, January 14, 1939.

57. Quoted passages are a reporter's description: "Barck Murder Trial Lawyer Held for Jury." On December 9, 1938, a Hudson County grand jury determined there was insufficient evidence for a full hearing and no-billed the Peterfreund case (returning no bill of indictment): "White card" No. 12060 for "Peterfreund, Joshua," defendant, "obstruction of justice" charge, Office of the Hudson County Prosecutor.

58. Impellitteri quote: "Barck Murder Trial Lawyer Held for Jury."

59. "Angry Mob Beats, Routs Red Orator in Hoboken: Workers Defense League Representative Pulled from Stand Before Crowd of 2,000, Finally Rescued by Police; Herman Matson Jailed on Charge of Inciting to Riot—Had Sought Before to Rouse Longshoremen," *HD*, September 16, 1938; and "Speaker Arrested Following Attack by Longshoremen," *JO*, September 16, 1938.

60. Alleged kickback scheme and local's corruption, as related by WDL-associated longshoremen: Milgram, statement to Madigan, May 4, 1939, file 7-77, pp. 16–18; and Herman Matson, statement to Madigan, May 4, 1939, file 7-77, p. 39. See also, as part of an ongoing effort to democratize Local 867, copy of "Hoboken Shape Up Rank & File" mimeograph, December 22, 1938, urging men to "use the shape up to tell the men things they should know," box 17594, folder 144-48-1, DOJ Subject File 144-48-1, Records of the DOJ (RG 60), NACP.

61. Matson's inability to secure local meeting hall: Herman Matson, statement to Madigan, May 4, 1939, file 7-77, pp. 25–26, 87–89. "Now Matson's Counsel Queries Him on His Belief in God," *JJ*, June 5, 1940; the location of Matson's platform is described in "Hoboken Mob Beats and Kicks 'Red' Speaker: His Wife Also Injured; Attack on Administration Is Cut Short When Police Break Through Crowd of 1,500," *JJ*, September 16, 1938.

62. Herman Matson, statement to Madigan, May 4, 1939, file 7-77, pp. 27–28. Elizabeth Matson, statement to Madigan, June 30, 1939, file 44-2, pp. 30–31, noted warning by supportive longshoreman, "Mr. Arcediano."

63. Morris Milgram, statement to Harold Grouls, attorney, September 15, 1938, regarding the beating of Herman Matson, submitted to John T. Madigan, FBI agent, Newark, NJ, office, June 30, 1939, file 44-2, p. 10, box 17593, folder 144-48-0, section 1 (4/5/39–9/5/39), DOJ Subject File, Records of the DOJ (RG 60), NACP; Elizabeth Matson, statement to Madigan, June 30, 1939, file 44-2, 31; Nicholas Piracci, statement to Madigan, June 30, 1939, file 44-2, p. 38. Sunset was at 7:06 PM that evening; see *NYT*, September 15, 1938.

64. Milgram's City College protest: Lawrence Van Gelder, "Morris Milgram, 81: Built Interracial Housing," obituary, *NYT*, June 26, 1997. As state secretary of the WDL of New Jersey he was quoted repeatedly; see, for example, "Circulars Again Barred," *NYT*, March 31, 1938. Grace Milgram's role as observer: Herman Matson, statement to Madigan, June 30, 1939, file 44-2, p. 21. Matson's assertion that Milgram's protests helped him regain his WPA position: Herman Matson, statement to Madigan, May 4, 1939, file 7-77, p. 44.

65. Milgram, statement to Grouls, September 15, 1938, file 44-2, p. 10; Herman Matson, statement to Harold Grouls, attorney, September 15, 1938, submitted to John T. Madigan, FBI agent, Newark, NJ, office, June 30, 1939, file 44-2, p. 13, box 17593, folder 144-48-0, section 1 (4/5/39–9/5/39), DOJ Subject File, Records of the DOJ (RG 60), NACP; Grace Piracci, Aurora Piracci, and Antoinette De L'Aquila, group statement to Harold Grouls, attorney, September 21, 1938, submitted to John T. Madigan, FBI agent, Newark, NJ, office, June 30, 1939, file 44-2, pp. 16–17, box 17593, folder 144-48-0, section 1 (4/5/39–9/5/39), DOJ Subject File, Records of the DOJ (RG 60), NACP; Michael Lemonie (age twelve), statement to Harold Grouls, attorney, September 20, 1938, submitted to John T. Madigan, FBI agent, Newark, NJ, office, June 30, 1939, file 44-2, pp. 15–16, box 17593, folder 144-48-0, section 1 (4/5/39–9/5/39), DOJ Subject File, Records of the DOJ (RG 60), NACP.

66. Milgram, statement to Madigan, May 4, 1939, file 7-77, p. 18 .

67. Milgram, statement to Grouls, September 15, 1938, file 44-2, p. 10.

68. "Angry Mob Beats, Routs Red Orator in Hoboken"; see also, for a lower estimate, "Hoboken Mob Beats and Kicks 'Red' Speaker." Officer seemed to be ignoring the growing swarm: Herman Matson, statement to Madigan, May 4, 1939, file 7-77, p. 29.

69. Description of start of meeting: Milgram, statement to Madigan, May 4, 1939, file 7-77, p. 18; Grace Piracci, Aurora Piracci, and Antoinette De L'Aquila, group statement to Grouls, September 21, 1938, file 44-2, pp. 16–17. Description of Matson's suit based on full-length mugshot taken by Hoboken Police Department, September 15, 1938, Hoboken Historical Museum archives, Hoboken, NJ, Hoboken Police Collection, 2002.0008.2000. Matson's lack of suits: author interview with Evelyn Olsen.

70. Herman Matson, statement to Madigan, May 4, 1939, file 7-77, p. 29.

71. Nicholas Piracci, statement to Madigan, June 30, 1939, file 44-2, p. 38.

72. Milgram, statement to Madigan, May 4, 1939, file 7-77, p. 19; and Herman Matson, statement to Madigan, May 4, 1939, file 7-77, p. 29.

73. Elizabeth Matson, statement to Madigan, June 30, 1939, file 44-2, p. 31.

74. Milgram, statement to Grouls, September 15, 1938, file 44-2, p. 11; Herman Matson, statement to Madigan, May 4, 1939, file 7-77, p. 29. See also Joseph F. McDonald, *Fifteenth Census of the United States, 1930, Population Schedule*, Hoboken, Hudson County, NJ, roll 1348, enumeration district 257, sheet 9B, via Ancestry.com.

75. "Hoboken Mob Beats and Kicks 'Red' Speaker."

76. Matson's plans to speak about relief and to call for a trial for Scutellaro: "McFeely Critic Beaten and Jailed for Hoboken Speech," *NYP*, September 16, 1938.

77. Milgram, statement to Grouls, September 15, 1938, file 44-2, p. 11.

78. "Speaker Arrested Following Attack by Longshoremen"; "Angry Mob Beats, Routs Red Orator in Hoboken"; "Hoboken Mob Beats and Kicks 'Red' Speaker." Orestes Cerruti, statement to Harold Grouls, attorney, September 21, 1938, regarding beating of Herman Matson, submitted to John T. Madigan, FBI agent, Newark, NJ, office, June 30, 1939, file 44-2, p. 15, box 17593, folder 144-48-0, section 1 (4/5/39–9/5/39), DOJ Subject File, Records of the DOJ (RG 60), NACP.

79. Herman Matson, statement to Madigan, May 4, 1939, file 7-77, p. 30; "Speaker Arrested Following Attack by Longshoremen."

80. Elizabeth's shoes: Herman Matson, statement to Madigan, May 4, 1939, file 7-77, p. 30; physical description of Elizabeth Matson from author interview with Evelyn Olsen. On Elizabeth's pregnancy: Elizabeth Matson, statement to Madigan, June 30, 1939, file 44-2, p. 33.

81. Elizabeth Matson, statement to Madigan, June 30, 1939, file 44-2, pp. 31–32; "Hoboken Mob Beats and Kicks 'Red' Speaker"; "Kicked, Says Mrs. Matson on Stand," *JJ*, June 6, 1940; David Knoll, statement to Harold Grouls, attorney, n.d., regarding beating of Herman Matson, submitted to John T. Madigan, FBI agent, Newark, NJ, office, June 30, 1939, file 44-2, pp. 17–18, box 17593, folder 144-48-0, section 1 (4/5/39–9/5/39), DOJ Subject File, Records of the DOJ (RG 60), NACP.

82. "Angry Mob Beats, Routs Red Orator in Hoboken"; "Speaker Arrested Following Attack by Longshoremen" reported the assailants were "grimly purposeful in their work."

83. Milgram, statement to Madigan, May 4, 1939, file 7-77, pp. 19–20; Dr. Harry Arons, statement to John T. Madigan, FBI agent, Newark, NJ, office, report dated August 1, 1939, file 44-2, pp. 1–2, box 17594, folder 144-48-1, DOJ Subject File, Records of the DOJ (RG 60), NACP.

84. Herman Matson, statement to Madigan, May 4, 1939, file 7-77, p. 30; Herman Matson, statement to Grouls, n.d., file 44-2, p. 12.

85. Herman Matson, statement to Madigan, May 4, 1939, file 7-77, p. 30.

86. Ibid.; also Lemonie, statement to Grouls, September 20, 1938, file 44-2, pp. 15–16.

87. Milgram, statement to Madigan, May 4, 1939, file 7-77, pp. 19–20; Milgram, statement to Grouls, September 15, 1938, file 44-2, p. 11; Herman Matson, statement to Grouls, n.d., file 44-2, p. 14.

88. Milgram, statement to Grouls, September 15, 1938, file 44-2, p. 11.

89. "Speaker Arrested Following Attack by Longshoremen"; Herman Matson, statement to Grouls, n.d., file 44-2, p. 14; and Herman Matson, statement to Madigan, May 4, 1939, file 7-77, p. 32.
90. Herman Matson, statement to Madigan, May 4, 1939, file 7-77, p. 32. On police brutality during the 1920s, see Marilynn S. Johnson, *Street Justice: A History of Police Violence in New York City* (Boston: Beacon Press, 2003), 122–35.
91. Herman Matson, statement to Madigan, May 4, 1939, file 7-77, p. 32.
92. "Angry Mob Beats, Routs Red Orator in Hoboken" and "Speaker Arrested Following Attack by Longshoremen." See also "Matson Convicted in Hoboken Trial," *NYT*, October 8, 1938.
93. See previously cited articles from New York and New Jersey newspapers. For additional New York coverage see "Hoboken Jails Speaker After Mob Beats Him," *Herald Tribune*, September 16, 1938. For coverage in other states: "Workers Defense Speaker Beaten," *The Lowell Sun* (Lowell, Massachusetts), September 16, 1938; and a variously titled syndicated column by Westbrook Pegler, "Neither Reds nor Nazis Will Save Civil Rights," *Appleton Post Crescent* (Appleton, Wisconsin), September 20, 1938; and "Fair Enough!" *Mansfield News-Journal* (Mansfield, Ohio), September 20, 1938. All via Ancestry.com. Nolan quoted in "Angry Mob Beats, Routs Red Orator in Hoboken"; "Speaker Arrested Following Attack by Longshoremen."
94. Harold Grouls, WDL attorney and counsel to Herman Matson, statement to John T. Madigan, FBI agent, Newark, NJ, office, June 30, 1939, file 44-2, p. 4, box 17593, folder 144-48-0, section 1 (4/5/39–9/5/39), DOJ Subject File, Records of the DOJ (RG 60), NACP.
95. "McFeely Critic Beaten"; Milgram, statement to Madigan, May 4, 1939, file 7-77, pp. 20–21; Morris Shapiro, attorney for the Worker's Defense League, to Grenville Clark, New York representative of the American Bar Association, September 24, 1938, regarding Matson case, included in WDL national office file shared with FBI agent John T. Madigan and quoted in his report dated April 11, 1939, file 7-77, pp. 24–25, box 17313, 4th folder (1/25/39–7/26/39), DOJ Central Files, Classified Subject Files, Correspondence, Records of the DOJ (RG 60), NACP; Grouls, statement to Madigan, June 30, 1939, file 44-2, pp. 4–6.
96. Herman Matson, statement to Madigan, May 4, 1939, file 7-77, pp. 32–33; Elizabeth Matson, statement to Madigan, June 30, 1939, file 44-2, pp. 32–33. In her statement, Elizabeth misrembers the date of the miscarriage, putting it on the first night of Herman's incarceration instead of the second. See also "Matson Case Off to Oct. 7: Defendant's Wife, Chief Witness, Too Ill to Appear in Court," *JJ*, September 21, 1938.

10. The Marble Halls of Justice

1. "McFeely Critic Beaten and Jailed for Hoboken Speech," *NYP*, September 16, 1938.
2. Morris Milgram to Harry Hopkins, Administrator, Works Progress Administration, Washington, DC, October 20, 1938, box 1878 (NJ I–R 1937–1938), folder 641 (NJ Ma–Mc), Central Files, State 1935–1944, Records of the Works Progress Administration 1922–1944 (RG 69), NACP. Employment Record of Herman Matson produced by the WPA, box 1878 (NJ I–R 1937–38), folder 641 (NJ Ma–Mc), Central Files, State 1935–1944, Records of the WPA 1922–1944 (RG 69), NACP.

3. Ragged hands: Author telephone interview with Evelyn Olsen, April 1, 2009. Surviving on charity and WDL assistance: Milgram to Hopkins, WPA, Washington, DC, October 20, 1938.

4. Babysitter: David Clendenin, Workers Defense League, to Laura B. Woodbridge, a donor to the Matson Defense Fund, October 1, 1938, The Workers Defense League Collection, box 130, folder 18, Archives of Labor and Urban Affairs, Wayne State University. "Had to submit to an operation": Elizabeth Matson, typed statement to John T. Madigan, FBI agent, Newark, NJ, office, report dated June 30, 1939, file 44-2, p. 33, box 17593, folder 144-48-0, section 1 (4/5/39−9/5/39), DOJ Subject File, Records of the DOJ (RG 60), NACP.

5. Author interview with Evelyn Olsen. Herman and Elizabeth's statements to FBI agent John T. Madigan contain many accounts of joint leafleting; for newspaper account of same, see "Defense League Head Distributes More Fliers in Hoboken," *JJ*, April 6, 1938.

6. Regarding the poll: Chad Alan Goldberg, *Citizens and Paupers: Relief, Rights, and Race, from the Freedmen's Bureau to Workfare* (Chicago: University of Chicago Press, 2007), 126.

7. On pauper's oath and exclusion laws, see Douglas H. MacNeil, *Seven Years of Unemployment Relief in New Jersey, 1930–1936* (Washington: Committee on Social Security, Social Science Research Council, 1938), 38–39; Goldberg, *Citizens and Paupers*, 125–26.

8. Ten million unemployed by the winter of 1937–38: David M. Kennedy, *The American People in the Great Depression: Freedom from Fear*, pt. 1 (New York: Oxford University Press, 1999), 350. "Conservative countermobilization" against WPA and Workers Alliance of America: Goldberg, *Citizens and Paupers*, 132–34, 139–52. Committee chairman Congressman Martin Dies's charge the Civil Liberties Union was a unit in the "'united front' of the communistic movement": Luther A. Huston, "Dies Inquiry Shaping Laws," *NYT*, August 28, 1938.

9. "Hoboken Mob Beats and Kicks 'Red' Speaker: His Wife Also Injured; Attack on Administration Is Cut Short When Police Break Through Crowd of 1,500," *JJ*, September 16, 1938; "Angry Mob Beats, Routs Red Orator in Hoboken," *HD*, September 16, 1938.

10. Herman Matson, statement to John T. Madigan, FBI agent, Newark, NJ, office, report dated May 4, 1939, file 7-77, p. 33, box 15205, folder 109-286, section 1 (3/25/39−5/4/39), DOJ Central Files, Classified Subject Files, Correspondence, DOJ (RG 60), NACP.

11. "Matson Denies Red, Criminal Accusations," *JJ*, October 18, 1940.

12. "Basis in reality" and account of "campaign against Communism": Goldberg, *Citizens and Paupers*, 139–40.

13. George's request for a struck jury: "Struck Jury in Barck Slaying," *JO*, September 19, 1938; "Grants Struck Jury in Killing of Poormaster," *HD*, September 20, 1938.

14. Leibowitz's antipathy to "blue ribbon juries": "Blue Ribbon Juries Debated in Albany," *NYT*, February 23, 1938, and Robert Leibowitz, *The Defender: The Life and Career of Samuel S. Leibowitz, 1893–1933* (Englewood Cliffs, NJ: Prentice Hall, 1981), 44.

15. For more on Leibowitz's reading of faces to select jurors: Fred D. Pasley, *Not Guilty! The Story of Samuel S. Leibowitz* (New York: G. P. Putnam's Sons, 1933), 128–29.

16. Before 1947 the "county prosecutor" was known as the "prosecutor of the pleas of the county"; I have used the shorter designation for clarity. On William George:

Isaac Undermine, DCL, PhD, *Jewish Personalities of Hudson County: Graphic Portraits and Character Sketches* (privately printed booklet, 1930), 77–79, from the collection of the New Jersey Room, Jersey City Public Library, Jersey City, NJ; *Social Security Death Index* for William George, establishing his birth date as July 18, 1890, number 136-32-1432, New Jersey, 1956–1958, via Ancestry.com; "Official on Trial in Jersey Tuesday," *NYT*, January 24, 1949, regarding allegiance to Hague and election to state assembly; "Job Created for Hague Aide," *NYT*, June 23, 1944, regarding Hague support; "Official from Jersey, Hissed Here, Retorts with Attack on New York," *NYT*, May 18, 1938, regarding public defense of Hague's anti–civil liberties actions; *U.S. World War II Draft Registration Cards, 1942*, roll WWII_2372038, Hudson, NJ, via Ancestry.com, reporting George's physical appearance, and photograph accompany "Barck Murder: George to Claim Slaying Planned," *HD*, January 9, 1939. On Hague's inclusion of representatives of ethnic groups in his administration, see Richard J. Connors, *A Cycle of Power: The Career of Jersey City Mayor Frank Hague* (Metuchen, NJ: Scarecrow Press, 1971), 95–97.

17. Physical description of Robert Kinkead from photograph and article, "Kinkead Takes New Post Today," *HD*, February 3, 1939, and *U.S. World War II Draft Registration Cards, 1942*, roll WWII_2372161, Hudson County, NJ, via Ancestry.com.

18. For biographical facts on Kinkead, see "Robert Kinkead, 83, Jersey Judge, Dead," obituary, *NYT*, June 18, 1975, and "Silzer Sends Nominations," *NYT*, February 13, 1923, which contains the description "a Democratic lawyer." On Governor George S. Silzer's connections to Frank Hague, see Alfred Steinberg, *The Bosses* (New York: Macmillan Publishing Co., 1972), 34–35. On Robert Kinkead's appointment as a way for Hague to draw close "former intra-party opponents," and Eugene Kinkead's opposition to Hague, see Connors, *A Cycle of Power*, 51–52, and "Eugene Kinkead, Banker, 84, Dies," *NYT*, September 7, 1960.

19. See Steinberg, *The Bosses*, 43–44, regarding Hague opponents James "Jeff" Burkitt and John R. Longo; Robert A. Ambry to the American Civil Liberties Union board, December 27, 1938, American Civil Liberties Union Records, Roger Baldwin Years, roll 177, vol. 2135, Public Policy Papers, Department of Rare Books and Special Collections, Princeton University Library; "Hague's Control Extends Even to Jury System," *NYP*, May 24, 1938; "Burkitt, Bail Denied, Wins Court Review," April 26, 1938; "Bail for Longo Denied, Kinkead Refuses to Release Hague Foe Pending Appeal," *NYT*, July 2, 1938.

20. "Struck Jury in Barck Slaying."

21. Complaint dated September 21, 1938, and signed by Joseph R. Scott, swearing Herman Matson "did indulge and utter aloud indecent and offensive language" and directed obscenities at Lt. Scott and Sergeant Arthur Marotta, submitted by Edward Stover to John T. Madigan, FBI agent, Newark, NJ, office, report dated June 2, 1939, file 7-77, p. 63, box 15205, folder 109-286, section 2 (6/2/39), DOJ Central Files, Classified Subject Files, Correspondence, Records of the DOJ (RG 60), NACP. On surprise of Matson and his lawyers at the new charge and their preparation for a different defense, see Morris Milgram, statement to John T. Madigan, FBI agent, Newark, NJ, office, report dated May 4, 1939, file 7-77, p. 21, box 15205, folder 109-286, section 1 (3/25/39–5/4/39), DOJ Central Files, Classified Subject Files, Correspondence, Records of the DOJ (RG 60), NACP.

22. Harold Grouls, WDL attorney and counsel to Herman Matson, statement to John T. Madigan, FBI agent, Newark, NJ, office, report dated June 30, 1939, file 44-2,

p. 6, box 17593, folder 144-48-0, section 1 (4/5/39–9/5/39), DOJ Subject File, Records of the DOJ (RG 60), NACP; Frank Romano, statement to John T. Madigan, FBI agent, Newark, NJ, office, report dated November 1, 1939, file 44-2, p. 11, box 17594, folder 144-48-1, DOJ Subject File, Records of the DOJ (RG 60), NACP.

23. Statements taken by Harold Grouls regarding September 15, 1938, incident in Hudson Square Park, submitted to John T. Madigan, FBI agent, Newark, NJ, office, file 44-2, pp. 9–18, box 17593, folder 144-48-0, section 1 (4/5/39–9/5/39) DOJ Subject Files, Records of the DOJ (RG 60), NACP. Biographical background, Harold Grouls: Grouls, statement to Madigan, June 30, 1939, file 44-2, p. 2; "Jersey Law School Awards 164 Degrees," *NYT*, June 8, 1932; "Wide Shake-Up Hits Police in Hoboken," *NYT*, May 28, 1947; "John H. Grouls Dies Suddenly," unidentified newspaper clipping, ca. 1935, collection of the Hoboken Historical Museum, catalog no. 20021110007.

24. Biographical background Edward Stover: Edward Quinton Keasbey, *The Courts and Lawyers of New Jersey, 1661–1912* (New York: Lewis Historical Publishing Co., 1912), 309; Edward Stover, *1920 United States Federal Census*, Ward 2, Hoboken, Hudson County, NJ, roll T625_1042, p. 1B, enumeration district 72, image 128, via Ancestry .com. On motives for entering the case, see Edward Stover to David L. Clendennin, National Treasurer for the WDL, October 14, 1938, submitted with statement by Clendennin to John T. Madigan, FBI agent, Newark, NJ, office, report dated April 11, 1939, file 7-77, pp. 22–24, box 17313, 4th folder (1/25/39–7/26/39), DOJ Central Files, Classified Subject Files, Correspondence, Records of the DOJ (RG 60), NACP. For Stover's self-identification as "anti-McFeely" see Stover to Madigan, June 2, 1939, file 7-77, p. 63.

25. "Matson Baby's Death Laid to Hoboken Mob," *New York Herald-Tribune*, September 22, 1938.

26. "Workers Defense Speaker Beaten," *The Lowell Sun*, September 16, 1938, via Ancestry.com.

27. Articles reprinted by WDL for publicity campaigns, see Milgram to Hopkins, October 20, 1938. Clippings include the undated *Post* headline "Baby Born Dead to Beaten Mother: Matson Trial Off."

28. Thomas's and Baldwin's role in establishing precursor to American Civil Liberties Union: Robert C. Cottrell, *Roger Nash Baldwin and the American Civil Liberties Union* (New York: Columbia University Press, 2000), 51, 121. Norman Thomas's failed attempt to secure bail: Milgram, statement to Madigan, May 4, 1939, file 7-77, p. 20; also "Thomas Wants Cummings to Watch Hoboken Trial," *NYT*, September 20, 1938.

29. Milgram, statement to Madigan, May 4, 1939, file 7-77, p. 20; "Thomas Wants Cummings to Watch Hoboken Trial," *NYT*.

30. Dorothy Dunbar Bromley, "Strike a Balance," *NYP*, September 22, 1938. Biographical background on Bromley, see "Dorothy Dunbar Bromley, 89, A Writer on Women's Issues," [obit] *NYT*, January 6, 1986.

31. Telegram from Arthur Garfield Hays, General Counsel, American Civil Liberties Union, to Mayor Bernard J. McFeely, September 16, 1938, American Civil Liberties Union Records, Roger Baldwin Years, roll 165, vol. 2094, Public Policy Papers, Department of Rare Books and Special Collections, Princeton University Library. Hays's telegram was released to the press and reprinted in several newspapers. On Thomas's advocacy, see: Donald S. Howard, *The WPA and Federal Relief Policy*

(New York: Russell Sage Foundation, 1943), 650, describing an appeal Thomas and other notables made to President Roosevelt on behalf of the National Unemployment League.

32. "Hague Is Attacked in Free Speech Ban," *NYT*, May 18, 1934. On his battles with Hague generally: Arthur Garfield Hays, *City Lawyer: The Autobiography of a Law Practice* (New York: Simon and Schuster, 1942), 197–99; on 1939 Supreme Court ruling in *Hague v. Congress of Industrial Organizations*, see Cottrell, *Roger Nash Baldwin and the American Civil Liberties Union*, 168.

33. Thomas's anti-Communism: Cottrell, *Roger Nash Baldwin and the American Civil Liberties Union*, 124. On the Jersey City "kidnapping" charge, see "Thomas's Charges Go to Grand Jury," *NYT*, September 29, 1938; Dayton David McKean, *The Boss: The Hague Machine in Action* (Boston: Houghton Mifflin Company, 1940), 236; Harry Fleischman, *Norman Thomas: A Biography* (New York: W. W. Norton & Co., 1964), 159–60.

34. Hague's recognized ability to bring in votes: Kennedy, *American People in the Great Depression*, 253; Steinberg, *The Bosses*, 62; Lyle W. Dorsett, *Franklin D. Roosevelt and the City Bosses* (Port Washington, NY: Kennikat Press, 1977), 10, 35, 101, 107. Norman Thomas, *"Last Night in Jersey City"* (New York: Workers Defense League, 1938), 4, booklet reproducing Thomas's May 8, 1938, speech, author's collection.

35. "Thomas Wants Cummings to Watch Hoboken Trial." The two men hated each other: Vilas J. Boyle, "Hoboken: A Look at McFeely, the Man," *NYP*, April 9, 1938.

36. Boyle, "A Look at McFeely."

37. Listed resolutions, except Methodist ministers': box 17313, 3rd folder, DOJ Central Files, Classified Subject Files, Correspondence; Records of the DOJ (RG 60), NACP. Herman Matson's flyer announcing his October 7, 1938, trial features ministers' resolution, box 1878 (NJ I–R 1937–38), folder 641 (NJ Ma–Mc), Central Files, States, 1935–1944, Records of the Works Progress Administration 1922–1944 (RG 69), NACP.

38. For background on trial of Herman Matson: "Court Finds Matson Guilty," *JJ*, October 7, 1938; "Court Hears Accounts of Park Affray," *JO*, October 7, 1938; "Matson Convicted, Sentence Stayed," *New York World-Telegram*, October 7, 1938; "Matson Convicted in Hoboken Trial," *NYT*, October 8, 1938; "Matson Convicted in Hoboken Riot," *Philadelphia (Pennsylvania) Record*, October 8, 1938; "Matson Guilty, Hays Rebukes Hoboken Court," *New York Herald-Tribune*, October 8, 1938; "Matson to Appeal Conviction," *JO*, October 9, 1938. See also "Hays Threatens Civil Suit Against Hoboken After Defying Court on Matson Conviction," *Bronx (New York) Home News*, October 8, 1938.

39. For height and weight of Stover and Hays: Edward J. D. Stover, *U.S. World War II Draft Registration Cards, 1942*, roll WWII_2372590, Hudson County, NJ, via Ancestry.com. Arthur Garfield Hays, *U.S. World War II Draft Registration Cards, 1942*, roll WW2_2283915, New York City, NY, via Ancestry.com. See also photo of Hays accompanying article, "Hague Speech Ban Is Defied by Hays," *NYT*, May 20, 1938. Stover's frugality is mentioned in "Matson to Appeal Conviction."

40. Background on Arthur Garfield Hays, generally: Hays, *City Lawyer*; biographical sketch, Arthur Garfield Hays Papers, Seeley G. Mudd Manuscript Library, Princeton University Library; and Cottrell, *Roger Nash Baldwin and the American Civil Liberties Union*, 123–24. Hays's and Darrow's involvement with NAACP on "Scottsboro Boys" case: James Goodman, *Stories of Scottsboro* (New York: Vintage Books, 1995),

37–38, and Kevin Tierney, *Darrow: A Biography* (New York: Thomas Y. Crowell Publishers, 1979), 403–5.

41. "Matson to Appeal Conviction"; and Arthur Garfield Hays, statement to John T. Madigan, FBI agent, Newark, NJ, office, report dated April 11, 1939, file 7-77, pp. 17–18, box 17313, 4th folder (1/25/39–7/26/39), DOJ Central Files, Classified Subject Files, Correspondence, Records of the DOJ (RG 60), NACP.

42. Quoted in Bernard Glick, attorney, Hoboken, NJ, statement to John T. Madigan, FBI agent, Newark, NJ, office, bureau, report dated May 4, 1939, file 7-77, p. 72, box 15205, folder 109-286, section 1 (3/25/39–5/4/39), DOJ Central Files, Classified Subject Files, Correspondence, Records of DOJ (RG 60), NACP. "Bar Association Picks Seven to Investigate Hoboken Police Court," *JO*, November 19, 1937.

43. "Matson Guilty, Hays Rebukes."

44. Years Allen served in City Law Department, see: "Horace Allen Dies: New Jersey Lawyer," obituary, *NYT*, January 7, 1940; Horace L. Allen, *1930 United States Federal Census*, Hoboken, Hudson County, NJ, roll 1349, p. 10A, enumeration district 267, image 189.0.

45. From an application for a writ of certiorari to review conviction of Herman Matson, provided by Harold Grouls to John T. Madigan, FBI agent, Newark, NJ, office, report dated August 1, 1939, file 44-2, p. 7, box 17593, folder 144-48-0, section 1 (4/5/39–9/5/39), DOJ Subject File, Records of the DOJ (RG 60), NACP.

46. "Matson Guilty, Hays Rebukes"; Stover to Clendennin, October 14, 1938, file 7-77, pp. 22–23.

47. Ibid.

48. Matson's assertions he did not use indecent language appear in various accounts of the trial; see "Court Finds Matson Guilty."

49. "Matson to Appeal Conviction."

50. Ibid.

51. Ages listed in group statement of Grace Piracci, Aurora Piracci, and Antoinette De L'Aquila, group statement to Harold Grouls, attorney, September 21, 1938, submitted to John T. Madigan, FBI agent, Newark, NJ, office, June 30, 1939, file 44-2, p. 16, box 17593, folder 144-48-0, section 1 (4/5/39–9/5/39), DOJ Subject File, Records of the DOJ (RG 60), NACP.

52. "Matson Guilty, Hays Rebukes."

53. "Matson to Appeal Conviction." See also "Court Finds Matson Guilty."

54. "Matson to Appeal Conviction."

55. Ibid., "Matson Guilty, Hays Rebukes."

56. "Matson to Appeal Conviction."

57. Ibid.

58. "Court Hears Accounts of Park Affray"; Morris Milgram, State Secretary, Workers Defense League of New Jersey, to Mrs. Margery Newhall Robinson, October 12, 1938, soliciting funds to send Elizabeth to a convalescent home, Workers Defense League Collection, box 130, folder 10, Archives of Labor and Urban Affairs, Wayne State University. Morris Milgram to Dorothy Dunbar Bromley, October 26, 1938, noting WDL's support of the Matsons and Elizabeth's admission to Theresa Grotta Convalescent Home, Caldwell, Workers Defense League Collection, box 130, folder 11, Archives of Labor and Urban Affairs, Wayne State University.

59. Nicholas Piracci, statement to John T. Madigan, FBI agent, Newark, NJ, office, report dated June 30, 1939, file 44-2, p. 39, box 17593, folder 144-48-0, section 1 (4/5/39–9/5/39), DOJ Subject File, Records of the DOJ (RG 60), NACP.

60. Stover to Clendennin, October 14, 1938, file 7-77, pp. 22–23.

61. Untitled news clippings, *JO*, October 22, 1938, and October 25, 1938, provided by Workers Defense League to John T. Madigan, FBI agent, Newark, NJ, office, and detailed in his report dated April 11, 1939, file 7-77, pp. 21–22, box 17313, 4th folder (1/25/39–7/26/39), DOJ Central Files, Classified Subject Files, Correspondence, Records of the DOJ (RG 60), NACP.

62. Herman Matson, statement to Madigan, May 4, 1939, file 7-77, pp. 38–39.

63. Stover to Clendennin, October 14, 1938, file 7-77, pp. 23–24.

64. Milgram letter to Hopkins, October 20, 1938. But even Milgram, who knew better because of his involvement in local politics, could not resist slanting his appeal by mentioning "the Hague machine." His letter to Hopkins became the basis of a news report headlined "WPA in Hoboken Accused: Workers' Group Says Anti-Hague Man Cannot Get Job," *NYT*, October 24, 1938. On Milgram's awareness of local politics, including McFeely's control over Hoboken: Milgram, statement to Madigan, May 4, 1939, file 7-77, p. 23.

11. A Jury of His Peers

1. "Barck Slayer Awaits Trial, Scutellaro Due to Face Murder Charge Next Monday," *JJ*, January 6, 1939.

2. "Tilts Mark Selection of Barck Jurors," *JO*, January 10, 1939. "Relief Murder Trial Put Off," *NYT*, November 13, 1938. Joe's physical state while in county jail from report prepared by Dr. Laurence M. Collins for Prosecutor's Office, November 5, 1938, *SVJS*. The November 1938 trial that returned Leibowitz to New York was *The People v. Irwin* (Court of General Sessions, Manhattan). Leibowitz's goal was not to free his client but to establish the man's insanity: Robert Irwin believed he had been decreed by God to kill three people. After a week's trial, Irwin pleaded guilty to second-degree murder, was officially declared insane, and was sent to a state facility for the criminally insane. On Irwin case: Diana Klebanow and Franklin L. Jonas, *People's Lawyers: Crusaders for Justice in American History* (Armonk, NY: M. E. Sharpe, 2003), 197; Quentin Reynolds, *Courtroom: The Story of Samuel S. Leibowitz* (New York: Farrar, Straus and Giroux: 1950), 107–50.

3. On Congressional conservatives, see David M. Kennedy, *The American People in the Great Depression: Freedom from Fear*, pt. 1 (New York: Oxford University Press, 1999), 348–50; Arthur Krock, "Taxpayers Revolt," *NYT*, November 10, 1938; Turner Catledge, "Relief to Confront Congress at Start," *NYT*, December 28, 1938. Comments of Senator Carter Glass: "Relief Proposals 'Shocking' to Glass," *NYT*, December 24, 1938.

4. "Relief Dimes Defend Poormaster Slayer," *DN*, January 9, 1939; "Barck Murder, George to Claim Slaying Planned," *HD*, January 9, 1939; "Barck Slayer Put on Trial for His Life," *JO*, January 9, 1939.

5. "Vivo interesse per il processo Scutellaro che si inizia stamane," *PIA*, January 9, 1939. On *Il Progresso Italo-Americano's* coverage generally, see: *The Italians of New York: A Survey Prepared by Workers of the Federal Writers' Project, Works Progress Administration in the City of New York* (New York: Arno Press and the *New York Times*, 1969

ed.), 123–24. "La causa di Giuseppe Scutellaro e la causa di tanti e tanti poveri," *PIA*, March 2, 1938; and "Due testi smentiscono che Miss Hartman [sic] vide Scutellaro ferire Barck," *PIA*, January 12, 1939. Italian-language articles translated for author by Elisa Varano.

6. On number of publications supported by Italian American readers: Ibid, 123. For leftist and centrist Italian language coverage of Scutellaro case, see for example, "Le rivolte della fame," *L'Adunata Dei Refrattari*, March 12, 1938; "Hague vuol mandar lo alla sedia elettrica," *Il Popolo*, January 14, 1939; "Chi sono i responsabili," *Il Popolo*, January 14, 1939.

7. "Chi sono i responsabili," *Il Popolo*.

8. Ibid.

9. McAlister Coleman, "Study in Relief," *Nation*, January 28, 1939, 119–21; "Killing and Suicide Mark Poverty Scene," *The Catholic Worker*, March 1938, 2.

10. See, for example, Associated Press reports "Seek to Free Relief Client," *San Antonio Light*, January 10, 1939; "On Trial in Poormaster's Slaying," *Kingston Daily Freeman* (Kingston, New York), January 10, 1939; "Relief Client Faces Manslaughter Term," *Oakland Tribune* (Oakland, California), January 16, 1939. And from the International News Service: "Escapes Chair, But Near Collapse," *San Antonio Light*, January 15, 1939. All via Ancestry.com.

11. "Top-paid African-American entertainer in the world" and biographical facts: Jim Haskins and N. R. Mitgang, *Mr. Bojangles: The Biography of Bill Robinson* (New York: William Morrow & Co., 1988), 192–194, 213, 215–16, 225, 241, 248. "A hundred-dollar bill": Author interview with Marie Scutellaro Werts.

12. Author interview with Marie Scutellaro Werts in Toms River, NJ, September 17, 2008.

13. "Barck Slayer Awaits Trial"; "May Ask Chair in Barck Case," *JJ*, January 7, 1939; and "Barck Murder, George to Claim Slaying Planned."

14. "Client of Leibowitz Dies in the Chair," *JO*, January 6, 1939; Klebanow and Jonas, *People's Lawyers*, 158.

15. "Trophy room": Klebanow and Jonas, *People's Lawyers*, 159; on Leibowitz's office, see Fred D. Pasley, *Not Guilty! The Story of Samuel S. Leibowitz* (New York: G. P. Putnam's Sons, 1933), 118–20. "So-called record": "Policeman's Slayers Fail to Win Appeal," *NYT*, November 23, 1938.

16. Background on Gati case, see: "Policeman's Slayers Fail to Win Appeal"; Reynolds, *Courtroom*, 347–59; "Two Thugs Guilty in Police Killing," *NYT*, June 30, 1938; Klebanow and Jonas, *People's Lawyers*, 185.

17. Leibowitz's concern he would be remembered "only for the Gati case": Klebanow and Jonas, *People's Lawyers*, 173; Reynolds, *Courtroom*, 357.

18. Size of crowd waiting for Scutellaro: "Cheered as Slayer of Overseer of Poor," *NYT*, January 10, 1939; "Barck Slayer in Court Room As Quiz Opens," *JJ*, January 9, 1939; and "Poormaster's Killer Goes on Trial as Hero," *DN*, January 10, 1939. See also photo "La prima udienza del processo di Scutellaro," *PIA*, January 10, 1939. The courthouse incorporated Italian Renaissance features, as well as elements of Greek and Roman style. See William G. McLoughlin, *Court Houses and Court Rooms, United States and New Jersey: Their History and Architecture* (Jersey City, NJ: John Marshall College, 1937), 15–16, in collection of New Jersey Room, Jersey City Public Library.

19. Two lines: "Tilts Mark Selection of Barck Jury."

20. "Barck Slayer in Court Room As Quiz Opens"; "Poormaster's Killer Goes on Trial as Hero."
21. Pasley, *Not Guilty!*, 127.
22. Information from struck jury cards: *SVJS.*
23. "Tilts Mark Selection of Barck Jurors"; Pasley, *Not Guilty!*, 128–29.
24. Pasley, *Not Guilty!*, 127.
25. *Norris v. Alabama* as a "landmark": see Klebanow and Jonas, *People's Lawyers*, 159.
26. Seating: "Barck Slayer in Court Room As Quiz Opens."
27. "Tilts Mark Selection of Barck Jurors."
28. Springlike temperatures, see "Mercury 24 Degrees Above Normal in January Thaw," *NYT*, January 7, 1939; "The Weather over the Nation and Abroad," *NYT*, January 8–10, 1939; and "Springlike Temperature Gives Way to Freezing Weather," *HD*, January 14, 1939. Marie's attire: "Confession Introduced in Evidence at Trial Here," *JJ*, January 11, 1939; "Tilts Mark Selection of Barck Jurors"; photograph of Anna, Marie, and little Joseph accompanying article, "Poormaster's Killer Goes on Trial as Hero"; author interview with Marie Scutellaro Werts.
29. "Cheered As Slayer of Overseer of Poor."
30. Longest "could ever recall": "Barck Slayer in Court Room As Quiz Opens." Six hours: "Tilts Mark Selection of Barck Jurors." Used a week: Klebanow and Jonas, *People's Lawyers*, 170. "Frequently judges": Pasley, *Not Guilty!*, 127.
31. "Hangers" and "let-livers" philosophy: Pasley, *Not Guilty!*, 127–28.
32. Ibid.
33. Leibowitz query regarding "testimony of a police officer": "Cheered as Slayer of Overseer of Poor." Leibowitz query regarding McFeely family: "M'Feelys Kept Off Record at Slaying Trial," *NYP*, January 9, 1939.
34. Foreman selected: "Tilts Mark Selection of Barck Jurors"; "Barck Slayer in Court Room As Quiz Opens."
35. Ibid.
36. "Dole Killer Hero on Trial in Jersey," *DN*, January 10, 1939.
37. "Tilts Mark Selection of Barck Jurors."
38. See for example, "Relief Client on Trial for Murder," *Newark Evening News*, January 9, 1939; ibid.
39. Struck jury cards, *SVJS.*
40. Harold D. Tompkins, *1930 United States Federal Census*, Jersey City, Hudson County, NJ, roll 1354, p. 22B, enumeration district 114, image 92.0, via Ancestry.com; "George G. Tennant, Retired Jurist, 79," *NYT*, February 4, 1948; "Harold D. Tompkins," obituary, *NYT*, November 28, 1951. Joseph C. Darrell, *1930 United States Federal Census*, Jersey City, Hudson County, NJ, roll 1252, p. 7A, enumeration district 84, image 807.0, via Ancestry.com. Henry A. F. Kelm, *1930 United States Federal Census*, Jersey City, Hudson County, NJ, roll 1356, p. 11B, enumeration district 180, image 796.0, via Ancestry.com. William Lindquist, *1930 United States Federal Census*, Bayonne, Hudson County, NJ, roll 1346, p. 4B, enumeration district 188, image 517.0, via Ancestry.com. Peter Nolan, *1930 United States Federal Census*, Jersey City, Hudson County, NJ, roll 1352, p. 37B, enumeration district 82, image 658.0, via Ancestry.com. Robert H. Sinclair, *1930 United States Federal Census*, Jersey City, Hudson County, NJ, Roll 1360, p. 13B, enumeration district 433, image 864.0, via Ancestry.com. Thomas Hamilton, *1930 United States Federal Census*, Bayonne, Hudson County, NJ, roll 1347, p. 15A, enumeration district 211, image 31.0, via Ancestry.com.

41. Tompkins, *1930 United States Federal Census,* Jersey City, NJ, Department of Revenue and Finance, Tax Assessment for Block 1814, Lot 9A-10, 132 Bentley Avenue, Jersey City, owner Harold D. Tompkins, inspected April 12, 1939, Tax Assessors' Office, City Hall, Jersey City. *Cornell Alumni News,* vol. 15, no. 36 (June 11, 1913): 436, notes inauguration of Tompkins's employment with Smooth-On Manufacturing, iron cements manufacturer in Jersey City.

42. Tompkins graduated from Cornell in 1910. See *Cornell Alumni News,* vol. 37, no. 23 (March 28, 1935): 11. On Leibowitz's years at Cornell University Law School, see Robert Leibowitz, *The Defender: The Life and Career of Samuel S. Leibowitz, 1893–1933* (Englewood Cliffs, NJ: Prentice Hall, 1981), 7. On Tompkins's father-in-law, see: "George G. Tennant, Retired Jurist, 79."

43. "Clashes Mark Scutellaro Jury Choice," *HD,* January 10, 1939.

44. Hotel Plaza background: "Jersey City, Past and Present, Hotel Plaza," www.njcu .ed/Programs/jchistory; "Hague Begs Nation to Ban C.I.O. Reds," *NYT,* January 13, 1938.

45. "Burkitt Watches 'King' Hague Fete," *NYT,* January 3, 1938.

46. "Clashes Mark Scutellaro Jury Choice."

47. Lining hallway: "Dole Killer Hero."

12. On Trial: The State's Case

1. Photographers pushing: "Confession Introduced in Evidence at Trial Here," *JJ,* January 11, 1939; author interview with Marie Scutellaro Werts in Toms River, NJ, September 17, 2008.

2. Quentin Reynolds, *Courtroom: The Story of Samuel S. Leibowitz* (New York: Farrar, Straus and Giroux, 1950), x; "Scutellaro Trial Gets Underway," *JJ,* January 10, 1939.

3. Excluding officers: "Scutellaro Trial Gets Underway." On Edward McFeely's ruddy complexion: Edward John McFeely, *U.S. World War II Draft Registration Cards, 1942,* roll WWII_2372200, Hudson County, NJ, via Ancestry.com. Leibowitz's awareness of police officers in the courtroom, see *SVJS,* partial trial testimony, January 10, 1939, Leibowitz cross-examination of Eleonore Hartmann, 8.

4. "Defense Hints Death of Barck Accidental," *JO,* January 11, 1939. See also Rudolph V. Magnus, *U.S. World War II Draft Registration Cards, 1942,* roll WWII_2372199, Hudson County, NJ, via Ancestry.com.

5. Braunstein: "Eye-Witness Gives Story of Murder," *JJ,* January 10, 1939; "Defense Hints Death"; autopsy report, February 25, 1938, performed at Hoffman's Morgue in Hoboken by Doctors Arthur P. Hasking, William P. Braunstein, Manuel Hernandez, and Thomas S. Brady, *SVJS.*

6. "Defense Hints Death."

7. Courtroom hat, see photograph of "Miss Eleanor Hartman [sic]" accompanying "Hint Fall on Spindle Fatal to Poormaster," *HD,* January 11, 1939; "Una teste d'accusa contro Scutellaro si contraddice," *PIA,* January 11, 1939. Hartmann as "star witness," see, for example: "Scutellaro Case to the Jury," *JO,* January 14, 1939. Unless otherwise noted, William George's direct examination of Hartmann is derived from *SVJS,* partial trial transcript, January 10, 1939, testimony of Eleonore Hartmann, 2–16. Hartmann's courtroom behavior and appearance: "Eye-Witness Gives Story of Murder"; "Saw Barck Slain, Woman Asserts," *NYP,* January 10, 1939.

8. Fred D. Pasley, *Not Guilty! The Story of Samuel S. Leibowitz* (New York: G. P. Putnam's Sons, 1933), 123. *SVJS*, partial trial transcript, testimony of Eleonore Hartmann, 16–75.

9. Hartmann's reddening face under cross-examination, see: "Una teste d'accusa contro Scutellaro si contraddice."

10. Photograph accompanying "Hint Fall on Spindle Fatal to Poormaster."

11. Pasley, *Not Guilty!*, 37.

12. "To go outside": "Eye-Witness Gives Story of Murder."

13. See especially Leibowitz's cross-examination: *SVJS*, partial trial transcript, testimony of Eleonore Hartmann, 38, 58–59.

14. Desk spindle in evidence: "Defense Hints Death"; and "Confession Introduced." Cerutti's date of birth: Adaline [sic] Cerutti, *1920 United States Federal Census*, Ward 1, Hoboken, Hudson County, NJ, roll T625_1041, p. 16A, enumeration district 66, image 1063, via Ancestry.com. "Hint Fall on Spindle Fatal to Poormaster."

15. "Defense Hints Death" and "Saw Barck Slain."

16. "Defense Hints Death."

17. He asked Romayne Mullin: "Hint Fall on Spindle Fatal to Poormaster."

18. "Hint Fall on Spindle Fatal to Poormaster"; statement of Josephine Shea to the Police Department, City of Hoboken, February 25, 1938, *SVJS*; "Confession Introduced"; "Defense Hints Death."

19. "Defense Hints Death." Ralph Corrado, *1920 United States Federal Census*, Ward 3, Hoboken, Hudson County, NJ, roll T6125_1042, p. 3B, enumeration district 83, image 540, via Ancestry.com. Ralph Corrado statement to Detective Sergeant Edward Fitzgerald, Police Department, City of Hoboken, February 25, 1938, 7:45 PM; "Confession Introduced."

20. Unless otherwise indicated, Corrado's direct examination, testimony, and cross-examination: "Una teste d'accusa contro Scutellaro si contraddice."

21. "Defense Hints Death."

22. "Confession Introduced."

23. Likely to call Impellitteri: "Defense Hints Death."

24. Headlines announcing cuts and lack of state relief funds included: Turner Catledge, "Voters Urge Curb," *NYT*, January 10, 1939; "Moore Lists Relief as Most Urgent Task for New Legislature Meeting Tomorrow," *NYT*, January 9, 1939; "Legislators Open Session in Jersey," *NYT*, January 11, 1939. See also Hudson County papers likely offered to jurors: "Congress to Take Up Future WPA Spending," and "'Cut Out Relief Chiselers'—Muir," *JJ*, January 9, 1939; "Committee Decide Today on Relief Cut," *JJ*, January 10, 1939; "Roosevelt Job Funds Slashed by 150 Million," *HD*, January 10, 1939.

25. Police presence: "Confession Introduced." On waiting spectators and applause, see: "Due testi smentiscono che Miss Hartman [sic] vide Scutellaro ferire Barck," *PIA*, January 12, 1939.

26. Statement of John Galdi to Hoboken Police, February 25, 1938. John Galdi, *1930 United States Federal Census*, Hoboken, Hudson County, NJ, roll 1349, p. 8B, enumeration district 288, image 777.0, via Ancestry.com.

27. Barck had the power: See Paul Tutt Stafford, *Government and the Needy: A Study of Public Assistance* (Princeton, NJ: Princeton University Press, 1941), 67–68, 172–73; and State Charities Aid and Prison Reform Association of New Jersey, *Poor Relief, A Manual for Overseers of the Poor, 1913*, passim.

28. Statement of John Galdi to Hoboken Police; "Confession Introduced"; "Barck Jurors Get Confession of Death Blow," *NYP*, January 11, 1939.

29. "Scutellaro Takes the Stand," *JO*, January 12, 1939.

30. Biographical background on Nicholas Russo: Russo statement to Hoboken Police Department, February 25, 1938, *SVJS*; and Nick Russo, *1930 United States Federal Census*, Hoboken, Hudson County, NJ, roll 1349, p. 3A, enumeration district 274, image 381.0, via Ancestry.com. Courtroom testimony: "Scutellaro Takes the Stand"; "'Confession' Is Used in Trial," *Newark Evening News*, January 11, 1939; "Barck Jurors Get Confession."

31. Diana Klebanow and Franklin L. Jonas, *People's Lawyers: Crusaders for Justice in American History* (Armonk, NY: M. E. Sharpe, 2003), 167. See also Reynolds, *Courtroom*, 81–82, regarding case of Alvin Dooley.

32. "Confession Introduced."

33. See, generally, Alva Johnston, "Let Freedom Ring," pt. 1, *New Yorker* (June 4, 1932): passim; Alva Johnston, "Let Freedom Ring," pt. 2, *New Yorker* (June 11, 1932): passim; Pasley, *Not Guilty!*, passim; Klebanow and Jonas, *People's Lawyers*, 162, 164. George's knowledge of Leibowitz's tactics: "State Summation Strikes at Accident Defense in Killing," *JO*, January 16, 1939.

34. On Leibowitz charging police brutality: Johnston, "Let Freedom Ring, pt. 1, 21. On public awareness of it: Marilynn S. Johnson, *Street Justice: A History of Police Violence in New York City* (Boston: Beacon Press, 2003), 114, 125, 132–33.

35. Asked officers to be excluded: "Confession Introduced." For Scott's physical description: Joseph R. Scott, *U.S. World War II Draft Registration Cards, 1942*, roll WWII_2372588, Hudson County, NJ, via Ancestry.com.

36. Ibid. Facing jury: "Scutellaro Takes the Stand"; statement, typed by Hoboken Police Department patrolman and signed by Joseph F. Scutellaro, February 25, 1938, *SVJS*.

37. "Barck Jurors Get Confession."

38. "State Rests in Surprise Move," *HD*, January 12, 1939.

39. "Looking at the girls": "Barck Jurors Get Confession."; "Scutellaro Takes the Stand."

40. "It was a matter of slipping your lieutenant's coat on": "Scutellaro Takes the Stand."

41. "Poormaster Slaying Confession Disputed," *DN*, January 12, 1939. Well-used strategy: Johnston, "Let Freedom Ring," pt. 1, 24. Tailor it for Scutellaro case: "State Rests in Surprise Move."

42. "Hot" courtroom: "Due testi smentiscono che Miss Hartman [sic] vide Scutellaro ferire Barck."

43. "Scutellaro Takes the Stand."

44. "State Rests in Surprise Move"; "Barck Jurors Get Confession."

45. McAlister Coleman, "Study in Relief," *Nation*, January 28, 1939, 120; "Scutellaro Takes the Stand."

46. "Scutellaro Takes the Stand."

13. On Trial: The Defense

1. "Pastor Claims Hoboken Poor Are Starving," *HD*, May 27, 1936. Other prominent locals would also gain seats in court. See "Tilts Mark Selection of Barck Jurors," *JO*, January 10, 1939.

2. "The Weather over the Nation and Abroad," *NYT*, January 13, 1939, records previous day's weather: 39 degrees and partly cloudy, as a winter storm moved in. Final witnesses: "State Rests in Surprise Move," *HD*, January 12, 1939. Leibowitz's earlier accusations of coached testimony: Diana Klebanow and Franklin L. Jonas, *People's Lawyers: Crusaders for Justice in American History* (Armonk, NY: M. E. Sharpe, 2003), 190–91.

3. Joe's appearance: "Una teste d'accusa contro Scutellaro si contraddice," *PIA*, January 11, 1939; and " 'Poor' Killer Faces 1 Year," *DN*, January 16, 1939.

4. "Scutellaro Takes the Stand," *JO*, January 12, 1939.

5. John R. Bott, "Scutellaro on Stand Tells Story of Killing," *NYP*, January 12, 1939.

6. "Scutellaro Quits Stand," *HD*, January 13, 1939.

7. Mentions illness, "funny ideas": "Scutellaro Case to the Jury," *JO*, January 14, 1939. On encephalitis: www.bbc.co.uk/health/conditions/encephalitislethargical1.shtml. See also, generally, on epidemics of the 1920s, Molly Caldwell Crosby, *Asleep: The Forgotten Epidemic That Remains One of Medicine's Greatest Mysteries* (New York: Berkeley Books, 2010).

8. Average American worker's family described as two parents with three children, living in an industrial city. Reports by Bureau of Labor Statistics and Labor Research, Inc., published in late 1928, see Mauritz A. Hallgren, *Seeds of Revolt: A Study of American Life and the Temper of the American People During the Depression* (New York: Alfred A. Knopf, 1933), 18–20.

9. "Scutellaro to Know His Fate by Tomorrow," *JJ*, January 13, 1939.

10. "Scutellaro Case to the Jury."

11. Scutellaro's difficulty in speaking at trial: "Scutellaro giura che la morte di Barck fu causata da un accidente," *PIA*, January 13, 1939; Bott, "Scutellaro on Stand"; and "Barck Trial Halts as Prisoner Faints," *NYT*, January 13, 1939.

12. "Scutellaro Says Death Was Accident," *JJ*, January 12, 1939.

13. See: Fred D. Pasley, *Not Guilty! The Story of Samuel S. Leibowitz* (New York: G. P. Putnam's Sons, 1933), 37, 121–22, 280. On his years at Cornell University Law School and theatricality of criminal law, see Robert Leibowitz, *The Defender: The Life and Career of Samuel S. Leibowitz, 1893–1933* (Englewood Cliffs, NJ: Prentice Hall, 1981), 7; Klebanow and Jonas, *People's Lawyers*, 161.

14. Use of props: Pasley, *Not Guilty!*, 55; "Scutellaro Says Death Was Accident."

15. Pasley, *Not Guilty!*, 55; "Scutellaro Says Death Was Accident;" "Scutellaro Quits Stand."

16. Bott, "Scutellaro on Stand"; "Scutellaro Says Death Was Accident."

17. Bott, "Scutellaro on Stand."

18. "Scutellaro Says Death Was Accident."

19. *SVJS*, partial trial transcript, January 12, 1939, testimony of Joseph Scutellaro, 31–32.

20. *SVJS*, partial trial transcript, testimony of Joseph Scutellaro, 18.

21. "Scutellaro Collapses," *JO*, January 13, 1939.

22. *SVJS*, partial trial transcript, testimony of Joseph Scutellaro, 35.

23. "Scutellaro Quits Stand"; "Scutellaro to Know His Fate by Tomorrow."

24. "Scutellaro to Know His Fate by Tomorrow."

25. See, generally, *SVJS*, partial trial transcript, January 12, 1939, testimony of Dr. Lawrence J. Kelly, 1–23.

26. *SVJS*, partial trial transcript, testimony of Dr. Kelly, 11. "Scutellaro Quits Stand."
27. *SVJS*, partial trial transcript, testimony of Dr. Kelly, 4.
28. Ibid., 5.
29. "Scutellaro Collapses."
30. *SVJS*, partial trial transcript, testimony of Joseph Scutellaro, 9, 17–18.
31. "Barck Trial Halts."
32. "Scutellaro Quits Stand"; *SVJS*, partial trial transcript, testimony of Joseph Scutellaro, 77.
33. Pedersen first mentions an unnamed, needy "family of five" in "Pastor Claims Hoboken Poor Are Starving." Articles thereafter mention the Hasties by name— see, for example, "Hoboken Families in Dire Need Specifically Cited by Clergyman," *HD*, May 28, 1936.
34. "Pastor Claims Hoboken Poor Are Starving"; "Scutellaro in Collapse," *JJ*, January 13, 1939; "Barck Trial Halts"; "Scutellaro Collapses"; "Scutellaro Quits Stand."
35. "Scutellaro sviene mentre rende l'interrogatorio," *PIA*, January 13, 1939, translated for the author by Elisa Varano: "he was stiff, as if in a state of catalepsy."
36. Ibid.; "Barck Trial Halts."
37. *SVJS*, partial trial transcript, testimony of Joseph Scutellaro, 79–82.
38. "Scutellaro Case Goes to Jury At 2 PM," *JJ*, January 14, 1939; "Jury Gets Scutellaro Case This Afternoon," *HD*, January 14, 1939; report prepared by Dr. Laurence M. Collins for Prosecutor's Office, November 5, 1938, *SVJS*.
39. "Scutellaro to Know His Fate by Tomorrow."
40. "Scutellaro Case to the Jury."
41. Pedersen's recent arrival in Hoboken: "Barck Claims Cleric Erred," *JO*, May 28, 1936. Years of Pedersen's service as Pastor (1935–39): First Baptist Church, Hoboken, *100th Anniversary Program*, Sunday, December 9, 1945, catalog number 2002.028.0003, Collection of the Hoboken Historical Museum, Hoboken, NJ.
42. Exchanges between Barck and Pedersen: "Says Nobody 'Is Starving in Hoboken,'" *HD*, May 26, 1936; "Pastor Claims Hoboken Poor Are Starving"; "Hoboken Families in Dire Need"; "Barck Claims Cleric Erred"; "Barck Denies Relief Asked," *HD*, May 29, 1936.
43. "Clark's Bolt Causes Change In 1935 Lineup," *HD*, May 4, 1934; "Scutellaro to Know His Fate by Tomorrow"; "M'Feely Dance Tonight to Be Without Clark," *HD*, May 5, 1934.
44. "Closest friend": Mayor Bernard N. McFeely, statement to John T. Madigan, FBI agent, Newark, NJ, office, report dated November 1, 1939, file 44-2, p. 4, box 17594, folder 144-48-1, DOJ Subject File, Records of DOJ (RG 60), NACP. "Clark Trial Adjourned After Lively Session," *JJ*, July 30, 1934.
45. "Scutellaro to Know His Fate by Tomorrow"; "Jury Gets Scutellaro Case This Afternoon," *HD*, January 14, 1939.
46. "Jury Gets Scutellaro Case"; "8-Inch Snow Blankets the City," *NYT*, January 14, 1939.

14. The Hand of God

1. "Winter's Second Heaviest Snowfall Brings Out Plows," *HD*, January 14, 1939; "8-Inch Snow Blankets the City," *NYT*, January 14, 1939.

2. "Jersey's Assembly Bars Relief Protest," *NYT,* January 14, 1939. On Newark's claim: "Cut in Relief Cost Is Voted in Jersey," *NYT,* February 6, 1939.

3. Two hundred and seventy-one of New Jersey's 567 municipalities received no state relief funds in 1938. New Jersey's relief formula and distribution: Donald S. Howard, *The WPA and Federal Relief Policy* (New York: Russell Sage Foundation, 1943), 54.

4. Men outside: "Jury Is Long Out in Barck Slaying," *NYT,* January 15, 1939.

5. Unless otherwise noted, details of Leibowitz's summation were derived from the following articles: "Leibowitz Makes Three-Hour Appeal to Save Scutellaro," *JO,* January 16, 1939; and "Scutellaro Will Be Sentenced on Thursday for Manslaughter," *JO,* January 16, 1939. For background on the Greenfield case, see: "Kills Imbecile Son As 'Act of Mercy,'" *NYT,* January 13, 1939; "Father on Trial as 'Mercy Killer,'" *NYT,* May 9, 1939; "Father Acquitted in Mercy Killing," *NYT,* May 12, 1939.

6. Fred D. Pasley, *Not Guilty! The Story of Samuel S. Leibowitz* (New York: G. P. Putnam's Sons, 1933), 122.

7. "Scutellaro Faces 10-Year Prison Term," *JJ,* January 16, 1939. The rest of the sentence, represented by ellipsis, is "and be told to have his wife become a prostitute."

8. "A man inured to suffering": "Jury Is Long Out in Barck Slaying." "Scutellaro Faces 10-Year Prison Term." Parents escape from tyranny: Pasley, *Not Guilty!,* 64–67. "Convict Scutellaro of Manslaughter," *HD,* January 16, 1939.

9. "Ask any American": "Jury Is Long Out in Barck Slaying." See Quentin Reynolds, *Courtroom: The Story of Samuel S. Leibowitz* (New York: Farrar, Straus and Giroux, 1950), 153–54, regarding Leibowitz's use of the "hand of God" defense to describe "tragedies . . . caused by forces outside the comprehension of man"; quote on p. 169.

10. "Convict Scutellaro of Manslaughter"; "Scutellaro Faces 10-Year Prison Term."

11. See: "Scutellaro Will Be Sentenced on Thursday for Manslaughter."

12. "Scutellaro Faces 10-Year Prison Term."

13. Ibid.

14. "Convict Scutellaro of Manslaughter."

15. Physical description of Louis Messano: Louis James Messano, *U.S. World War II Draft Registration Cards, 1942,* roll WWII_2372201, Hudson County, NJ, via Ancestry .com. In 1942, when Messano registered, he was five foot seven and weighed 190 pounds.

16. "State Summation Strikes at Accident Defense in Killing," *JO,* January 16, 1939.

17. "Convict Scutellaro of Manslaughter."

18. "State Summation Strikes at Accident Defense in Killing."

19. "'Poor' Killer to Cheat Chair," *Sunday (Daily) News,* January 15, 1939; "Convict Scutellaro of Manslaughter"; "Scutellaro Faces 10-Year Prison Term."

20. "Scutellaro Faces 10-Year Prison Term" and "State Summation Strikes at Accident Defense in Killing." On Scutellaro's crying: "Jury Is Long Out in Barck Slaying."

21. "Convict Scutellaro of Manslaughter"; "Scutellaro Faces 10-Year Prison Term." "An upright man": Leibowitz statement to Kinkead after verdict was announced and jury excused; see "Scutellaro Will Be Sentenced on Thursday for Manslaughter."

22. "Convict Scutellaro of Manslaughter"; "Scutellaro Faces 10-Year Prison Term"; "La giuria indecisa sul fato di Giuseppe Scutellaro," *PIA,* January 15, 1939; "Scutellaro Will Be Sentenced on Thursday for Manslaughter."

23. "La giuria indecisa sul fato di Giuseppe Scutellaro"; "Scutellaro Will Be Sentenced on Thursday for Manslaughter."

24. "Scutellaro Faces 10-Year Prison Term."

25. "Convict Scutellaro of Manslaughter."

26. "Scutellaro Guilty of Manslaughter: Slayer of Hoboken Poormaster is Calm as Jury Reports After Ten Hours," *NYT*, January 16, 1939; "Scutellaro Faces 10-Year Prison Term"; "Barck's Slayer Awaits Sentence," *NYP*, January 16, 1939.

27. The act of manslaughter, explained by Judge Kinkead: "Jury Is Long Out in Barck Slaying"; "Convict Scutellaro of Manslaughter."

28. "Agreed at the outset": "Convict Scutellaro of Manslaughter." "Pig-headed" juror: "Viva attesa fra gli Italiani per la sorte di G. Scutellaro," *PIA*, January 16, 1939, identified as Lyon. See however, *PIA* article published the day before, "La giuria indecisa sul fato di Giuseppe Scutellaro," which names Tompkins as the holdout. A report by the *DN* confirmed Tompkins as such; see "Poormaster's Slayer Guilty, Faces a Year," *DN*, January 16, 1939.

29. "Scutellaro Will Be Sentenced on Thursday for Manslaughter"; "'Poor' Killer Faces 1 Year"; "Scutellaro Guilty of Manslaughter."

30. "Scutellaro Faces 10-Year Prison Term"; "Scutellaro Will Be Sentenced on Thursday for Manslaughter"; "Weigh Appeal by Scutellaro," *JO*, January 17, 1939.

31. "Un commento della difesa di Scutellaro sul verdetto che fu emesso domenica dai giurati," *PIA*, January 18, 1939.

32. "The Shape of Things," *Nation*, January 21, 1939.

33. McAlister Coleman, "Study in Relief," *Nation*, January 28, 1939, 121.

34. "Convict Scutellaro of Manslaughter."

35. "Two Women Can't Forget Poor Office Slaying Tragedy, Relatives Shield Barck Widow in Dover: Mrs. Scutellaro Won't Reveal Feelings," *HD*, January 16, 1939.

36. "Scutellaro condannato a due anni," *PIA*, February 3, 1939.

37. "Kinkead Hints He May Be Lenient with Scutellaro," *JO*, January 20, 1939; "Scutellaro to Hear His Sentence Today," *HD*, February 2, 1939; "Scutellaro condannato a due anni."

38. "Could provoke a wave of rebellion": "Scutellaro condannato a due anni"; "Scutellaro Gets 2 to 5 Years," *JJ*, February 2, 1939.

39. "Billions are spent for roads and bridges": "Given Two Years in Barck Killing," *Newark Evening News*, February 2, 1939. New Jersey State Legislature consideration of bill to offset Newark's relief reimbursement with its highway construction debt: "Cut in Relief Cost Is Voted in Jersey" and "Jersey Bill Seen Forcing Needy to 'Eat Route 21,'" *NYT*, February 8, 1939.

40. "Jersey Relief Tax Urged in Program," *NYT*, January 17, 1939.

41. Would be well rid: "Scutellaro Gets 2 To 5 Years." Leibowitz taking cases to win: Pasley, *Not Guilty!*, 268, 272. "A scapegoat": "Scutellaro condannato a due anni."

42. "Scutellaro Gets 2 To 5 Years."

43. "Scutellaro condannato a due anni."

44. "Scutellaro Gets 2 To 5 Years."

45. "Scutellaro Gets 2 Years in Killing," *NYP*, February 2, 1939.

46. Ibid.; "Given Two Years in Barck Killing."

47. "Scutellaro Gets 2–5 Year Term," *HD*, February 3, 1939; "Scutellaro condannato a due anni."

48. Transcript of telegram from Cary Euwer, Office of Attorney General to Morris Milgram, Executive Secretary, Workers Defense League of NJ, February 2, 1939, and Morris Milgram to Attorney General Frank Murphy, January 25, 1939, box 17313, 4th folder (1/25/39–7/26/39), DOJ Central Files, Classified Subject Files, Correspondence, Records of the DOJ (RG 60), NACP. See also "Labor Group Asks Hague Indictment," *NYT*, February 12, 1939.

Epilogue

1. Richard Lowitt and Maurine Hoffman Beasley, eds., *One Third of a Nation: Lorena Hickok Reports on the Great Depression* (Urbana: University of Illinois Press, 1981), 330. "3rd Ward Club Hails McFeely, Aids at Affair: Father of Joseph Scutellaro Bespeaks Friendship for Mayor at Rally," *HD*, April 3, 1939.

2. In interview with author in Toms River, NJ, September 17, 2008, Marie Scutellaro Werts noted contracts restoration but had no firm date.

3. Obituary for Mrs. Augusta Barck, *Daily Record*, November 25, 1945.

4. "Matson to Appeal Conviction"; Arthur Garfield Hays, statement to John T. Madigan, FBI agent, Newark, NJ, office, report dated April 11, 1939, file 7-77, pp. 17–18, box 17313, 4th folder (1/25/39–7/26/39), DOJ Central Files, Classified Subject Files, Correspondence, Records of the DOJ (RG 60), NACP. See also ACLU minutes of the Board of Directors, October 10, 1938, American Civil Liberties Union Records, Roger Baldwin Years, roll 165, vol. 2044, Public Policy Papers, Department of Rare Books and Special Collections, Princeton University Library.

5. Herman Matson, statement to John T. Madigan, FBI agent, Newark, NJ, office, report dated May 4, 1939, file 7-77, pp. 34–35, box 15205, folder 109-286, section 1 (3/25/39–5/4/39), DOJ Central Files, Classified Subject Files, Correspondence, DOJ (RG 60), NACP.

6. "Pair Accused by Matson Freed," *JJ*, November 8, 1938; Morris Milgram, statement to John T. Madigan, FBI agent, Newark, NJ, office, report dated May 4, 1939, file 7-77, pp. 21–22, box 15205, folder 109-286, section 1 (3/25/39–5/4/39), DOJ Central Files, Classified Subject Files, Correspondence, Records of the DOJ (RG 60), NACP.

7. ACLU pamphlet, *The Bill of Rights, 150 Years After, the Story of Civil Liberty, 1938–39* (New York, June 1939): 11, 32, in author's collection. Herman Matson's speech at WDL meeting in Newark: "Matson Attacks Hoboken Relief," *JJ*, October 7, 1938. WDL flyer announcing Mass Meeting, Wednesday, November 30 (1938) at the YCLA Auditorium, NYC, The Workers Defense League Collection, box 33, folder 14, Archives of Labor and Urban Affairs, Wayne State University; another WDL flyer announcing Matson as a speaker at a Friday, September 8, 1939 WDL-related meeting to prevent "deportation" from NJ of relief clients who had not attained residency: The Workers Defense League Collection, box 95, folder 7, Archives of Labor and Urban Affairs, Wayne State University. Flogging of Joseph Shoemaker: Robert P. Ingalls, "The Tampa Flogging Case, Urban Vigilantism," *Florida Historical Quarterly*, vol. 55, no. 1 (July 1977): 13–27.

8. Mimeographed, undated flyers of Hoboken Independent Citizens Committee: "Stop This Relief Hoax!" "The Hoboken Citizen," "Ai cittadini di Hoboken,"

"McFeely Silent on Relief Funds," box 17594, folder 144-48-1, DOJ Subject File 144-48-1, Records of the DOJ (RG 60), NACP. Flyers were stamped, noting receipt by Office of the Attorney General, December 21, 1939.

9. See "Labor Group Asks Hague Indictment," *NYT*, February 12, 1939. In addition to Herman Matson and Morris Milgram, the WDL of NJ delegation included others known for civil liberties activism: Episcopal minister William C. Kernan; progressive journalist McAlister Coleman; Socialist Party activist Clara Handelman; and outspoken Hague opponent Robert Ambry. Miss Kate Small, Hoboken, NJ, to Henry Schienhaupt [sic], DOJ, December 29, 1939, box 17594, folder 144-48-0, section 2 (9/8/39–6/26/40), DOJ Subject File 144-48-0, Records of the DOJ (RG 60), NACP.

10. Dorothy Dunbar Bromley, "Strike a Balance: Matson, Jersey's Persecuted WPA Worker," *NYP*, May 12, 1939. Memorandum for acting assistant attorney general Hopkins from J. Edgar Hoover, director of the Federal Bureau of Investigation, Washington, DC, May 24, 1939, box 17313, 4th folder (1/25/39–7/26/39), DOJ Central Files, Classified Subject Files, Correspondence, Records of the DOJ (RG 60), NACP.

11. David Clendenin, Workers Defense League, to Henry Schweinhaut, Bureau of Civil Liberties, DOJ, May 8, 1939, The Workers Defense League Collection, box 37, folder 22, Archives of Labor and Urban Affairs, Wayne State University. "Charges Against Matson Dropped," *JJ*, May 18, 1939.

12. Mrs. Florence Keator, Hoboken, NJ, to Mr. Henry Schweinhaupt [sic], DOJ, Washington, DC, January 6, 1940, box 17594, folder 144-48-0, section 2, 9/8/39–6/26/40, DOJ Subject File 144-48-0, Records of the DOJ (RG 60), NACP. On Clark's arrest and its aftermath: "Armed Groups, McFeely Critic Held," *JJ*, May 9, 1939; "Clark on Stand in Trial for Poll Fracas," *JJ*, May 22, 1939; "Clark Found Guilty, Fined for Poll Row," *JJ*, May 23, 1939, lists Mrs. Elizabeth Matson as one of the witnesses to Clark's beating: "Clark Appeals in Poll Case," *JJ*, May 31, 1939; "Clark Drops Damage Suit Against Cops," *JJ*, April 5, 1940, stating Clark dropped his damage suit after his disorderly conduct conviction was set aside.

13. City hall protests, late spring-summer 1939: "Matson Pickets," *JJ*, May 15, 1939; "Hoboken Relief Standards Low, Matson Holds," *JJ*, July 12, 1939; "Matson Again Speaks on Steps of City Hall," *JJ*, July 22, 1939.

14. US Attorney General's speech: "Murphy, In Jersey, Denounces Hague," *NYT*, June 22, 1939. James A. Hagerty, "Big Cities Drop Boss Rule: With Pendergast Under Sentence, Only Hague Is Left with Dictatorial Power," *NYT*, May 28, 1939.

15. "Kicked, Says Mrs. Matson on Stand," *JJ*, June 6, 1940; "Suit Against Hoboken by Matson Fails," *JJ*, June 8, 1940.

16. Author interviews with Raymond Matson, April 15, 2009, and Evelyn Olsen, April 1, 2009. "Ex-Commissioner Clark Leaves Hoboken for North Bergen," *JJ*, October 7, 1940.

17. Author interview with Evelyn Olsen; e-mail communication from Raymond Matson Jr. to author, March 19, 2010. "Brooklyn Navy Yard" is popular, colloquial name of officially titled (1801–1966) New York Naval Shipyard.

18. Author interview with Daniel Matson, April 8, 2009; "The McFeely," *Time*, May 26, 1947, www.time.com/time/magazine/article/0,9171,793712,00.html.

19. Background on testimony of rebel police officers and resulting indictments: "Common-Law Criminal Conspiracy as a Weapon Against Corrupt Political

Organizations," *University of Chicago Law Review*, vol. 15, no. 4 (Summer 1948): 939–44. "Mayor of Hoboken, 10 Others Indicted," *NYT*, October 16, 1946; "Hoboken Officials Deny Conspiracy," *NYT*, October 26, 1946. Role of rebel officers in forming 1947 opposition slate: Alexander L. Crosby, "The Bosses Leave Town," *New Republic*, March 22, 1948, 17–18; Richard J. Connors, *A Cycle of Power: The Career of Jersey City Mayor Frank Hague* (Metuchen, NJ: Scarecrow Press, 1971), 150–51; "End of a Boss," *Life*, May 26, 1947, 40–41. The indictments went nowhere; see: "Mayor of Hoboken Will Go on Trial," *NYT*, April 30, 1947; "McFeely Dies in Hoboken," *JJ*, August 9, 1949; "Court Finally Gets 1946 Hoboken Case," *NYT*, November 2, 1954; "All Charges Ended Against E. J. M'Feely," *NYT*, December 8, 1954; "Edward M'Feely Dies," *NYT*, November 24, 1956.

20. Bartletta quote: "Ask High Court to Stop McFeely War on Italians," *JJ*, December 19, 1928. "The McFeely"; "30-Year McFeely Rule over Hoboken Closes," *Joplin Globe*, May 21, 1947, accessed via Ancestry.com; "10,000 In Hoboken Hail New Regime," *NYT*, May 31, 1947.

21. Thomas H. Reed and Doris D. Reed, *The Government of Hoboken: A Report of an Administrative and Financial Survey of the City of Hoboken, New Jersey* (New York: National Municipal League, January 1948), 140.

22. "Chief Quits on Eve of Hoboken Trial," *NYT*, May 16, 1947. Director of Welfare in Department of Public Welfare: Reed and Reed, *The Government of Hoboken*, 49.

23. Diana Klebanow and Franklin L. Jonas, *People's Lawyers: Crusaders for Justice in American History* (Armonk, NY: M. E. Sharpe, 2003), 185.

24. "Sentencing Sam": "Jurist Before the Bar," *Time*, November 15, 1963, 71. "Leibowitz Envisions Death Penalty Here," *NYT*, January 12, 1970. Forty men sent by Leibowitz to electric chair: Martin Arnold, "Parole in Capital Offenses Less Likely, Officials Say," *NYT*, June 30, 1972. For "A Brief History of the Death Penalty in New York," see: Joseph Lentol, Helene Weinstein, and Jeffrion Aubry, *A Report on Five Public Hearings on the Death Penalty in New York Conducted by the Assembly Standing Committees on Codes, Judiciary and Correction, December 15, 2004–February 11, 2005*, 12–13. http://assembly.state.ny.us/comm/Codes/20050403/deathpenalty.pdf, accessed March 31, 2010.

25. Author interview with Marie Scutellaro Werts; unless otherwise noted, all personal details about the Scutellaro family are from this source.

26. Relief clients dropped for "talking politics": James A. Weschler, "Hoboken: Story of a Sick City," *PM*, vol. 1, no. 40 (August 12, 1940): 16. Quoted chairman is William Haber of the National Resources Planning Board's Committee on Relief Policy: Donald S. Howard, *The WPA and Federal Relief Policy* (New York: Russell Sage Foundation, 1943), 51.

27. Chad Alan Goldberg, *Citizens and Paupers: Relief, Rights, and Race, from the Freedmen's Bureau to Workfare* (Chicago: University of Chicago Press, 2007), 149–50; Josephine C. Brown, *Public Relief, 1929–1939* (New York: Henry Holt and Company, 1940), 391–92; and Howard, *WPA and Federal Relief*, 631–32.

28. Goldberg, *Citizens and Paupers*, 161; Larry W. DeWitt, Daniel Beland, and Edward D. Berkowitz, *Social Security: A Documentary History* (Washington, DC: CQ Press, 2008), 93, 131–39; Mimi Abramovitz, *Regulating the Lives of Women: Social Welfare Policy from Colonial Times to the Present* (Boston: South End Press, 1996), 253–54, 265, 315–17; Michael B. Katz, *In the Shadow of the Poorhouse: A Social History of Welfare in America* (New York: Basic Books, 1986), 254–55; David M. Kennedy, *The American*

People in the Great Depression: Freedom from Fear, pt. 1 (New York: Oxford University Press, 1999), 270–72; Frances Fox Piven and Richard A. Cloward, in *Regulating the Poor: The Functions of Public Welfare* (New York: Vintage Books, 1993), 92, 117.

29. Hoboken's impoverished state, summer of 1940: Weschler, "Story of a Sick City," 13, 16. Joe's earnings from August 1940 to March 1941: "Poormaster's Killer Is Now a Landlord: His Wife Buys Tenement, but Denies Using Defense Fund," *NYT*, March 9, 1941.

30. Quotes from: "Man Convicted in Poormaster Slaying Buys Apartment," *JJ*, March 10, 1941. Identical quotes appear in "Poormaster's Killer Is Now a Landlord."

31. Hoboken's decline, including its population: Weschler, "Story of a Sick City," 13; Crosby, "The Bosses Leave Town"; Federal Writers' Project of the Works Progress Administration for the State of New Jersey, *New Jersey: A Guide to Its Present and Past* (New York: The Viking Press, June 1939), 262–64.

32. "Man Convicted in Poormaster Slaying Buys Apartment."

33. Scutellaro's comments on being "a sick man" and concerns about being too ill to survive imprisonment: "Weigh Appeal by Scutellaro," *JO*, January 17, 1939. Work at shipyard: Hoboken Historical Museum, Bethlehem Steel Shipyard Employee Archive, 2001.002.003.

34. Author interview with Marie Scutellaro Werts, as is reference below to the morning routine of Joe and Anna.

INDEX